Rocks and Rock Minerals

ROCKS AND ROCK MINERALS

Richard V. Dietrich
Central Michigan University

Brian J. Skinner
Yale University

JOHN WILEY & SONS
New York · Chichester · Brisbane · Toronto

Library of Congress Cataloging in Publication Data:

Dietrich, Richard Vincent, 1924-
  Rocks and rock minerals.

  Includes bibliographical references and index.
  1. Petrology. 2. Mineralogy. I. Skinner,
Brian J., 1928- joint author. II. Title.

QE431.2.D53   552   79-1211
ISBN 0-471-02934-3

Printed in the United States of America

10 9 8 7 6 5 4 3

preface

The first volume entitled *Rocks and Rock Minerals* was written by Louis V. Pirsson and published in 1908. That book was widely used as both a text and a reference by a whole generation of geologists. By 1926, however, so many changes had taken place in petrography that a second edition was needed. That edition was prepared by Pirsson's successor on the Yale faculty, Adolph Knopf. Twenty more years brought the need for a third edition, this time with a thorough revision by Dr. Knopf, just five years before his retirement from Yale.

Both the second and third editions of *Rocks and Rock Minerals* were obviously direct descendents of Dr. Pirsson's original volume. The outline and order of topics were little changed; many illustrations and even long sections of the text appeared in each edition.

This version of *Rocks and Rock Minerals* is really a new book. Petrology, mineralogy and, indeed, all of geology have changed tremendously since 1946. With the exception of a few brief paragraphs that deal with mineral descriptions and some crystal drawings, the text and the illustrations are new. The order and emphasis of topics differs from previous editions and entirely new subjects have been added. Nevertheless, it will soon become evident to those who are familiar with earlier editions that the present version of *Rocks and Rock Minerals* is a member of the same family, and that the authors of this version owe a deep debt of gratitude to both Dr. Pirsson and Dr. Knopf. One of us (RVD) also wishes to acknowledge the fact that several of the anecdotes we relate were told to him by Dr. Knopf. We only hope that this book will prove as useful to the next generation of geologists as the previous versions did to earlier generations.

Rocks and Rock Minerals is intended to be both a text-book and a reference for those who need to identify rocks and minerals without relying on sophisticated laboratory equipment. We strongly believe that all geologists should possess the capability to identify rocks and rock-forming minerals in hand-specimen. Megascopic field identifications can be made, not only by geologists, but by anyone interested in or working with rocks, and we consider it most unfortunate that the skills needed to make them so often remain undeveloped in many graduates. We sincerely hope that this book will encourage future students to develop the necessary skills.

One does not need to know all minerals or all the mineralogical techniques to identify the minerals that may be encountered in the field. The amount of crystallography and the details of physical properties discussed in Chapter 1 are sufficient to allow identification of the minerals mentioned in Chapter 2. Each family of rock-forming minerals, or mineral species, is discussed in narrative style in Chapter 2; once your skills in mineral identification have been developed, however, you will need only the tabulated mineral properties given in Chapter 3, and Chapter 2 can be used as a reference. This kind of presentation necessarily leads to a certain amount of repetition, but we think it will greatly speed up your use of the book.

Chapters 4, 5, 6, and 7 are devoted to igneous, sedimentary, metamorphic, and unusual rocks, respectively. In Chapter 8, we outline a procedure and provide tables to help you identify the common rocks. For each common rock-type we have attempted to mention one or more localities where the rock can be observed in the field. We have had to rely on literature references to some extent and have not been able to check each locality personally. Some discrepancies may therefore have crept in; we will appreciate hearing of our errors.

Many books define each new term as it is introduced. Because *Rocks and Rock Minerals* discusses both minerals and rocks, we have not been able to follow this practice. You will, for example, find a number of simple rock terms used in Chapter 2 before they are defined in a later chapter. We do not believe this will cause confusion, mainly because the book is intended for use by people who already have some familiarity with rocks.

Naturally, a book such as this must draw a great deal from the accumulated experience of our profession, from our friends, and from our colleagues. To them we owe a great debt of gratitude. We express our sincere thanks for especial assistance, reviews, and opinions from Richard Fiske, Robert Ginsburg, Maunu Härme, Brian Mason, J. Stewart Monroe, Raymond Murray, Philip Orville, Jack Rice, John Schilling, A. L. Streckeisen, John Suppe, Tommy Thompson, Marion Whitney, and Ray Wilcox.

Richard V. Dietrich
Brian J. Skinner

New Haven, Connecticut

CONTENTS

ROCKS AND
ROCK MINERALS

introduction

Beneath the loose mantle of soil, vegetation, streams, and ponds that are draped like a cloth over the surface of the earth, there is a foundation of solid rock, usually called *bedrock*. Here and there, in cliffs, on mountain sides, in road cuts, on barren islands, the rocky foundation juts through the mantle and forms *outcrops*. Samples taken from outcrops, together with samples recovered in mines, tunnels, wells and drill holes, provide the evidence upon which an important branch of the science of geology is built. *The special branch of geology that deals with the occurrence, origin, and history of rocks* is called **petrology**.

What do we mean by the term *rock*? At first glance it seems ridiculous to ask such a question, but any attempt to explain rock soon leads us to borderline cases and the need for a definition. For example, rock suggests a hard or firm substance to most people, so the particles in rock must be consolidated into a coherent aggregate. But at what stage of compaction do we describe an aggregate of particles as being firm? The best we can do is to recognize the ambiguities and to define **rock** in general terms as being *any naturally formed, solid material, composed of one or more minerals (and/or mineraloids) and having some degree of chemical and mineralogical constancy*. The definition of a rock immediately leads us to another question—What is a mineral?

Unfortunately, mineral is also a term subject to ambiguities. To some, for example, it can mean certain chemical elements, such as iron, in vitamin pills. For our purposes we define a **mineral** as *any naturally formed chemical substance having a definite chemical composition and a characteristic crystal structure*. Most minerals are inorganic substances, and indeed some people include the word *inorganic* in the definition. There are, however, a number of natural organic substances that fulfill the requirements of definite composition and characteristic crystal structure, and to deny them the right to be called minerals merely leads to confusion. But there also are many naturally occurring mineral-like substances that do not fulfill either the composition or crystal structure requirement of minerals. Examples are natural resins and glasses, both of which have wide composition ranges and are amorphous (meaning they lack crystal structure), and opals, which have a more-or-less constant composition but are amorphous. We use the term *mineraloid* to describe these mineral-like substances.

EXAMINATION OF ROCKS

From the definition of a rock it is evident that any characterization of a specimen must begin with an examination of the minerals and/or mineraloids present. Indeed, the kinds and amounts of these constituents, together with the textures resulting from the way they are packed, are the most important properties used in classifying rocks. The first step in an examination is the selection of a conveniently sized *hand-specimen* of the rock under study. If too small (less than about 5 centimeters on an edge), some of the textural patterns may not be apparent; if too large, the specimen is awkward to handle.

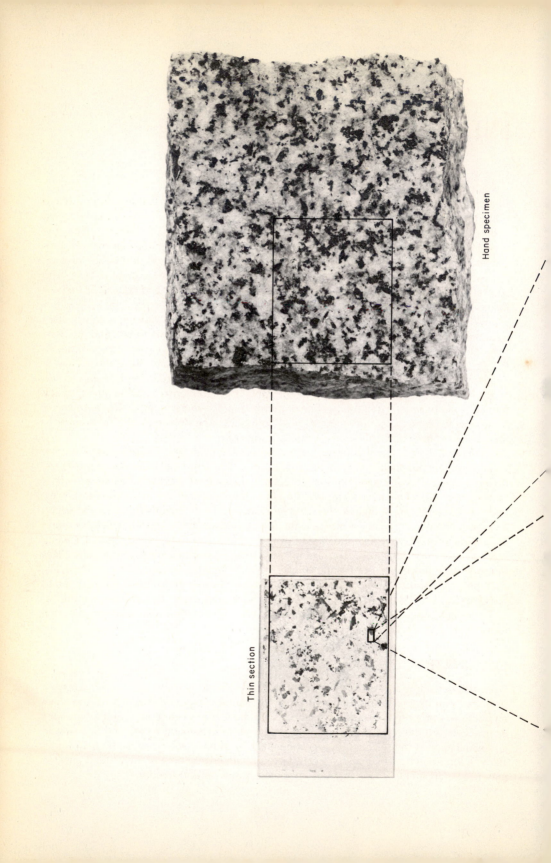

Hand specimen

Thin section

Area magnified with a microscope

Plane polarized light

Doubly polarized light

Biotite

Plagioclase

Quartz

FIGURE I-1 In the study of rocks, polished surfaces and thin sections reveal textures and distributions of minerals to great advantage. The specimen here is a granodiorite containing quartz, plagioclase, hornblende, and biotite. The magnified area on the left is in plane polarized light, that on the right in doubly polarized light, which enhances features such as twinning.

Two useful terms, *megascopic* and *microscopic,* are used to describe the features of a rock. Megascopic refers to those characteristics of rocks that can be perceived by the unaided eye, or by the eye aided by a simple handlens with a magnification up to 10×. Microscopic refers to those features that require high magnification and the preparation of special microscopic sections. When carefully glued to a glass slide and ground to a paper-thin wafer about 0.03 millimeters thick, even most opaque-looking rocks become transparent (Figure I-1). Microscopic properties are determined by examination of the thin sections with specially designed microscopes called *polarizing* or *petrographic micro-scopes.* By use of a polarizer similar to those used in certain kinds of sunglasses, light passing through the thin sections is polarized. The minerals in the thin sections have crystal structures that influence the polarized light in measurable ways; this allows one to identify even the tiniest grains in a rock.

Petrographic microscopy is an extraordinarily powerful tool and at a number of places in this book we will make use of thin sections to illustrate a feature being described. Our present understanding of petrology would be impossible without the input of microscopic petrography. Thus a field examination of megascopic properties is very commonly fol-lowed by a laboratory study of microscopic ones. Manifestly, however, a classification based as much on microscopic features as on megascopic ones cannot be used in deter-mining rocks in the field. Frequently, it is important that we name rocks when we examine them in the field. This book supplies a field classification based on megascopic characters of rocks, determinable by eye or with a handlens, aided by a few simple tests using readily available and easily carried tools and chemicals.

THE ROCK FAMILIES

Most rocks, based on the way they are formed, can be grouped into one of three large families. The first family is the **igneous rocks** (from the Latin word *igneus,* meaning fire), which are *rocks formed by the consolidation of molten or partly molten rock material.* The second family is the **sedimentary rocks**, which are *rocks formed by cementation of transported and sedimented materials derived from the physical and chemical breakdown of pre-existing rocks, or from diverse chemical or biochemical processes.* The third large family is the **metamorphic rocks**, those *rocks formed as a result of solid-state transfor-mations of pre-existing rocks under conditions of high temperature, high pressure, and/or a changed chemical environment.*

Several kinds of rocks, however, do not fit conveniently into the three major families. Instead they appear to occupy transitional places between two of the families, incorpo-rating characteristics of both. Three transitional groups are particularly important (Figure I-2). **Pyroclastic rocks** are *rocks made up of fragments of material ejected from volcanoes that are sedimented and then cemented or welded to a coherent aggregate.* Pyroclastic rocks are transitional between igneous and sedimentary rocks. **Diagenetic rocks,** a term applied to the second transitional group, are *rocks formed by low-temperature changes in composition and/or texture of sediment that leads to lithification* (meaning "conversion to solid rock"). Although diagenetic rocks resemble sedimentary rocks in many aspects of composition, texture, and mode of occurrence, they are, strictly speaking, transitional between sediments and metamorphic rocks. Rocks of the third important transitional group are **migmatites**, the *rocks that are composite mixtures of metamorphic and igneous, or igneous-appearing components.* Many migmatites are apparently formed under conditions of intense metamorphism, where rock melting is just commencing.

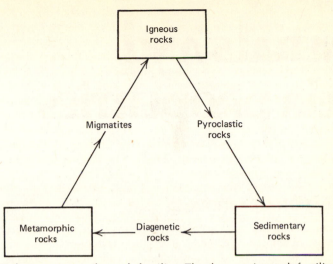

FIGURE I-2   Relations among the rock families. The three major rock families are plotted at each apex of the triangle. Rock families that are transitional in character fall on the sides of the triangle. For example, pyroclastic rocks contain fragments of material ejected from volcanoes and thus are igneous. But the fragments are sedimented and welded or cemented to form a rock, so pyroclastic rocks are also sedimentary rocks.

To simplify this volume, we have not allotted a separate chapter to each transitional rock group. Rather, we have treated them along with the rocks of the major group from which they are derived: pyroclastic rocks with igneous rocks; diagenetic rocks with sedimentary rocks; migmatites with metamorphic rocks.

To provide as complete a coverage as possible, we have added a chapter dealing with "Other Rocks and Pseudo-rocks." In it we describe such unusual rocks as meteorites, tektites, impactites and fulgurites, together with veins and ores and certain *man-made materials that resemble rocks*, which we term **pseudo-rocks.**

Useful References

Gary, M., Mc Afee, R., Jr., and Wolf, C. L., eds. (1972), *Glossary of Geology*, Washington, D.C.: American Geological Institute, 805 pp. This volume is the standard dictionary reference for geological terms of all kinds.

Holmes, A. (1971), *The Nomenclature of Petrology*, New York: Hafner Publishing Co., 284 pp. This is a reprinted edition of a famous 1920 book in which most of the older, petrological terms can be found even if they are no longer in common use.

CHAPTER 1
MINERALS AND THEIR PROPERTIES

CLASSIFICATION OF MINERALS

Every mineral contains one or more of the 91 chemical elements that occur naturally on earth. Hundreds of thousands of chemical analyses have proved this point and have also established another important fact: Every mineral is either a single element (in which case we call it a *native element*) or a compound in which two or more elements are combined. These chemical properties afford the basis for a primary classification of minerals.

Chemical elements combine to form compounds by the transfer or sharing of one or more of the orbiting electrons. When an element gives up or donates electrons, it is said to be acting as a *cation*. In chemical symbols that aspect is recorded by a positive superscript indicating the number of donated electrons. Thus Pb^{+2} indicates a lead atom that has donated two negatively charged electrons and hence is electrically unbalanced by having a net positive charge of two units. When an atom receives electrons, it is said to be acting as an *anion*, and that fact is recorded by a negative superscript recording the number of accepted electrons. Thus S^{-2} indicates a sulfur atom that has accepted two electrons. The reasons for donation and acceptance of electrons relate to the stability of the orbits in which electrons move around an atomic nucleus (some configurations being more stable than others). Space restricts us from pursuing this topic here, but most introductory chemistry books will provide an adequate introduction to the topic of electron orbits and atomic stability. For our purposes it serves to point out that anions and cations combine in such a way that the electrical charges are balanced. For example, Pb^{+2} and S^{-2} may combine to form the compound PbS, which is the mineral galena.

A few elements are chemically ambivalent and may sometimes act as a cation and sometimes as an anion. Additionally, two elements may sometimes combine or bond together in such a way that unsatisfied electrical charges still remain. An excellent example is afforded by silicon, Si^{+4}, which combines with four oxygens, O^{-2}, to form the group $(SiO_4)^{-4}$. Such complex groups are called *complex anions* or *complex cations*. The *silicate anion*, $(SiO_4)^{-4}$, and $(NH_4)^{+1}$, the ammonium cation, are examples. Complex anions and cations combine to form electrically neutral compounds in the same way that simple anions and cations do. For example, the silicate anion may combine with two Mg^{+2} cations to form the compound Mg_2SiO_4, which is the mineral forsterite.

Minerals, other than the native elements, are classified on the basis of their anions. Thus, the oxides are grouped together, and so are the sulfides, the silicates, the carbonates, and so on. This is a convenient method of grouping because many chemical properties prove to be much more sensitive to the anions present than to the cations. For example, the properties of calcite, $CaCO_3$, are much more like those of magnesite, $MgCO_3$, than they are like those of fluorite, CaF_2.

FREQUENCY OF MINERAL GROUPS

By the use of the 88 chemical elements known to occur on earth, it is theoretically possible to make millions of compounds. But only about 2400 different minerals have been discovered thus far, and for the last several years no more than about four dozen new minerals have been discovered each year. The seeming disparity between the almost infinite number of compounds that could possibly be formed and the number of minerals we actually find reflects two things. First, only 12 chemical elements are sufficiently abundant so they comprise 0.1 percent or more of earth's crust. These 12 elements (Table 1-1), collectively, make up 99.23 percent of the entire crust. Of the 12 elements, only four act readily as anions or form complex anions. Thus the silicate $(SiO_4)^{-4}$, oxide O^{-2}, hydroxide $(OH)^{-1}$, and phosphate $(PO_4)^{-3}$ anions all form common minerals. Many other elements can also form anions or serve as partners in complex anions, but only a few are sufficiently abundant to form minerals found in relatively common rocks. These elements are carbon, sulfur, chlorine, and fluorine. Therefore, the first controlling factor of mineral abundance is element abundance. In actual fact, some of the 88 chemical elements are so rare that they are not known to form minerals under any circumstance.

The second factor that controls mineral abundance has to do with the sizes of ions. A chemical element can be present in the earth but not form a mineral because of the *principle of atomic substitution,* sometimes called *solid solution.* Provided that the sizes

TABLE 1-1   The 12 most abundant chemical elements in the earth's continental crust estimated from a weighted average of the compositions of common rocks. Hydrogen and oxygen are not analyzed directly but are calculated from their constant combining proportions with other elements. After K. K. Turekian (1971).

Element	Weight %
Oxygen (O)	45.20
Silicon (Si)	27.20
Aluminum (Al)	8.00
Iron (Fe)	5.80
Calcium (Ca)	5.06
Magnesium (Mg)	2.77
Sodium (Na)	2.32
Potassium (K)	1.68
Titanium (Ti)	0.86
Hydrogen (H)	0.14
Manganese (Mn)	0.10
Phosphorus (P)	0.10
Total	99.23

of two cations or two anions are reasonably close, one can substitute for the other without appreciably changing the chemical properties of a mineral. For example, in the mineral forsterite, Mg_2SiO_4, Fe^{+2} can readily substitute for Mg^{+2} because the two cations are almost the same size and because the substitution maintains electrical neutrality. Much more complex atomic substitutions, involving three or four different kinds of atoms to preserve electrical neutrality are also possible, but the principle is the same. One result of such substitution is that most of the relatively scarce chemical elements are, so-to-speak, hidden as only trace amounts in minerals as atomic substitutes for more common elements. For example, most analyses of forsterite reveal the presence of trace amounts of Ni, Cu, and many other elements as well as a few percent of Fe, all substituting for Mg atoms.

Although nearly 2400 minerals have been discovered, fewer than 40 account for the great bulk of the earth's crust. These common minerals are *the major mineral constituents of common rocks* and thus are called the **rock-forming minerals.** Not surprisingly, considering the abundance of silicon and oxygen, the most abundant rock-forming minerals are silicates. Besides the rock-forming minerals there is a group of minerals, numbering about 30 that are also widespread as minor constituents in many kinds of rocks. Usually comprising less than 5 percent of a rock, these minerals are rather widely referred to as *accessory minerals.* Finally, there is a group of rather rare, but widespread minerals, most of them oxides or sulfides, that are locally found concentrated into the ore deposits we mine and process for industrial metals. These minerals are loosely referred to as the *ore minerals,* wherever they occur.

REPRESENTATION OF MINERAL COMPOSITION

Minerals are chemical compounds so the common rules of formula representation are used. The first common rule is to reduce a formula to its lowest common denominator. Thus we write the formula for chalcopyrite as $CuFeS_2$, not as $Cu_2Fe_2S_4$. The second common practice is to list cations before anions—galena is written PbS rather than SPb.

When complex anions and cations are present in a mineral, that fact is recorded by grouping the constituent atoms of the complex ion together. For example, we write the formula of dolomite as $CaMg(CO_3)_2$ to show that dolomite contains the carbonate anion $(CO_3)^{-2}$; this fact would not be apparent if we wrote C_2CaMgO_6. When two or more complex ions are present, the formula is written to reflect that fact, even if it contravenes the rule for listing cations before anions. Epidote, for example, contains three different kinds of complex anions—(Si_2O_7), (SiO_4), and (OH)—so its formula is written $CaFeAl_2O(Si_2O_7)(SiO_4)(OH)$.

Representation of Solid Solutions

Unlike synthetic chemicals, most minerals are complex solid solutions. Two different methods are commonly used to indicate the existence of solid solutions. The first, the site occupancy method, is a simple extension of the standard chemical formula. When one element substitutes for another by atomic substitution, that fact can be recorded by putting parentheses around the two elements in the mineral formula. For example, Fe and Mg replace each other in the mineral olivine, so we write the formula $(Mg, Fe)_2SiO_4$. The comma between the Mg and Fe indicates that the replacement occurs in the same cation sites in the mineral structure and thus does not produce a new mineral. If, by chemical analysis, we can establish the proportions of Mg and Fe atoms that are present in the olivine, we record the proportion by subscripts. For example, $(Mg_{0.6}, Fe_{0.4})_2SiO_4$ indicates that 60 percent of the cation sites are occupied by Mg ions and 40 percent by Fe ions. The method seems straightforward, but it can be quite complex when a crystal structure contains two or more nonequivalent cation sites. For example, a pyroxene may have the formula (Ca, Mg) (Mg, Fe) $(SiO_3)_2$ because Mg can occupy either of two nonequivalent sites.

The second common way of representing solid solutions is to use the concept of end-member compositions. By end-member we mean the unsubstituted or limiting compositions of a complex solid solution. Separate names are commonly given to end-members. For example, the pure magnesian olivine, Mg_2SiO_4, is called forsterite, whereas the pure iron olivine, Fe_2SiO_4, is called fayalite. An alternate way of describing the formula, $(Mg_{0.6}, Fe_{0.4})_2 SiO_4$, is to say that it contains 60 percent of the forsterite end-member and 40 percent of the fayalite end-member—that is, we can write $(Mg_2SiO_4)_{0.6}(Fe_2SiO_4)_{0.4}$. For convenience, however, we frequently abbreviate forsterite to Fo and fayalite to Fa and record the formula as a percentage of either or both of the end-members—that is, as $Fo_{60}Fa_{40}$, or even as Fo_{60} with Fa_{40} being understood.

The two ways of representing solid solutions are completely interchangeable. Which method one uses can be a matter of individual choice. In general, compositions are written in terms of end-members when the end-members exist as real minerals rather than as imaginary ones. In this way we avoid having to assign names to imaginary compounds. Examples of minerals usually expressed in terms of the compositions of end-members are the garnets, olivines, feldspars, and pyroxenes. When the extent of solid solution is limited so that end-member compositions apply only to imaginary compounds, mineral compositions are usually recorded in terms of percentage site occupancy.

Graphical Representation of Compositions

Graphical representation of a mineral composition containing two solid-solution end-members only requires the use of a straight line, as shown in Figure 1-1. One end of the line corresponds to 100 percent of one component, the other end to 100 percent of the second component. The composition $Fo_{60}Fa_{40}$ is plotted in Figure 1-1 as an example.

When three components are used to represent a composition, three lines, arranged to form a triangle, are needed. For convenience, we usually use an equilateral triangle so that each line segment is the same length. Because triangular diagrams are useful for representing not only mineral compositions, but also many rock compositions that may be expressed in terms of three end-members, they deserve special attention.

For convenience, let the three end-member components in Figure 1-2 be A, B and C. In order to plot them on a triangular diagram, it is essential that the percentages of $A + B + C = 100$. Each corner of the triangle represents 100 percent of the component plotted there. Point 1 in Figure 1-2, for example, is 100 percent B, 0 percent A, and 0 percent C. Along the sides of the triangle we can plot mixtures of the two components at

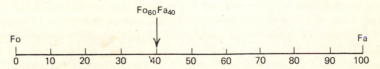

FIGURE 1-1 Graphical representation of the olivine composition $Fo_{60}Fa_{40}$ in terms of the two end-member compositions Mg_2SiO_4 (Fo) and Fe_2SiO_4 (Fa).

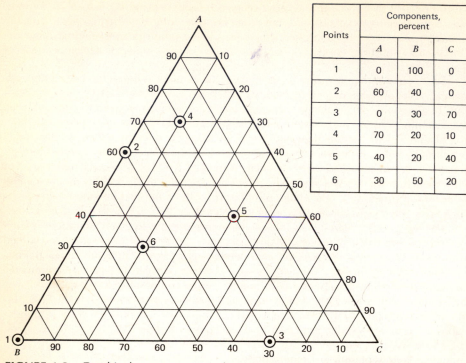

Points	Components, percent		
	A	B	C
1	0	100	0
2	60	40	0
3	0	30	70
4	70	20	10
5	40	20	40
6	30	50	20

FIGURE 1-2 Graphical representation of composition expressed in terms of three components, A, B and C. Numbers indicating percentages apply as follows: along AB—percentages of A, along BC—percentages of B, and along AC—percentages of C.

either end, just as was done in Figure 1-1. Point 2 in Figure 1-2 represents a composition 60 percent A, 40 percent B, 0 percent C, while point 3 is 70 percent C, 30 percent B, 0 percent A.

Compositions containing each of the end-members are plotted inside the triangle. The percentage of each component is indicated by a line parallel to the zero line of that component. That is to say, all points on the line AC contain 0 percent B, so the composition lines for component B are all parallel to AC. Similarly, all points on AB contain 0 percent C and all points on BC contain 0 percent A. Points 4 and 5 in Figure 1-2 both represent compositions that contain 20 percent B because they lie on a line 20 percent of the distance from the line AC (0% B) to the vertex B (100% B). Point 4 also lies on a line 10 percent of the distance from the line AB to vertex C, and on a line 70 percent of the distance from BC to vertex A. Therefore, the composition at point 4 is 70 percent A, 20 percent B, 10 percent C (or, in end-member notation $A_{70}B_{20}C_{10}$). The composition at point 5 is $A_{40}B_{20}C_{40}$.

In most printed diagrams, only the outline of the triangle and the composition points are plotted. This means that for interpretation or measurement, one must visualize or construct a grid of composition lines, or use a template overlay to read the exact compositions.

When more than three end-member components are needed to represent a composition, we can sometimes employ more complex geometric figures; for example, four components can be plotted by using a tetrahedron. In this book, though, we limit ourselves to the use of three components.

MINERAL PROPERTIES

Mineral properties are controlled by mineral compositions (meaning the kinds and proportions of the atoms present) and by the way the constituent atoms are packed together. We define a mineral as having a definite composition and a characteristic crystal structure. Definite composition includes the possibility that solid solution may occur because the anions and cations in a mineral always combine in definite ratios, whether or not partial substitution has occurred. All specimens of a given mineral have the same crystal structure. This simply reflects the fact that the atoms in a given mineral are always packed in the same geometric pattern and hence that the internal atomic configuration of each mineral is a unique characteristic of that mineral. But megascopic examination will not reveal the atomic packing and internal structure of a mineral. This requires specialized laboratory procedures involving X-rays. Thus we must utilize megascopic expressions of the unseen, orderly packing of atoms. Actually, the atomic packing is most obviously expressed by the external shape and form of a crystal. In order to use this property, it is helpful to briefly discuss the geometry of crystals.

Crystal Symmetry

If you are fortunate enough to be able to examine a perfect specimen of a mineral, you will observe that it is a complex geometric form, completely bounded by plane surfaces. The plane surfaces are called *crystal faces*. Few mineral specimens are perfect, however. Most mineral grains, especially in rocks, will not reveal any of their own faces but will instead be bounded by surfaces developed as a result of growth impeded by the presence of other mineral grains (Figure 1-3). We refer to grains that have none of their own crystal faces as being *anhedral*. If, on the other hand, a mineral has a few, but not all, of its own crystal faces, the grain is said to be *subhedral*. Also, in the relatively rare cases where a grain is bounded completely by its own faces, it is said to be *euhedral*. As the definition of a mineral indicates, however, the characteristic geometric packing of atoms is present in all mineral grains, no matter what their external shape. Nevertheless, as might be expected, the laws of crystal geometry are demonstrated best by euhedral grains.

Although a cursory study of euhedral crystals reveals great diversity among them, further study usually shows that similar-appearing faces may be seen in two or more places on a given crystal, and hence that some underlying symmetry must be present. Further study will reveal that the same symmetrical arrangement of faces is present in every euhedral crystal of the same mineral.

Careful examination of a variety of different crystals shows that there are three different types of symmetry elements (Figure 1-4). They are

1. *Plane of symmetry*, which is an imaginary plane dividing a crystal in half so that each half is a mirror image of the other. Some crystals (for example, one that has the shape of a cube) have as many as nine planes of symmetry, other crystals have none.

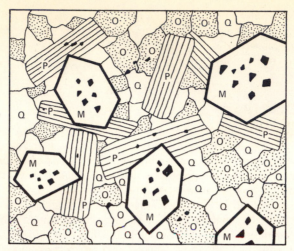

FIGURE 1-3   Texture of interlocking grains in which grains labeled *M* (for mica) are euhedral; those labeled *P* (for plagioclase) are subhedral; and those labeled *O* (for orthoclase) and *Q* (for quartz) are anhedral.

2. *Axis of symmetry,* which is an imaginary line through a crystal about which a crystal can be rotated in such a way that a viewer will see identical faces repeated two or more times during a complete revolution. There are 2-, 3-, 4-, and 6-fold axes of symmetry. Some crystals have several kinds of axes (a cube has six 2-fold axes, four 3-fold axes and three 4-fold axes), others have none.

3. *Center of symmetry,* which is present in a crystal if an imaginary straight line can be passed from any point on the surface, through its center, to a similar point on the opposite side. Most, but not all, crystals have a center of symmetry.

Fortunately, the possible combinations of symmetry elements needed to describe the geometry of crystal faces is limited—there are only 32 possible combinations and these we refer to as the *32 crystal classes*. It is even more fortunate for the student of mineralogy that only 12 of the 32 classes are represented by relatively common minerals.

The study of crystals, as you look for the symmetry elements, frequently leads to confusion because crystals do not always look like perfect geometric figures. Nonetheless, even though the relative sizes of faces may vary, *the angles between the faces are always the same*. Figure 1-5 shows an example of a perfect geometric form, an octahedron, compared with two malformed octahedrons such as one might observe when studying a crystal of the mineral fluorite (CaF_2). The symmetry elements are the same for each of the three cases. In seeking to identify symmetry elements on a malformed crystal, we must mentally construct a perfect crystal with faces parallel to those of the malformed specimen.

The 32 crystal classes can be grouped, because of the similarities in the symmetry elements they contain, into 6 larger groups, called the *crystal systems*. A useful property of the crystal systems is that all crystals in the same system, whether or not they have the same number of symmetry elements, can be described geometrically in terms of the same

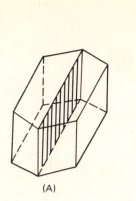

(A)

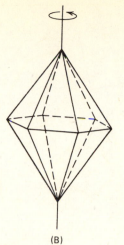

(B)

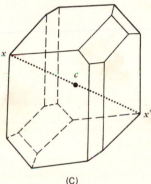

(C)

FIGURE 1-4 The three kinds of symmetry. (A) A plane of symmetry. The crystal also has two other planes of symmetry. (B) An axis of symmetry. The position of a 6-fold axis of symmetry is indicated. The crystal also has six 2-fold axes of symmetry. (C) Center of symmetry. The crystal lacks both planes and axes of symmetry.

geometric axes, commonly called the *crystallographic axes*. The crystallographic axes of the 6 crystal systems are illustrated in Figure 1-6.

Because most of the mineral grains we find in rocks are either anhedral or subhedral, a study of crystal symmetry may seem to be a waste of time. Indeed, a very detailed study of crystallography is not particularly helpful to one who wishes to identify the common minerals in rocks quickly and simply. Nonetheless, so many of the properties of a crystalline solid are influenced by crystal symmetry that some familiarity with the concepts of crystallography is extremely helpful. One such property is habit, which is one of the more obvious expressions of the internal arrangement of the atoms.

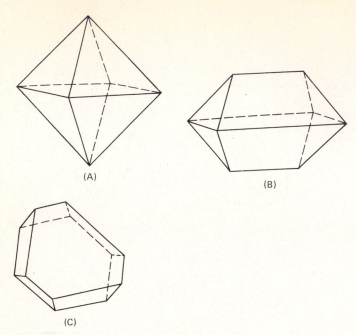

(A)

(B)

(C)

FIGURE 1-5 Shapes of crystallographically equivalent octahedra. (A) A perfect octahedron. (B) and (C) Two malformed octahedra. The same faces are present in each of the crystals; the
angles between the faces are always the same.

Habit means the common and characteristic form assumed by a mineral as it grows.
We are all familiar with the long, fibrous habit of asbestos, and the flat, sheetlike habit of
micas. In both cases, the typical growth habit reflects the internal geometry of the constituent atoms and, therefore, the crystal system of the mineral. Not all minerals have
distinctive growth habits that are useful in their identification. Those that do will be mentioned specifically where the mineral is described.

Cleavage is the easy breakage of a mineral along a plane surface. The geometric
arrangement of atoms in a mineral grain is generally such that the force of cohesion is less
along some particular plane or planes than along others. A chemist would describe the
same thing by saying that the bonds holding the atoms together are weaker in some
directions than in others. If we break a mineral with a hammer or knife edge, the weakest
bonds give away, resulting in a smooth, planar surface of breakage. We refer to each
distinct plane of breakage as a *cleavage plane* (Figure 1-7). Because a mineral will cleave
down to atomic levels, we usually observe a multiplicity of parallel cleavage planes. The
direction of parallel cleavage planes is usually referred to as a *cleavage direction*. Clearly,
since they arise from the internal arrangement of atoms, cleavage planes must obey the
same laws of symmetry that crystal faces do. Not all cleavage planes are parallel to
commonly observed crystal faces, however.

If the cleavage is very good, the new surfaces are smooth and shiny and the cleavage
is said to be *perfect*. If the new surfaces are broken by frequent, irregular steps, the cleavage

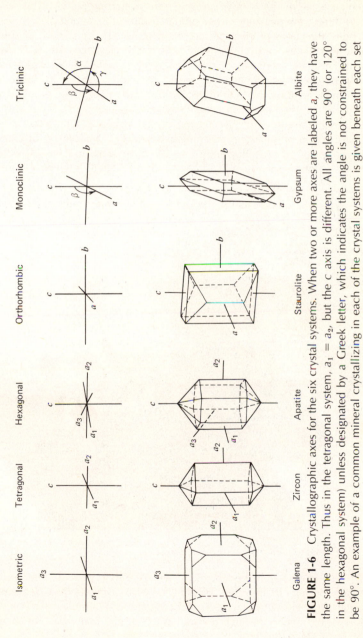

FIGURE 1-6 Crystallographic axes for the six crystal systems. When two or more axes are labeled a, they have the same length. Thus in the tetragonal system, $a_1 = a_2$, but the c axis is different. All angles are 90° (or 120° in the hexagonal system) unless designated by a Greek letter, which indicates the angle is not constrained to be 90°. An example of a common mineral crystallizing in each of the crystal systems is given beneath each set of axes.

is said to be *distinct.* If the breakage is generally rough, with only a few planar areas, the cleavage is *indistinct.*

A mineral may have more than one direction of cleavage. When this happens, the angle between cleavage planes is often an important diagnostic property. We can use it, for example, to distinguish pyroxenes from similarly appearing amphiboles. In some minerals, the different directions of cleavage are exactly alike so far as ease of splitting; in others, the two are unlike—for example, one direction of cleavage may be perfect while the other one is indistinct. There may be three differently oriented planes parallel to which cleavage can be produced—again, all alike in ease of splitting, such as in calcite ($CaCO_3$), or all unlike, as in barite ($BaSO_4$). Some minerals have four or even six cleavages. Whether they are alike or unlike when more than one cleavage is present depends not only on their direction in the mineral grain, but also on the crystal system in which the mineral has crystallized. Description of all of the relations involved in the geometry of cleavage requires greater discussion of crystallography than we have space to cover. The following, however, will be helpful so far as your understanding of certain commonly used terms.

1. *Good cleavage parallel to one plane only*: the mineral grains in the rock tend to occur as tablets, folia, or scales, the surfaces of which are parallel to the cleavage.

(A)   0 ⊢————————⊣ 2 cm

FIGURE 1-7 Two examples of perfect cleavage. (A) Single perfect cleavage plane in muscovite breaks the mineral into thin, parallel flakes (B) Three perfect cleavage planes, not at right angles, are typical of calcite. The photograph is of a broken surface of calcite, magnified as it would appear through a handlens. Note the many parallel surfaces that indicate a single cleavage direction. (B. J. Skinner)

(See Figure 1-7A.) This tendency is well shown in such minerals as the micas and chlorite (see Table 1-2).

2. *Good cleavage parallel to two systems of planes and both alike in ease of splitting*: representative minerals are likely to be *prismatic*—that is, to occur in elongate forms parallel to the cleavages. Elongate forms determined by prismatic cleavage are exemplified by minerals in the amphibole family. Even if the two cleavages are not exactly alike, the mineral still is typically elongate in the direction of the

(B)

0   5 mm

edge produced by the meeting of the two cleavage planes. This is so even though the cleavage is commonly tabular, with the largest faces parallel to the better cleavage. The feldspars, which form the free-developed crystals in many porphyries (see Chapter 4), typically exhibit such tabular or columnar cleavage forms.

3. *Good cleavage in three systems of planes and all alike in ease of splitting*: if the three planes are at right angles to each other, the mineral may break into cubes or rectangular blocks and the cleavage is *cubic* or apparently so. If all planes are at some other angle, rhombohedrons will be produced and the cleavage is termed *rhombohedral*. Cubic cleavage is well shown by galena (PbS), the common ore-mineral of lead, and by halite (NaCl). Rhombohedral cleavage is characteristic of the common rock-making carbonates calcite ($CaCO_3$) (see Figure 1-7B) and dolomite [$CaMg(CO_3)_2$]. Four directions of cleavage are of little importance in

TABLE 1-2   Some Common Minerals with Prominent Cleavages.

A. *One Prominent Cleavage*
   chlorite
   clay (usually too fine-grained to be visible)
   gypsum
   mica (muscovite and biotite)
   serpentine
   talc
   topaz

B. *Two Prominent Cleavage Planes*
   amphibole (at or near 126° and 54°)
   feldspar (at or near 90°)
   kyanite
   pyroxene (near 90°)

C. *Three Prominent Cleavage Planes*
   1. Cleavage planes mutually perpendicular:
      anhydrite
      galena
      halite
   2. Cleavage planes not mutually perpendicular:
      calcite
      dolomite
      magnesite   (rhombohedral cleavage)
      siderite
      barite (two planes at 78°, the third perpendicular to the other two)

D. *Four Prominent Cleavage Planes*
   fluorite (octahedral cleavage)

E. *Six Prominent Cleavage Planes*
   sphalerite (dodecahedral cleavage)

megascopic petrography, because only one common accessory mineral, fluorite, shows them.

When a rock made up of mineral grains sufficiently large to be readily studied with the aid of a handlens is examined carefully, the surfaces of the minerals will be found, almost without exception, to be full of minute cracks and fissures. The cracks are parallel to at least one cleavage and generally to all of the cleavage directions that the mineral has. Besides the cleavage cracks, there commonly are irregular lines of fracture that do not correspond to any definite direction. Actually, most mineral grains in rocks contain not only these relatively large cleavage cracks and irregular fractures that can be perceived with the eye or with the aid of a handlens, but, in addition, are everywhere rifted by cracks so minute that they can only be detected in thin sections of rocks under high powers of the microscope. The reflection of light from these minute microscopic cracks renders many minerals, which would otherwise be colorless and transparent, white and essentially opaque. These cracks and fissures have been produced by various forces to which the rocks have been subjected. Some rifts in metamorphic and igneous rocks are apparently caused by contraction during cooling from a high temperature stage. Others reflect the intense pressures and strains to which many rocks of the earth's crust have been subjected. In any case, minute as the rifts are, they are of great importance in geologic processes. For example, it is by means of these rifts that water is drawn, by capillary action, to penetrate not only the rocks but even the interiors of the individual mineral grains, to alter them into other minerals and thus, for example, to change the rocks into soil.

Fracture

The appearance of a surface obtained by breaking a mineral in a direction other than that of cleavage, or by breaking a mineral that has no cleavage, is called the *fracture* of the mineral. If the mineral is fibrous in structure, the fracture may be termed *fibrous;* or fracture may be rough and uneven, or *hackly;* or perhaps *conchoidal*—that is, it breaks with smooth, shell-like surfaces like those of broken glass, which resemble the inside of a clam shell. Quartz is the most common mineral that gives a good conchoidal fracture (Figure 1-8).

Twinning

One of the most interesting and useful types of crystal aggregates that can be observed consists of units that are related to each other by some simple geometric relation—for example, two halves of an aggregate may be mirror images of each other, or may be rotated 90° around a common plane. Such crystal aggregates are called *twinned crystals* (Figure 1-9).

Twinning is a property that usually develops while a mineral is growing. It can arise in various ways, usually involving a small strain or distortion. It is rarely possible to determine the cause and decide why a mineral has grown as a twin, but we can, nevertheless, use the geometry of twinning as a diagnostic characteristic. This is particularly true for the feldspars. A distinctive type of fine-scale, regularly repeated twinning (commonly called albite twinning) is rather common in the plagioclase feldspars and may be used to distinguish the plagioclases from otherwise similarly appearing alkali feldspars. (See Figure 2-8.)

FIGURE 1-8 Irregular fracture, generally termed conchoidal, of a stream-rounded pebble of quartz. Its curved surfaces resemble broken glass. (B. J. Skinner)

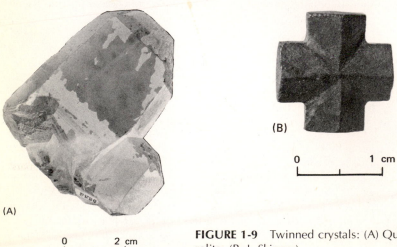

FIGURE 1-9 Twinned crystals: (A) Quartz; (B) staurolite. (B. J. Skinner)

Hardness

The hardness of a mineral, by which we mean its resistance to scratching, is of great value as an aid in identifying minerals and is likewise useful in making rough field tests on rocks (see Chapter 8). For field tests we use a relative scale of hardness, in which 10 minerals (listed in Table 1-3) are arranged in an order, from softest to hardest, so that each mineral can scratch all minerals below it on the scale. If, for example, a fragment of an unknown mineral is found to scratch calcite, its hardness is greater than 3. If it will not scratch fluorite, but on the contrary is, in itself, scratched by fluorite, its hardness is less than 4. Therefore, it must have a hardness of between 3 and 4, or approximately 3.5.

TABLE 1-3 Mohs' hardness scale. Minerals arranged according to relative hardness, starting with the softest mineral, talc.

Mohs' Hardness Scale	Mineral	Common Object for Comparison
1	Talc	
2	Gypsum	
(2.2)		Fingernail
3	Calcite	
(3.5)		Copper penny
4	Fluorite	
5	Apatite	
(5.1)		Geological hammer
(5.2)		Pocketknife
(5.5)		Window glass
6	Feldspar	
7	Quartz	
8	Topaz	
9	Corundum	
10	Diamond	

Both a geological hammer (5.1) and the point of an ordinary pocketknife blade (5.2) have a hardness of a little over 5, and fragments of common window glass have a hardness of about 5.5. Both pocketknives and glass are useful aids in determining mineral hardness. For softer minerals, a common copper penny, with a hardness of about 3.5, and a fingernail, with a hardness of 2.2 are very helpful.

For one skilled in its use, hardness can be a particularly valuable property. With a little practice anyone can develop the necessary skills. Indeed, it will soon become apparent that hardness testing can be performed with a knife blade alone. With a little practice, one can estimate the hardness of any mineral at 5 or below simply by the ease with which it is scratched by the blade.

When applying the hardness test, two precautions should be taken. First, be sure that the surface being tested is clean and fresh. Most surface contaminants and thin layers of alteration products are softer than the underlying mineral. Second, be sure that a single mineral grain is being tested. If the test is applied to an aggregate of small grains, the knife blade may simply separate the grains or even crush them, suggesting too low hardness.

Specific Gravity

The specific gravity of a substance is the ratio of its density to the density of water, or, stated another way, it is the number of times heavier a given volume of the substance is than an equal volume of water. It is rather easily measured by weighing a piece of the mineral or rock in air and then in water; the difference between the two is equal to the weight of an equal volume of water (Archimedes Principle). Thus, we have

$$\frac{\text{weight in air}}{\text{weight in air} - \text{weight in water}} = \text{specific gravity}$$

The operation can be carried out with one of the special apparatuses devised for determining specific gravity and described in most manuals of determinative mineralogy, or it may be done with a chemical assay (Figure 1-10) or jeweler's balance. The specimen is first weighed in the pan and then suspended from the pan by a hair or fine thread and weighed in water. A specimen about 1 centimeter in diameter is convenient for minerals, although a smaller fragment is generally selected in order to obtain pure homogeneous material. Without such purity, it is perhaps needless to say that the determination of specific gravity is of little value. Adherent air bubbles and air in cracks, which also lead to incorrect values, are best eliminated by boiling the fragment in water and then allowing it to cool before weighing.

If a mineral has an essentially fixed chemical composition, as, for example, quartz (SiO_2), its specific gravity has a fixed value, such as 2.65 for quartz, and any departure from that value must be due to the presence of impurities. Most minerals, however, are solid solutions and, therefore, range considerably in chemical composition. In accordance with such variations the specific gravity of such a mineral also has a range of values. The pyroxenes, amphiboles, garnets, and olivines exemplify minerals with such ranges of specific gravity. In fact, solid solution accounts for most of the ranges in specific gravity given for the minerals in Table 1-4.

The inconvenience of carrying equipment in the field means that direct determination of specific gravity is not a convenient field test. Fortunately, it is possible to train oneself to estimate the specific gravity of unknown specimens simply on the basis of how "heavy they feel." A good way to develop this skill is to hold specimens of known specific gravity in the palm of the hand, curling the fingers over to lightly touch the specimen and thus sense its volume. A little practice will soon allow one to distinguish, for example, specific gravity of 2.5 from one of 3.0.

Color and Streak

The color of a mineral, if used with caution, may be a useful property for helping with its identification. Color may depend on overall chemical composition, in which case it is said to be *inherent,* or it may be due to some foreign substance distributed through the mineral as a pigment, and thus is termed *exotic.* It is because the color of many minerals is exotic, or is a combination of inherent and exotic substances, that caution must be used

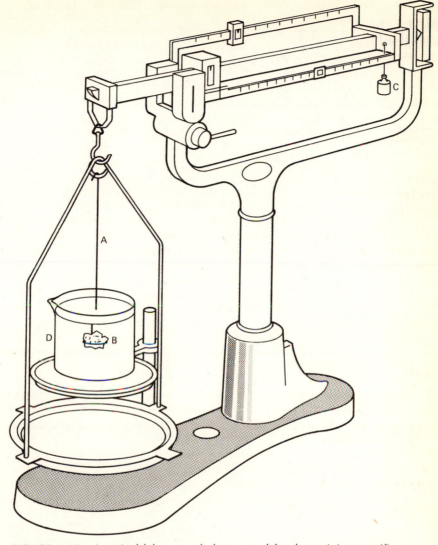

FIGURE 1-10 A typical laboratory balance used for determining specific gravity of a mineral sample. Three separate steps are needed in this calculation: (1) Balance with support wire A but minus sample B is balanced at 0 grams with counterweight C; (2) sample B is placed in the support wire and weighed in air; and (3) the beaker of water (D) is raised to completely cover the sample and the weight of the sample is then taken in water.

TABLE 1-4   Specific gravities of some common minerals. Ranges in values reflect compositional variations due to solid solution.

Numerical Order		Alphabetical Order	
Name	Specific Gravity	Name	Specific Gravity
Halite	2.16	Albite (pure)	2.62
Gypsum	2.32	Amphibole	3.0–3.5
Orthoclase		Anhydrite	2.89–2.98
microcline (pure)	2.54	Apatite	3.15
Serpentine (massive)	2.5–2.7	Beryl	2.65–2.80
Albite (pure)	2.62	Biotite	2.9–3.2
Quartz	2.65	Calcite	2.71
Beryl	2.65–2.80	Copper	8.9
Calcite	2.71	Dolomite	2.87
Labradorite	2.71	Epidote	3.2–3.5
Muscovite	2.7–3.0	Galena	7.5
Talc	2.7–2.8	Garnet	3.5–4.3
Dolomite	2.87	Gold	19.3
Anhydrite	2.89–2.98	Gypsum	2.32
Biotite	2.9–3.2	Halite	2.16
Tourmaline	2.9–3.2	Hematite	5.26
Amphibole	3.0–3.5	Ilmenite	4.4–4.9
Apatite	3.15	Kyanite	3.56–3.67
Epidote	3.2–3.5	Labradorite	2.71
Olivine	3.22–4.39	Magnetite	5.18
Pyroxene	3.2–3.7	Muscovite	2.7–3.0
Garnet	3.5–4.3	Olivine	3.22–4.39
Kyanite	3.56–3.67	Orthoclase and	
Staurolite	3.75	microcline (pure)	2.54
Ilmenite	4.4–4.9	Pyrite	5.0
Pyrrhotite	4.58–4.65	Pyroxene	3.2–3.7
Pyrite	5.0	Pyrrhotite	4.58–4.65
Magnetite	5.18	Quartz	2.65
Hematite	5.26	Serpentine (massive)	2.5–2.7
Galena	7.5	Staurolite	3.75
Copper	8.9	Talc	2.7–2.8
Gold	19.3	Tourmaline	2.9–3.2

in employing color as a means of identification. Such caution is particularly necessary when one is observing transparent and translucent minerals.

Color can be influenced greatly by even trace amounts of cations in solid solution. Quartz, for example, is colorless in its pure form, but by slight compositional variations may be black, brown, red, pink, green, opalescent blue, milky-white, smoky-gray, purple or yellow. The most important thing to remember in using color as an aid is that you should not rely on color alone. In fact, there are a number of well-known mineralogists, and petrologists who are color-blind and hence can not use color for identification, but who are, nevertheless, highly skilled in mineral identification.

One way to reduce, but not eliminate errors in judgment about color, is to determine the color of the powdered form of the mineral. This eliminates spurious color effects, such as those attributable to grain size differences. The color of a powder is usually referred to as the *streak* of a mineral.

A powder can be obtained by grinding a small fragment in a mortar, but is more easily produced by scratching a point or edge of a mineral across a plate of unglazed porcelain. The color of the resulting streak is, of course, that of the powdered mineral. Although any piece of unglazed porcelain will serve fairly well, small plates, called streak plates, are specially made for this purpose and are available from many mineral dealers and university bookstores.

The color shown by most minerals in the powdered state is much lighter than that which they display in the mass; for other minerals the streak is a completely different color. Streak is most useful in helping to discriminate certain dark-colored minerals, especially the metallic oxides and sulfides of the heavy metals that are used as ores. Its application to the light-colored silicates and carbonates that comprise the rock-forming minerals is much less helpful. Nonetheless, even in these minerals it is sometimes useful in distinguishing exotic colors from inherent colors because the color of the streak is generally that of the mineral substance itself—that is, pigments that produce exotic colors must be present in greater than typical amounts to exert any perceptible influence on the color of the streak. Thus yellow, brown, or red varieties of calcite, which are inherently colorless or white, will all tend to exhibit a white streak. Feldspars are typically white or light-colored, but in some rocks, such as anorthosite, may appear nearly black and be easily mistaken for an iron-bearing mineral. Even these dark-colored feldspars, however, give a white streak that discloses their true nature.

In the field, the bruised surface of a rock, where struck by the hammer, generally shows patches of powder—thereby giving, in a rough manner, the color of the mineral streaks. Alternatively, a small piece of a mineral can be ground between two hammer surfaces and the resulting powder then rubbed on white paper to show its streak.

Luster

Another property of light reacting with a mineral is luster. Unlike color, which is due to absorption of light rays of certain wavelengths by the mineral, luster is the appearance of the fractured or cleaved surface, independent of the color, which is caused by the way the light is reflected. Different kinds of luster may be readily described as follows:

1. *Metallic luster,* which resembles the luster of a metallic surface like iron, copper or gold. Only opaque minerals possess metallic luster, so it is most commonly observed on sulfide and oxide minerals.
2. *Nonmetallic luster,* which is present in all transparent and translucent minerals.

Most adjectives used to describe nonmetallic lusters are straightforward and self-explanatory, such as *vitreous* (meaning glassy-looking), *silky* (like a bundle of silk fibers), *resinous* (like a piece of resin), *pearly, waxy,* and *dull.*

Luster is not a useful property for all minerals, but for certain ones, as noted under the individual mineral descriptions, it can be exceedingly helpful.

Other Properties

Mineral texts describe a number of other properties that can be helpful in identifying minerals. Most of these properties, however, are not sufficiently helpful to warrant separate discussion here. A few of these properties, such as magnetism, are noted in the individual mineral descriptions. Full treatment can be found in some of the books listed at the end of the chapter.

Useful References

For those wishing to pursue the topic of mineral properties beyond the elementary level of the preceding chapter, the following books will be helpful.

Bloss, F. D. (1971), *Crystallography and Crystal Chemistry*, New York: Holt, Rinehart and Winston, 545 pp. Advanced and detailed, but an excellent text.

Dana, E. S. (1932), *A Text Book of Mineralogy*, 4th ed., revised by W. E. Ford, New York: John Wiley & Sons, Inc., 851 pp. A classic reference and text, the first half of which discusses physical properties and their use in determinative mineralogy.

Dana, E. S. (1949), *Minerals and How to Study Them*, 3rd ed., revised by C. S. Hurlbut, Jr., New York: John Wiley & Sons, Inc., 323 pp. An older and very elementary text.

Hurlbut, C. S., Jr., and Klein, C. (1977), *Manual of Mineralogy,* 19th ed., New York: John Wiley & Sons, Inc., 532 pp. An excellent introduction to mineralogy and a widely used text.

Mason, B. and Berry, L. G. (1968), *Elements of Mineralogy,* San Francisco: W. H. Freeman and Company, Publishers, 550 pp. A widely used introductory text in mineralogy, but not quite as up-to-date as the preceding reference.

Sinkankas, J. (1964), *Mineralogy for Amateurs,* New York: Van Nostrand Reinhold Company, 585 pp. An interesting introductory text that is very popular with nonprofessionals.

chapter 2
THe ROck-foRMiNG MiNERALs

I. SILICA AND THE SILICATES

CLASSIFICATION OF SILICATE MINERALS

Oxygen and silicon are the two most abundant elements in the crust. It is not surprising, therefore, that silicate minerals, in which the complex anion $(SiO_4)^{-4}$ is the major structural unit, are the most abundant group of rock-forming minerals.

The only rational way to classify silicate minerals is on the basis of the way the silicate anions are packed in the mineral structures. The shape of a silicate anion is not a sphere, like a simple anion; it is a regular tetrahedron because the four large oxygen ions are arranged so that their centers form the vertices of a tetrahedron (Figure 2-1). The small silicon cation sits among the four oxygens, in the open space at the center of the tetrahedron. We generally refer to the silicate anion as the *silica tetrahedron*. The crystal structures of all silicate minerals can be described as a regular array of silica tetrahedra with cations sitting in the openings among tetrahedra. Silicate mineral structures are therefore controlled by the ways tetrahedra pack together. There are certain rules that govern the packings.

Each silicate anion $(SiO_4)^{-4}$ has four unsatisfied negative charges. This is so because the silicon cation has a charge of +4, while each oxygen has a charge of −2. Each oxygen satisfies one of its charges by a bond to the silicon ion at the center of the tetrahedron, so each oxygen still has one unsatisfied charge remaining. To make a stable mineral structure, each oxygen must satisfy both of its charges. This can happen in two ways.

First, charges can be satisfied by bonding with cations. For example, in the mineral forsterite, two Mg^{+2} cations completely satisfy the four negative charges of each silicate anion, leading to the formula Mg_2SiO_4. The crystal structure of forsterite can consequently be described as isolated silica tetrahedra surrounded by magnesium cations in such a way that each oxygen is bonded both to a silicon and to a magnesium ion.

A second, and entirely different way to satisfy charges is for two adjacent tetrahedra to *share* an oxygen. That is, an oxygen is bonded to two silicon ions, each of which sits at the center of its own tetrahedron. By sharing, two or more tetrahedra become joined together to form an even larger complex anion. The process is called *polymerization*. Simple cases of polymerization, in which discrete groups are formed by the joining of two, three, four, and six silica tetrahedra, to form $(Si_2O_7)^{-6}$, $(Si_3O_9)^{-6}$, $(Si_4O_{12})^{-8}$, and $(Si_6O_{18})^{-12}$ groups, respectively, have been discovered in some minerals (Figure 2-2). Most minerals in which large, discrete polymerized anions occur contain only one kind of anion. For example, beryl, $Be_3Al_2(Si_6O_{18})$, contains only the $(Si_6O_{18})^{-12}$ six-member rings. A few minerals contain two different kinds of discrete anion groups—for example, epidote, $CaFeAl_2O(Si_2O_7)(SiO_4)(OH)$, contains both $(Si_2O_7)^{-6}$ and $(SiO_4)^{-4}$ anion groups.

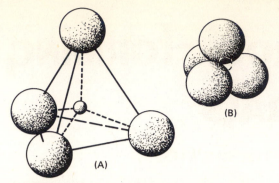

FIGURE 2-1 Silica tetrahedron. (A) Expanded view showing large oxygen ions at the corners of a tetrahedron with a small silicon ion at the center of the tetrahedron, equidistant from each oxygen. Short dashed lines represent the bonds between silicon and oxygen ions. (B) Tetrahedron as it really is, with oxygen ions touching each other. A silicon ion (dashed circle) occupies the central space.

One of the rules that governs polymerization of silicate tetrahedra is that two adjacent tetrahedra can never share more than one oxygen between them; that is, tetrahedra can only be joined at corners, never along edges or faces. On the other hand, there is no requirement that polymerized anions must be discrete, closed rings. Therefore, infinitely polymerized chains, sheets, and frameworks are possible. For example, chains of tetrahedra can readily form if each tetrahedron shares two oxygens to give the general anion formula $(SiO_3)_n^{-2}$ (see Figure 2-2). Similarly, sheet structures result when each tetrahedron shares three oxygens to give $(Si_4O_{10})_n^{-4}$. And complete, three-dimensional frameworks arise as a result of the sharing of all four oxygens, thus satisfying all charges, as in the mineral quartz $(SiO_2)^0$.

Atomic substitutions lead to even more complex mineral formulas than are predicted by consideration of simple polymerization. Many elements have similar ionic radii and, as a result, whole families of minerals can arise. For example, the olivine family is expressed by the general formula X_2SiO_4, where X may be Mg^{+2}, Fe^{+2}, or Mn^{+2} and solid solutions between these end-members. Additionally, Si^{+4} ions in tetrahedra can be replaced, *to a limited extent*, by somewhat larger Al^{+3} ions. The general formula for an Al^{+3} tetrahedron is $(AlO_4)^{-5}$. As a consequence, substitution of an $(AlO_4)^{-5}$ tetrahedron for a $(SiO_4)^{-4}$ tetrahedron must be balanced by the addition of more or different cations to the structure. For example, in the feldspar albite, $Na(AlSi_3O_8)$, all oxygens are shared to give a continuous, three-dimensional network of tetrahedra. But because ¼ of the Si^{+4} ions are replaced by Al^{+3}, Na^{+1} ions must be added to maintain neutrality of charge. The feldspar anorthite, $Ca(Al_2Si_2O_8)$, and albite are end-members of the plagioclases, a continuous solid solution series. The series demonstrates coupled replacement to maintain charge balances so that $Na^{+1} + Si^{+4}$ are completely interchangeable with $Ca^{+2} + Al^{+3}$.

Arrangement of silica tetrahedra		Formula of complex anion	Typical mineral	
			Name	Composition
Isolated tetrahedra		$(SiO_4)^{-4}$	Olivine	$(Mg, Fe)_2 SiO_4$
Isolated polymerized groups	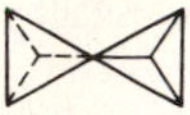	$(Si_2O_7)^{-6}$	Lawsonite	$CaAl_2 (Si_2O_7) (OH)_2 H_2O$
	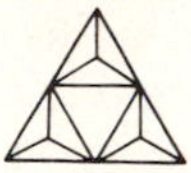	$(Si_3O_9)^{-6}$	Benitoite	$BaTi Si_3O_9$
	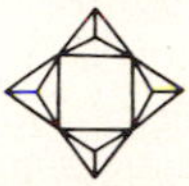	$(Si_4O_{12})^{-8}$	Axinite	$Ca_3 Al_2 (BO_3) (Si_4O_{12}) OH$
	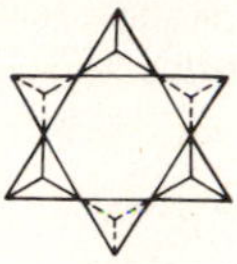	$(Si_6O_{18})^{-12}$	Beryl	$Be_3 Al_2 (Si_6 O_{18})$
Continuous chains of tetrahedra	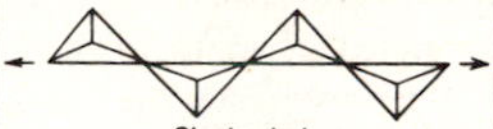 Single chain	$(SiO_3)_n^{-2}$	Enstatite (a pyroxene)	$(Mg, Fe) (SiO_3)$
	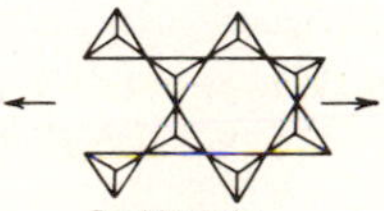 Double chain	$(Si_4O_{11})_n^{-6}$	Tremolite (an amphibole)	$Ca_2 Mg_5 (Si_4 O_{11})_2 (OH)_2$
	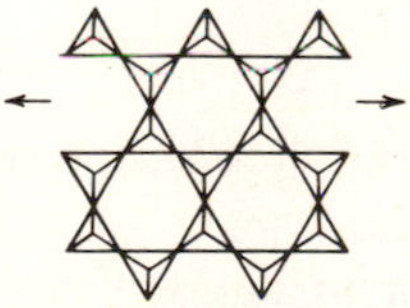 Triple chain	$(Si_3O_8)_n^{-4}$	Jimthompsonite	$(Mg, Fe)_5 (Si_3 O_8)_2 (OH)_2$
Continuous sheets	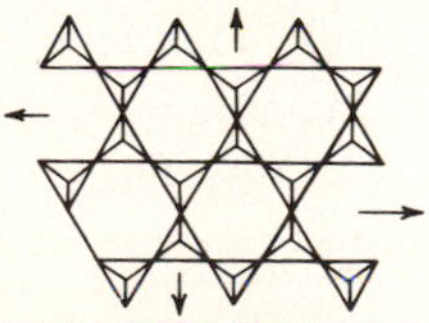	$(Si_4O_{10})_n^{-4}$	Muscovite (a mica)	$K Al_2 (Si_3 AlO_{10}) (OH)_2$
Three-dimensional networks	Too complex to be shown by a simple two-dimensional drawing.	$(SiO_2)^0$	Quartz	SiO_2

FIGURE 2-2 By sharing an oxygen, two silica tetrahedra can polymerize to form a larger anion. For simplicity, oxygens and silicons are not shown. An oxygen would sit at each apex and a silicon at the center of each tetrahedron. Complex anions are drawn as viewed from above. Solid lines are in or above the plane of the page, dashed lines below the page.

All of the important kinds of silicate anion polymerizations, together with an example of each, are shown in Figure 2-2. By compositional changes arising from solid solution, and by slight variations in the packings of tetrahedra, many hundreds of individual silicate minerals are formed. Fortunately, just 11 common mineral groups account for more than 95 percent of all silicate minerals.

It might seem, at first glance, that all we need to do is learn to identify the common minerals and ignore the less-common ones. The fault in this assumption is that mineral properties are so strongly controlled by atomic structure that many relatively uncommon minerals can look like and be confused with the more common minerals that have the same basic structures. We must, therefore, learn to recognize both the common and less-common silicate minerals, lest we draw incorrect conclusions about the rocks in which they occur.

The structural classification of silicate minerals given in Figure 2-2 and Table 2-1 is used as an organizing framework for the mineral discussion that follows. Within each structure group, we will first discuss the common minerals and then, in alphabetical order, the less-common ones.

TABLE 2-1   Silicate anion polymerizations and compositions of important silicate minerals. The most common mineral groups are printed in boldface.

Arrangement of Silica Tetrahedra	Mineral or Mineral group	Composition
	The Ortho- and Ring Silicates	
Isolated tetrahedra, $[SiO_4]^{-4}$	Alumino-silicates; kyanite, andalusite, sillimanite	$Al_2O[SiO_4]$
	Chloritoid	$(Fe^{+2}, Mg)_2(Al, Fe^{+3})Al_3O_2[SiO_4](OH)_4$
	Garnet group	$Mg_3Al_2[SiO_4]_3$ var. pyrope
	Humite group	$Mg(OH, F)_2Mg_4[SiO_4]_2$ var. chondrodite
	Olivine group	$Mg_2[SiO_4]$ var. forsterite
	Sphene	$CaTi[SiO_4](O, OH, F)$
	Staurolite	$(Fe^{+2}, Mg)_2(Al, Fe^{+3})_9O_6[SiO_4]_4(O, OH)_2$
	Topaz	$Al_2[SiO_4](OH, F)_2$
	Zircon	$Zr[SiO_4]$
Isolated $[Si_2O_7]^{-6}$ groups	Lawsonite	$CaAl_2[Si_2O_7](OH)_2H_2O$
	Melilite group	$Ca_2Al[SiAlO_7]$ var. gehlenite
Isolated $[Si_4O_{12}]^{-8}$ groups	Axinite	$(Ca, Mn, Fe^{+2})_3Al_2BO_3[Si_4O_{10}]OH$
Isolated $[Si_6O_{18}]^{-12}$ groups	Beryl	$Be_3Al_2[Si_6O_{18}]$
	Cordierite	$Al_3(Mg, Fe^{+2})_2[Si_5AlO_{18}]$
	Tourmaline	$NaMg_3Al_6(BO_3)_3[Si_6O_{18}](OH, F)_4$ var. dravite

TABLE 2-1 **Silicate anion polymerizations and compositions of important silicate minerals. The most common mineral groups are printed in boldface. (Continued)**

Arrangement of Silica Tetrahedra	Mineral or Mineral group	Composition
	The Ortho- and Ring Silicates	
Mixed groups of $[SiO_4]^{-4}$ and $[Si_2O_7]^{-6}$	**Epidote group**	$Ca_2FeAl_2O[Si_2O_7][SiO_4](OH)$ var. epidote
	Pumpellyite	$Ca_4MgAl_5O[Si_2O_7]_2[SiO_4]_2(OH)_3 \cdot 2H_2O$
	Vesuvianite	$Ca_{10}(Mg, Fe)_2Al_4[Si_2O_7]_2[SiO_4]_5(OH, F)_4$
	The Chain Silicates	
Single chain, $(SiO_3)_n^{-2}$	**Pyroxene group**	$CaMg[SiO_3]_2$ var. diopside
	Wollastonite	$Ca[SiO_3]$
Double chain, $(Si_4O_{11})_n^{-6}$	**Amphibole group**	$Ca_2Mg_5[Si_4O_{11}]_2(OH)_2$ var. tremolite
Triple chain $(Si_3O_8)_n^{-4}$	Jimthompsonite	$(Mg, Fe)_5[Si_3O_8]_2(OH)_2$
	The Sheet Silicates	
Sheet structure, each tetrahedron shares 3 oxygens; $(Si_4O_{10})_n^{-4}$	**Chlorite group**	$(Mg, Al, Fe)_6[(Si, Al)_4O_{10}](OH)_8$
	Clay group	$Al_4[Si_4O_{10}](OH)_8$ var. kaolinite
	Mica group	$K_2Al_4[Si_3AlO_{10}]_2(OH, F)$ (var. muscovite)
	Prehnite	$Ca_2Al[Si_3AlO_{10}](OH)_2$
	Pyrophyllite	$Al_2[Si_4O_{10}](OH)_2$
	Serpentine group	$Mg_6[Si_4O_{10}](OH)_8$
	Stilpnomelane	$(K, Na)Fe_6^{+3}[Si_4O_{10}]_2(OH)_5O_3$ (approximate formula)
	Talc	$Mg_3[Si_4O_{10}](OH)_2$
	The Framework Silicates	
Three-dimensional framework; all oxygens shared; $(SiO_2)^0$	Analcite	$Na[AlSi_2O_6]H_2O$
	Feldspar group	$Na[AlSi_3O_8]$ var. albite
	Leucite	$K[AlSi_2O_6]$
	Nepheline	$Na_3(Na, K)[AlSiO_4]_4$
	Scapolite group	$Ca_4[Al_6Si_6O_{24}]CO_3$ var. meionite
	Silica group	$[SiO_2]$ var. quartz
	Sodalite group	$Na_4[AlSiO_4]_3Cl$ var. sodalite
	Zeolite group	$Ca[Al_2Si_4O_{12}]4H_2O$ var. laumontite

COMMON SILICATE MINERALS WITH FRAMEWORK STRUCTURES

When each of the four oxygens in a silicate tetrahedron is shared with an adjacent tetra-hedron, all charges are balanced and the formula (SiO_2) results. This is the case for quartz and its less-common polymorphs, tridymite and cristobalite. The way that other framework silicate minerals form is by Al^{+3} substitution for some of the Si^{+4} ions and the addition of extra cations to balance the formula. This is the case for the feldspar group. Both quartz and feldspar are common minerals—indeed, they are the two most common minerals in the earth's crust.

Quartz and the Silica Minerals

Quartz follows the feldspars as the second most abundant mineral in rocks of the conti-nental crust. It is one of the easiest minerals to identify and, therefore, is a good candidate to start our discussion of individual minerals.

Form and habit. Quartz crystallizes in the trigonal subdivision of the hexagonal sys-tem, which means that it has a 3-fold axis of symmetry instead of a 6-fold axis. Most crystals are bounded by six prism faces (the *m* faces in Figure 2-3A) that are parallel to the 3-fold axis. The prisms are capped at either end by combinations of positive rhombohedra (the *r* faces) and negative rhombohedra (the *z* faces). The *r* and *z* faces, which are not crystallographically identical, are the most obvious expression of the 3-fold symmetry axis. The *z* faces are usually much smaller than the *r* faces—in fact, they are sometimes barely visible. This form of quartz, known as *low-quartz*, is common as crystals in veins. It is the stable form of quartz at the earth's surface. Above 573°C, however, a slight rearrangement of the silica tetrahedra occurs and the 3-fold axis becomes a 6-fold axis. Thus quartz grown above 573°C has slight crystallographic differences from quartz grown below 573°C. The high-temperature form of quartz is called *high-quartz*. Crystals of high-quartz rarely have large prism faces and instead of rhombohedra we observe six identical pyramid faces capping each end of the crystal (see Figure 2-3B).

When low-quartz is heated above 573°C, or high-quartz is cooled below 573°C, a very rapid rearrangement of the silica tetrahedra occurs. Nonetheless, the external crystal form is not changed by the internal rearrangement because faces do not appear and

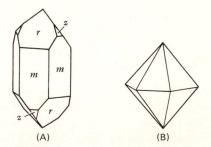

(A)   (B)

FIGURE 2-3 Commonly observed crystal forms of quartz: (A) Low-quartz; (B) high-quartz.

disappear on crystals simply by heating and cooling. Thus the presence of high-quartz crystal forms indicates that the rock in which the crystals are found must have formed above 573°C. Similarly, low-quartz crystals indicate an origin below 573°C. Not surprisingly, most high-quartz crystals are found as phenocrysts in volcanic rocks.

In certain igneous and pyroclastic rocks, especially those containing quartz phenocrysts, it is possible to observe euhedral and subhedral grains. Generally, however, rock-forming quartz occurs as anhedral grains.

Microcrystalline varieties of quartz, usually deposited by precipitation from water solutions, occur as cements and fillings in the openings of many rocks, particularly volcanic and certain sedimentary rocks. The microcrystalline varieties are massive and, although their internal structure cannot be distinguished megascopically, they may be seen microscopically to be either fibrous or granular. The fibrous varieties, all called *chalcedony*, commonly display color banding. The granular varieties, usually uniform in color, are called *chert*, or sometimes *flint* if dark gray; they are commonly found as nodules in limestones—these, actually rocks, are described in Chapter 5.

Cleavage and fracture. Quartz has so poor a cleavage that for all practical purposes it can be regarded as not having any. Instead, it has a good conchoidal fracture. That fracture is a great help in distinguishing quartz within granitic rocks because the somewhat similarly appearing minerals all have at least one good direction of cleavage. When quartz occurs in fine-grained masses, the fracture surface is commonly uneven and splintery.

Color. Rock-making quartz (as distinct from the crystals found in veins) ranges in color from milky white through shades of gray and dark smoky gray, brown to black or, less commonly, is bluish-gray. The gray and smoky tones are common in igneous rocks and the white color is most common in sedimentary and metamorphic rocks, but no absolute rule exists. Black quartz is rare and is mostly confined to igneous rocks. Bluish-gray quartz is also rare and is generally found in high-grade metamorphic rocks. Colorless, limpid quartz, common as crystals in veins and geodes, is rare as a rock-making mineral, but does occur in certain very fresh lavas. Rose, purple, and other exotically colored quartz crystals are found in veins but not as rock-forming components.

The *luster* of quartz varies from glassy to oily or greasy. Its *streak* is white or very pale-colored and not distinctive.

Hardness and specific gravity. Quartz has a hardness of 7. It will scratch feldspar and glass, so it is too hard to be scratched by a knife. The specific gravity varies little from 2.65 because compositional variations are slight.

Composition. Common, rock-forming quartz is essentially pure SiO_2. Some chalcedony contains impurities, usually as intergrown minerals, that give rise to distinctive colors.

Occurrence. Quartz is such a common mineral that it is universally distributed, occurring in rocks of all classes. In some rocks—pure sandstones and quartzites—quartz is essentially the only mineral present. Indeed, quartz is so common that, except in limestones, marbles, and dark, heavy igneous rocks such as peridotite and basalt, its presence should always be suspected.

Tridymite, Cristobalite, Opal, and Coesite

Tridymite and *cristobalite* are both framework minerals with the formula SiO_2 and thus are polymorphs of quartz. The packing of the silica tetrahedra is considerably more open than in quartz and as a consequence cations can more readily fit into the cristobalite and tridymite structures. Analysis usually shows them to contain some Na and Al.

Tridymite is the stable polymorph of pure SiO_2 from 870 to 1470°C, while cristobalite is the stable form from 1470°C to the melting point at 1723°C. Natural tridymites and cristobalites are rarely pure and as a consequence they can form well below 870 and 1470°C, respectively. Their presence in a rock cannot, therefore, be relied upon to indicate temperature of formation.

Tridymite and cristobalite both occur in siliceous, volcanic rocks as linings of cavities or, in some cases, as fine-grained, ground-mass minerals. They have hardnesses between 6.5 and 7 and when massive may be difficult to distinguish megascopically from quartz and from each other. Crystals, when seen, are hexagonal (tridymite) or cubic (cristobalite), but most specimens are massive and colorless with a vitreous luster. When the presence of tridymite and cristobalite are suspected in a rock, it is wise to submit the specimen to laboratory tests for verification.

Opal is a cryptocrystalline form of cristobalite with submicroscopic pores that contain water. Chemical analysis of opal always reveals several percent water, and because the amount is variable it is usual to classify opal as a mineraloid. Opal is always massive, commonly as botryoidal or rounded masses, and is colorless, milky white, yellow, tan, red, green, blue or black in color. Precious opal displays a play of delicate colors arising from scattering and interference of light waves by the internal structures of the crypto-crystalline cristobalite particles.

Opal ranges in *hardness* from 5 to 6, has a *specific gravity* of 2.0 to 2.2, and almost always will fluoresce under ultraviolet light. These three properties can be used to distinguish opal from quartz.

Coesite is a dense, high-pressure polymorph of silica found in some impactites. It has also been observed in a fragment of a deep-seated rock brought up in a kimberlite pipe. Coesite is usually so fine-grained that it cannot be distinguished from quartz, which it resembles in color and form. *Hardness* is 7 and *specific gravity* is 3.01.

The Feldspar Group

The feldspars are a group of minerals that have a general similarity in atomic structure and, therefore, in their chemical and physical properties. The feldspars are so much alike in appearance and general properties that some cannot be told apart megascopically, except in certain favorable circumstances.

Composition. When an Si^{+4} is replaced by Al^{+3} in a framework of tetrahedra, another cation must be added to maintain balanced charges; $Na(AlSi_3O_8)$ and $K(AlSi_3O_8)$ are both feldspars. Up to half of the Si^{+4} ions can be replaced so $Ca(Al_2Si_2O_8)$ is also a feldspar. These three compositions are the end-members of the complex series of solid solutions that are found in the feldspars. We express the end-member $K(AlSi_3O_8)$ as Or, $Na(AlSi_3O_8)$ as Ab, and $Ca(Al_2Si_2O_8)$ as An.

Solid solutions of the kind $(K, Na)(AlSi_3O_8)$, between Ab and Or, are complete and the family of minerals so formed are called the *alkali feldspars*. Because K-rich alkali feldspars are very common, it has become a widespread practice to use the terms alkali feldspar and *potassium feldspar* more or less interchangeably. Solid solutions between Ab and An are also complete and arise because of a coupled substitution by which Na^{+1} + Si^{+4} are replaced by Ca^{+2} + Al^{+3}. The family of minerals so-formed are called the *plagioclase feldspars*. There is very little solid solution between Or and An (Figure 2-4).

A complication arises when we consider how Al replaces Si in the structure. The replacement can happen in an ordered fashion so that only specific tetrahedra contain Al, or it can be essentially random. Because Al and Si atoms are different, an ordered or nearly ordered substitution will yield a different symmetry than a random, or disordered one will. We observe this particularly in the alkali feldspars: those grown at high temperatures and quenched rapidly, as in lavas, are disordered and have monoclinic symmetries; those grown at lower temperatures, or that cool slowly from high temperatures, allow the Al atoms sufficient time to become ordered and are triclinic. Thus we not only have compositional families of feldspars, we also have structural families that reflect the ordering of Al and Si atoms.

The subject of atomic ordering is a complex one. If we ignore those feldspars made in the laboratory and consider only those found in common rocks, the feldspars can be summarized as follows: The plagioclase feldspars are more nearly ordered than the alkali feldspars, regardless of the temperature of formation, and are always triclinic. High-temperature alkali feldspars that are cooled rapidly are disordered and are monoclinic; examples are *sanidine* and *anorthoclase* (Figure 2-4A). Potassium feldspars grown at either intermediate temperatures or at high temperatures but cooled slowly are only partly ordered and are also monoclinic; the relatively common mineral *orthoclase* is formed in this fashion (Figure 2-4B). Potassium feldspars grown at low temperatures or cooled very slowly are more nearly ordered and are triclinic; the common mineral *microcline* is an example. (See Figure 2-4B.)

The temperature of growth also influences composition because the extent of solid solution is temperature-dependent. At high temperatures, there is a complete solid solution in both the alkali feldspars and the plagioclases, as shown in Figure 2-4A. At lower temperatures, however, the extent of solid solution in the alkali feldspar compositional range decreases. Therefore, when a high or intermediate temperature alkali feldspar cools slowly, an unmixing of the solid solution occurs and we observe an intergrowth of potassium feldspar and plagioclase. A potassium feldspar with laths, lamellae or irregular masses of plagioclase within it is called a *perthite* (Figure 2-5). The reverse case, in which laths of potassium feldspar occur within a plagioclase host is called *antiperthite*. In the classification of igneous rocks given in Chapter 4, perthites and potassium feldspars, as well as high-temperature alkali feldspars, are all considered alkali feldspars.

Other compositional variations in feldspars are possible but are rarely important. The rare feldspar *celsian*, $Ba(Al_2Si_2O_8)$ forms a complete solid solution with potassium feldspar, so most potassium feldspars contain at least trace amounts of barium. They also contain trace amounts of Fe^{+3}, which, to a limited extent, can replace Al^{+3}. This latter substitution is more common in potassium feldspar than in plagioclase, and for this reason potassium feldspar is commonly pink or reddish-colored.

Form and habit. When observed as crystals, all feldspars look alike. The most common forms are illustrated in Figure 2-6. In the monoclinic feldspars sanidine and orthoclase, the angle between the faces labeled *c* and *b* is exactly 90°. In the triclinic feldspars, the angle is so close to 90° that it can scarcely be perceived by the eye. Under most circumstances, therefore, we cannot use crystal form as a megascopic means of differentiating between feldspars.

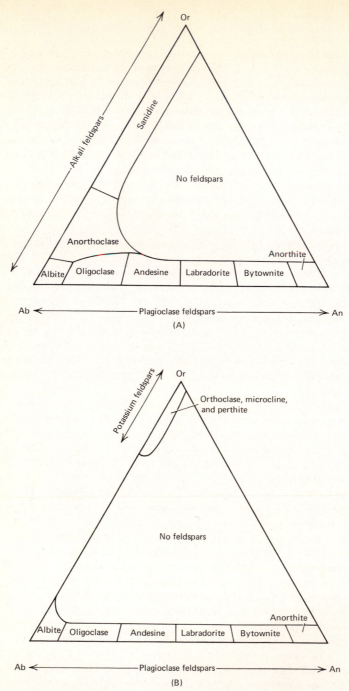

FIGURE 2-4 Nomenclature for the feldspars. (A) High-temperature feldspars. (After Deer, Howie, and Zussman, 1963, *Rock Forming Minerals*, v. 4.) (B) Intermediate and low-temperature feldspars. The plagioclase feldspars and microcline are triclinic, the remainder are monoclinic.

FIGURE 2-5 Interdigitation appearance typical of rock-forming perthites. The plagioclase lamellae are the darker colored streaks. Note how irregular they are compared to the perfection of the albite twins in Figure 2-8D. Specimen from Limpopo belt, southern Zimbabwe. (R. V. Dietrich).

Only as phenocrysts in porphyritic igneous rocks and as projecting crystals in miarolitic cavities in granular igneous rocks have the feldspars had the opportunity to assume free crystal forms. Ordinarily they are interfered with during crystallization by either the growth of adjacent minerals or of other crystals of feldspar, and consequently, they occur as irregularly shaped grains. Nevertheless, in some rocks feldspars tend to assume their free crystal forms—for instance, in syenites, which are composed mainly of feldspar, the individual grains commonly have the shape of flat tablets or of rude laths that approximate those shown in Figures 2-6B and C.

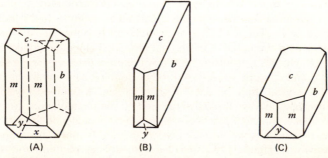

(A)   (B)   (C)

FIGURE 2-6 Commonly observed crystal forms of feldspars.

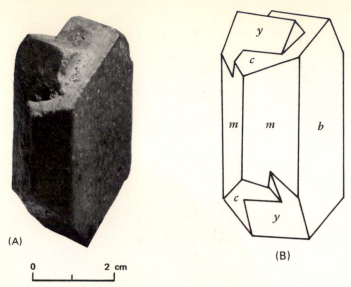

(A)

(B)

0   2 cm

FIGURE 2-7   Carlsbad twin in feldspar. (A) Alkali feldspar crystal, Gunnison Co., Colorado. (B. J. Skinner) (B) Sketch in the same orientation as the photograph with faces labeled in the same way as in Fig. 2-6.

Twinning. Feldspars are generally twinned. There are several different kinds of twinning possible. Many crystals are twinned in two or more ways at the same time so the subject is complex. One of the most common forms of twinning is known as *Carlsbad twinning* (Figure 2-7), named for the town in Bohemia where excellent specimens of twinned feldspar have been found. Carlsbad twinning looks as if a crystal, such as that shown in Figure 2-6A, were cut through parallel to the face labeled *b*. Then, one of the parts was revolved 180° around a vertical axis parallel to the edge *mb*; and finally, the two parts were pushed together so that they would mutually penetrate each other. Because one of the cleavage surfaces in feldspar is parallel to face *c*, Carlsbad twinning can be readily observed on a cleaved crystal. The two *c* faces in a twinned crystal slope away from each other and a sharp boundary is apparent between the two twin elements. Carlsbad twins are common in both monoclinic and triclinic feldspars.

Another common and distinctive form of twinning may be observed only in triclinic feldspars. It is a form of multiple or repeated twinning. It is so common in albite and other members of the plagioclase feldspars that it is called *albite twinning*. In the triclinic system, the face *c* (Figure 2-8A) makes an oblique angle with face *b* so that face *a*, instead of being a rectangle, is actually a rhomboid. If this crystal is divided along the dotted line in Figure 2-8A, and one of the halves is revolved 180°, it will present the appearance seen in Figure 2-8B. The faces *c* and *c'* slope toward each other, forming a re-entrant angle, while on the bottom of the crystal, they produce a salient angle. A twinned crystal is thereby produced, and because cleavage is parallel to *c* and *c'*, sharp undulations can be observed on the cleaved surface. In actual practice, we rarely find a single albite twin in nature. In the rock-making plagioclases we observe crystals that are twinned again and again into thin slices as shown in Figure 2-8C. On cleavage surfaces parallel to *c*, the *multiple twinning* can be observed as a distinctive set of fine, parallel lines (Figure 2-8D).

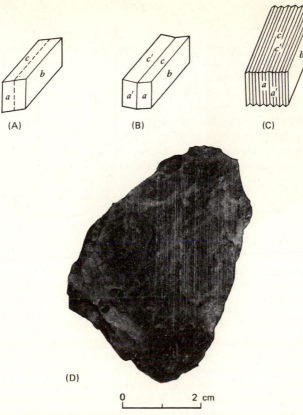

(A)   (B)   (C)

(D)

0   2 cm

FIGURE 2-8   Albite twinning: (A) Untwinned crystal; (B) single twin; (C) multiple twin. (D) Albite twinning on the cleavage surface of plagioclase, from Tvedestrand, Norway. (B. J. Skinner)

Albite twinning descends to such a remarkable degree of fineness that twins may be less than 0.0025 millimeter thick and can scarcely be perceived, even in thin sections in polarized light under the highest powers of the microscope. Frequently, however, especially in the more calcic feldspars, such as labradorite, the twinning is coarse enough to be readily seen by the unaided eye. Also, even if the lines are exceedingly fine and occur only on a small cleavage surface of a plagioclase feldspar grain that is embedded in a rock, they can be distinctly seen by properly adjusting the light that is reflected from the cleavage surface.

Many plagioclase feldspars are twinned according to both the Carlsbad and the albite laws. Such feldspars can be seen to be divided into the Carlsbad halves by the reflection of light from the cleavage surfaces, and each of these halves may be seen to exhibit fine lines manifesting multiple albite twinning.

Some of the already-mentioned perthitic mixtures have their microcline or orthoclase and albite constituents arranged so they roughly resemble multiple albite twinning. Close examination, however, generally serves to distinguish the two because most perthites may be seen to have an irregular interdigitation appearance rather than one exhibiting parallel lines (compare Figure 2-5 and Figure 2-8D).

Cleavage. All the feldspars are alike in that they have two good cleavages. The better one is parallel to the base, or c face in Figure 2-6; the other cleavage is parallel to the b face. Since, in the monoclinic feldspars, the b and c crystal faces intersect at a right angle, so also do the cleavages. It is from this fact that the monoclinic potassium feldspar, orthoclase, takes its name (Greek, *orthos,* straight or right, *klasis,* a break or fracture). In the triclinic feldspars the b and c faces are slightly oblique and so are the cleavage planes. Hence the name plagioclase (Greek, *plagios,* oblique, *klasis,* a break or fracture) was given to the most common of triclinic feldspars. Microcline, which is also triclinic, is so named because the cleavage planes are only inclined a microamount away from the perpendicular.

Cleavage surfaces on large feldspar grains in rocks can readily be seen by reflected light; they commonly have a steplike appearance. Even if the grains are small, cleavage can usually be detected with a lens and a bright light. In cleavage fragments, as in crystals that show distinct faces, the amount of obliquity of the plagioclase and microcline are far too small to be used to distinguish them from orthoclase, either by eye or with a handlens.

Color, luster, and streak. Feldspars have no inherent color; hence, they should normally be either limpid and colorless or white. Transparent, colorless, glassy feldspars in rocks, however, are confined to fresh and recent lavas, in which they commonly occur as conspicuous phenocrysts. Their luster in fresh lavas may be strongly vitreous. But more commonly, feldspars are semitranslucent or opaque and white, grayish white or yellowish, and of a somewhat porcelainlike appearance.

Potassium feldspars generally have a tinge of red, ranging from a pale flesh tint to a strong brick red or brownish red. A distinct flesh color, best described as pale pink mixed with a little yellow, is most common. It is this color of the feldspars that gives many granites used for building stones their color. The red tint of the potassium feldspars may be either inherent because of Fe^{+3} substitution for Al^{+3}, or exotic because of finely disseminated particles of hematite. On the other hand, plagioclase feldspars are commonly gray but rarely red. This distinction can be used, to some extent, as a means of identification, but it is not an absolute criterion, so it must be used with care. Nonetheless, in general if a rock contains two feldspars, one of which is red and the other not, the red feldspar is almost certainly orthoclase, microcline or perthite.

Some potassium feldspars, especially the variety of microcline called amazonstone, where occurring in distinct crystals in the miarolitic druses of granites, have a green color—pale to bright green.

Some rock-forming feldspars are gray, bluish gray, violet brown or even black. The dark colors are especially common in the calcic plagioclase feldspars, especially labradorite. They are caused by minute black particles that are disseminated through the feldspars. The particles, which act as a pigment, may be magnetite dust but are much more commonly ilmenite. Some labradorites also exhibit a pearly play of colors. Fine examples of dark feldspars, many with the just-mentioned play of colors, occur in the anorthosites from the Adirondack region of New York and Labrador.

The *luster* of feldspar is vitreous, rarely glassy (glassiness is limited chiefly to sanidine) or pearly. Feldspars that are more or less altered commonly have a waxlike appearance and a waxy luster. If completely altered, however, they are dull or chalky and lusterless.

The *streak* is white and is not characteristic.

Hardness and specific gravity. Feldspar has a hardness of 6; it is scratched by quartz, scratches glass, and is not scratched by the knife. The specific gravity of ideally pure orthoclase is 2.539; that of albite is 2.62 and that of anorthite is 2.76. The specific gravity of the actual minerals, which are mixtures and solid solutions, ranges between these limits. Thus the alkali feldspars average about 2.57, whereas the plagioclase feldspars have specific gravities that range from 2.62 to 2.76, depending on the relative amounts of Ab and An. If, therefore, the specific gravity of a fragment of feldspar can be determined with accuracy to the second decimal, measuring the specific gravity of a sample provides a fairly good method of ascertaining its composition.

Alteration. When feldspars are acted on by slightly acid water, such as surface waters percolating downward through the rocks or hot waters rising from the depths below, they may be altered to clay minerals or muscovite, accompanied by separation of free silica and removal of alkalis in solution. In a general way, one can say that weathering produced by surface waters generally forms clays, whereas the change to muscovite is likely to result from subsurface reactions. For example, in mines it is often seen that the solutions that deposited the ores have altered the rocks enclosing the ore bodies, in some cases to kaolinite, but in many more cases to a fine scaly form of muscovite called *sericite*.

All feldspars may undergo changes, but the calcium-bearing feldspars tend to alter to more complex mixtures of minerals than the alkali feldspars. Calcite and epidote are sometimes among the alteration products. Other alterations are also known. For example, under some circumstances the feldspars are changed into zeolites, and in metamorphic processes the feldspars containing calcium may react with other minerals to form epidote and garnet.

When the alteration of feldspar, particularly to muscovite or a clay, is more or less complete, the feldspars lose their original vitreous luster and become dull and earthy. If the change is pronounced, they are soft and can be cut or scratched with the knife or even with the fingernail. As a result, the plagioclase feldspars take on a faint, glimmering luster, become semitranslucent and of a pale bluish or grayish tone, lose to a great extent their property of cleavage, and resemble wax or paraffin. These changes as a rule, however, do not take place uniformly throughout the entire crystal: In some, the border is altered or only the center is attacked. In others, especially the plagioclase feldspars, intermediate zones are altered. If the feldspars of a rock do not show bright, glistening cleavage surfaces, they are manifestly in a more or less altered state. These alterations of the feldspars are of great importance in many geologic processes, including the formation of soils.

Occurrence. The feldspars are widely distributed, more so than any other minerals. They occur in all classes of rocks and in a very large percentage of rock types within both igneous and metamorphic rocks that constitute most of the continental crust beneath the veneer of sedimentary beds. It is no exaggeration to say that there is more feldspar in the earth's crust than any other substance.

Determination. Because of the abundance of feldspar and the difficulties of identification, it is useful to summarize what can be done as far as identification is concerned.

In general, the two cleavages nearly at right angles, the vitreous to pearly luster, the light color and the hardness, which resists the point of the knife, enable one to recognize the feldspar grains in rocks and to distinguish them from other common minerals, especially quartz, with which they are typically associated. Sometimes the crystal form is of assistance, especially in porphyries.

Determining the different varieties of feldspar that are present in a rock is often a difficult task, however, when only megascopic means are used. As we previously mentioned, color is sometimes of assistance. If the cleavage surfaces are closely examined with a lens and perthitic intergrowths are seen we know alkali feldspar is present, or if the cleavage surfaces are examined and the delicate albite twinning lamellae can be seen, then we know that plagioclase feldspar is present. If, however, albite twinning cannot be detected on the cleavage surface of a feldspar, we cannot safely conclude that the feldspar is a potassium feldspar and not, instead, a plagioclase feldspar. This is so because some albite twinning lamellae, as already stated, are so thin that they cannot be seen with the lens or they may even be missing. Furthermore, in fine-grained rocks the multiple twinning is extremely difficult to detect. Nonetheless, good training of the eye by studying rocks in which twins are easily seen on the feldspars helps greatly and eventually enables one to perceive most twinning rather clearly, even where at first it was not recognized.

In sum, if perthitic intergrowths are clearly seen in several feldspar grains in a rock, we can safety say that much alkali feldspar is present; indeed alkali feldspar may be the only feldspar present. Similarly, if albite twinning is clearly perceptible in several of the feldspar grains of a rock, we can safety conclude that much plagioclase is present; in fact, that plagioclase may be the only feldspar present in the sample. But, if neither perthitic mixtures nor albite twinning can be seen, we cannot draw a definite conclusion about composition of the sample from megascopic examination.

One possible way to distinguish between potassium feldspar and plagioclase, even when both are present in the same rock, utilizes selective staining techniques. The method requires access to a laboratory, but the equipment needed is readily obtained and the procedure does not require special training. All of the chemicals can be obtained from chemical supply houses.

To prepare a rock for staining, it must first be cut and finely ground (not polished) to give a smooth, flat surface. If the specimen is very porous, it is helpful to first impregnate it with paraffin or a quick-setting plastic. Next, the surface must be activated by etching with hydrofluoric acid (HF) vapors. This is a hazardous step because HF is one of the most dangerous and corrosive chemicals known. Hydrofluoric acid will dissolve silicate glasses, so it must always be stored and used in plastic vessels. Because its vapor is extremely reactive, it must only be used in a well-ventilated hood. Even a small drop of HF will cause such a serious burn that persons using the substance should not only exercise extreme care but should always wear plastic gloves and safety glasses. Once the rock surface is etched and activated by HF vapors, a series of straightforward steps can be followed to selectively stain potassium feldspars bright yellow and plagioclases more An-rich than An_3 brick red. The steps, as laid out by Bailey and Stevens (1960) are as follows:

1. In a well-ventilated hood, pour concentrated hydrofluoric acid (52 percent HF) into a shallow, plastic etching vessel. The acid should be about 5 millimeters from the top of the vessel.

2. Place the cut and ground rock surface across the top of the vessel, face down, being careful not to get the surface dirty from finger prints or into contact with the acid.

3. Cover the etching vessel and the specimen with an inverted plastic cover to prevent drafts, and allow the HF vapors to etch and activate the surface for at least 3 minutes.

4. Remove the specimen from the etching vessel using plastic or metal tongs, dip

in clean cold water, then dip twice, quickly, in and out of a 5 percent solution of barium chloride.

5. Again, quickly rinse the specimen in clean water and then immerse it, face down for 1 minute, in a saturated solution of sodium cobaltinitrite.

6. Remove the specimen and rinse it by gently tilting it back and forth under running tap water until the excess sodium cobaltinitrite solution is removed. If the specimen has been adequately etched, the potassium feldspar will be stained bright yellow. If the potassium feldspar is not bright yellow, remove the etch residue by rubbing the surface under running water, dry the specimen, and return to step 2 and etch it for a longer period. When a bright, yellow stain has developed, proceed to step 7.

7. Briefly rinse the yellow stained surface with distilled water, then cover the surface with a *freshly made* solution of potassium rhodizonate. The solution is made by dissolving 0.05 gram of potassium rhodizonate in 20 milliliters of distilled water. It is convenient to keep the solution in plastic topped dropping bottles so it can be applied with a dropper. Because the solution is unstable, it should not be stored.

8. A few seconds after covering the specimen with the rhodizonate solution, the plagioclase feldspar will turn brick red. When the red color is intense enough, rinse the specimen in tap water to remove the excess solution.

It is important to remember that *all* steps must be followed, even if potassium feldspar is not present. Steps 5 and 6, therefore, must always precede step 7. Other staining reagents have also been described, particularly for plagioclase. One widely used reagent that replaces, and is less expensive than, potassium rhodizonate is the dye called amaranth, known as F.D. and C. Red No. 2 fruit dye. The steps are the same as those listed above, except that step 7 uses a solution of 28 grams of the dye in 2 liters of water. The stain color is red, as it is with the rhodizonate etch, but unfortunately the reaction is not specific for plagioclase. Other calcium-bearing minerals will also react.

LESS-COMMON SILICATE MINERALS WITH FRAMEWORK STRUCTURES

The Feldspathoid Group
The feldspathoid group (commonly called *foids*) is so named because it consists of minerals, which are silicates of aluminum with sodium, potassium, and calcium (like the feldspars), that accompany or take the place of the feldspars in rocks. Like feldspars, the feldspathoids have framework structures, but unlike the feldspars, the actual arrangements of silica tetrahedra vary from mineral to mineral within the feldspathoid group. Also unlike the feldspars, the feldspathoids are relatively rare, being restricted to special kinds of igneous rocks that are so rare that they make up less than 1 percent of the total of the igneous rocks of the world. Thus feldspathoids are far less important than the feldspars, although in problems regarding the origin of igneous rocks, they are highly significant. The more abundant feldspathoids are *leucite* and *nepheline;* less common are *analcime, cancrinite, hauyne, nosean,* and *sodalite.*

Leucite. Leucite, which crystallizes in the isometric system, commonly occurs as trapezohedrons, a form also commonly observed in garnets (Figure 2-14B). The crystals, when imperfect, appear nearly spherical. On cooling, leucite reverts to a tetragonal form, but this fact cannot be seen megascopically because the high temperature, isometric crystal form is retained.

The *composition* of leucite is $K(AlSi_2O_6)$, but up to 10 percent of the K is commonly replaced by Na in solid solution. The mineral has imperfect *cleavage*, conchoidal *fracture*, white to gray *color*, vitreous to dull *luster*, a hardness of 5.5 to 6, and a *specific gravity* of 2.5.

Some crystals that appear at first to be leucite can, on close examination, be found to be intergrowths of alkali feldspar and nepheline. The intergrowths, many of which have zonal patterns, are known as *pseudoleucite* because they are formed by the breakdown or alteration of leucite.

Leucite occurs almost wholly in igneous rocks, principally lavas but also intrusive rocks. Pseudoleucite is practically confined to lavas, especially those with high contents of potassium.

Nepheline. Although nepheline crystallizes in short, thick, hexagonal prisms having flat bases and tops, it rarely shows distinct crystal form in rocks. Instead, it generally occurs as anhedral grains, like quartz. Its normal *color* is white, but it is commonly gray, ranging from light smoky to dark in tone; some is flesh colored or brick red. The white color may shade into yellowish, the gray into bluish or greenish. The *streak* is light and not characteristic. Nepheline is translucent; its *luster,* when fresh, is vitreous, with a somewhat oily or greasy cast. Larger grains have weak *cleavage;* its fracture is conchoidal. Small glassy grains are, therefore, likely to resemble quartz. It is brittle. The *hardness* is nearly that of feldspar, 6. The *specific gravity* is 2.55 to 2.61. Its *composition* is $Na_3(Na, K)(AlSiO_4)_4$, with a small, varying amount of potassium proxying for sodium.

On weathered surfaces of rocks, nepheline tends to be etched out, a feature that at once distinguishes it from feldspar and quartz.

Nepheline and quartz are mutually incompatible; that is, the presence of one in a rock excludes the other. This incompatibility is indicated in the following equation.

$$\underset{\text{Nepheline}}{Na_3(Na)(AlSiO_4)_4} \; + \; \underset{\text{Quartz}}{8\,SiO_2} \; = \; \underset{\text{Albite}}{4\,NaAlSi_3O_8}$$

Nepheline is the most common feldspathoid and is characteristic of many feldspathoidal igneous rocks, both intrusive and extrusive.

Analcime. Analcime is isometric and occurs as well-formed crystals (often the same 24-sided trapezohedral form seen in leucite), as radiating fibrous aggregates, and as granular masses. The *composition* is $Na(AlSi_2O_6) \cdot H_2O$ and small amounts of potassium and calcium can substitute for sodium. The *cleavage* is weak and imperfect; the *fracture* is conchoidal, and the *hardness* is 5 to 5.5. The *specific gravity* of analcime is 2.2 to 2.3; the *color* is white to colorless; and the *luster* is vitreous. Analcime closely resembles leucite but can often be distinguished from it by occurrence, that is, where it is found. Leucite is always embedded in a rock matrix whereas analcime, although a primary mineral in some volcanic rocks (principally, alkali-rich basalts), is much more commonly seen in vesicles in association with zeolites. Analcime also occurs as a product of diagenetic mineral growth in certain tuffaceous, sedimentary rocks.

Cancrinite. Cancrinite is hexagonal and resembles nepheline in both form and *composition*, $Na_6Ca(CO_3)(AlSiO_4)_6 \cdot 2H_2O$. Commonly, it has a yellowish color and is megascopically visible in a rock. It is rarely observed in crystals and, because cancrinite occurs with nepheline or in alkaline igneous rocks in which nepheline might be expected, special care must be exercised in its identification. The best test is application of an acid, such as 1 : 1 HCl, which causes evolution of CO_2, a feature that distinguishes cancrinite from all other minerals except the carbonates.

Hauyne, nosean, and sodalite. These three minerals have identical structures and differ only in *composition:*

Sodalite	$Na_8(AlSiO_4)_6\ Cl_2$
Nosean	$Na_8(AlSiO_4)_6\ SO_4$
Hauyne	$(Na, Ca)_{4-8}\ (AlSiO_4)_6\ (SO_4, S)_{1-2}$

Often referred to as the sodalite group, the minerals are isometric and crystallize in do-decahedrons, a form commonly seen in garnets. (See Figure 2-14A). Crystals are rare in this group and as rock-forming minerals, the sodalite group minerals demonstrate typically anhedral grains. *Color* may be white but is more commonly some shade of blue, generally a bright sky blue to a dark, rich blue. The *cleavage* is dodecahedral but is not striking as a megascopic property; the *fracture* is uneven; the *luster* is vitreous to greasy; the *hardness*, 5.5 to 6; and *specific gravity*, 2.2 to 2.3. The sodalite group minerals are found in association with nepheline, cancrinite, and other foids in feldspathoidal igneous rocks, mainly syenites and phonolites.

Alteration. The feldspathoids, like the feldspars, are readily altered by weathering as well as by other agents. They become converted into kaolinite or muscovite and also, commonly, into zeolites.

The Scapolite Group

The scapolites, found in metamorphic rocks, have compositions similar to feldspars. The end-member compositions are *marialite*, $Na_4(AlSi_3O_8)_3Cl$, and *meionite*, $Ca_4(Al_2Si_2O_8)_3(CO_3, SO_4)$. The compositional relationship to feldspar can be readily seen by writing the formula for marialite $3NaAlSi_3O_8 \cdot NaCl$. All rock-forming scapolites are intermediate solid solutions.

Scapolites are tetragonal and where crystals are seen they are usually four-sided prisms. Most grains, however, are irregular. The *cleavage* is imperfect but distinct and useful, especially in distinguishing scapolite from quartz. The *hardness* is 5 to 6; the *specific gravity* is 2.55 to 2.75. The *luster* is vitreous when fresh; the *color* is white, gray or pale green; minerals of the group are transparent to translucent and commonly fluoresce in ultraviolet light. Scapolite can be confused with feldspar but is slightly softer. It is found only in high-grade metamorphic rocks, mainly schists, gneisses, and amphibolites, and in contact metamorphic rocks in association with diopside and grossular.

The Zeolite Group

The zeolites are a group of hydrous silicates composed, like the feldspars, of aluminum, calcium, sodium, and potassium. They are mostly secondary minerals formed at the expense of feldspars and feldspathoids by the action of hot circulating water but they are also found as early diagenetic minerals in some sediments, and as metamorphic minerals in some low-grade metamorphic rocks. Consequently, they are found chiefly in igneous and pyroclastic rocks, especially in volcanic rocks. As a group, they are not so closely interrelated in crystallography and other properties as the feldspars, but they still have many properties in common by which they can be distinguished.

The zeolites are generally well crystallized, the crystals presenting the forms characteristic of the different species. They have a vitreous *luster* and most are colorless or white, but some are yellow or red. Most are of inferior *hardness* and can be scratched by the knife. Their *specific gravity* is low, 2.1 to 2.4. They dissolve in hydrochloric acid, some of them gelatinizing and some yielding slimy silica. The more common zeolites are *natrolite*, *stilbite*, and *heulandite*.

Natrolite crystallizes into orthorhombic prisms, generally long, slender, and even needlelike clusters that are commonly arranged in divergent bunches or compacted into fibrous, radiating masses. The composition is $Na_2(Al_2Si_3O_{10}) \cdot 2H_2O$.

Stilbite crystallizes into complex monoclinic crystals, which are generally aggregated to form a sheaf. It has a perfect cleavage in one direction, along which it has a characteristic pearly luster. It may also occur in divergent or globular groups. It is white or, more rarely, red. The composition is essentially a hydrous calcium-aluminum silicate: $Ca(Al_2Si_7O_{18}) \cdot 7H_2O$.

Heulandite crystallizes in flat monoclinic crystals that aggregate into compound individuals, the crystals having grown side by side with their flat surfaces together. It commonly has a tan color and a perfect cleavage parallel to this flat side, upon which it has a pearly luster. The cleavage plates are generally curved and have a lozenge-shaped outline. The composition of heulandite is essentially $Ca(Al_2Si_7O_{18}) \cdot 6H_2O$.

Occurrence. As stated above, the zeolites are secondary minerals occurring chiefly in igneous rocks but they occur as well in diagenetic and metamorphic rocks. They occur where igneous rocks have been subjected to the action of steam or hot circulating waters that attacked the feldspars and feldspathoids. Hence feldspathic rocks that have been somewhat altered are likely to contain zeolites in at least small amounts scattered through them. In some rare instances, the rocks are composed largely of zeolites plus analcime. Ordinarily, fine-grained zeolites cannot be detected megascopically, but they may be discovered by heating some of the powdered rock in a closed glass tube. Thereafter, the presence of zeolites is indicated by the easy evolution of abundant water.

The especial home of relatively coarse-grained zeolites is in lavas, particularly basalts. Here they coat the walls of cavities and the sides of joint planes, and they fill the vesicles. In these cavities, they commonly occur as bundles of radiating needles. They may be associated with crystals of quartz, calcite, and prehnite in such occurrences. As well as those already mentioned, many other zeolites may occur. Descripiton of the less commmon zeolites can be found in the larger manuals on minerals.

COMMON SILICATE MINERALS WITH SHEET STRUCTURES

All of the silicate minerals with sheet structures have, as their basic building unit, a polymerized sheet of silica tetrahedra in which three of the four oxygens are shared. All of these sheet minerals have a pronounced cleavage parallel to the sheet (Figure 2-9A). Differences between sheet structure minerals arise from the way the sheets are stacked, from the cations that balance the unsatisfied charges, and from extensive solid solutions. Because the micas are the most common group of sheet minerals, we shall discuss them first.

The Mica Group

The micas are characterized by a remarkably fine cleavage in one direction and by the thinness, toughness, and flexibility of the elastic flakes into which the cleavage permits them to be split.

For practical purposes of megascopic rock study, micas can be divided into the *light-colored* micas, of which *muscovite* is the most common, and the *dark-colored* micas, of which *biotite* is the common variety.

Form and habit. Micas crystallize in six-sided tablets with flat bases. These tablets seem to be short, hexagonal prisms (Figure 2-9B); in reality they are monoclinic. Their side faces are rough and striated; the flat bases, which are usually cleavage faces, are bright and glittering. In some crystals two of the side faces are much elongated, as in Figure 2-9C. Although the distinct crystals are often seen in rocks, particularly igneous rocks, the micas are much more common as irregular flakes and scales having flat, shining cleavage faces. Some folia, or leaves, are curled or bent.

Cleavage. The cleavage is perfect in a direction parallel to face c in Figure 2-9B. An example of this perfect cleavage can be seen in Figure 1-7A. When mica occurs as an aggregate of fine scales, its cleavage is not so apparent but can generally be seen by close observation.

Color and luster. Muscovite is colorless, white to gray or light brown, commonly with greenish tones. The other light-colored micas are similar, except that the lithium mica (lepidolite), which occurs in the pegmatites of some localities, is generally pink or lilac-colored. In thin sheets the micas are transparent.

Biotite and its congeners are black. In thin sheets, however, they are translucent, with strong brown, red-brown or deep-green colors. *Phlogopite* is pale brown, but some varieties are coppery. The luster of micas is splendent. On cleavage faces its luster is sometimes pearly, and in the minutely crystalline variety of muscovite, called *sericite,* it is silky.

Hardness and specific gravity. The hardness of micas ranges from 2 to 3; all are easily scratched with the knife. Specific gravity is least for muscovite, namely, 2.76; and greatest for iron-rich biotite, namely, 3.2.

Composition. Chemically, the rock-forming micas fall into two main groups: the dark-colored, iron- and magnesium-bearing biotite micas and the light-colored muscovite group, which are iron- and magnesium-free. The two groups can be represented as follows:

1. Muscovite $KAl_2(AlSi_3O_{10})(OH)_2$
   Paragonite $NaAl_2(AlSi_3O_{10})(OH)_2$
   Lepidotite $K(Li, Al)_{2-3}(AlSi_3O_{10})(O, OH, F)_2$
2. Biotite $K(Mg, Fe)_3(AlSi_3O_{10})(OH)_2$
   Phlogopite $KMg_3(AlSi_3O_{10})(OH, Cl, F)_2$

FIGURE 2-9   Sheet structure minerals. (A) Electron micrograph of kaolinite. Vesuvius, Virginia. (Pennsylvania State University) (B) and (C) Biotite crystals.

Alteration. Biotite under the action of weathering becomes leached of its alkalis, loses its elasticity, and eventually becomes decolorized to grayish silvery flakes. In the intermediate stages it has a bronzy luster and is golden yellow. In fact, it is often mistaken by the inexperienced for flakes of gold. Muscovite strongly withstands the processes of weathering, and its scales commonly occur in soils that are made up of weathered rocks, the other constituents of which have been greatly altered.

Occurrence. The common micas are widely distributed as rock components. *Biotite* is abundant in many igneous rocks, especially those rich in feldspar, such as granites and syenites. It is abundant in many metamorphic rocks, such as gneisses and schists, and is frequently one of the products of contact metamorphism. Because it alters easily, it does not figure as a component of sedimentary beds, but its bleached derivative is probably abundant. *Phlogopite*, the member of the biotite group containing little iron, is rare in igneous rocks. It occurs chiefly as a product of contact metamorphism of carbonate-rich rocks. *Glauconite*, which has a very complex formula due to solid solution, is closely related to biotite. It occurs as green flakes and pellets in certain marine sedimentary rocks.

Muscovite occurs in granites, especially in pegmatites and in miarolitic druses of granites, and in places where the igneous rocks have been subjected to later fumarole action that furnished water and fluorine. It is especially common in metamorphic rocks, being widely distributed in gneisses and schists. In some metamorphic rocks, especially in phyllites, it is in the form of aggregates of minute scales that have a silky luster and lack the ordinary megascopic characters of the mineral, such as its cleavage. This important variety is called *sericite*. When feldspars are altered to muscovite rather than to kaolinite, sericite is the common form. In sedimentary rocks, such as conglomerates and sandstones, muscovite is fairly common, being an unchanged remnant of the original rocks from which the material of the sedimentary rocks was derived. *Lepidolite* is practically restricted to granite pegmatites and is commonly accompanied by tourmaline. *Paragonite* is known to occur in only a few places—for example, in certain schists, where it plays the role ordinarily taken by muscovite.

Determination. The micas can be distinguished from most rock-forming minerals by their appearance, especially their high luster and prominent cleavage. The last-named quality and the hardness can readily be tested in the field by the knife point. The micas can be distinguished from chlorite and from talc—which resemble them—by the elasticity of their split-off laminae. The thin flakes of the chlorites and talc are, in contrast, flexible but not elastic. From *chloritoid*, a micaceous-appearing mineral of a gray or green color that commonly occurs as distinct crystals in low-rank metamorphic rocks, they can readily be distinguished because of the superior hardness (6.5) and the brittleness of chloritoid.

The Chlorite Group

The chlorites are a large and complex group of micaceous silicates, so named because of their green color (Greek *chloros*, green). They are mostly secondary in origin, formed at the expense of previously existing silicate minerals that contain aluminum, iron, and magnesium. Outwardly, they resemble the micas but differ from them in that chlorite folia are not elastic. The chlorites have certain properties in common by which they can be recognized as a group. To distinguish the disparate members of the group is difficult, however, and for megascopic purposes of little importance. In the description that follows, then, it is the group properties that are given, although those properties are actually based largely on the species *clinochlore*, perhaps the most common member of the group.

Form and habit. The chlorites are really monoclinic in crystallization, but, as in the case of the micas, when they show crystal form, they are in six-sided plates and tablets. Generally, however, they occur in irregular leaves and scales that are massed together in aggregates ranging from finely granular to coarsely massive, or less commonly in fanlike or rosettelike groups. The scales may be flat or in bent and curled forms.

General properties. Chlorite, like mica, has a perfect *cleavage* in one direction parallel to the flat base of the plates. The cleavage leaves are flexible and tough, but, unlike those of mica, they are not elastic. The *luster* of cleavage faces is rather pearly. The *color* is a variable green, usually a rather dark green. Most chlorite is translucent. Its *hardness* is 2 to 2.5—just scratched by the fingernail. The *specific gravity* is about 2.7. The *streak* is pale green to white. The *composition,* which is extremely variable and complex because of solid solution, is $(Mg, Fe, Al)_6[(Si, Al)_4O_{10}](OH)_8$.

Occurrence. The chlorites are abundant and occur wherever previously existent rocks that contain iron-magnesian silicates—such as biotite, amphibole and pyroxene—have been altered by geologic processes. Many altered igneous rocks owe their green color to their content of chlorite, the original ferromagnesian silicates having altered more or less completely into this mineral.

Chlorite is also abundant in many schistose rocks. In chlorite schist, it is the prominent megascopic component and other finer-grained foliates—as, for example, green slates—owe their green color to its presence. Thus, as finely disseminated particles, it is a common coloring matter. Some of the iron-rich chlorites occur abundantly in sedimentary iron formations.

The Clay Group

The clays are one of the most difficult of all groups to deal with. They are so fine-grained that it is virtually impossible to see individual grains, even with a handlens, so that megascopic identification cannot be made. The general properties of the group can be described in terms of the common clay mineral, *kaolinite*.

General properties. Kaolinite, in common with most of the clays, crystallizes in the monoclinic system, forming small, thin plates or scales. The plates have hexagonal outlines (see Figure 2-9A) and are flexible but inelastic. The scales are generally so minute and so closely aggregated together, however, that the crystal form is no help in megascopic determination. All of the clays commonly occur in compact, friable, or mealy masses. The *color* is white but may become yellow, brown or gray. Neither the *hardness* (2 to 2.5) nor the *specific gravity* (2.6) can be used for practical tests. Rubbed between the fingers, the clay minerals have a smooth, unctuous, greasy feel that helps to distinguish them from fine aggregates of other minerals. Most aggregates of clay minerals have a musty odor when damp or breathed on.

Composition. On the basis of physical properties, such as the ability to absorb liquids, and the chemical composition, four main families of clay minerals are recognized. They are

1. *Kaolinites* $Al_4(Si_4O_{10})(OH)_8$
2. *Illites* $KAl_4(AlSi_7O_{20})(OH)_4$
3. *Montmorillonites* $(\frac{1}{2}Ca, Na)_{0.7}(Al, Mg, Fe)_4[(Si, Al)_4O_{10}]_2(OH)_4 \cdot n\ H_2O$
4. *Vermiculites* $(Mg, Ca)_{0.7}(Mg, Fe, Al)_8[(Si, Al)_4O_{10}]_2(OH)_4 \cdot 8H_2O$

Within individual families, compositions vary widely by solid solution and by addition or subtraction of water (particularly, in the montmorillonites).

Occurrence. Clays are all secondary minerals formed by weathering or by hydro-thermal alteration of previously existent aluminous minerals or volcanic glass. Although the properties of clays do not allow us to separate them megascopically, their mode of occurrence is sometimes an indication of which clay group is present.

The *kaolinites,* probably the most common clay minerals, are formed mainly by hydrothermal alteration and weathering of feldspars and feldspathoids. Thus the kaolinites occur in alteration zones around ore bodies, in hydrothermally altered masses of igneous rocks, and in soils where the parent materials were micas or alkali feldspars. *Illites* are the common clay minerals present in siltstone, claystone, mudstone, and shale. They are also common in small amounts in limestones. *Montmorillonites,* also known as smectites, are widespread, although occurring in small amounts. They are mixed with other clays in soils, particularly in those soils derived by weathering of basalts and other mafic rocks. Montmorillonite is also the principal constituent of *bentonite clay deposits,* which are formed by alteration of tuffs and volcanic ash. *Vermiculite* is derived by weathering or hydrothermal alteration of biotite, so it is commonly found as pseudomorphs after biotite; it also occurs in soils.

The Serpentine Group

The serpentines are three minerals—*chrysotile, lizardite,* and *antigorite*—all of which have similar compositions based on $Mg_6(Si_4O_{10})(OH)_8$ and which differ slightly in the degree of substitution of magnesium by iron. Other than chrysotile, which has a fibrous habit and is the common asbestos of commerce, the three serpentines cannot be distinguished megascopically.

General properties. Serpentine occurs in an amazing variety of forms and colors. It is usually massive, ranging from minutely to coarsely granular. Some samples are fibrous—the fibers being fine, flexible, and easily separable. Massive varieties have a conchoidal or splintery fracture and a smooth, greasy feel. The *color* of massive varieties is green, bright yellowish green, olive green, blackish green or nearly black. The fibrous varieties are generally brownish, yellowish brown, pale brown, or nearly white. The *luster* of the massive varieties is greasy, waxlike, glimmering, and typically feeble to dull; the luster of fibrous varieties is pearly to opalescent. Serpentine is translucent to opaque. The *hardness* is 2.5 to 3.0; an apparent greater hardness may be caused by the presence of traces of the original mineral or by infiltrated silica. The *specific gravity* is somewhat variable: for the fibrous varieties, 2.2 to 2.4; for the massive, 2.5 to 2.7.

Serpentine is easily distinguished from epidote and other common green silicates that may resemble it, by its greasy feel and softness.

Occurrence. Serpentine is a secondary mineral formed by the alteration of previously existing silicates that were rich in magnesium. Thus pyroxene, amphibole, and especially olivine are commonly found to be altered to serpentine. The process with olivine can be illustrated by the following equation:

Olivine	Water	Carbon dioxide	Serpentine	Magnesite

$$4Mg_2SiO_4 \;+\; 4H_2O \;+\; 2CO_2 \;=\; Mg_6(Si_4O_{10})(OH)_8 \;+\; 2MgCO_3$$

The equation suggests why *magnesite* ($MgCO_3$) is commonly associated with serpentine.

Another method of alteration to serpentine is by the action of aqueous solutions containing dissolved silica:

$$3Mg_2SiO_4 + 4H_2O + SiO_2 = Mg_6(Si_4O_{10})(OH)_8$$

Therefore, as an alteration product of such minerals, especially as the result of the action of hydrothermal solutions, serpentine is a common and widely distributed mineral that occurs both in igneous and in metamorphic rocks. It is commonly disseminated as small masses within rocks or forms large independent bodies, as noted in Chapters 4 and 6.

LESS-COMMON SILICATE MINERALS WITH SHEET STRUCTURES

Prehnite

One of the minerals commonly present as a secondary mineral lining cavities in basalts and related volcanic rocks has an attractive bright green color. It is prehnite, $Ca_2Al(Si_3AlO_{10})(OH)_2$. Crystals of prehnite are rare; most of it occurs as rounded groups of intergrown tabular crystals or in rough, rounded masses. *Hardness* is 6 to 6.5; *specific gravity* is 2.8 to 3.0; *color* is typically light green but may be white.

Pyrophyllite

In certain alumina-rich metamorphic rocks, frequently in association with kyanite, one may observe foliated or radiating masses of pyrophyllite, $Al_2(Si_4O_{10})(OH)_2$. It has a single perfect cleavage and yields folia that are somewhat flexible but not elastic. *Hardness* is distinctive at 1 to 2 and *specific gravity* is 2.8. *Luster* is pearly and *color* is usually white but also can be light green, gray or brown. Pyrophyllite has a distinctive greasy feel and is easily confused with talc.

Stilpnomelane

A rare, but important, mineral that resembles biotite is frequently observed in iron- and manganese-rich rocks subjected to low-grade regional metamorphism. The mineral is stilpnomelane, a micalike mineral in which ferric iron, Fe^{+3}, is a predominant component. A generalized formula for stilpnomelane is $K(Fe_5^{+3} Fe^{+2})(Si_4O_{10})_2(OH)_4O_4$, but actual compositions are much more complex because of substitutions for K, Fe^{+3}, and O. The basal *cleavage* of stilpnomelane is less perfect than that of biotite, and a second, imperfect cleavage occurs at right angles to it. The folia are brittle, a fact that distinguishes stilpnomelane from both biotite and chlorite. The *color* is black, greenish black or brown; the *hardness* is 2 to 3; and the *specific gravity* is 2.8 to 3.0. It typically occurs as micalike masses and flakes, but it may also be massive. It is generally associated with other iron minerals such as magnetite and pyrite.

Talc

General properties. Talc rarely occurs in distinct crystals. It is usually in compact or strongly foliated masses, or in scaly or platy aggregates grouped into globular or rosettelike forms. Like mica, it has a perfect *cleavage* in one direction, but, unlike mica, the resulting laminae, although flexible, are not elastic. It is sectile (capable of being cut smoothly with a knife). It has a smooth, greasy feel. The cleavage face has a mother-of-pearl-like *luster*. The *color* is white, often inclining to green, apple green, or, in some cases, gray to dark gray. It is typically translucent. The *hardness* is 1 to 1.5 and is easily scratched with the fingernail. The *specific gravity* is 2.7 to 2.8. The *streak* is white. Talc marks a cloth, the marking being best seen on dark color. This feature is the single distinctive megascopic test for talc. The *composition* is hydrous magnesium silicate: $Mg_3(Si_4O_{10})(OH)_2$. It is easily recognized by the properties mentioned above. When in fine scales, however, talc cannot be distinguished from sericite except by laboratory tests.

Occurrence. Talc is a secondary mineral produced by the action of hot circulating fluids on magnesium silicates, especially those free from aluminum, such as olivine and some pyroxenes and amphiboles. The process is illustrated by the following equation.

$$\underset{\text{Enstatite}}{4MgSiO_3} + \underset{\text{Water}}{H_2O} + \underset{\text{Carbon dioxide}}{CO_2} = \underset{\text{Talc}}{Mg_3(Si_4O_{10})(OH)_2} + \underset{\text{Magnesite}}{MgCO_3}$$

Thus talc commonly occurs in the igneous rocks, especially in peridotites and pyroxenites, as an alteration byproduct of such silicate minerals. The place, however, where talc is particularly abundant is in the metamorphic rocks where it forms large masses, as in soapstone. Or, it occurs as an important component of several varieties of schistose rocks, as in talc schists.

COMMON SILICATE MINERALS WITH CHAIN STRUCTURES

The chain-structure minerals have, as their basic building units, open-ended polymerized chains of silica tetrahedra. The chains may be single strands, as in the pyroxenes; double strands, as in the amphiboles; or triple strands, as in the mineral jimthompsonite. Despite the underlying differences in chain structures, all of the chain minerals look alike and are commonly difficult to distinguish one from another. Because of their family similarities in composition and structure, the chain minerals are frequently referred to, collectively, as the *pyriboles* from the names of the two most common members, the pyroxenes and the amphiboles.

The Pyroxene Group
The pyroxenes are common in igneous rocks; in fact, some igneous rocks (logically called pyroxenites) are composed almost entirely of pyroxene. Yet it is often difficult to recognize pyroxenes in rocks and to distinguish them from several other minerals, notably the amphiboles, by purely megascopic methods. It is generally impossible to tell apart, by megascopic means, many varieties of the pyroxenes recognized by mineralogists and petrographers. This is so because the varieties differ in chemical composition and in crystallographic properties that can only be detected by optical or X-ray means. For the practical purpose of identifying rock-forming pyroxenes, we therefore limit ourselves to the five most important members: *bronzite-hypersthene*, *diopside-hedenbergite*, *augite*, *aegirine*, and *jadeite*.

Composition. Pyroxenes are solid solutions of great complexity, all of which have the basic formula $XY[(Si, Al)O_3]_2$, where X may be Na^{+1}, Ca^{+2}, Mn^{+2}, Fe^{+2}, Mg^{+2}, and Li^{+1}; and Y may be Mn^{+2}, Fe^{+2}, Mg^{+2}, Fe^{+3}, Al^{+3}, Cr^{+3}, and Ti^{+4}. Additionally, there are crystallographic differences among the pyroxenes that lead to two large families.

One family is the *orthopyroxenes*, crystallizing in the orthorhombic system, of which bronzite and hypersthene are the most common members. The orthopyroxenes are a relatively simple solid solution in that only Mg^{+2} or Fe^{+2} are present and the same kinds of ions fill both the X and Y positions. Thus the end-members of the orthopyroxenes are *enstatite*, $MgSiO_3$ and *ferrosilite*, $FeSiO_3$, abbreviated to En and Fs, respectively. All rock-forming orthopyroxenes have intermediate compositions. The composition range for the two commonest ones are *bronzite,* $En_{87.5}Fs_{12.5}$ to $En_{70}Fs_{30}$, and *hypersthene,* $En_{70}Fs_{30}$ to $En_{50}Fs_{50}$.

The other family of pyroxenes, which embrace all of the remaining pyroxenes, is the *clinopyroxenes,* crystallizing in the monoclinic system. Among the clinopyroxenes, we separate individual members by composition. *Diopside* has the formula $CaMg(SiO_3)_2$, and significant amounts of Fe^{+2} can replace the Mg^{+2}. (The end-member, $CaFe(SiO_3)_2$ is *hedenbergite*). *Augite,* the most common of all pyroxenes, has the general formula, $(Ca, Na)(Mg, Fe, Al, Ti)[(Si, Al)O_3]_2$. Common rock-forming augite usually contains about 60 percent of the diopside end-member. *Aegirine* (sometimes also called acmite) is ideally $NaFe^{+3}(SiO_3)_2$, but extensive solid solution occurs by the coupled substitution $Na^{+1}Fe^{+3} = Ca^{+2}Mg^{+2}$ to give *aegirine-augite.* *Jadeite* is $NaAl^{+3}(SiO_3)_2$ with a limited substitution of Fe^{+3} for Al^{+3}

Form and habit. Crystals of bronzite and hypersthene are so rare that the distinction between orthorhombic and monoclinic pyroxene crystals is rarely employed in megascopic determination. The common form in which the monoclinic pyroxenes crystallize is a prism, short and thick as a rule, although some are longer and more slender. Such a prism is shown in Figure 2-10A, with the ends modified by pyramidal faces. Generally, however, the edges of the prism *mm* are truncated by a front face *a* and a side face *b*. These truncations may be small, with the result that *a* and *b* are narrow faces (Figure 2-10B), but as a rule the *a* and *b* faces are broad and the prism faces are narrow. Although these faces are generally well developed and lustrous, the pyramidal faces may be imperfect or wanting. The crystal, instead, is rounded at the ends. In rare cases, other pyramidal faces are present and the ends are more complex than shown in the figures. The augite crystals in igneous rocks, especially in porphyries and lavas, generally have the appearance and development shown in Figure 2-10C. The most important crystallographic feature of the pyroxenes is that the angle *m* on *m* is nearly a right angle so that the prism is almost square in cross section. When truncated by *a* and *b*, the prism is eight-sided, as shown in Figure 2-11. Besides occurring as prismatic crystals, the pyroxenes are common as grains or as more or less irregularly shaped masses; this is usually the way they appear in massive igneous rocks, such as gabbros and peridotites.

Cleavage and fracture. All of the pyroxenes have cleavage parallel to the two prism faces (*m* in Figure 2-10). The cleavage is generally good, but not perfect. In the ortho-

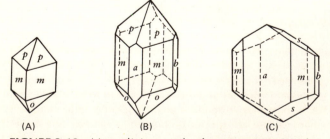

(A)   (B)   (C)

FIGURE 2-10 Monoclinic crystals of pyroxene. (A) Simple prism (*m* faces) truncated by pyramids *p* and *o*. (B) and (C) Most common form of pyroxene in which prism faces are modified by *a* and *b* faces.

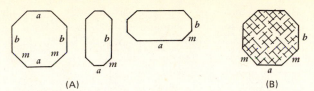

FIGURE 2-11   Cross sections of pyroxene crystals. (A) As commonly observed in igneous rocks. (B) Relation between cleavage and prism faces (*m*).

rhombic pyroxenes, the faces and cleavages are at an angle of 88.25°; in the monoclinic pyroxenes, at 87°. These differences are so close to 90° that pyroxene cleavages all seem to be at right angles (See Figure 2-11B). The nearly right-angled cleavage of pyroxenes serves to distinguish the group from the amphiboles. Some pyroxenes, as the result of pressures to which they have been subjected, have a good parting. The parting resembles cleavage, but its direction differs from that of the cleavage. The parting causes the mineral to appear lamellar, almost micaceous, as in the pyroxenes of some gabbros. Fracture is uneven and the mineral is brittle.

Color and luster. The pyroxenes range from white through shades of green to black, according to the amount and proportion of ferrous and ferric iron present. *Diopside* is white when pure, is rarely colorless and transparent, and is generally pale green and more or less translucent. *Augite* is dull green to black. *Aegirine* is black and opaque. *Bronzite* and *hypersthene* are gray, yellowish to greenish-white or brown and commonly have a bronzelike luster, which accounts for the name bronzite. *Jadeite* has a pearly luster on cleavage surfaces, a vitreous luster on fractures and is white, apple-green or emerald green in color. Less commonly, it is white with spots of green. The streak of most pyroxenes is white to pale gray green.

Hardness and specific gravity. The hardness of the orthorhombic pyroxenes and of diopside and augite, ranges from 5 to 6—some varieties can just be scratched by the knife. The hardness of jadeite and aegirine is between 6 and 7. The specific gravities of the pyroxenes range from 3.2 to 3.6.

Alteration. The pyroxenes are prone to alter into other substances, the nature of which depends partly on the kind of process to which they are subjected and partly on their own composition. Thus under the action of weathering, some pyroxenes may be converted into carbonates, such as calcite, whereas others, for example, those containing much iron, may break down completely into limonite plus carbonates.

Another important change is one that they undergo when subjected to metamorphic processes. In this change they are transformed into chlorite or to masses of fibrous or felty hornblende needles and prisms, usually of distinct but variable green colors. This process is of great geologic importance. By means of such change, whole masses of pyroxenic rocks, generally of igneous origin (such as basalts, gabbros, and peridotites), have been changed into chloritic and amphibole-rich rocks—rocks to which various names, such as greenstone, amphibolite and amphibole schist, have been applied.

Occurrence. The pyroxenes occur chiefly in igneous rocks, especially in those rich in calcium, iron, and magnesium. They should always be looked for in the dark-colored rocks of this class. They are sparse in most igneous rocks that contain much quartz; hence they are rare in granites and felsic porphyries.

Augite is common in basaltic lavas and allied rocks as well-formed crystals, but in gabbros and peridotites it generally occurs as irregularly shaped grains. Hypersthene is prominent in some varieties of gabbro and peridotite. Aegirine occurs chiefly in nepheline syenites and in the aphanite called phonolite. Some normal syenites and related rocks contain a diopsidelike pyroxene.

In the metamorphic rocks diopside occurs either as scattered well-formed crystals in recrystallized impure limestones and dolostones, or aggregated into large masses. Augite is abundant in many high-grade metamorphic rocks and hypersthene is a characteristic mineral of the problematic charnockitic suite rocks.

Being readily decomposed by weathering, pyroxenes play no part in sedimentary beds.

Determination. If the mineral under examination is in well-formed crystals, careful observation usually shows whether or not it is a pyroxene by the presence or absence of the forms previously described. Whether the cross section of the prism is square or not should be especially noted. Common rock-forming minerals with which pyroxenes may sometimes be confused are hornblende, epidote, and tourmaline. The lack of good cleavage, superior hardness, high luster, coal-black color, and triangular shape of the prism cross section of tourmaline readily distinguish that mineral from pyroxene. Epidote has one perfect cleavage and one poor one; it is much harder than the common pyroxenes, 6 to 7; and, although green, it commonly has a yellow tone, giving a yellowish green color unlike any of the pyroxene greens. The distinction between pyroxene and hornblende, which is more difficult to recognize, is treated in the section devoted to the determination of amphiboles.

To distinguish the several varieties of pyroxene from one another is always difficult. The only certain methods involve access to laboratory instruments.

The Amphibole Group

The amphiboles, as the pyroxenes, are a large and complex group within which both compositional and crystallographic differences are recognized. Many varieties recognized by mineralogists using laboratory tools simply cannot be discriminated by megascopic means. Thus, as with the pyroxenes, we limit our identification clues to the most common and distinctive amphiboles. They are *anthophyllite, tremolite-actinolite, cummingtonite, hornblende, glaucophane-riebeckite,* and *arfvedsonite.*

Composition. The amphiboles have a double chain of silica tetrahedra in which some substitution of silicon by aluminum may occur. Three additional cation groups are present so the general formula for the amphiboles is $X_{0-1}Y_2Z_5[(SiAl)_4O_{11}]_2(OH, F)_2$, where X may be Na^{+1} and K^{+1}; Y denotes Ca^{+2}, Na^{+1}, Mn^{+2}, Fe^{+2}, Mg^{+2}, and Li^{+4}; and Z denotes Fe^{+2}, Mg^{+2}, Fe^{+3}, Al^{+3}, and Ti^{+4}.

The most common orthorhombic amphibole is *anthophyllite,* $Mg_7(Si_4O_{11})_2(OH)_2$, in which X is zero and Mg occurs in both the Y and Z sites. About 30 percent of the Mg^{+2} ions can be replaced by Fe^{+2}.

The other amphiboles noted are monoclinic. *Tremolite* is $Ca_2Mg_5(Si_4O_{11})_2(OH)_2$ and replacement of Mg^{+2} by Fe^{+2} is possible, giving *actinolite*. *Cummingtonite*, $(Fe, Mg)_2 (Mg, Fe)_5 (Si_4O_{11})_2 (OH)_2$ has an obvious compositional relationship with anthophyllite, but cummingtonite is always more Fe-rich and is monoclinic. *Hornblende* has an extremely complex composition that can be simplified to $(Ca, Na)_2 (Mg, Fe^{+2}, Al)_5 [(Si, Al)_4O_{11}]_2(OH)_2$, but Ti^{+4} and Fe^{+3} can also be present. *Glaucophane* is $Na_2Mg_3Al_2(Si_4O_{11})_2(OH)_2$ with possible substitution of Fe^{+2} for Mg^{+2} and of Fe^{+3} for Al^{+3} to give *riebeckite* $Na_2Fe_3^{+2}Fe_2^{+3} (Si_4O_{11})_2(OH)_2$. *Arfvedsonite*, written in the form of the general formula above, is $NaNa_2(Fe_4^{+2}Fe^{+3})(Si_4O_{11})_2(OH)_2$, because Na occurs in both the X and Y sites, while both Fe^{+2} and Fe^{+3} are found in the Z site.

Form and habit. Crystals of both monoclinic and orthorhombic amphiboles look alike. Additionally, crystals of anthophyllite are so rare that for all practical purposes we can confine our discussion of amphibole crystals to the monoclinic varieties.

The crystals are generally long and bladed, formed by two prism faces *mm* (Figure 2-12A) that meet at angles of 54 and 126°. Some have terminal faces *rr*, but many crystals are imperfect at the ends and have no terminal faces; such imperfect crystals are common in rocks. The side face *b* is generally present, truncating the prism edge and giving the crystal a nearly hexagonal cross section, as in Figure 2-12B and D. The hornblendes conspicuous as phenocrysts in andesites commonly have a fairly long prism and appear as in Figure 2-12C; they are the hornblendes that as a rule have distinct terminal planes. If present, the prismatic faces *mm* and the *b* face tend to be shiny, whereas the ends are generally dull.

Amphibole rarely occurs as crystals whose planes can be seen distinctly. If recognizable crystals do occur, they are mostly the hornblendes forming the phenocrysts in aphanite porphyries and the amphiboles occurring in limestones and dolostones altered by metamorphism. Amphibole commonly appears as long, slender blades with rough irregular ends, as, for example, in hornblende schists where the crystals are aggregated together in more or less parallel positions. They may be so small as to be mere shining needles, so minute that the individual prisms can hardly be discerned with the lens; the aggregate then has a silky appearance. In felsic aphanites and porphyries, the hornblende phenocrysts range from short prisms, like those in the figures, to slender needles. In massive granular rocks, such as diorite, the amphibole generally occurs as irregular grains.

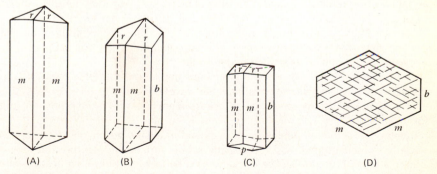

(A)   (B)   (C)   (D)

FIGURE 2-12 Amphibole crystals. (A), (B), (C) Common crystal forms. (D) Cross-section of amphibole showing the position of cleavage.

Cleavage and fracture. Amphiboles have a perfect cleavage parallel to the prism faces *mm,* as illustrated in the cross section in Figure 2-12D. Like the prism faces *mm,* these cleavages meet at angles of 126° and 54°, a feature of great importance in distinguishing all the amphiboles. The glittering prismatic faces seen on the blades and needles of broken rock surfaces are commonly due to this perfect cleavage. Other fracture is uneven.

Color and luster. The color varies with the amount of iron from purest white and gray in tremolite, through gray green or bright green in actinolite, to dark green and black in common hornblende, and brown in anthophyllite and cummingtonite. Arfvedsonite is black. Glaucophane and riebeckite are unique in that they have a deep lavender blue and a blue color, respectively. Some varieties of amphibole in igneous rocks seem to be black but are really deep brown. The amphiboles range from opaque in the deeper-colored varieties to translucent in the lighter ones. The luster is bright and vitreous to somewhat pearly on the cleavage surfaces; it is dull on other surfaces of large grains; it is silky for very fine, needlelike or fibrous varieties; and a few of the black amphiboles have an almost metallic luster. The streak of all amphiboles, regardless of their color, is white to gray-green or brownish.

Hardness and specific gravity. The hardness ranges from 5 to 6; some specimens can be scratched with the knife. The specific gravity ranges, chiefly with the amount of iron, from 3.0 to 3.5.

Alteration. The amphiboles alter much as the pyroxenes do. Under the action of various agents they are changed into serpentine or chlorite or both, with an accompanying formation of carbonates, sometimes of epidote and also of quartz. Under the continued action of weathering they break down into limonite, carbonates, and quartz. Thus on much-weathered rock surfaces, only rusty-looking holes and spots may be left to indicate the former presence of amphiboles.

Occurrence. Amphiboles are common and widely distributed minerals playing an important role in both igneous and metamorphic rocks.

Tremolite occurs chiefly in impure, crystalline marbles in contact-metamorphic zones and in a few schistose metamorphic rocks. In such occurrences it may have an extraordinarily finely fibrous structure and is capable of being split into long, flexible asbestiform fibers of great fineness and strength. *Actinolite* has its true home in the schists; it is the characteristic light green to bright green amphibole of many amphibolites, amphibole schists and greenstones. In many of these, it is secondary after the original pyroxene of a former gabbro or basalt, as described under uralite.

Common hornblende occurs both in igneous and in metamorphic rocks. It is found in granites, syenites, and diorite. It is abundant as phenocrysts in felsic porphyries. It is rare in basalt. In the metamorphic rocks, it occurs in gneisses and is the prominent mineral of hornblende schists.

Arfvedsonite occurs in nepheline syenites and in alkalic porphyries. *Glaucophane* is found only in metamorphic rocks, especially schists formed by high-pressure, low-temperature metamorphism. *Riebeckite* is also formed by metamorphism, particularly of iron-rich sedimentary rocks. The asbestiform variety *crocidolite,* mined in Australia and South Africa, is formed by metamorphism of a Precambrian siliceous iron-formation. Riebeckite also occurs in alkali-rich igneous rocks, particularly syenites and certain granites.

Anthophyllite is always a product of metamorphism, particularly of ultramafic igneous rocks.

Uralite is a name given to fibrous or fine-needlelike, columnar hornblende, secondary after pyroxene, and produced from it by metamorphic processes. The outward crystal form of the pyroxene is retained, but the substance is now hornblende in parallel bundles of needlelike prisms. Generally, the secondary amphibole is in aggregates, which may be very fine and feltlike, lying in the plane of schistosity. It is especially likely to occur when mafic pyroxenic igneous rocks have been subjected to deformation attended with squeezing and shearing. It varies in composition from actinolite to common hornblende, depending on the kind of pyroxene from which it was derived. Obviously, this change cannot be a simple rearrangement of the pyroxene molecule, which has twice as much calcium as the hornblende and lacks the necessary water and fluorine. Calcium separates out during the alteration of pyroxene to hornblende and forms a carbonate (calcite) or other calcium mineral. The availability of water is also necessary to produce the amphibole.

Determination. Amphibole is likely to be confused in megascopic observations with pyroxene, tourmaline, and epidote. To distinguish it from tourmaline and epidote, use should be made of the various physical properties mentioned under the determination of pyroxene. The excellent cleavage distinguishes at once an amphibole from tourmaline. Color differences usually suffice to distinguish amphibole from epidote. To distinguish amphibole from pyroxene is much more difficult, because these minerals have rather similar chemical compositions and physical properties. The following points will be found to be useful in this connection. If the mineral is in tolerably distinct crystals, its form should be carefully studied, especially the outline of the cross section of the prism, which can often be seen on a fractured surface of a rock. Comparison should be made with Figures 2-11 and 2-12.

If the crystal form is imperfect or wanting, the angle at which the cleavage surfaces meet should be carefully studied; the cleavage prism, as already described, is nearly square in pyroxene and highly oblique in amphibole (See Figures 2-11B and 2-12D). Further, the perfection of the cleavage in amphibole and the resulting bright, glittering surfaces give indications not often seen in pyroxene, the cleavage of which is only fairly good. Furthermore, amphibole tends to occur in needles or long-bladed prisms whereas pyroxene is commonly in short prismoids or blocky grains.

Finally, it must be realized that it is often impossible, especially in examining fine-grained igneous rocks, to tell by purely megascopic means whether the dark ferromagnesian mineral present is amphibole or pyroxene or, as is common, a mixture of both. To recognize this difficulty frankly, simply call the dark mineral *pyribole*, implying thereby that one or the other or both are present, but that they have not been distinguished. Examined under the microscope in a thin section or as powder immersed in an index oil, they can, of course, be easily and reliably identified.

LESS-COMMON SILICATE MINERALS WITH CHAIN STRUCTURES

Astrophyllite

In certain nepheline-syenites and alkali-rich granites one may observe elongate crystals, blades or starlike groups of a bronze-yellow mineral. It is astrophyllite, $(K, Na)_3 (Fe, Mn)_7$

$Ti_2 [SiO_3]_8(O, OH, F)_7$. The mineral has a perfect, micalike *cleavage*, but brittle laminae; a *hardness* of 3 and a *specific gravity* 3.3. It is commonly associated with the pyroxene aegirine and the amphibole arfvedsonite.

Chesterite and Jimthompsonite
Both the pyroxenes and amphiboles have been recognized as mineral groups for a long time. But the difficulty of identifying the pyriboles in fine-grained masses obscured the fact that another family of pyribole minerals, one with triple chains as the basic building block, also exists. The triple-chain silicates were only discovered in 1975, intergrown with talc, anthophyllite, cummingtonite, and tremolite. The triple-chain minerals are *chesterite*, $(Mg, Fe)_{17}(Si_{10}O_{27})_2(OH)_6$ and *jimthompsonite*, $(Mg, Fe)_5 (Si_3O_8)_2(OH)_2$. The fact that the minerals were only recognized in 1975 means that the triple-chain silicates are impossible to distinguish from their associated magnesian-amphiboles by megascopic means. It also suggests that whenever assemblages containing anthophyllite, cummingtonite, tremolite, and other magnesian-amphiboles are encountered, the presence of triple-chain silicates should be suspected and appropriate laboratory tests carried out.

Wollastonite
One of the minerals often encountered in contact metamorphosed limestones is *wollastonite*, $CaSiO_3$. Although wollastonite has a single chain of silica tetrahedra as its basic structural unit, the tetrahedra are twisted in such a way that wollastonite is not a true pyroxene. Wollastonite crystallizes in the triclinic system; has two perfect *cleavages*, which cause it to break into splintery fragments; has a *hardness* of 5 to 5.5, a *specific gravity* of 2.8, a *luster* that is vitreous to pearly on cleavage surfaces, and is white or less commonly gray in *color*. The common *habit* of wollastonite is as masses of silky-looking fibers; more rarely it occurs as tabular crystals. It is solely a metamorphic mineral and is commonly associated with calcite, diopside, tremolite (with which it is easily confused), andradite, and epidote.

COMMON SILICATE MINERALS WITH ISOLATED TETRAHEDRA OR TETRAHEDRAL GROUPS

Three large and important mineral families have isolated silica tetrahedra or tetrahedral groups—the *garnets*, the *olivines*, and the *epidotes*. All of the remaining members of this group are less common.

The Epidote Group
The epidotes are unusual in that they contain an isolated tetrahedral group (Si_2O_7) *and* a single tetrahedron, (SiO_4), in their structures.

Form and habit. Epidote crystallizes in the monoclinic system, the simplest form being that shown in Figure 2-13; its crystals, however, tend to be more complex, having many more faces. Well-developed crystals as a rule occur only in druses, in seams, and in cavities, and thus the crystal form is a character generally of not much use in megascopic determination. Epidote is common as bladed prisms extended in the direction of the edge *ac*. Slender needlelike forms are common, especially aggregated in bundles or sheaves. Terminations of prisms are generally rounded. Epidote also occurs as spherical and angular grains and as aggregates of such grains. The individual grains are commonly microscopic.

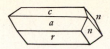

FIGURE 2-13 Common crystal form of epidote.

General properties. The *cleavage* is perfect in the direction parallel to the face *c*. The *fracture* is uneven. Epidote is brittle with a *hardness* of 6 to 7. The *specific gravity* is 3.2 to 3.5. The *color* is green, generally a peculiar yellowish green, ranging from the distinctive pistachio green to olive and very dark green; it is rarely brownish. The *luster* is vitreous and the *streak* whitish. It is translucent to opaque.

Composition. Epidote is a solid solution. The end-member is *clinozoisite* $Ca_2Al_3O[SiO_4][Si_2O_7](OH)$; common epidote has approximately one third of the Al^{+3} replaced by Fe^{+3} to give $Ca_2FeAl_2O[SiO_4][Si_2O_7](OH)$. Other substitutions are possible. When Mn^{+3} replaces Fe^{+3}, the purplish pink-colored epidote called *piemontite* results. When cesium and rare earth elements replace calcium, *allanite*, a pitch-black epidote is formed.

Occurrence. Epidote is characteristically a product of alteration of other minerals. When mafic igneous rocks undergo metamorphism of a relatively mild kind, epidote is likely to form. The most notable occurrences, however, are those in which impure limestones containing sandy, clayey, and limonitic impurities have been subjected either to regional or contact metamorphism. Epidote was then developed and was typically associated with other silicates that were apparently formed at the same time. In places the epidote is so abundant as to make extensive masses consisting almost entirely of it.

Determination. The peculiar yellow-green color, superior hardness, and perfect cleavage in one direction only generally suffice to distinguish epidote from olivine, hornblende, pyroxene, and tourmaline, with which it might be confused. The hardness distinguishes it at once from varieties of serpentine that resemble it in color.

A related mineral species, *zoisite*, has nearly the same chemical composition as epidote, to which it is closely related. It consists almost wholly of the Ca-Al silicate molecule of epidote and contains little or no Fe^{+3}. It is orthorhombic, but with regard to the crystals in rocks this characteristic can be ascertained only by optical methods. Zoisite occurs as aggregated blades or prisms, parallel or divergent, or as grains and masses. Its color is usually gray of varying shades. It can be told from epidotes lacking in iron only by optical or crystallographic investigation.

The Garnet Group

Form and habit. Garnets crystallize in the isometric system in the simple form of the rhombic dodecahedron shown in Figure 2-14A or of the trapezohedron shown in Figure 2-14B. Crystals are common and some show these forms well developed; other excellent crystals are complicated by bevelings of the edges of the dodecahedron. Commonly, however, the faces are not well developed and the garnet appears as a roughly spherical mass or grain.

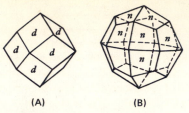

(A)   (B)

FIGURE 2-14   Common crystal forms
of garnet: (A) Dodecahedron; (B) trapezohedron.

Cleavage and fracture. Cleavage is absent. In some garnets occurring in sheared
rocks, however, a parting can be seen that causes a suggestion of lamellar structure. The
fracture is uneven. The mineral is brittle, but rocks composed largely of massive garnet
are very tough.

Hardness and specific gravity. The hardness ranges from 6.5 to 7.5; the specific
gravity, from 3.53 in grossular to 4.32 in almandine.

Composition. Garnets all have the general formula $X_3^{+2} Y_2^{+3} (SiO_4)_3$, where X may be
Ca^{+2}, Mg^{+2}, Fe^{+2}, Mn^{+2}; and Y may be Al^{+3}, Fe^{+3}, or Cr^{+3}. The compositions of end-
members are

Name	X	Y
grossular	Ca	Al
pyrope	Mg	Al
almandine	Fe	Al
spessartine	Mn	Al
andradite	Ca	Fe

Extensive solid solutions exist between the end-members. The most common garnet is one
in which almandine is the principal component.

Color and luster. Grossular is sometimes white but is generally pale green or yellow;
some is yellowish or reddish brown to brown. *Pyrope* is deep red to black. *Almandine*
and most "common garnet" is deep red to brownish red; *andradite* is honey yellow to
black, but may resemble grossular. *Spessartine* is brownish red to red. Unfortunately,
however, color is not a reliable guide to the composition of the garnets. The streak is light-
colored and not significant. The luster is vitreous, but some garnets tend to appear resinous.

Alteration. Garnets are resistant to weathering. Those containing iron are by far the least
resistant and may alter into rusty spots of limonite and other products of decomposition. The
manganese garnet (spessartine) has weathered under tropical conditions to form large bodies
of manganese oxide ore in India and Brazil.

Occurrence. *Almandine* is widely distributed as a component of metamorphic rocks. Its most striking occurrence is in mica schists, though it is also found in related rocks—for example, in many hornblende schists and in gneisses. It is present in some granite pegmatites and rarely in granite itself, as sporadic scattered crystals. *Pyrope,* the garnet chiefly used as a gemstone, occurs in eclogites and is a minor component of some peridotites and the serpentinites derived from them. *Grossular* occurs especially in metamorphosed impure limestones as a result of either contact or regional metamorphism. *Andradite* occurs in enormous masses in certain ores of contact-metamorphic origin.

Determination. The crystal form, appearance, color, and hardness generally suffice to enable one to recognize the garnets. Refined tests of a quantitative nature are necessary, however, if it is desired to ascertain the exact composition of a garnet.

The Olivine Group

Form and habit. Olivine crystallizes in the orthorhombic system, but the form is not a matter of practical importance, because olivine is rare as well-developed crystals in rocks but occurs instead as grains or as small, irregular masses of grains.

General properties. The single cleavage is poor and is not perceptible megascopically. The *fracture* is conchoidal. The *color* is green, ranging from olive green to yellow green; bottle green is common. A beautiful golden iridescence is often seen on fractured surfaces. Olivine is transparent, or translucent, but becomes brown or dark red and more or less opaque on oxidation of its iron content. It has a vitreous *luster,* white to yellowish *streak,* and a *hardness* of 6.5 to 7.0. The *specific gravity* ranges with the iron content from 3.22 to 4.39.

Composition. Olivine is a group name given to a continuous series of solid solutions ranging from *forsterite,* Mg_2SiO_4, to *fayalite,* Fe_2SiO_4. These end-members occur in rocks but are rare. Olivine is abundant in basalts, gabbros, and peridotites. In all of these the olivine is strongly magnesian, being composed predominantly of the forsterite molecule.

Alteration. When olivine alters by oxidation of the iron, it turns reddish or brownish, and eventually becomes a mass of limonite, accompanied by carbonates and some form of silica. The rusty iron product is the most noticeable result of the process.

Much olivine is found to be altered into serpentine, not as the result of weathering at the Earth's surface, but by more deep-seated processes. Other minerals, such as magnesite, magnetite, and quartz are likely to occur as by-products in the process.

Occurrence. Olivine is highly characteristic of the igneous rocks rich in ferromagnesian minerals. On the other hand, it so rarely occurs in igneous rocks composed chiefly of alkali feldspars—in granites or feldspathic porphyries—that for practical purposes it need not be sought in them. Anorthosite is the only feldspathic rock in which it may be at all abundant. Thus its true home is in gabbros, peridotites, and basalts, and the igneous rock known as dunite is a peridotite that consists almost wholly of olivine. In basalts, most olivine occurs as bottle-green grains; in gabbros and peridotites, it is commonly darkened by inclusions. Fine transparent crystals of olivine from basaltic lavas are cut for gems, commonly called peridots. The mineral is also found in meteorites.

Forsterite occurs in metamorphic rocks, especially in dolomitic marbles and in other rocks composed of varying quantities of other magnesian (and calcic) silicates, such as amphibole, pyroxene, and talc. Its origin is ascribable to reactions such as that between dolomite and diopside. For example:

Dolomite		Diopside		Forsterite		Calcite		Carbon dioxide

$$3CaMg(CO_3)_2 \; + \; CaMg(SiO_3)_2 \; = \; 2Mg_2SiO_4 \; + \; 4CaCO_3 \; + \; 2CO_2$$

Determination. The appearance, associations, and characters described above generally suffice to identify olivine. Although it can be confused with greenish, more or less transparent grains of pyroxene, its lack of cleavage and superior hardness generally enable one to distinguish it from that mineral.

Olivine can also be confused with epidote. Both minerals have similar hardnesses, but epidote has one good cleavage, while olivine lacks any. Also, because epidote is formed by alteration of other minerals, it is commonly associated with chlorite, calcite, and quartz, none of which is likely to be associated with olivine.

LESS-COMMON SILICATE MINERALS WITH ISOLATED TETRAHEDRA OR TETRAHEDRAL GROUPS

The Alumino-Silicates and Staurolite

Four aluminum-rich minerals are characteristically found in rocks developed by intense metamorphism of clay-rich shales; they are the three polymorphs andalusite, kyanite, and sillimanite, (see Figure 6-2B) and the iron-bearing mineral staurolite.

Andalusite is orthorhombic in crystallization and is generally in rough prisms, nearly square in cross section. The prisms may occur in radiated groups. The *cleavage* parallel to the prism is good; the other directions are poor. The *fracture* is uneven to subconchoidal. The normal *color* is white to pink or red to brown, but andalusite is likely to contain impurities, especially particles of carbonaceous matter, which color it dark or even black. Commonly, the particles are arranged in a symmetrical manner in the crystal so that, when it is broken or cut, the resulting cross section displays a remarkable symmetric pattern, such as a black cross in a white square. This feature helps to identify the mineral. It is usually subtranslucent in thin splinters. It is brittle and has a *hardness* of 7.5, a *specific gravity* of 3.2, and a white *streak*. The *composition* is Al_2SiO_5.

Andalusite is especially characteristic of the contact-metamorphic zones surrounding intrusive igneous rocks, such as granite. It occurs also in regionally metamorphosed tracts by the alteration of slates and shales. Rarely, it occurs in granite as the result of contamination—that is, the granite magma dissolved some aluminous sedimentary rock and the excess alumina thus acquired caused andalusite to form along with the normal minerals of the granite.

Kyanite is generally in long bladed crystals, which rarely show distinct end faces, or in coarsely bladed columnar masses. It is triclinic. It has one perfect *cleavage* and another less so; the angle between these is about 74°. The *color* is white to pure blue and the center of a blade may be blue bordered by white margins or rarely, gray or green to black. The *streak* is white. The crystal is transparent to translucent with a vitreous to pearly *luster*. *Hardness* varies in different directions from 5 to 7; it is softer (5) parallel to the length of the blade and harder (7) in the transverse direction. The *specific gravity* is 3.56 to 3.67. Its *composition* is Al_2SiO_5.

Kyanite is a mineral characteristically developed in regions subjected to intense metamorphism. It occurs in gneisses and in mica schists. In the latter the mica is mostly muscovite (commonly, a Cr-rich green variety) and in part, possibly the soda-bearing variety, paragonite. Kyanite is generally associated with garnet and staurolite or with corundum.

Kyanite is easily distinguished from other minerals, especially andalusite, which has the same chemical composition, by its form, its color, its having different hardness in different directions, and its specific gravity.

Sillimanite occurs as slender, four-sided prisms, commonly as parallel groups called *fibrolite,* or as radiating aggregates of prisms forming brushlike masses. It is orthorhombic, has one perfect *cleavage,* a *hardness* of 6 to 7, and a *specific gravity* of 3.2 The *color* is typically white or light gray; the *luster* is vitreous; and the *composition* is Al_2SiO_5.

Sillimanite is a product of intense metamorphism, being formed at higher temperatures and/or lower pressure than kyanite. It is found in gneisses that are commonly associated with muscovite, biotite, quartz, and plagioclase.

Staurolite is orthorhombic and generally occurs as distinct crystals of the form shown in Figure 2-15A. They are stout and thick, rarely long and slender but not strikingly so. The angle of the prismatic faces *m* on *m* is 50° 40′. They are terminated by flat bases *c,* but these cannot, as a rule, be seen in the rock. Staurolite commonly forms cruciform twinned crystals, as shown in Figure 2-15B and C. From this striking feature its name is derived, from the Greek, *stauros,* meaning a cross. Staurolite has a weak but distinct *cleavage* parallel to the face *b;* the fracture is subconchoidal. The *color* is dark reddish, yellowish brown, or almost black; the light transmitted through thin splinters appears almost blood red. The *streak* is white to gray; the *hardness* is 7 to 7.5; the *specific gravity,* 3.75.

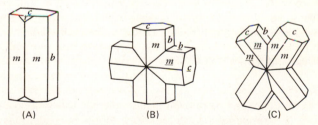

(A)   (B)   (C)

FIGURE 2-15   Commonly observed crystal forms of stau- rolite. (A) Untwinned crystal. (B) and (C) Twinned crystals. See also Figure 1-9B.

Staurolite has the end-member *composition* $Fe_2Al_9O_6(SiO_4)_4(OH)_2$, but a number of substitutions occur in nature: Mg^{+2} can replace Fe^{+2}, Fe^{+3} can replace Al, and O can replace OH.

Staurolite occurs in metamorphic rocks. It is a characteristic mineral of the crystalline schists. It is found in phyllites of argillaceous origin and in the corresponding mica schists and gneisses. It is commonly associated with dark-red garnets.

Axinite

In cavities in certain granites, and in contact metamorphic zones surrounding felsic igneous intrusives, one sometimes observes the distinctive mineral axinite. It is not a rock-forming mineral, but it deserves mention because it is one of two boro-silicate minerals that one is likely to see. The other is tourmaline.

Axinite has the ideal *composition* $Ca_3Al_2(BO_3)(Si_4O_{10})(OH)$ but Mn^{+2} and Fe^{+2} are both common substitutes for Ca. The mineral is triclinic. It commonly forms thin, wedge-shaped crystals with sharp edges but it also occurs as massive or granular aggregates. The *cleavage* is distinct; the *hardness* is 6.5 to 7; the *specific gravity* is 3.3; the *luster* is vitreous and the *color* is clove brown, violet or gray.

Beryl

Another mineral that does not qualify as a rock-forming mineral, but is distinctively present in many granite pegmatites, is beryl, $Be_3Al_2[Si_6O_{18}]$. The basic structural unit of beryl is a six-sided ring of tetrahedra, and this fact is reflected in the beautiful, six-sided, prismatic crystals of beryl that are often found. The *cleavage* is imperfect; the *hardness* is 7.5 to 8; and the *specific gravity* is 2.65 to 2.8. The *color* is commonly bluish green or green, but may be white or yellow. When transparent and not fractured, beryl is a gemstone—emerald, aquamarine, and morganite are the three best-known color varieties. Granite pegmatites are the most common location for beryl, but schists adjacent to granites and altered rocks associated with certain tin ores may also harbor beryl crystals.

Chloritoid

The mineral chloritoid may develop during metamorphism of iron- and aluminum-rich sedimentary rocks. The end-member *composition* is $Fe_2Al_4O_2(SiO_4)(OH)_2$, but most natural chloritoids have some Mg^{+2} replacing the Fe^{+2} and up to 25 percent of the Al replaced by Fe^{+3}. Chloritoid is monoclinic but rarely occurs as crystals. The common *forms* are coarsely foliated masses or thin scales. *Cleavage* is good but not as perfect as in the micas and the flakes are brittle. *Hardness* is 6.5; *specific gravity* is 3.5 to 3.8; and *color* is dark green, sometimes grassy green. The *streak* is white. Chloritoid is often associated with and confused with chlorite, but is much harder. In low to medium grades of metamorphism, most iron-rich rocks contain chloritoid. Commonly associated minerals are muscovite, chlorite, staurolite, and garnet.

Cordierite

Few minerals are misidentified more often than cordierite. This is so because it looks so much like quartz. The *composition* is $(Mg, Fe)_2Al_3(Si_5AlO_{18})$, but water may also be present because it can fit loosely into the centers of the six-sided rings of tetrahedra in the structure. Squat, prismatic, six-sided crystals are common, and although they are actually orthorhombic, they are called pseudohexagonal because of their shape. Cordierite is also rather commonly massive. The *cleavage* is poor and for identification purposes, it is absent. The *hardness* is 7 to 7.5; the *specific gravity* is 2.6 to 2.7; the *color* is various shades of blue or bluish gray; and the *luster* is vitreous. Unlike quartz, cordierite is commonly altered to mica, chlorite or talc. It is a common constituent of regionally metamorphosed argillaceous rocks, especially gneisses.

Eudialyte

In many nepheline syenites and nepheline-bearing pegmatites, one observes a distinctive cherry-red, accessory mineral. It is eudialyte, which has the ideal formula $Na_6Zr(Si_3O_9)_2$ (OH, F, Cl). Tabular or rhomhedral crystals are common; *hardness* is 5 to 5.5; and *specific gravity* is 2.9 to 3.0. The cherry-red *color* is common and distinctive, but pink, reddish-brown, and yellow varieties may be encountered. Eudialyte is commonly associated with astrophyllite.

The Humite Group
The humites are a small group of minerals so closely allied in all of their general properties that megascopically they are indistinguishable and should all be called humite.

The properties of one of the humites, *chondrodite,* can be applied to all humites. Although chondrodite is monoclinic, it rarely shows any definite crystal form that is of value in determining it. Instead, it appears as embedded grains and lumps. The *cleavage* is not marked, but may be distinct in one direction. It is brittle with a subconchoidal fracture. The *color* is yellow, honey yellow to reddish yellow, or brownish red. The *luster* is vitreous, the *hardness* is 6 to 6.5; and the *specific gravity* is 3.1 to 3.2. In *composition,* chondrodite is closely allied to olivine, but differs in containing fluorine and hydroxyl; it is $Mg(OH, F)_2Mg_4[SiO_4]_2$. As in olivine, the Mg is partly replaced by Fe^{+2}.

The characteristic mode of occurrence of humite is in dolostone that has been subjected to metamorphism. It forms yellowish or reddish imbedded grains associated with other metamorphic minerals, such as pyroxene, vesuvianite, magnetite, spinel, and phlogopite. In some rocks it is partially altered to serpentine.

Lawsonite
Lawsonite is a common associate of glaucophane in metamorphic rocks formed under high pressures and low temperatures. It is common as tabular or prismatic crystals. It has two good *cleavages;* the *hardness* is 8; the *specific gravity* is 3.1; the *color* is pale blue to bluish gray, sometimes colorless or mottled; and the *composition* is $CaAl_2(Si_2O_7)(OH)_2H_2O$.

The Melilite Group
The composition of melilite can be expressed in terms of two end-member compositions, those of *gehlenite,* $Ca_2Al(AlSiO_7)$, and *akermanite,* $Ca_2Mg(Si_2O_7)$. Melilite is tetragonal and most commonly occurs in short, square, prismatic crystals. The *cleavage* is good in one direction; the *fracture* is conchoidal; the *hardness* is 5; the *specific gravity* is 2.9 to 3.1; and the *color* is white, pale yellow or reddish brown. Some melilite occurs as a product of metamorphism of impure carbonate rocks. The most common occurrence, however, is as a constituent of nepheline basalts and other silica-deficient igneous rocks including melilitolites.

Pumpellyite
This mineral commonly is associated with prehnite and zeolites but is usually difficult to recognize. It is found with zeolites both in amygdules and in metamorphic rocks associated with glaucophane. Pumpellyite has a good *cleavage;* it is commonly observed in minute fibers or narrow plates. Its *hardness* is 5.5; its *specific gravity* is 3.2; its *color* is bluish green and its *composition* is $Ca_4MgAl_5O(Si_2O_7)_2(SiO_4)_2(OH)_3 \cdot 2H_2O$.

Sphene
Sphene is a common accessory mineral in granites and other silica-rich phaneritic igneous rocks, especially nepheline syenites. It also occurs in some metamorphic rocks. Sphene crystallizes in the monoclinic system and forms characteristic wedge-shaped crystals. The *composition* is $CaTiSiO_5$, and both iron and manganese may substitute for calcium. The

cleavage is distinct in one direction; the *hardness* is 5 to 5.5; the *specific gravity* is 3.4 to 3.5; the *color* is gray, brown, green or black; and the *luster* is resinous. The name *sphene* comes from a Greek word meaning "wedge" because the crystal form is the single most distinctive property of the mineral.

Topaz

Topaz crystallizes in the orthorhombic system and the *form* in which it is generally seen is in pointed prisms. It has one perfect *cleavage* and the *fracture* is uneven. The mineral is very *hard* (8) and brittle. The *specific gravity* is about 3.5. It is generally transparent or colorless, and in rare samples, is yellow to brown yellow or white and translucent. The *luster* is vitreous. The *composition* is $Al_2(SiO_4)(F, OH)_2$. Although topaz is not a common or important rock-forming mineral, it is interesting because it is particularly characteristic of the end stages in the formation of igneous rocks, when gases are being evolved. It occurs as crystals in miarolitic cavities of granites where the vapors have collected and it also occurs in essentially the same way in felsic aphanites, especially in rhyolite. Topaz also occurs in some pegmatites and in the fissures of the surrounding rocks that served as channelways for the hot escaping gases. In these occurrences it is generally associated with quartz, mica, and tourmaline and in some places with cassiterite.

The form, color, cleavage, and great hardness of topaz, together with its mode of occurrence, serve to distinguish it readily from other minerals.

Tourmaline

Tourmaline is a mineral of which there are many varieties distinguished by color, which in turn depends on the chemical composition of each variety. The chief ones are black, green, brown, and red. The black variety, known also as *schorl*, is the most common species.

Form. Tourmaline crystallizes in the rhombohedral division of the hexagonal system. The faces are, therefore, in threes or multiples of three. A simple form is shown in Figure 2-16A. The same form, as it appears to an observer looking down upon the upper end, is in Figure 2-16B. It consists of the three-cornered prism *m*, its edges beveled by the prism faces *a*, and terminated by the rhombohedron *r*. The crystals are more complex than this, if well developed, because more faces are present; if both ends are perfect, they have unlike faces. Most crystals are long, thin prisms; they are rarely short and thick. Generally, the prism faces *a* and *m* alternate repeatedly so that the prism is striated or channeled, as shown in Figure 2-16C, and the outline and appearance from above are as shown in Figure 2-16D. This cross section, resembling a spherical triangle, is very characteristic of the prisms of rock-making tourmaline. Tourmaline rarely occurs as formless grains or large irregularly shaped masses. The slender prisms and needles are commonly assembled together into bundles, sheaves or radiate groups.

General properties. Tourmaline has no *cleavage* and its fracture is rather conchoidal. It is brittle. Schorl is coal black; the *luster* is glassy, commonly dull; the *streak* is uncolored and hence not characteristic; the mineral is opaque; the *hardness* is 7 to 7.5; and the *specific gravity* is 2.9 to 3.2. Tourmaline becomes electrified—for example, it will pick up small bits of paper when briskly rubbed with wool.

Composition. Tourmaline is a complex solid solution with the general formula $(Na, Ca)(Mg, Li, Al)_3(Al, Fe, Mn)_6(BO_3)_3(Si_6O_{18})(OH, F)_4$.

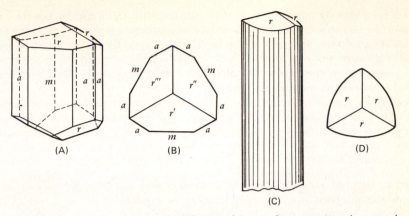

FIGURE 2-16 Common crystal forms of tourmaline. (A) Simple crystal showing characteristic prism faces (*m*). (B) End-view of crystal shown in (A). (C) Striations commonly observed on tourmaline caused by multiple growth of *a* and *m* faces. (D) End-view of crystal form shown in (C).

Occurrence. Tourmaline is abundant in the pegmatite dikes associated with intrusive masses of granites. Its presence in granite indicates, as a rule, nearness to the contact; it is very likely to occur in rocks that have been altered by contact metamorphism. It is not infrequently associated with certain ore deposits. It also occurs in certain gneisses, schists, and marbles.

Determination. The coal-black color, crystalline form, and mode of occurrence of common tourmaline generally suffice to identify it. It is easily distinguished from black hornblende by its lack of good cleavage, by its superior hardness, and especially by the shape of the cross section of its prism.

Vesuvianite
Vesuvianite is a tetragonal mineral whose typical habit is that of a short, thick, square prism that is terminated by a cut-off pyramid, as illustrated in Figure 2-17. It also occurs in lumps or grains. The *cleavage* is poor and is perceptible, if at all, in the direction parallel to the prism faces *m*. *Fracture* is uneven. The *color* is generally apple green, yellow, or brown. The *luster* is vitreous; the *hardness* is 6.5; and the *specific gravity* is about 3.4. The mineral is subtransparent to subtranslucent. The *composition* is $Ca_{10}(Mg, Fe)_2Al_4(Si_2O_7)_2(SiO_4)_5(OH, F)_4$.

FIGURE 2-17 Common crystal form of vesuvianite.

As a rock-forming mineral, vesuvianite characteristically occurs in limestones that have become coarsely crystalline through the contact-metamorphic action of igneous magmas. Formation of the mineral was evidently determined by emanations of steam and fluorine that issued from the magmas and reacted with the limestones. In these occurrences, vesuvianite is commonly associated with garnet, pyroxene, tourmaline, chondrodite, and other contact-metamorphic minerals.

Vesuvianite can be easily confused with garnet and epidote, which it resembles in color and general appearance, and also with pyroxene. Its crystal form (if definitely square prismatic) and its other physical characters generally serve to distinguish it from those minerals.

Zircon

Another widespread accessory mineral in igneous and metamorphic rocks is zircon, $ZrSiO_4$. Commonly seen in small, tetragonal prismatic crystals, zircon has a poor *cleavage*, a *hardness* of 7.5, a *specific gravity* of 4.7, an adamantine *luster*, and is commonly *colored* a shade of brown, but may be colorless, gray or green. Zircon is little affected by weathering so tends to pass unchanged into sedimentary rocks where its high specific gravity leads to its concentration in placers. It is relatively common in both river and beach sands.

II. THE NONSILICATE MINERALS

Although there are many compositional families, only eight, in addition to the silicates, are of even passing importance in megascopic petrography. These are the oxides, hydroxides, sulfides, sulfates, carbonates, phosphates, halides, and the native elements.

THE OXIDE MINERALS

The most widespread group of minerals, after the silicates, are the oxides. Among them, the oxides of iron and of titanium are by far the most common and important.

Magnetite and the Spinels

Magnetite crystallizes in the isometric system, most commonly in octahedrons, as in Figure 2-18A, in dodecahedrons, and rarely in a combination of both (Figure 2-18B). It may occur as distinct crystals in rocks but is generally in small grains, the forms of which cannot be distinguished. It also occurs in larger, irregular masses.

General properties. Magnetite has no *cleavage*. Some, however, has a parting parallel to the octahedral faces that resembles cleavage. This rift appears to be a pressure effect, since it has been produced experimentally. The *fracture* is uneven. Magnetite is opaque and has a dark-gray to iron-black *color*. The *luster* is metallic and fine to dull. Magnetite commonly resembles bits of iron or steel in rocks and is always *strongly magnetic*. The *streak* is black; the *hardness* is 6; and the *specific gravity* is 5.18. The *composition* is Fe_3O_4 ($= Fe^{+2}O \cdot Fe^{+3}_2O_3$).

Occurrence. Magnetite is one of the most widely distributed of all minerals. It occurs in igneous rocks of all kinds, generally as small grains. In some places, however, it is aggregated into considerable masses—some large enough to be rich ore bodies. It also occurs in rocks produced by contact metamorphism and in crystalline schists, sometimes in large bodies. Though common in unmetamorphosed sedimentary rocks, it is rarely abundant. It is not likely to be confused with any other mineral except ilmenite.

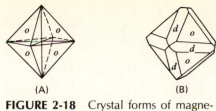

(A)   (B)

FIGURE 2-18 Crystal forms of magnetite: (A) Octahedron; (B) octahedron modified by faces of the dodecahedron (*d*)

Magnetite is resistant to weathering. It may alter to limonite, and, under the conditions of lateritic weathering, it may alter to pseudomorphs that consist of ferric oxide and are called *martite*.

The spinels. Magnetite is actually a member of a large family of minerals called the spinels. The family has the general formula $X^{+2}O \cdot Y_2^{+3}O_3$. All of them crystallize in the isometric system, typically as octahedrons. The *compositions* of the more important members of the family are

Name	X^{+2}	Y^{+3}
chromite	Fe	Cr
hercynite	Fe	Al
magnetite	Fe	Fe
spinel	Mg	Al

Although extensive solid solutions are possible, only magnetite is magnetic. *Chromite* is common in peridotites and other ultramafic rocks, and may occasionally be aggregated sufficiently to form rock masses called chromitite. Its *color* is iron-black to brown black, resembling magnetite, but its *streak* is dark brown. Its *hardness* is 5.5 and its *specific gravity* is 4.6. *Spinel* and *hercynite,* the aluminous varieties, are much harder, ranging from 7 to 8. They may be colorless, black, green or other colors; they lack cleavage; and they generally have a high luster. Spinel is commonly present in Al-rich metamorphic rocks, in many cases with diopside and forsterite. Hercynite has a similar mode of occurrence but is found in more Fe-rich rocks. It also occurs in some ultramafic igneous rocks.

Hematite

Form. Hematite crystallizes in the rhombohedral division of the hexagonal system, but it is so rarely in distinct, well-formed crystals of observable size as a rock constituent that crystal form is not a matter of practical importance. It occurs as a rock-making mineral in three different guises: *specular hematite* (also called specularite), *micaceous hematite,* and *common red hematite.* As specular hematite, it forms masses and plates; the latter are commonly hexagonal in outline. Its *color* is black to steel gray and in rare cases, with a faint reddish tone. It is opaque and has a metallic *luster,* which, as a rule, is brilliant or splendent so that it resembles polished steel. Some of it, however, is rather dull but still metallic looking. The *fracture* is subconchoidal. There is no *cleavage.*

As micaceous hematite, it occurs in thin flakes that somewhat resemble mica. The flakes may be so thin that they are translucent and they are then deep red. The *luster* is submetallic to metallic, but it may be splendent like that of the specular form. The thin leaves generally have ragged outlines, but some are hexagonal.

Common red hematite does not appear crystallized, although it is minutely crystalline. In appearance, it is massive, columnar, granular, in stalactitic or mammillary masses, or earthy. It is dull, without metallic *luster,* opaque, and dark red.

General properties. The *streak* of all hematite is red, from bright red to brownish red. This furnishes the most convenient method of distinguishing hematite from magnetite and limonite.

The *composition* is Fe_2O_3. The *hardness* ranges from 5.5 to 6.5, but the red ocherous variety, because of its fine state of division, seems to be much softer than 5.5. The *specific gravity* of specularite is 5.26.

Occurrence. Hematite is one of the most widely distributed of minerals. Micaceous hematite is a common accessory component of feldspathic igneous rocks, such as granite. It occurs abundantly in megascopic form in certain crystalline schists and in the quartz-hematite schists formed by metamorphism of Precambrian iron formations. Also, as minute microscopic scales, it forms the red coloring matter in igneous and metamorphic rocks. Just as the red color of many potassium feldspars is attributable to its presence, so is the color of many slates.

Common red hematite occurs as beds and masses, many of them of great size, in both sedimentary and metamorphic rocks. Some of the beds and masses constitute valuable ores of iron. Hematite also occurs as the interstitial cement of many stratified rocks, such as red sandstones. As a red pigment in the form of powder, it is distributed ubiquitously in rocks of all classes and in soils.

Ilmenite

General properties. Ilmenite crystallizes in the hexagonal system but it is so rarely in good megascopic crystals within rocks that its crystal form is not important. It typically occurs as embedded grains and masses or as plates that are irregular or hexagonal in outline. It is brittle and has no *cleavage.* *Fracture* is conchoidal. The *color* is iron black, and in rare instances, with a faint reddish or brownish tinge. The luster is submetallic and the *streak* is black to brownish red. Ilmenite is opaque. It has a *hardness* of 5.5 to 6 and a *specific gravity* of 4.7. The *composition* is $FeTiO_3$. In general, ilmenite is not pure but is more or less mixed with hematite. Some specimens of ilmenite are weakly magnetic.

Occurrence. Ilmenite is widely distributed as an accessory component in igneous rocks in the same general manner as magnetite, which it generally accompanies. It also occurs as a widespread minor component in gneisses and schists. Unless the embedded grains are of such size that they can be easily tested, especially for magnetism, ilmenite cannot usually be distinguished from magnetite by simple inspection. The most important occurrences of megascopic ilmenite are in the coarse-grained gabbros and anorthosites where it is very common. In fact, in some places ilmenite occurs in such large quantities that it is a commercial source of titanium—for example, in the Adirondacks and in Québec. Ilmenite also occurs in many coarse-grained sediments and in placers.

Corundum

Corundum crystallizes in the hexagonal system. The form generally assumed is either a thick six-sided prism, swelling out in the middle into a barrel-like shape, or a six-sided tablet. Corundum also occurs in grains or shapeless lumps. The thick barrel-like forms are most common when it occurs in massive rocks such as the syenites. On some parting faces a multiple twinning, resembling that illustrated as occurring on feldspars, can be seen. Corundum does not have a *cleavage,* but it does have one parting, which simulates a perfect cleavage parallel to the base. Also poor, additional partings occur in three other directions at an angle to the base. (They are parallel to the unit rhombohedron.) In large pieces of corundum these latter partings, or pseudo-cleavages, appear to be at nearly right angles. Rock-making corundum is dark gray, bluish gray or smoky in *color.* It is very rarely blue, forming the variety *sapphire.* Even more rarely, it is red, giving the variety *ruby,* which is extremely rare. The *luster* is adamantine to vitreous but may be dull or greasy in rock grains. Corundum is translucent to opaque. It is the hardest of the rock-forming minerals (9). It is brittle, though sometimes very tough. The *specific gravity* is 4.

Corundum is an important primary mineral in the igneous rocks of a few regions, such as in the nepheline syenites of Ontario and in the pegmatites associated with those syenites. It also occurs in some contact zones of igneous rocks, where it typically occurs as thin tabular crystals. It is present in some metamorphic rocks, in some places in thick layers of the rock called emery.

Rutile

Most rutile occurs as tetragonal prismatic crystals, commonly with striations parallel to the length of the prism. Compact and massive varieties are also known, but crystals are more common. The *cleavage* is distinct; the *hardness* is 6 to 6.5; the *specific gravity* is 4.2; and *color* is red, reddish-brown or black. The *streak* is pale brown and the *luster* is adamantine. The *composition* of rutile is TiO_2, but considerable amounts of iron may be present.

Rutile is very common as an accessory mineral, especially in greisens, granite pegmatites, gneisses, and schists. It also is fairly common in some coarse sediments, especially beach sands, where it collects by virtue of its resistance to weathering and its high specific gravity.

Pyrolusite and Psilomelane

Manganese, like iron, occurs in two common oxidation states in minerals. In silicate and carbonate minerals, the Mn^{+2} state is important, whereas by weathering and reaction with the atmosphere, the Mn^{+4} state develops. Two Mn^{+4} minerals, pyrolusite and psilomelane, may be encountered.

Pyrolusite is rarely seen as crystals. Most of it occurs as radiating fibers, dendritic films on joint surfaces (See Figure 5-12) or earthy masses. When crystalline, its *cleavage* is perfect and its *hardness* is 6 to 6.5. In the common earthy varieties, its *hardness* is 1 to 2 and it will soil the hand. The composition is MnO_2. *Color* and *streak* are both iron black.

Pyrolusite is present in the black manganese nodules on the deep-sea floor (Figure 5-31), in bogs, and in lake bottoms. Most commonly, pyrolusite occurs as a stain or thin film on joint and fracture surfaces where it has been deposited by circulating waters.

Psilomelane, $Ba_3Mn_8O_{16}(OH)_6$, resembles pyrolusite in many ways, and is commonly intermixed with it. Most psilomelane is massive, botryoidal or in amorphous-looking films and masses. The *hardness* is 5 to 6; the *specific gravity* is 3.7 to 4.7; and the *color* is black. The *streak* is brown-black. The common origins and associations of psilomelane are the same as those of pyrolusite. The best way to distinguish between the two minerals is by streak.

THE HYROXIDE MINERALS

Limonite and Goethite
For many years limonite was considered to be an amorphous colloidal form of ferric hydroxide mixed with silica and other fine-grained material. X-ray studies, however, have shown that the main constituent of limonite is a microcrystalline form of *goethite*, $FeO \cdot OH$, and that little or no amorphous material is present. Nonetheless, analysis of limonite usually shows more water than the 10.1 percent indicated by the formula of goethite. Presumably, the additional water is held by capillary forces between the micro-crystalline grains. In addition, fine-grained substances, such as hematite and other iron minerals, may also be present. Thus unless pure goethite fibers can be seen megascopi-cally, the name *limonite* remains a convenient field term.

Limonite occurs as films and coatings, in earthy masses, and, when in considerable deposits, commonly shows stalactitic or mammillary shapes and concretionary forms. Limonite has no *cleavage*. Although the *luster* of compact varieties is silky to submetallic, it generally is dull and earthy. The *color* is a shade of brown, ranging from very dark to yellowish brown. The surface of the compact stalactitic or mammillary forms may have a varnishlike skin. It is opaque. The *streak* is yellow-brown. The *hardness* of the compact mineral ranges from 5 to 5.5 and the *specific gravity* from 3.6 to 4.0. The yellow-brown streak is the most convenient means of distinguishing limonite from similarly appearing hematite.

Gibbsite and Diaspore
The high alumina-type of laterite, formed by extreme tropical leaching, is called *bauxite*. The high Al-content is attributable to the presence of either *gibbsite* $[Al(OH)_3]$, or diaspore $(AlO.OH)$, or both. Neither mineral is common as large crystals, though diaspore may be found as bladed masses or as thin, platelike crystals associated with corundum. The common forms are the same—earthy, clay-like mixtures that are commonly pisolitic. Both minerals are white, gray, yellow or reddish in *color* and have a hardness of 1 to 3. The pisolitic character (Figure 7-4) is a tip-off, but not certainly diagnostic. When gibbsite or diaspore are suspected, analysis and laboratory tests are called for.

THE SULFIDE MINERALS

Only the three sulfides of iron—pyrite, marcasite, and pyrrhotite—are common and wide-spread minerals in ordinary rocks. Chalcopyrite may be encountered in some igneous and metamorphic rocks. The remaining sulfide minerals are usually observed only in ores.

Pyrite

Form. Pyrite is by far the most common sulfide mineral, and the first to be suspected and tested for whenever a sulfide mineral is encountered.

Pyrite occurs almost invariably as crystals, and rarely as grains and masses. It crystallizes in the isometric system. It is frequently seen in cubes or in the twelve-sided form shown in Figure 2-19A, which is called the pyritohedron because pyrite so commonly demonstrates this type of crystallization. Combinations of the cube and pyritohedron are also common. (See Figure 2-19B). The cubic faces are generally striated by fine lines, as shown in Figure 2-19C and the striae are produced by an oscillatory combination of the pyritohedron on the cube faces. The octahedron is far less common; it is likely to be modified by the pyritohedron, as shown in Figure 2-19D. Other more complex forms also occur.

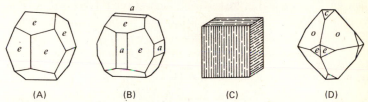

(A)   (B)   (C)   (D)

FIGURE 2-19 Common crystal forms of pyrite. (A) Pyritohedron. (B) Pyritohedron modified by cube faces (a). (C) Cube, striated by oscillatory development of pyritohedron faces. (D) Octahedron (o) modified by pyritohedron, (e).

General properties. There is no *cleavage*. The *fracture* is conchoidal to uneven; the *color* is brass yellow; and the *luster* is metallic and splendent, although duller when tarnished. Pyrite is opaque. The *streak* is brownish or greenish black. The *hardness* is notably high for a sulfide: 6 to 6.5. The *specific gravity* is 5.0. The *composition* is FeS_2.

The color and crystallization usually suffice at once to identify pyrite and to distinguish it from other minerals. Pyrite is readily distinguished from pyrrhotite and chalcopyrite by the test for hardness: chalcopyrite, at 3.5, can be readily scratched with the knife and furthermore gives reactions for copper. Pyrrhotite also is scratched by the knife and, in addition, has a bronze color and is commonly magnetic.

Occurrence. Pyrite has many different modes of origin. Consequently, it occurs in rocks of all kinds as a scattered component, generally in small distinct crystals or, less commonly, is aggregated. The largest masses of pyrite are found in ore deposits, chiefly formed by the action of hydrothermal solutions. In igneous rocks it occurs in small amounts. In sedimentary rocks it is common as replacements of fossils. It is also common in coal beds, forming many of the so-called coal brasses.

Marcasite

Marcasite, a polymorph of pyrite, FeS_2, is orthorhombic. It is often seen as radiating masses or tabular crystals that are commonly twinned to look like a cocks-comb. The *hardness* is 6 to 6.5; the *specific gravity* is 4.89; and the *color* is pale bronze-yellow and considerably lighter than pyrite on a freshly broken surface. *Streak* is grayish-black. Marcasite is opaque. It is much less common than pyrite, with which it is easily confused. Marcasite most frequently occurs as concretions in clays and shales. It may also be observed as replacements of fossils and along joints and fractures in some limestones. It readily oxidizes and breaks down to a corrosive, white powder.

Pyrrhotite

Pyrrhotite has a variable composition, ranging from FeS to Fe_7S_8. It is common as small anhedral grains in rocks, but may be massive in some ores. The *color* is bronzy brown and on freshly broken surfaces, it is distinctly different from pyrite or marcasite. On tarnished surfaces, however, it can be iridescent and may be confused with either pyrite or marcasite. The *streak* is black and the *luster* is metallic. It is opaque. The *hardness* is 4, softer than pyrite, and the *specific gravity* is 4.6. Pyrrhotite is magnetic, though the strength of the magnetism varies and is greatest with highest sulfur content. Pyrrhotite is common in mafic igneous rocks, especially gabbros. It also occurs in contact metamorphic rocks and in many ores.

Chalcopyrite

Chalcopyrite is the most common and widely occurring mineral of copper. It is rarely seen in crystal form. Instead, it occurs as massive pieces or anhedral grains. *Color* is brass-yellow, commonly tarnished bronzy or iridescent and thus is easily confused with pyrite and pyrrhotite. *Streak* is greenish black; *hardness* is 3.5 to 4; and *specific gravity* is 4.2. *Composition* is $CuFeS_2$. Chalcopyrite can be distinguished by its color on freshly fractured surfaces, its relative softness, and its streak and lack of magnetism. It occurs as small, accessory grains in mafic igneous rocks and in many schists, but chalcopyrite is most common in veins and copper ores. It is a common ore mineral in porphyry-copper deposits.

Other Sulfide Minerals

A number of other sulfide minerals may be encountered, mainly in ores. Most can be readily recognized.

Arsenopyrite, $FeAsS$, is common as prismatic, pseudo-orthorhombic crystals. *Cleavage* is poor to absent; *color* is silver-white; *streak* is black; *hardness* is 5.5 to 6. *Specific gravity* is 6.1; *luster* is metallic; and it is opaque. It has a garlic-like odor when ground or beaten. It occurs in contact metamorphic rocks, in pegmatites, and in ore deposits, most commonly associated with tin and tungsten minerals.

Bornite, Cu_5FeS_4, is a soft (3), massive, copper mineral that occurs in many ores. It is rare in common rocks. It has no *cleavage*; the *color* on fresh surfaces is copper-red to bronze-brown, but tarnish forms rapidly, giving iridescence. The *streak* is pale grayish brown. Bornite may be confused with pyrrhotite, which is magnetic, or with chalcocite, which differs in color.

Chalcocite and *digenite* are two copper sulfides, Cu_2S and Cu_9S_5, respectively. They are essentially impossible to distinguish one from the other megascopically. They rarely occur as crystals, but are generally massive. Both are important ore minerals. Their *color* is shiny lead gray (digenite has a bluish tinge), but they tarnish to a dull black on exposure. *Streak* is grayish black; *hardness* is 2.5 to 3; and *specific gravity* is 5.5 to 5.8. *Luster* in both types of copper sulfide crystals is metallic and they are both opaque.

Covellite, CuS, is typically massive, but also occurs as anhedral grains and as coatings in copper ores. It has perfect *cleavage,* a distinctive indigo-blue *color,* a lead-gray *streak,* and a hardness of 1.5 to 2. It is opaque. Although covellite is a distinctive mineral, it can be confused with tarnished forms of bornite.

Galena, PbS, is the only important lead mineral. It commonly occurs as cubic crystals. *Cleavage,* which is perfect and parallel to cube faces, gives distinctive cube-shaped cleavage fragments. The *hardness* is 2.5; the *specific gravity* is 7.4 to 7.6; the *luster* is metallic; and the *color* and *streak* are both shiny lead-gray. Galena is a distinctive mineral because of its cleavage. It is common in veins and massive ores and is generally associated with sphalerite. In many places, it is also found with pyrite and chalcopyrite.

Molybdenite, MoS_2, occurs as thin hexagonal plates, which are found commonly as foliated masses or scales. Molybdenite is an accessory mineral in some granites and pegmatites, but it is most common in ore deposits. *Cleavage* is perfect and yields flexible laminae; *hardness* is 1 to 1.5; and *specific gravity* is 4.6 to 4.7. *Luster* is metallic; *color* is lead gray; and *streak* is grayish black; molybdenite is *opaque.* Molybdenite may be distinguished from graphite, which it resembles, because of its higher specific gravity and its streak. On *glazed porcelain,* molybdenite gives a greenish streak, whereas graphite produces a black streak.

Sphalerite, ZnS, is the most important zinc mineral. It is common as tetrahedral crystals, which are typically complex because of numerous modifying forms and/or twinning. It also may be massive. *Cleavage* is perfect; *hardness* is 3.5 to 4; and *specific gravity* is 3.9 to 4.1. *Luster* is submetallic and distinctively resinous. *Color* of sphalerite is commonly brown, yellow or black, but in some cases it can be red or green. *Streak* is white to pale brown. It is transparent to translucent. Sphalerite can be identified by its luster, hardness, and cleavage. It is common in ore deposits.

Tetrahedrite, $Cu_{12}(Sb, As)_4S_{13}$, has a complex formula because of complete substitution of antimony and arsenic and the replacement of copper by iron, zinc, silver, and mercury. Tetrahedrite is a common and important ore mineral in many ore deposits. It generally occurs as tetrahedral crystals, but also may be massive and granular. Tetrahedrite lacks *cleavage,* has a *hardness* of 3 to 4.5, a *specific gravity* of 4.6 to 5.1, a metallic *luster,* a grayish-black to black *color,* a black to brown *streak* and is opaque. The most distinctive property is its crystal form, but luster, color, and streak are also helpful in identifying it.

THE SULFATE MINERALS

Only two sulfates, anhydrite and gypsum, are sufficiently abundant to be called rock-forming minerals. Barite and alunite, however, are important accessory minerals.

Gypsum

Gypsum crystallizes in the monoclinic system. The common form of the crystal is shown in Figure 2-20A. The same crystal is shown in Figure 2-20B, revolved so that the side face *b* is parallel with the plane of the paper. Such crystals can be roughly tested by placing them on the diagram and seeing if the angles coincide. Twin crystals are common; they tend to assume fishtail or arrowhead forms, as shown in Figure 2-20C. More commonly, as a rock constituent, gypsum is granular. Less commonly, it is foliated, with curved surfaces. Some gypsum is fibrous.

Gypsum has a perfect *cleavage* parallel to the side face *b*. By means of it, very thin sheets with perfect luster can be split off, almost as in mica. Such sheets break in one direction along straight lines but with a subconchoidal fracture. This rift is a result of

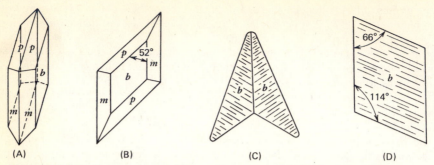

FIGURE 2-20 Common crystal forms of gypsum. (A) Simple monoclinic crystal. (B) Side-view of (A). (C) Twinned crystal forming distinctive fishtail or arrowhead shape. (D) Cleavage rhomb of gypsum.

another cleavage that is parallel to the edge between the prismatic faces *mm*. If the sheets are bent, cracks will appear in them, making angles of 66 to 114° with the straight fracture edge just mentioned. If bending parallel to this direction is continued, the sheets will break with a fibrous fracture, and a cleavage rhomb like that shown in Figure 2-20D will be obtained. In massive, coarsely crystalline gypsum, the cleavages can usually be obtained, and they furnish one means of helping to identify it. In compact massive forms, it is likely that no cleavage can be seen. Fibrous gypsum simply cleaves parallel to the fibers.

Gypsum is generally colorless or white and most crystals are transparent to translucent. Massive varieties, however, may be red, orange, yellow, brown or black, because of the presence of impurities, and may range from translucent to opaque. The *luster* of the cleavage face is glassy to pearly; that of fibrous varieties is satiny; and massive forms are glistening and glimmering to dull. The *streak* is white. The *hardness* is 1.5 to 2.0, easily scratched by the fingernail. The *specific gravity* of pure crystals is 2.32. The *composition* is $CaSO_4 \cdot 2H_2O$. Heated moderately (not above 200°), gypsum loses some water and becomes plaster of Paris. When moistened, the powder absorbs water again and sets, becomes solid, and thus turns back into gypsum. Gypsum is widely distributed in sedimentary rocks, commonly forming thick and relatively pure beds, as a result of evaporation of seawater. It also occurs in lake deposits, in shale and muds, as an alteration product where sulfide minerals are oxidizing, and as deposits from volcanic fumaroles.

Anhydrite

Anhydrite crystallizes in the orthorhombic system. In the rocks in which it occurs, it is granular, ranging from coarse to extremely fine grained or, less commonly, it is fibrous. It has *cleavages* in three directions at right angles, and in coarsely crystalline anhydrite the cleavage can be seen to produce cubelike forms. Most anhydrite is white, but some is tinted blue. The *luster* of the cleavage faces is pearly to glassy but in massive varieties, it ranges to dull. Anhydrite is harder (3 to 3.5) than gypsum but anhydrite is easily cut by a knife. The *specific gravity* is 2.95. The *composition* is $CaSO_4$.

Because anhydrite reacts with near-surface waters to form gypsum, it is much less common in outcropping rocks than in equivalent subsurface rocks. Like gypsum, anhydrite forms beds that are interstratified in sedimentary sequences, especially in those that are predominately limestones and shales. It is also found in masses and in geodes. It is a common associate of rock salt and gypsum. A completely different occurrence of anhydrite is as an alteration product in the central zones of many porphyry copper deposits.

Alunite

Usually found in massive form or as disseminated powders, alunite has the composition $KAl_3(SO_4)_3(OH)_6$. It forms as a byproduct when acids act on alkali feldspars or muscovite. The *hardness* is 4; the *specific gravity* is 2.6 to 2.8; and the *color* is white, gray or reddish. The fact that alunite, dispersed in water, gives an acid solution serves as a distinctive test. Alunite is found around fumaroles and as a byproduct or alteration product in many ore deposits.

Barite

Barite, $BaSO_4$, can be seen in many ore deposits, around hot springs or as veins or irregular masses in limestones. It may occur as tabular crystals, as groups of crystals, or it may be massive and earthy. The *cleavage* is perfect; *hardness* is 3 to 3.5; and *specific gravity* is 4.5, which is distinctively heavy for a nonmetallic mineral. *Color* of barite is white, light blue, yellow or colorless; and the *luster* is pearly to vitreous.

THE CARBONATE MINERALS

The two important rock-making carbonates are calcite and dolomite but the structurally related accessory minerals, siderite, magnesite, and ankerite can easily be confused. Aragonite, a polymorph of calcite, is an important constituent of many seashells. Additionally, the two highly colored copper carbonates, azurite and malachite, make bold showings on outcrops and should be recognized.

Calcite

Form. Calcite crystallizes in the trigonal subdivision of the hexagonal system. Its crystals, are, as a rule, well developed and perfect, and some are of large size. It has a great variety of crystal forms, many of which are complex. Some simple crystals are shown in Figure 2-21. Figure 2-21A shows a simple flat rhombohedron, three faces above and three below. Figure 2-21B shows the unit rhombohedron, so called because its faces are parallel to the cleavage. Figure 2-21C shows a short prism having six prism faces *m* and the flat rhombohedron *e* above and below. Figure 2-21D is similar to Figure 2-21C, but the prism faces *m* are elongated. Figure 2-21E is an acutely pointed form, the scalenohedron. All these crystal forms are commonly shown by calcite. They occur where calcite lines cavities in rocks, in druses, in amygdaloids, in geodes, and on the surface of joint planes and fissures. Calcite also forms in caves—in short, in all places where calcite has been deposited by infiltrating water carrying the dissolved mineral in solution.

As a rock-making mineral, calcite is massive. It is coarse to finely granular in marble, compact in ordinary limestone, or loose and powdery in chalk. It has an open-work or spongelike structure in travertine and a rounded, stalactitic structure in the dripstone of cave deposits and in concretions. Uncommonly, it is fibrous.

Cleavage. Calcite has a perfect rhombohedral cleavage in three directions parallel to the rhombohedral faces *r* of the crystal shown in Figure 2-21B. Although this cleavage is best produced in isolated crystals, it can also be readily seen on the fractured surfaces of

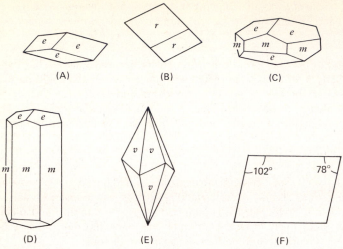

FIGURE 2-21   Common crystal and cleavage forms of calcite.
(A) Flattened rhomb. (B) Common rhomb showing *r* faces that are
parallel to cleavage planes. (C) and (D) Rhomb (*e*) modified by
prism (*m*). (E) Scalenohedral crystal. (F) Face of a cleavage rhomb.

coarsely crystalline massive rocks, as in many marbles and related rocks, and in the
massive calcite of veins (Fig. 1-7B). The angles of the face of the rhombs produced by
cleavage are 78 and 102°, as shown in Figure 2-21F. Small cleavage pieces can be readily
tested by applying them to the edges of the figure on the paper.

General properties. The *hardness* is 3, so calcite is readily scratched or cut by the
knife. The *specific gravity* is 2.71. Calcite is generally colorless or white, but it also displays
a great variety of exotic colors owing to the presence of impurities. Thus, it may be reddish
or yellowish from iron oxides, gray to black from organic matter, or green, purple, or blue
from other substances. The *streak* is white to gray. Crystallized calcite has a vitreous *luster*
and massive forms are glimmering to dull. It ranges from transparent through translucent
to opaque. The *composition* is $CaCO_3$. Fragments effervesce freely in *cold,* very dilute
hydrochloric acid. This test will distinguish calcite from dolomite, which will only effervesce if finely powdered.

Occurrence. Calcite is one of the most abundant and widely distributed of all minerals. It occurs in the igneous rocks as the result of alteration of the calcium-bearing
silicates by water containing dissolved carbon dioxide. The calcite thus formed may remain
for a time in the rock, but eventually, as the rock breaks down into soil, the calcite is, to
a greater or lesser extent, carried away in solution.

Calcite also occurs in minute cavities in unaltered igneous rocks, especially intrusive
ones. Its presence is probably attributable to infiltration and deposition of material derived
from neighboring rock masses. In many such cavities, the calcite is ordinarily not observable megascopically, but its presence is easily ascertained by immersing a fragment of the

rock in cold dilute acid and by seeing if it effervesces. Calcite also occurs in amygdaloidal cavities in lavas, especially in basalts.

In the sedimentary and metamorphic rocks, calcite is much more important. It is very commonly distributed through them either in fine particles or by forming a cement to other mineral grains. From this minor role, it increases more and more in abundance as a constituent, until finally, there are enormous rock masses, such as the chalks, limestones, and marbles that are composed largely or wholly of calcite. Such rocks are described in their appropriate places. It suffices here to mention that in the sedimentary rocks, calcite is an important constituent of chalk, limestone, calcareous marls, and calcareous sandstones. It is also an important part of travertine, dripstones, and veins; and in the metamorphic rocks, it comprises many marbles and occurs in rocks that are mixtures of calcite and various silicate minerals.

Determination. Calcite, if sufficiently coarsely crystallized, is easily recognized by its inferior hardness and rhombohedral cleavage. This determination may be confirmed chemically by its ready solubility in cold dilute acids with effervescence of carbon dioxide gas. For the distinction from dolomite, see the following entry.

Dolomite

Form. Dolomite like calcite, crystallizes in the trigonal division of the hexagonal system and, like calcite, occurs as simple rhombohedral crystals, the faces of which are parallel to the cleavage. Unlike calcite, dolomite rarely forms complex crystals and the simple rhombohedron, which is the prevalent habit when dolomite shows crystal form, usually has curved instead of flat faces. Moreover, the curved crystals are likely to be compound—that is, they are made up of several subindividuals. This is the habit dolomite has where it lines druses and cavities. As a rock-making mineral, dolomite—like calcite—is generally massive and ranges from coarsely granular to exceedingly fine grained.

Cleavage. The cleavage, like that of calcite, is perfect in three directions parallel to the faces of the simple rhombohedron. The angles of the cleavage rhombs (approximately 74° and 106°) differ only a few degrees from those of calcite and, accordingly, they cannot be distinguished from those of calcite by the unaided eye.

General properties. The natural *color* is white, and though this is common, dolomite is likely to be tinted some exotic color by other substances. Thus it may be reddish, brown, greenish, gray or even black. The *luster* is vitreous, pearly to dull or glimmering in compact varieties. Dolomite is translucent to opaque. The *hardness* is 3.5 to 4.0, harder than calcite but easily scratched with a knife. The *specific gravity* of the pure mineral is 2.87. The *composition* is $CaMg(CO_3)_2$.

If unpowdered, dolomite reacts feebly, if at all, in cold, dilute hydrochloric acid. If powered, it effervesces, though not as briskly as calcite. Even lump dolomite effervesces in hot acid and dissolves rapidly. The difference in action of cold acid on powdered, as contrasted with its effect on unpowdered dolomite, is a convenient means of distinguishing dolomite from calcite in the field.

Occurrence. Dolomite is a scattered accessory component of certain crystalline schists and in beds of gyprock. Its great importance as a rock-making mineral lies in the fact that it forms thick, areally extensive beds in both sedimentary and metamorphic rock series—that is, there are rocks that are composed predominately to wholly of dolomite. Thus dolomite parallels calcite, and in limestones and dolostones (and in the marbles derived from them), we have every degree of association between the two minerals—rocks that are composed of calcite alone, rocks that have both in all percentages, and rocks that are pure dolomite. These are described in more detail in chapters 5 and 6.

Determination. The rhombohedral cleavage and inferior hardness separate dolomite, like calcite, from other common rock-making minerals. The commonly curved surfaces help to distinguish it from calcite, but the already mentioned test with acid is the best distinction.

Unfortunately, simple tests do not always serve to distinguish calcite from dolomite, nor, when fine-grained samples are involved, either calcite or dolomite from aragonite. In such circumstances selective staining with organic dyes may be used. The equipment and materials needed to carry out the staining tests are readily available from chemical supply houses and it is not even necessary to have a chemical laboratory available. Many etching reagents can be used, as discussed by Friedman (1959), but two in particular—Harris' hematoxylin and Feigl's solution—are the easiest to use and are the most reliable. Samples to be tested can be chips, a freshly broken hand specimen, or a cut surface. The surface should be etched for 3 to 5 minutes in a hydrochloric acid (HCl) solution prepared by diluting one part of concentrated HCl with ten parts of distilled water. After etching, the sample is washed in running water and then is either immersed in or painted with a solution of Harris' hematoxylin. That solution can be prepared by adding 3 milliliters of 10 percent HCl to 50 milliliters of commercial grade Harris' hematoxylin. The solution must be well shaken before using. After application of the solution, nine to ten minutes are generally required for the development of an even coat of purple color on the calcite. Dolomite remains unaffected.

If Harris's hematoxylin is unavailable, calcite will stain a deep red when it is immersed in a solution containing 0.1 gm of Alizarin Red S that is dissolved in 100 milliliters of 0.2 percent cold HCl. The stain develops in two to three minutes, during which time dolomite remains unaffected.

To distinguish dolomite and calcite from aragonite, use Feigl's solution. Etch and wash the sample to be tested as previously described. Prepare the solution by dissolving 11.8 grams of $MnSO_4 \cdot 7H_2O$ in 100 cc of water, by adding more solid Ag_2SO_4 than will dissolve, and by boiling the solution. Allow the solution to cool, filter it to remove any undissolved Ag_2SO_4, and add one or two drops of a concentrated solution of NaOH. A precipitate will form, and after 1 or 2 hours the solution should again be filtered before being stored in tightly stoppered, *dark* glass bottles. When samples are immersed in this solution for a few minutes, aragonite will stain black while calcite and dolomite remain unchanged.

Siderite, Magnesite, and Ankerite

Each is a rhombohedral carbonate showing the same crystal and cleavage forms as calcite and dolomite. *Siderite*, $FeCO_3$, is commonly light to dark brown in *color* and usually is more or less massive. In sedimentary beds, it commonly occurs as concretions called "clay ironstone." *Magnesite*, $MgCO_3$, typically occurs as white, compact masses in veins and as irregular pods derived by alteration of Mg-rich igneous and metamorphic rocks.

Ankerite, CaFe(CO$_3$)$_2$, which is closely related to dolomite, is generally massive, but rarely occurs as crystals. Its *color* is commonly pink, but it may be colorless or gray to brown. Ankerite is most common in sedimentary iron formations and in hydrothermal veins. Both magnesite and ankerite react to cold acids as dolomite does; siderite reacts more like calcite.

Aragonite

Aragonite, which is orthorhombic, occurs as radiating masses of steep-sided pyramidal crystals, as tabular plate-like crystals, and in some cases as pseudohexagonal crystals formed by twinning. Massive, columnar, and stalactitic aggregates are also known. *Cleavage* is distinct in one direction, poor in a second. *Luster* is vitreous and *color* is white, yellow to colorless or rarely gray. *Hardness* is 3.5 to 4; *specific gravity* is 2.95; and it is transparent to translucent. Aragonite is CaCO$_3$ and like calcite, effervesces in cold, dilute hydrochloric acid. It can be distinguished from calcite by cleavage and specific gravity and from both calcite and dolomite as described under dolomite. It is the common, fine-grained carbonate in the shells of many molluscs. It also occurs as crusts in serpentinites and as crystals in druses in basalts. It is associated with glaucophane as massive bodies in certain metamorphic rocks that have been affected by high pressure and low temperature metamorphism.

Azurite and Malachite

Azurite and malachite, Cu$_3$(CO$_3$)$_2$(OH)$_2$ and Cu$_2$CO$_3$(OH)$_2$, respectively, are the bright azure blue and bright green carbonates formed as products of weathering of copper minerals. Both are soft (3.5 to 4) and both effervesce readily with cold dilute acids. That simple test distinguishes them from other secondary copper minerals.

THE PHOSPHATE MINERALS

Only one phosphate mineral is common—apatite. Monazite is an important secondary mineral.

Apatite

Apatite crystallizes in hexagonal prisms either rounded at the ends or capped by a six-sided pyramid. It is scratched by the knife, has a vitreous *luster* and is white, green or brown. There is no good *cleavage*. It is brittle. It is transparent in small crystals but ranges to opaque in large masses. The *composition* is Ca$_5$(PO$_4$)$_3$(F, OH).

Apatite occurs in large, even huge, crystals in pegmatites and in metamorphosed limestones interlayered with schists. These may be said to be its chief megascopic modes of occurrence. In these, however, apatite cannot be said to function as a rock-forming mineral of wide or general importance. Apatite also occurs as minute microscopic crystals in essentially all kinds of igneous rocks and in many metamorphic rocks. Microscopic study of the thin sections of such rocks has shown that, in this form, apatite is almost universally distributed as an accessory component. A rare, but important form of chemical sedimentary rock, phosphorite, consists largely of apatite in crusts or in small shapeless masses and/or nodules. Phosporite is the world's principal source of phosphorus for fertilizers. Phosphorus is essential for plant growth and for our own well being since apatite is the main constituent of bones and teeth.

Monazite

Monazite, $(Ce, La, Y, Th)PO_4$, is a distinctive and widespread mineral. It occurs as an accessory mineral in many granites, pegmatites, nepheline syenites, and gneisses and as a persistent placer mineral in coarse, clastic sediments. It lacks distinctive *cleavage*, has a hardness of 5 to 5.5, a *specific gravity* of 4.6 to 5.4, a red-brown to yellow *color*, and a distinctive resinous *luster*. It may be confused with zircon and sphene, but monazite is softer than zircon and more dense than sphene. Also, monazite is typically massive or anhedral, whereas zircon and sphene tend to form distinct crystals.

THE HALIDE MINERALS

Halite

Halite NaCl, is the chief chloride that occurs as a rock-forming constituent in such amounts as to be important. It is easily recognized by its cubic crystals, perfect cubic *cleavage*, solubility in water, and saline taste. Halite is colorless and transparent or white and translucent; it also may be tinted various colors by impurities. The *hardness* is 2.5.

Halite occurs in beds, some of which are of enormous extent, in sedimentary evaporite formations. It is generally accompanied by gypsum and anhydrite, and in a few places by other valuable chlorides, such as *sylvite* (KCl) and *carnallite* $(KMgCl_3 \cdot 6H_2O)$. Perhaps more remarkable than even the great salt beds are the salt domes, the intrusive plugs and stocks of salt, that have risen up from deeply buried salt beds to dome and pierce through the sedimentary rocks above them.

Fluorite

Fluorite is a common and widely distributed mineral, but always in accessory amounts. It is isometric and commonly forms cubic crystals; it also may be massive and granular. *Cleavage* is perfect parallel to octahedral faces (Figure 1-5) and distinctive; the *hardness* is 4; and *specific gravity* is 3.18. *Color* is light green, blue, yellow, purple or colorless. *Composition* is CaF_2 and it is transparent to translucent. Fluorite is common in many hydrothermal veins and in cavities in limestones and marbles.

THE NATIVE ELEMENTS

No native elements are common rock-forming minerals, but several are accessory minerals, and thus may be encountered.

Graphite

Graphite is hexagonal but is rarely seen as crystals. Typically, it occurs as foliated or scaly masses. *Cleavage* is perfect and so easy that graphite has a distinctive slippery feel. *Hardness* is 1–2—so soft that graphite soils the hand and marks paper. *Specific gravity* is 2.23; *color* and *streak* are black; and *luster* is generally metallic. In some cases, however, luster is dull and earthy. Graphite occurs most commonly in metamorphic rocks, where it is apparently the endstage product in metamorphism of carbonaceous matter. Graphite may be confused with molybdenite—see that entry for distinctions.

Native Metals

Several native metals may be encountered in rocks.

Copper, Cu, occurs as flakes, irregular masses, plates, and scales of secondary origin, especially in cavities in basalts. It also is present in oxidized zones of some ore deposits. Native copper can be distinguished by its red color on fresh surfaces, its high *specific gravity* (8.9), its *hardness* (2.5 to 3), and its malleability. It is readily cut with a knife, exposing a fresh surface on which the color can be observed.

Gold, Au, is rarely seen as cubic or octahedral crystals; it generally occurs as tiny, irregular grains in quartz veins and in stream placer deposits. Gold is soft (2.5 to 3) and it is chemically resistant so it does not alter or tarnish. It has a distinctively high *specific gravity* (19.3) and a characteristic gold *color.* Its extreme malleability and ductility serve to distinguish gold from similar-looking materials.

Iron, Fe, is rare in rocks but common in many meteorites and in man-made slags. Iron has a poor *cleavage;* a *hardness* of 4.5; and *specific gravity* of 7.3 to 7.9. It is opaque, malleable, steel-gray to black in *color* and strongly magnetic—it is, in fact, the only malleable, strongly magnetic mineral. Native iron occurs as small grains in some serpentinites and in basalts that have assimilated organic matter.

Platinum, Pt, only rarely occurs as crystals; it generally occurs as anhedral grains and rough masses. It has a *hardness* 4 to 4.5 and *specific gravity* of 21.4 when pure, but specific gravity can be as low as 14 because of solid solution of other elements, such as iron and palladium. It is malleable and ductile, has a steel-gray *color* with a bright, shiny metallic *luster,* which is undiminished by tarnishing since platinum is practically resistant to weathering. Platinum occurs as tiny grains in some ultramafic rocks, commonly associated with chromite. It also is present in placers formed by weathering of such rocks.

Silver, Ag, is rare as crystals but is fairly common as masses, plates, wires, and scales. The *hardness* is 2.5 to 3; the *specific gravity* is 10.5; the *color* is silver-white, but is often tarnished brown to black. It is malleable and readily cut by a knife, which allows the true color to be observed. Silver is rather widely distributed in small amounts as both a primary mineral and in oxidized zones of silver-rich ore bodies.

MINERALOIDS

Certain materials resemble minerals in many ways and even have distinctive properties, but are *not* minerals. They are either amorphous or they are mixtures and are, therefore, mineraloids. The mineraloids most likely to be encountered are *opal,* which has already been discussed under the entry for tridymite and cristobalite, *glass, resin, tars,* and *pitches.*

Glass

Glass has an extremely wide range of compositions, depending on origin. Natural glasses are most commonly formed by rapid cooling of rhyolitic or andesitic lavas, but glasses of basaltic composition are also well known. Man-made glasses are very widespread, both as discarded articles of commerce and household use and as waste products from smelters (many slags are glassy) and furnaces.

The *luster* of all glasses is vitreous when fresh but may become dull with age due to spontaneous crystallization, a process called devitrification. *Color* ranges from colorless, white, black, and brown to red, orange, yellow, green, blue, purple, and several diverse combinations. *Streak* is white. *Fracture* in all glasses is conchoidal; *hardness* ranges between 5 and 6. *Specific gravity* is variable, depending on composition; commercial and natural glasses tend to be in the range 2.4 to 2.8, whereas many slags and furnace wastes are higher, some reaching as high as 4.4.

Resin

Natural gums or resins can be encountered in certain sedimentary beds, particularly those of terrestrial origin. When transparent and pleasantly colored, resin is called *amber* and is used for jewelry. The *color* is yellow, red or brown; the *streak* is white. *Luster* is distinctive, hence the term resinous. The *fracture* is conchoidal; the *hardness* is 2 to 2.5; and the *specific gravity* is about 1.05. Resins are organic matter and will readily melt in a flame, often giving off dense white fumes that are irritating to the nostril.

Tar

Tar, pitch, asphalt, and bitumen are all names for solid petroleum materials that are formed when evaporation of the more volatile hydrocarbons from petroleum leave a residue of large molecule compounds with low volatility. Tars are brown to black in *color,* and have brown *streaks,* distinctive pitchlike *lusters,* and conchoidal *fractures.* All tars are soft, with a *hardness* of 1+. The specific gravity ranges from 1 to 1.8. Tar melts in a flame and will ignite and burn with a bright orange flame. Tar is also soluble in many organic solvents such as benzene.

Useful References

Bailey, E. H. and Stevens, R. E. (1960), "Selective Staining of K-feldspar and Plagioclase on Rock Slabs and Thin Sections," *American Mineralogist,* Vol. 45, pp. 1020–1025.

Dana, E. S. (1932), *A Text Book of Mineralogy,* 4th ed., revised by W. E. Ford, New York: John Wiley & Sons, Inc., 851 pp. An old but very reliable text that covers all known minerals up to 1932.

Deer, W. A., Howie, R. A., and Zussman, J. (1966), *An Introduction to the Rock-Forming Minerals,* New York: John Wiley & Sons, Inc., 528 pp. A handy, abbreviated version of the following five-volume work. Tends to deal more with chemistry and microscopic properties than with megascopic characteristics.

Deer, W. A., Howie, R. A., and Zussman, J. (1962), *Rock Forming Minerals,* Vol. 1, *Ortho- and Ring Silicates,* 333 pp.; Vol. 2, *Chain Silicates,* 379 pp.; Vol. 3, *Sheet Silicates,* 270 pp.; Vol. 4, *Framework Silicates,* 435 pp.; Vol. 5, *Non-Silicates,* 371 pp., New York: John Wiley & Sons, Inc. The standard modern reference for the common, rock-forming minerals. Remarks about previous entry also apply to these volumes.

Dietrich, R. V. (1969), *Mineral Tables—Hand Specimen Properties of 1500 Minerals,* New York: McGraw Hill Book Company, 237 pp. A useful, compact set of tables. Some knowledge of mineralogy is assumed.

Friedman, G. M. (1959), "Identification of Carbonate Minerals by Staining Methods," *Jour. Sed. Petrol.,* Vol. 29, pp. 87–97.

Pough, F. H. (1976), *A Field Guide to Rocks and Minerals,* 4th ed., Boston: Houghton Mifflin Co., 317 pp. A low-level, nonprofessional book. Popular with amateur rock and mineral collectors.

Roberts, W. L., Rapp, G. R., Jr., and Weber, J. (1974), *Encyclopedia of Minerals,* New York: Van Nostrand Reinhold Company, 693 pp. A colorful and authoritative reference work. Good coverage of all minerals discovered since the 1932 publication date of Dana's *Textbook of Mineralogy.*

See also, references listed at end of Chapter 1.

CHAPTER 3
determination of the rock-forming minerals

The most important physical properties of the rock minerals have been described in the preceding chapter. Some people have difficulty in remembering all of the mineral properties, so this chapter tabulates the most useful ones in order to help you make systematic tests that will result in correct identification.

The tables can be used only to distinguish the minerals that are named in them, one from another; they cannot be used to distinguish these minerals from all other minerals. If doubt arises and a mineral seems to be something other than one of those described here, larger volumes of descriptive and determinative mineralogy should be consulted or the mineral should be taken to a laboratory for microscopic or X-ray examination.

The tables are based entirely on megascopic and easily determinable physical properties that can be used to advantage in the field. The only equipment needed is a hammer for collecting samples, a handlens, a pocket knife (preferably with a magnetized blade), a copper penny and a fragment of quartz for making hardness tests, and possibly a streak plate. In actual practice, a streak plate is not necessary because the color of the powdered mineral can be checked by grinding a small piece of the mineral between two hammer faces, by pouring the resulting powder on a piece of white paper, and then by rubbing the dust with a finger or knife blade to observe the color produced.

The most obvious feature about a mineral, generally seen at first sight, is its luster— it is either metallic to submetallic or it is nonmetallic. We use this feature as the separating property in the first two of the following tables.

Table 3-1 includes only minerals with metallic or submetallic lusters. Most of these minerals are opaque. In any case, the transparency, translucency, or opacity, if not obvious in a mineral enclosed in a rock, can be tested by holding a fragment or sliver of the mineral against a light and observing whether light is or is not transmitted through its thinnest edges. Because the most readily applied tests are hardness and streak, these properties are used to further organize the table. Minerals softer than a copper penny (3.5), are separated from those with hardnesses between 3.5 and the hardness of the knife blade (5.2), and again from those that are harder than a knife blade. After having found the correct portion of Table 3-1 on the basis of hardness, the next step is to locate the specific mineral by its streak. Then, the remarks column may be indicative. Finally, all of the mineral's properties should be checked on the basis of data given in Chapter 2.

TABLE 3-1 Determinative table for minerals with metallic or submetallic luster. Minerals are arranged in order of increasing hardness. Group I minerals are scratched by a copper penny; group II, by a knife blade; group III minerals are harder than a knife blade. Page for mineral entry in Chapter 2 follows name.

I. Hardness below 3.5. Can be scratched by a copper penny

H	Streak	Color	Mineral, page	Remarks
1–1.5	Grayish to greenish black (on glazed porcelain)	Lead-gray	**Molybdenite**, p. 77	Perfect cleavage; greasy feel; hexagonal flakes. Marks paper
1–2	Gray to black	Shiny black	**Graphite**, p. 84	Greasy feel; perfect cleavage. Marks paper
1–2	Iron-black	Iron-black	**Pyrolusite**, p. 73	Earthy and fibrous varieties. May mark paper
1.5–2	Lead-gray	Indigo-blue	**Covellite**, p. 76	Platy masses; perfect cleavage
2–5	Red-brown	Brick-red	**Hematite**, p. 71	Earthy variety. Compare with crystalline hematite, which is harder
2.5	Lead-gray	Lead-gray	**Galena**, p. 77	Perfect cubic cleavage
2.5–3	Grayish black	Lead-gray	**Chalcocite**, p. 76	Easily tarnished; conchoidal fracture. Digenite is closely related and has bluish tinge
2.5–3	Shiny copper-red	Copper-red	**Copper**, p. 85	Malleable; easily tarnished
2.5–3	Shiny silver-white	Silver-white	**Silver**, p. 85	Malleable; tarnishes black
2.5–3	Gold-yellow	Gold-yellow	**Gold**, p. 85	Malleable
3	Gray-black	Brownish bronze	**Bornite**, p. 76	Tarnishes rapidly to peacock colors. Typically, with other copper minerals

II. Hardness between 3.5 and 5.2. Scratches a copper penny but is scratched by a knife

H	Streak	Color	Mineral, page	Remarks
3–4.5	Brown to black	Gray-black	**Tetrahedrite**, p. 77	Typically with other copper minerals, especially

Hardness	Streak	Color	Mineral	Remarks
				chalcopyrite. Some varieties can be scratched by a copper penny
3.5–4	Greenish black	Brass-yellow	**Chalcopyrite**, p. 76	Typically massive. Occurs with pyrite or other copper minerals
3.5–4	Pale yellow to dark brown	Brown to black	**Sphalerite**, p. 77	Perfect cleavage; distinctive submetallic resinous luster
4	Black	Brownish bronze	**Pyrrhotite**, p. 76	Magnetic; freshly broken surfaces tarnish quickly
4–4.5	Shiny gray	White to steel-gray	**Platinum**, p. 85	Malleable; unusually hard for a native metal
5–5.5	Yellow-brown	Yellow-brown	**Goethite (Limonite)**, p. 74	Massive; radiating fibers; some can be scratched, some cannot

III. Hardness greater than 5.2. Not scratched by knife

Hardness	Streak	Color	Mineral	Remarks
5–6	Brown-black	Black	**Psilomelane**, p. 74	Some can be scratched, most cannot; commonly botryoidal
5.5	Dark brown	Brownish black	**Chromite**, p. 71	Good cleavage; not magnetic
5.5–6	Black	Silver-white	**Arsenopyrite**, p. 76	Pseudo-orthorhombic crystals; garlic odor when scratched or crushed
6	Black	Black	**Magnetite**, p. 70	Strongly magnetic
6–6.5	Greenish to brownish black	Brass-yellow	**Pyrite**, p. 75	Striated cubes and pyritohedrons common
6–6.5	Gray-black	Pale brass-yellow	**Marcasite**, p. 75	Common as radiating masses; most specimens are easily broken because of alteration
6–6.5	Iron-black	Iron-black	**Pyrolusite**, p. 73	Well-crystallized variety. Note soft, earthy variety. Common as dendrites
6–6.5	Pale brown to reddish brown	Brown to black	**Rutile**, p. 73	Striated crystals common; submetallic, adamantine luster; some translucent

Table 3-2 lists the minerals with nonmetallic lusters. Most of them are transparent or translucent. Few of them have distinctive streaks—in fact, the only distinctive streaks are the green and blue of malachite and azurite, respectively, and the brownish streak of siderite. Some minerals with submetallic lusters, principally limonite, earthy hematite, sphalerite, and rutile, may be mistakenly judged to be nonmetallic. Thus Tables 3-1 and 3-2 should be used in conjunction with each other. Minerals in Table 3-2 are arranged in four groups in the order of hardness.

Hardness is best tested on a smooth, lustrous cleavage face or on a freshly fractured surface, using the knife point, a sharp-pointed fragment of quartz, or the edge of a copper penny. In some cases, however, hardness can be checked by using a corner or edge of the mineral to see if it will scratch the knife blade or other material of known hardness. For those who wish to use hardness testing to its fullest, it will often be helpful to have a fragment of feldspar (H = 6) available.

Table 1-2 lists many of the common minerals according to the number of cleavages they have. Since it is difficult to tell, from megascopic examination of grains in a rock, how many cleavage planes a given mineral has, a most useful diagnostic property of a mineral is whether or not it displays any prominent cleavage or whether cleavage seems to be entirely lacking. Accordingly, Table 3-3 lists those minerals for which a prominent cleavage is usually observed and Table 3-4 lists those minerals that rarely, if ever, display prominent cleavage. If cleavage is not well shown on the originally fractured rock surface but is still thought to possibly exist, it is wise to remove a fragment of the mineral in question and to crack it into smaller pieces for observation of the breakage characteristics with a handlens.

By careful and systematic use of Tables 3-1 to 3-4, all of the common minerals in rocks may be identified. A certain amount of practice is needed to develop adequate skills, however, so the tables should only be relied on once some knowledge of mineralogy has been gained.

TABLE 3-2 Determinative table for minerals with nonmetallic luster. The minerals are arranged in the order of increasing hardness. Group I minerals are scratched by a copper penny; group II, by a knife blade; group III, by quartz; group IV minerals are harder than quartz. Page for mineral entry in Chapter 2 follows name.

I. Hardness below 3.5. Can be scratched by a copper penny.

H	Colors	Remarks	Name, page
1	White, gray, green	Greasy feel; commonly foliated	**Talc**, p. 52
1–2	White, gray, green	Greasy feel; cannot be easily separated from talc. Commonly seen in radiating masses	**Pyrophyllite**, p. 52
2	White, colorless, gray	Perfect cleavage; commonly fibrous; scratched by fingernail	**Gypsum**, p. 77
2–2.5	White	Compact, earthy, clayey or musty odor when breathed on	**Kaolinite**, p. 50
2–2.5	Green	Cleavage perfect, plates not elastic	**Chlorite**, p. 49
2–2.5	Colorless, white, greenish, yellowish, light brown,	Perfect cleavage; plates elastic	**Muscovite**, p. 47
2–5	Green, yellow, black, white	Massive or fibrous, commonly mottled. Some varieties too hard to be scratched by a penny	**Serpentine**, p. 51
2.5	Colorless, white, blue	Soluble, salty taste	**Halite**, p. 84
2.5–3	Dark brown, dark green, black	Perfect cleavage; plates flexible	**Biotite**, p. 47
2.5–3	Brown, yellow	Common in foliated masses; cannot easily be distinguished from biotite	**Phlogopite**, p. 47
3	Gray, white, colorless	Effervesces in cold, dilute HCl; perfect rhombohedral cleavage	**Calcite**, p. 79
3–3.5	White, colorless, blue	Commonly massive; may show three cleavages at right angles	**Anhydrite**, p. 78

91

TABLE 3-2 Determinative table for minerals with nonmetallic luster. (Continued)

IIA. Hardness between 3.5 and 5.2. Scratches a copper penny but is scratched by knife blade.

H	Colors	Remarks	Name, page
2–5	Green, yellow, black, white	Massive or fibrous, commonly mottled. Most varieties are soft and can be scratched by a penny	**Serpentine,** p. 51
3.5–4	Brown to black	Perfect cleavage, distinctive submetallic resinous luster, but light-colored varieties may be mistaken for nonmetallic luster	**Sphalerite,** p. 77
3.5–4	Blue	Light blue streak	**Azurite,** p. 83
3.5–4	Green	Light green streak	**Malachite,** p. 83
3.5–4	White, colorless	Effervesces in cold, dilute HCl; poor cleavage	**Aragonite,** p. 83
3.5–4	White, yellow	Radiating or sheaflike aggregates	**Zeolite minerals,** p. 45
3.5–4	Gray, white, colorless	Effervesces in cold, dilute HCl only when powdered; perfect rhombohedral cleavage	**Dolomite,** p. 81
3.5–4	Light to dark brown	Effervesces in cold, dilute HCl; perfect rhombohedral cleavage	**Siderite,** p. 82
3.5–4	Yellowish white	Effervesces in cold, dilute HCl; rhombohedral cleavage; commonly massive	**Magnesite,** p. 82
3.5–4	White, colorless, blue	Two good cleavages at right angles; high specific gravity (4.5)	**Barite,** p. 79
4	Violet, yellow, colorless, green	Cubic crystals; octahedral cleavage	**Fluorite,** p. 84
4	White, gray, yellow	Typically massive; dissolves in water to give acid solution	**Alunite,** p. 79
5	Green, blue, yellow, violet, colorless	Hexagonal crystals commonly with rounded edges and terminations; cleavage poor and rarely seen	**Apatite,** p. 83

IIB. The following minerals can sometimes be scratched by a knife, sometimes not. All can be scratched by feldspar. .

H	Colors	Remarks	Name, page
5–5.5	Brown, yellow, red	Small grains in sands; resinous luster	**Monazite,** p. 84
5–5.5	Brown, gray, green	Wedge-shaped crystals	**Sphene,** p. 67
5–5.5	White, colorless	Prismatic crystals, commonly as radiating groups in cavities in basalt	**Natrolite,** p. 46
5–5.5	White, colorless	Good cleavage; fibrous	**Wollastonite,** p. 60
5–6	White, gray, pink, brown, colorless	Prismatic, tetragonal crystals; commonly altered. Most common in metamorphic rocks, but also as trapezohedral crystals in cavities in basalt; commonly fluoresces in ultraviolet light	**Scapolite,** p. 45
5–6	White, yellow, colorless, red	A mineraloid. Conchoidal fracture	**Opal,** p. 34
5–6	Black, green, blue, white	Good intersecting cleavages at approximately 126° and 54°	**Amphibole** (see Chapter 2 for varieties), p. 56
5–6	Black, green, blue, white	Good intersecting cleavages at approximately 90° angle	**Pyroxene** (see Chapter 2 for varieties), p. 53
5–7	Blue, white	Long, bladed crystals; hardness 5 parallel to blade, 7 across blade. In metamorphic rocks	**Kyanite,** p. 64

III. Hardness greater than 5.2 but less than 7. Not scratched by knife blade but can be scratched by quartz (Continued)

H	Colors	Remarks	Name, page
5.5–6	Light gray, greenish, colorless	Greasy luster, typically massive. Does not occur with quartz. Commonly weathers to areas of negative relief	**Nepheline,** p. 44
5.5–6	Gray, white	Trapezohedral crystals in lavas. May be altered to pseudoleucite	**Leucite,** p. 44
5.5–6	Blue, gray, white	Dodecahedral cleavage; commonly mottled blue-white	**Sodalite** (see also hauyne and nosean), p. 45

TABLE 3-2 Determinative table for minerals with nonmetallic luster. (Continued)

III. Hardness greater than 5.2 but less than 7. Not scratched by knife blade but can be scratched by quartz (Continued)

H	Colors	Remarks	Name, page
6	Pink, gray, white, green, colorless	Good cleavage, lacks albite twinning, may show perthitic intergrowths	**Alkali feldspar**, p. 34
6	White, gray, bluish, colorless	Good cleavage; multiple albite twinning, if present, is diagnostic	**Plagioclase**, p. 34
6–6.5	Brown, yellow, orange	Lacks cleavage; commonly globular. Common in marbles as disseminated grains	**Humite**, p. 67
6–6.5	Green, gray, white	Color is diagnostic. Commonly associated with zeolites	**Prehnite**, p. 52
6–6.5	Brown to black	Striated crystals are common; submetallic, adamantine luster, but some translucent varieties may appear nonmetallic	**Rutile**, p. 73
6–7	White, pale brown, gray, colorless	Fibrous crystals. In high-grade metamorphic rocks	**Sillimanite**, p. 65
6–7	Yellowish green, yellow, white	Prismatic, striated grains, good cleavage	**Epidote**, p. 60
6.5	Brown, green, yellow	Prismatic, square crystals. Most common in marbles	**Vesuvianite**, p. 69
6.5–7	Olive to apple-green, brown	Resembles quartz except for color. Common in mafic igneous rocks	**Olivine**, p. 63
6.5–7	Clove-brown, gray, green	Striated wedge-shaped crystals	**Axinite**, p. 65
7	White, colorless	Crystals in cavities in light-colored aphanites	**Tridymite** and/or **cristobalite**, p. 34
7	Smoky, colorless, white	Conchoidal fracture; no cleavage; some occurs as hexagonal crystals	**Quartz**, p. 32

IV. Hardness greater than 7. Not scratched by quartz

Hardness	Color	Description	Mineral
6.5–7.5	Red, brown, yellow, green, off-white	Dodecahedrons and trapezohedrons. Common garnets are harder than quartz; rarer forms are softer	**Garnet** (see Chapter 2 for varieties), p. 61
7–7.5	Brown, red, black	Prismatic, cruciform-twinned crystals common	**Staurolite**, p. 65
7–7.5	Light blue	Resembles quartz but typically is much altered	**Cordierite**, p. 66
7–7.5	Black, brown, green	Elongate, striated crystals with cross-sections resembling spherical triangles	**Tourmaline**, p. 68
7.5	Reddish brown	Prismatic crystals; square cross-section	**Andalusite**, p. 64
7.5	Brown, red, gray, green	Small, tetragonal crystals. Always accessory	**Zircon**, p. 70
7.5–8	Green, blue	Prismatic hexagonal crystals; no cleavage. In pegmatites	**Beryl**, p. 66
8	Yellow, colorless	Orthorhombic crystals common; one perfect cleavage; some are striated parallel to length	**Topaz**, p. 68
8	Black, red	Octahedral grains. Accessory mineral, especially in marbles	**Spinel**, p. 70
8	Pale blue, colorless	Tabular or prismatic crystals in metamorphic rocks with purplish amphibole, glaucophane	**Lawsonite**, p. 67
9	Gray, brown, blue, white	Barrel-shaped hexagonal prisms with good parting (pseudo-cleavage)	**Corundum**, p. 73

TABLE 3-3 Common minerals with prominent cleavage. Many less-common minerals also display excellent cleavage and should be considered if observed properties do not match those of a common mineral. Page for mineral entry in Chapter 2 follows name.

I. Minerals with a Single, Well-Developed Cleavage

Name, page	Remarks
Chlorite, p. 49	Green; nonelastic flakes; H 2–2.5
Graphite, p. 84	Dark gray, black; greasy feel; marks paper, H 1–2; opaque. Accessory mineral
Gypsum, p. 77	Colorless or white; H 2, easily scratched with fingernail
Hematite (micaceous variety), p. 71	Black; red-brown streak; H 5.5–6.5; metallic luster; opaque. Displays parting rather than cleavage. Typically accessory
Kyanite, p. 64	Blue; white; bladed crystals; H 5 and 7. In schists and gneisses
Mica, p. 47	Tough, elastic, flakes; H 2–3. *Muscovite* is white, light brown, green; *biotite* dark brown, dark green, black; *phlogopite* is typically medium brown
Molybdenite, p. 77	Lead-gray; greenish black streak on glazed porcelain; greasy feel; H 1–1.5; metallic luster; opaque; easily confused with graphite (check streak). Accessory
Sillimanite, p. 65	White, pale brown, colorless; fibrous crystals; H 6–7. In schists and gneisses
Talc, p. 52	White, gray, green; H 1; greasy feel; marks cloth

II. Minerals with More than One Well-Developed Cleavage

Name, page	Remarks
Amphibole, p. 56	Two cleavages at 126° and 54°; H 5–6; *hornblende* and *arfvedsonite* are dark green or black; *actinolite* is green; *glaucophane* is blue; *anthophyllite* is gray or clove brown; *tremolite* is white. Easily confused with pyroxenes

Anhydrite, p. 78
White; colorless; H 3–3.5; three cleavages at right angles. Commonly with gypsum

Barite, p. 79
White, colorless, blue; two cleavages at right angles; H 3.5–4; specific gravity 4.5; unusually heavy for white mineral. Generally accessory

Calcite, p. 79
Gray, white, colorless; H 3; three rhombohedral cleavages; effervesces with cold, dilute HCl. *Siderite* is similar, but light to dark brown in color. Compare with dolomite

Dolomite, p. 81
Gray, white, colorless; H 3.5–4; three rhombohedral cleavages; will effervesce with cold dilute HCl only when powdered

Feldspar, p. 34
Two cleavages at about 90°; H 6. *Alkali feldspar* is white, pink or colorless; does not display albite twinning. *Plagioclase* is white, gray, colorless, or bluish; generally displays multiple albite twinning

Fluorite, p. 84
Violet, yellow, colorless, green; H 4; four octahedral cleavage planes. Typically accessory

Galena, p. 77
Metallic luster; color and streak lead-gray; opaque; H 2.5; three cleavages at right angles. Occurs in ores and veins

Halite, p. 84
White, colorless, blue; H 2.5; three cleavages at right angles; salty taste

Pyroxene, p. 53
Two cleavages at approximately 90°; H 5–6. *Augite* dark green to black; *hypersthene* and *bronzite* are brown, gray, bronze; *diopside* is green or white; *aegirine* is green or brown; *jadeite* is white, green, or gray and cleavage is less well developed

Sphalerite, p. 77
Brown, red, pale yellow to black; submetallic, resinous luster; H 3.5–4; six cleavages parallel to dodecahedral faces. Occurs in ores and veins

Wollastonite, p. 60
White, colorless; H 5–5.5; fibrous habit common. Two cleavages; resembles pyroxene. Easily confused with tremolite and sillimanite

TABLE 3-4 Common minerals that do not display prominent cleavage. Minerals with metallic lusters are tabulated separately from those with nonmetallic lusters. Many less common minerals also lack prominent cleavage and should be considered if the observed properties do not match those of a common mineral. Page for mineral entry in Chapter 2 follows name.

I. Minerals with Metallic Luster

Name, page	Remarks
Chalcopyrite, p. 76	Brass-yellow with greenish black streak; H 3.5–4; often confused with pyrite (H 6–6.5)
Hematite (massive type), p. 71	Brick-red color; red-brown streak; H 2–5, depending on grain size
Ilmenite, p. 72	Iron-black with dark brown streak; H 5.6–6; may be slightly magnetic; can be confused with magnetite
Limonite, p. 74	Brown to black with yellow brown streak; H 5–5.5; commonly fibrous or earthy
Magnetite, p. 70	Color and streak black; H 6; strongly magnetic
Pyrite, p. 75	Brass-yellow with greenish black streak; H 6–6.5; common as striated cubes and pyritohedrons; sometimes confused with chalcopyrite (H 3.5–4)
Pyrrhotite, p. 76	Brownish bronze on fresh surface but tarnishes quickly; streak black; H 4; magnetic
Rutile, p. 73	Brown to black, or reddish, with pale brown streak; submetallic luster; H 6–6.5; common as striated crystals; also as grains in sand

II. Minerals with Nonmetallic Luster

Name, page	Remarks
Andalusite, p. 64	Reddish brown; H 7.5; common in crystals with square cross sections. In high-grade metamorphic rocks

98

Apatite, p. 83 — Green, blue, violet, yellow, colorless; H 5; hexagonal crystals, commonly with rounded edges and ends. Typically accessory

Beryl, p. 66 — Green, blue; H 7.5–8; prismatic hexagonal crystals. Accessory in pegmatites

Garnet, p. 61 — Red, brown, yellow, green, off-white; H 6.5–7.5; common as dodecahedral and trapazohedral crystals (see Chapter 2 for varieties)

Leucite, p. 44 — Gray, white; H 5.5–6. Commonly, as trapezohedral crystals in aphanites

Nepheline, p. 44 — Colorless, gray, green; greasy luster; H 5.5–6. Not in same rock with quartz

Olivine, p. 63 — Olive to apple green, brown; H 6.5–7. Common in mafic igneous rocks associated with pyroxenes

Opal, p. 34 — Colorless, white, yellow, red; H 5–6; a mineraloid so crystals do not exist; conchoidal fracture

Quartz, p. 32 — Smoky, colorless, white; conchoidal fractures; crystals are hexagonal. Common in many rocks

Scapolite, p. 45 — White, gray, pink, brown; H 5–6; tetragonal crystals; commonly altered. In metamorphic rocks. Sometimes as trapezohedral crystals in cavities in basalts. Commonly fluoresces in ultraviolet light

Staurolite, p. 65 — Brown, reddish, black; H 7–7.5; prismatic, twinned crystals, commonly cruciform. In high-grade metamorphic rocks

Tourmaline, p. 68 — Black, green, brown; H 7–7.5; elongate crystals, commonly striated, with roughly triangular cross sections. Accessory

Zircon, p. 70 — Brown, green, red, gray; H 7.5; small tetragonal crystals. Accessory

CHAPTER 4
igNeous aNd pyroclastic rocks

MAGMA: ITS GENERATION, COMPOSITION, AND CONSOLIDATION

All igneous rocks are formed by the consolidation of magma. Usually called *lava* when it flows on the earth's surface, **magma** is *molten or partially molten rock material plus dissolved gases.* Most magma is siliceous in composition and is formed by partial to complete melting of rocks in which silicate minerals are the main constituents. A much less common class of magma is formed by the melting of carbonate-rich rocks.

The composition of magma ranges widely, and as a result the compositions of igneous rocks also range widely. These compositional variations, together with rock textures, provide the best basis on which to classify igneous rocks and to distinguish igneous rocks from other rock types. Composition and texture of igneous rocks, when combined with information on the geological environment in which an igneous rock occurs, also provide important evidence about the history of a magma—how and where it was generated, how it moved and reacted, and how it cooled and consolidated to form rock.

Generation of Magma

Magma is generated wherever the requisite pressure and temperature conditions for rock-melting are reached. For most of geological time this means that magma can only have formed deep below the earth's surface. Some magmas have formed in the earth's mantle; other magmas have been formed when rocks of the lower part of the crust were melted; still other magmas have apparently consisted of mixtures from the mantle and the crust.

The melting processes that form magma, however, are complex and beyond the scope of this book. Not only do they involve high temperatures and pressures, but also the presence of gases such as water (H_2O) and carbon dioxide (CO_2). Such gases can exert a profound influence on the way a rock melts (much the way the presence or absence of water can cause a profound influence in how a piece of meat is cooked). Additionally, the melting process is rarely complete. (See Figure 4-3B.) Because the melting of a mixture of minerals takes place over a temperature interval of about 200° Celsius, the first formed liquid will often rise up and separate from the unmelted residue, perhaps carrying a few scattered mineral grains with it. In such cases, the composition of the magma depends on the fraction of the parent rock that is melted before separation occurs.

Chemical Composition of Magma

Compositions of 11 representative magmas, as deduced from analyses of the igneous rocks formed from them, are given in Table 4-1. Several general relationships are immediately

TABLE 4-1. Chemical analyses of some common igneous rocks. (From *The Data of Geochemistry* (5th ed.) by F. W. Clarke—U.S. Geol. Sur. Bull. 770, 1924; all analyses by W. F. Hillebrand.)

	SiO_2	Al_2O_3	Fe_2O_3	FeO	MgO	CaO	Na_2O	K_2O	H_2O^+	Others	Total
Phanerites											
1. Peridotite	39.37	4.47	4.96	9.13	26.53	3.70	0.50	0.26	7.08	3.94	99.94
2. Gabbro	55.87	13.52	2.70	5.89	6.51	8.87	2.42	1.72	1.56	1.02	100.08
3. Diorite	57.97	15.65	0.73	2.80	4.96	10.93	3.03	3.16	0.38	1.08	100.69
4. Granodiorite	68.42	15.01	0.97	1.93	1.21	2.60	3.23	4.25	0.73	1.60	99.95
5. Granite	71.90	14.12	1.20	0.86	0.33	1.13	4.52	4.81	0.42	1.06	100.35
6. Nepheline Syenite	54.34	19.21	3.19	2.11	1.28	4.53	6.38	5.14	1.17	2.42	99.77
Aphanites											
7. Basalt	52.40	13.55	2.73	9.79	5.53	10.01	2.32	0.40	1.05	2.21	99.99
8. Andesite	56.63	16.85	3.62	3.44	4.23	7.53	3.08	2.24	0.51	2.05	100.18
9. Dacite	62.33	17.30	3.00	1.63	1.05	3.23	4.21	4.46	0.75	2.37	100.33
10. Rhyolite	74.24	14.50	1.27	0.67	0.25	0.11	3.00	3.66	2.04	0.54	100.28
11. Phonolite	56.24	21.43	2.01	0.55	0.15	1.38	10.53	5.74	0.86	0.97	99.86

(1) Near Opin Lake, Michigan; (2) Emigrant Gap, California; (3) Crazy Mountains, Montana; (4) Hailey, Idaho; (5) Mount Ascutney, Vermont; (6) Cripple Creek, Colorado; (7) Pine Hill, South Britain, Connecticut; (8) Unga Island, Alaska; (9) Near Clover Meadow, Tuolumne Co., California; (10) Near Willow Lake, Plumas Co., California; (11) Pleasant Valley, Colfax Co., New Mexico.

apparent. In going from peridotite to granite and from basalt to rhyolite, the SiO_2-content increases; FeO and total Fe decreases; MgO decreases; and both Na_2O and K_2O tend to increase. Furthermore, it is equally apparent that the nepheline syenite and phonolite—both of which are generally termed feldspathoidal (or alkalic) rocks—have low SiO_2 contents and low SiO_2/Al_2O_3 ratios, as well as relatively high Na_2O and K_2O contents. Bulk rock compositions are, of course, reflections of the mineralogical contents of the rocks which, in turn, reflect the compositions of the magmas from which they crystallized.

When we consider the frequency with which different kinds of igneous rocks occur, we observe that a very large percentage are one of three kinds: basalt, granite, and andesite. For the most part, the origin of the three magmas giving rise to these common igneous rocks are thought to be the result of partial melting rather than magmatic differentiation, as follows: Basaltic magmas are formed as the result of partial melting of essentially any rock material in the upper mantle. Granitic magmas are derived by partial melting of pre-existing rocks deep in the continental crust; in most, if not all, cases, the melting has been enhanced by the presence of water vapor and other volatiles. Andesitic magmas are of enigmatic origin; some are apparently the result of partial melting of subducted oceanic crust, whereas others may represent sections of crustal material that has been melted—and perhaps mixed with basaltic magma—within the upper mantle.

Consolidation of Magma

Some magmas cool and consolidate essentially where they are formed. Most, however, move, generally upward because liquids tend to be less dense than solids, to consolidate elsewhere. Some magmas that have moved appear to have retained their original compositions, whereas others have been modified by reactions with the enclosing rocks—generally termed country rocks—through which they have passed. Evidence of these reactions can be seen in *xenoliths,* which are inclusions of rocks that have been engulfed by moving magma (Figure 4-1). As a group, xenoliths exhibit all degrees of reaction with their host magma: Some have been unaffected; others have been partially to almost completely assimilated, with consequent modification of the magma that engulfed them; and presumably still others have been completely dissolved.

Magmas, being solutions, obey well-known physical-chemical laws. For example, the solubility rather than the melting point of a mineral determines the conditions and concentrations at which the mineral will crystallize. In general, as the temperature falls, first one or more minerals, then others, and still others . . . crystallize. In some cases, one mineral may be completely crystallized before some other mineral even starts to crystallize. In most cases, several minerals have overlapping periods of crystallization. In any case, just as might be expected, the major mineral constituents of igneous rocks have been found to crystallize and then to react or not react according to predictable sequences (see Figure 4-2).

N. L. Bowen was led to his hypothesis of sequential reactions (now called Bowen's Reaction Series) by work with his colleagues at the Geophysical Laboratory in Washington, D.C. They discovered that in cooling silicate melts, some minerals, once crystallized can react with the remaining melt. The reactions are of two kinds—discontinuous, whereby old minerals react to form new ones, and continuous, whereby a mineral continually changes composition through solid solution, but retains its basic crystal structure.

Bowen realized that both kinds of reactions can proceed side-by-side in the same cooling magma and can explain many of the features observed in igneous rocks. He demonstrated his hypothesis by describing the sequence of events in a cooling magma of

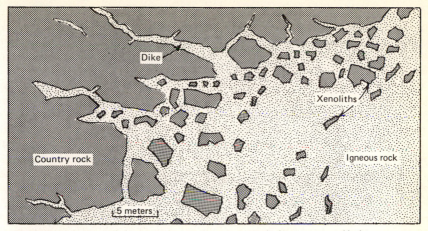

FIGURE 4-1   Xenoliths are pieces of country rock that are engulfed in magma during intrusion.

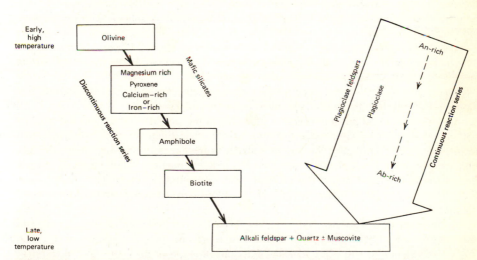

FIGURE 4-2   Bowen's Reaction Series. The first minerals that crystallize from a cooling basaltic magma are olivine and An-rich plagioclase. As crystallization proceeds, the olivine (upper left) reacts with the remaining molten magma to form pyroxene, while the early formed plagioclase (upper right) reacts by merely changing its composition towards a more Ab-rich plagioclase. With continued crystallization, the pyroxene reacts to form amphibole, generally hornblende, that subsequently reacts to form biotite while the plagioclase continues to react and change towards an Ab-rich form. Near the end of the cooling process, alkali feldspar and quartz, and in some cases muscovite, are crystallized.

basaltic composition as shown in Figure 4-2. The first minerals to crystallize are olivine and an An-rich plagioclase. As the magma cools, the olivine reacts with the liquid to form a more silica-rich mineral, pyroxene; pyroxene, in turn, will eventually react to form an amphibole. . . . This is a discontinuous reaction series. If the reaction is complete, no trace of the original olivine will remain.

The early formed plagioclase also reacts with the cooling magma, but it does so by exchanging Ca + Al atoms in the crystals for Na + Si atoms in the magma, thereby making the plagioclase more and more Ab-rich. This is a continuous reaction series.

If cooling and reacting proceeds at equilibrium, the process ceases when all the liquid has reacted. For a typical basalt, this will happen when a pyroxene and a plagioclase of about An_{45-50} are present. However, equilibrium is not always attained. For example, an early formed olivine may be rimmed by pyroxene and thus effectively prevented from reacting completely with the melt. So, too, may an early formed An-rich plagioclase be rimmed by a zone of a more Ab-rich plagioclase, preventing it from reacting with the liquid. As a consequence, the remaining liquid can become enriched in SiO_2 and Na. Bowen showed that if partial reactions occurred, an original basaltic magma could produce a small volume of residual melt that would be so SiO_2-rich and so enriched in sodium, potassium and volatile elements, that a granitic magma would result. He also pointed out that if a partly cooled melt were separated from the crystals, consisting of, say, olivine and An-rich plagioclase, perhaps by tectonic forces squeezing out the liquid or by the crystals settling to the floor of the magma chamber (see Figure 4-3), the result would be chemically similar to partial reaction between a melt and the crystals suspended in it. Because the two reaction series operate, a parent magma could therefore give rise to a large number of diverse daughter magmas, depending on the details of cooling, reaction, and crystal separation.

Processes by which a separation occurs between crystallized minerals and the remaining liquid are termed **magmatic differentiation.** The most important are *crystal settling* and *filter pressing.* In crystal settling, early formed minerals separate from the rest of the magma by sinking or floating, because their densities differ from that of the liquid. (See Figure 4-3D). The resulting rocks are called *cumulates.* Actually, the crystals aggregate to form a rock with a composition different from that of the parent magma, and the residual magma, whether it then consolidates or undergoes further differentiation, also has a composition different from that of the parent magma. In filter pressing, forces—generally tectonic—squeeze the liquid fraction out of a consolidating magma, leaving a mesh of early formed minerals (Figure 4-3E). The residual mesh constitutes a *"residuate."* Again, each of the fractions comprises rock material with a composition different from that of its parent magma.

Because melting processes that form magmas are controlled both by temperature and pressure (including both the pressure of overlying rocks and the gas pressures of H_2O and CO_2), it should not be surprising to learn that consolidation of magma is also dependent on temperature and pressure. Under some conditions, magma may consolidate and crystallize very slowly, allowing dissolved gases to escape gradually and large mineral grains to form. Under other conditions, cooling may be so rapid that crystals cannot form and a glass results, sometimes with bubbles of still escaping gas trapped within it.

The consolidation history of a magma can vary so greatly as a result of temperature and pressure differences that we use a special term, **heteromorphism,** to describe the *consolidation of essentially identical magmas to form different rocks* (Figure 4-4). The term is somewhat analogous to polymorphism in minerals. Good examples would be a granite

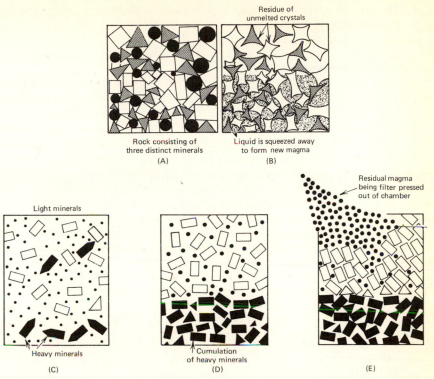

FIGURE 4-3 Generation and differentiation of magma. Rock that consists of three minerals (A) is heated to the temperature at which one of the minerals is melted completely and portions of the other two minerals dissolve in the melt (B). The generated magma, if squeezed out, leaves a residue of unmelted grains having a distinctly different composition from the departed magma. Subsequently, the magma may be differentiated to form two or more different rocks during cooling—for example, some early-crystallized minerals may sink or float to form cumulate rocks (C and D) and/or some of the remaining magma may be squeezed off (E) to be cooled and consolidated into still another different igneous rock.

and a glassy obsidian with identical compositions, or even two granites—one containing biotite, the other hypersthene—that have the same chemical compositions except for their water contents.

Thus both the composition and texture of the igneous rocks that we examine have been influenced by many different variables; the most important are

1. The composition of the rock material that was melted to form the parent magma and the degree to which the rock was melted.
2. Reactions between the magma and the rocks lining the passageways through which it moved.
3. The degree to which magmatic differentiation separated early-formed crystals from the residual liquid as the magma cooled and consolidated.

4. The way in which temperature and pressure combined to control the rate of consolidation of the magma.

Alteration of Igneous Rocks

Besides the primary magmatic effects, we often observe that igneous rocks have been subjected to post-consolidation alterations. Because many of these effects occur in response to end-stage magmatic activities, they may conveniently be considered as part of the cycle relating to igneous rocks. Some of the more common processes have widely accepted designations:

Chloritization—alteration of hornblende, biotite, and less commonly other mafic minerals, to form chlorite.

Saussuritization—alteration of a calcic plagioclase, such as labradorite, to a mixture made up largely of albite and one or more epidote-family minerals plus or minus calcite, sericite and one or more zeolites (greasy-appearing light green phenocrysts in some basalts are exemplary).

Serpentinization—alteration of mafic minerals, especially olivine, to serpentine.

Spilitization—alteration of calcic plagioclase, especially in basalts, to albite.

Uralitization—replacement of pyroxene by a hornblende-like amphibole called uralite.

The results of each of these processes, with the possible exception of spilitization, are frequently recognizable by megascopic means.

TEXTURE

Texture is the overall appearance that a rock has because of the size, shape, arrangement, and crystallinity of its constituents. Igneous rocks are often described by such textural terms as "subhedral coarse-grained phanerites," "aphanitic porphyries," and "flow-banded glasses."

Grain size has two aspects: First, the actual size of the grains and second, whether or not all of the grains of the major constituents have approximately the same size or a distinct range of sizes. Referring first to actual grain size, we use **phanerite** to describe a

FIGURE 4-4 Three rocks with essentially the same chemical composition, but different grain sizes. (A) Porphyritic rhyolite containing phenocrysts of sanidine, quartz, and muscovite; (B) Medium-grained granite containing quartz, alkali feldspar, plagioclase, and biotite; (C) Coarse-grained granite with the same mineral assemblage as (B). (B. J. Skinner)

(A)

0   2 cm

(B)

0   2 cm

(C)

0   2 cm

rock in which the component grains are distinguishable megascopically, and the term **aphanite** *for a rock in which the component grains cannot be distinguished with the naked eye or even with the aid of a simple handlens*. Phanerites may be further described as fine-, medium-, or coarse-grained when the average grain diameters are < 1 millimeter, 1–5 millimeter, and > 5 millimeter, respectively (see Figures 4-4B and C). A few geologists utilize a third term, microphanerite, for fine-grained phanerites. Fortunately, this self-contradictory term appears to be coming obsolete.

So far as equality of grain size is concerned, rocks in which grains are approximately equal in size are said to be *equigranular* whereas rocks consisting of obviously larger crystals that are surrounded by significantly smaller grains (Figure 4-5) are referred to as being porphyritic and the rock itself is called a *porphyry*. The relatively large crystals in a porphyry are called *phenocrysts*; the finer grained matrix material is termed *groundmass*. In the past, both the term porphyry and the adjective porphyritic have been applied in different ways. Some geologists have given the noun and the adjective identical connotations. Others have restricted the term, porphyry, to rocks with more than 50 percent phenocrysts and have used the adjective, porphyritic, to refer to rocks with less than 50 percent phenocrysts. We consider the former usage to be less confusing. That is, any igneous rock may be called a porphyry *or* may be said to be porphyritic if it contains conspicuous phenocrysts in a finer-grained groundmass.

The shapes and arrangements of grains comprise patterns commonly referred to as

FIGURE 4-5 A fine-grained gabbro porphyry with large phenocrysts of plagioclase. *(Ward's Natural Science Establishment)*

rock fabric (Figures 1-3 and 4-6). Three groups of descriptive terms that have been applied to mineral grains with different degrees of perfection of crystal form are given in Figure 4-6.

So far as crystallinity is concerned, some igneous rocks consist wholly of glass, others consist wholly of mineral grains, and still others are a mixture of glass and mineral grains. Those that are wholly glass have their own particular names (page 151). Essentially all phanerites are wholly crystalline, whereas aphanites and aphanitic porphyries may be either wholly crystalline or may contain a significant amount of glass. In most aphanitic mixtures, glass can only rarely be distinguished from crystalline aggregates by megascopic examination. Unambiguous identification requires, therefore, that the rocks be examined under a microscope.

When one interprets the origin of igneous textures, a useful rule of thumb is *the faster a rock cools and consolidates, the finer the grain size.* Considering the different geological environments where magma may cool, this generalization can be extended to say that magma cooled at great depth within the crust tends to cool slowly and to form coarse-grained rocks, whereas magma erupted onto the surface of the earth tends to cool fairly rapidly and to form fine-grained rocks or even to quench to form glass.

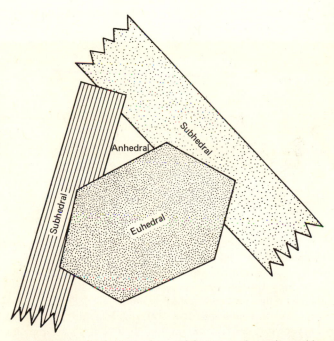

FIGURE 4-6 Perfection of crystal form may be indicated by the terms euhedral, subhedral, and anhedral (see also Figure 1-3). Some petrologists refer to the same degrees of crystal form development as idiomorphic or automorphic (= euhedral), hypidiomorphic or hypautomorphic (= subhedral), and allotriomorphic or xenomorphic (= anhedral).

Igneous rock formed from magma that has consolidated below the earth's surface is referred to as *intrusive igneous rock*. The shapes of intrusive igneous rock masses and their relationships with surrounding rocks have led to the introduction of several common terms (Figure 4-7). Igneous rocks formed from magma that consolidated above the surface are called *extrusive* or *volcanic igneous rocks*. Extrusive igneous rock formed by consolidation of lava is sometimes also loosely referred to as lava.

Another control of grain size is the ratio of the volume to surface area of the cooling mass of magma. Other things being equal, large masses cool more slowly than smaller ones. As a consequence, we find that most large intrusive masses are made up of medium- to coarse-grained phanerites, whereas small intrusives typically consist of fine-grained phanerites or porphyries, and extrusives are predominantly constituted by either aphanites, aphanitic porphyries, or glasses. Exceptions to these generalizations include the glassy and aphanitic border zones of some shallow intrusives and the phaneritic cores of some relatively thick lava flows. In addition, even some igneous masses that are phaneritic throughout have finer grained border zones.

Many porphyries are thought to reflect consolidation under two rather different cooling conditions. The phenocrysts are believed to have grown in a deeply buried, slowly

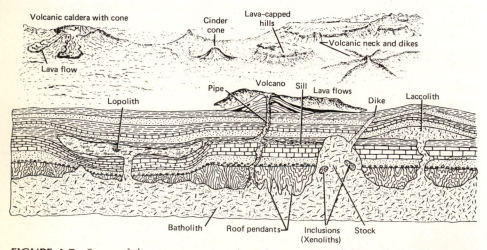

FIGURE 4-7 Some of the more common intrusive masses and their relationships to the surrounding country rock. (Modified after R. G. Schmidt and H. R. Shaw, U.S. Geological Survey.) Intrusive igneous masses are named on the basis of their size, shape, and/or geometric relationships with the surrounding country rock. Masses with no known bottoms are called batholiths if their bedrock surface is more than 100 square kilometers , but are known as stocks if they measure less than 100 square kilometers. Floored, generally lenticular shaped masses that are concordant (*i.e.*, their contacts are parallel to the bedding of the country rock) are laccoliths. Tabular masses that are concordant are sills; tabular masses that are discordant (*i.e.*, they cut across the bedding or foliation of the invaded country rocks) are dikes. Lopoliths may be described as generally concordant, basin-shaped masses that typically have their component rocks arranged in a stratified fashion. Several other kinds of igneous massses have been recognized and named—a historical review is given by R. A. Daly in his *Igneous Rocks and the Depths of the Earth*.

cooling magma. Then, when only partly crystallized, the magma and the early-formed crystals are thought to have been suddenly moved into another environment where the remaining fluid was cooled much more rapidly to form the finer grained groundness.

The relationship between cooling rate and grain size is termed a ''rule of thumb'' rather than a principle or law because there are several other controls of grain size. Probably the most important of these is the overall composition of the magma. For example, a magma of basaltic composition will consolidate to a crystalline aphanite or to a fine-grained phanerite under the same pressure-temperature conditions that a granitic composition magma will cool to a glass. In addition, the overall composition controls the amount of dissolved gases a magma can hold and, in turn, the gas content can depress the consolidation temperature of the magma and control such things as the magma's viscosity and potential explosivity. As a consequence, a magma's composition may be indirectly responsible for such additional textural features as flow banding and vesiculation.

The silica content, in particular, controls many properties of magma. The influence of silica content on viscosity is especially noteworthy (Table 4-2). This is so because silica tetrahedra in a magma can polymerize by sharing oxygens, just as they do in mineral structures. The more silica-rich a magma, the larger the polymerized groups of tetrahedra and the more viscous a magma becomes. Water and gases dissolved in magma tend to reduce the viscosity, offsetting to a certain extent the effect of silica, and thus to enhance the ability of a magma to flow. As might be expected from the data in the table, relatively viscous rhyolitic lavas tend to form domes and short, fairly thick flows, whereas more fluid basaltic lavas form rather long, much thinner flows.

TABLE 4-2   Viscosity of magma. (Values for water and hot pitch are given for comparison.)

Material	Approximate SiO_2-content, weight percent	Temperature, degrees Celsius	Pressure, bars	Approximate viscosity, poises
Water	—	30°C	1	0.8
Hot pitch	—	100°C	1	100
Basaltic magma	51.	1150°C	1	650
Andesitic magma	60.	1050°C	1	80,000
Rhyolitic magma	77.	800°C	1000	5,000,000

CLASSIFICATION

By the middle of the twentieth century, more than 1500 names and several classification systems had already been proposed for igneous rocks. Only a few of the names, however, have gained wide acceptance. The rest have been used only a few times and have proved to be essentially superfluous. The classification schemes have been based on such diverse aspects as mineralogical composition, overall chemical composition, and interpretations of the origins of the rocks. None has been universally accepted, so different petrologists use different schemes. Unfortunately, several of the widely used names have been used with different meanings in different classifications. As might be expected, misunderstandings and confusion have often resulted.

In the late 1960s, in an attempt to reduce the ever increasing confusion, the International Union of Geological Sciences (IUGS) created a Subcommission on the Systematics of Igneous Rocks and charged the group to formulate recommendations for the nomenclature of igneous rocks. The subcommission's recommendations relating to the plutonic rocks (phanerites) were approved by IUGS in 1972 and have been published rather widely. Although those recommendations carry no mandate, and it is possible that some geologists do not yet follow them, we believe that the system will ultimately prevail as the first internationally accepted nomenclature for any rocks. Therefore, we have used it as the basis for our coverage of the phanerites.

At a meeting held in August 1976, the subcommission also agreed upon root-names for volcanic rocks—that is, the aphanites. We use those root-names in anticipation of the formal recommendations and their probable approval.

So far as porphyries are concerned, some geologists have used rock names as adjectives to describe porphyries (e.g., granite porphyry), whereas others have used the identity of the phenocrysts as modifiers (e.g., quartz porphyry). We believe that if the bulk mineral composition of the rock can be determined, the porphyry should be named on the basis of that composition and the grain size of the groundmass—for example, granitoid porphyry and fine-grained gabbroid porphyry. For porphyries with aphanitic groundmasses, we suggest either the use of such terms as felsite porphyry or use of the scheme given on page 147.

The system for phanerites, largely plutonic rocks, is given on pages 116 and 139. That suggested for aphanites, predominantly volcanic rocks, is given on pages 147 and 148. Descriptions of the lamprophyres, a group of rocks that fall outside the general classification, are included at the end of the section dealing with phanerites (p. 147).

Before turning to the charts, a few additional terms warrant definition:

Felsic—mnemonic adjective (noun–felsite), from feldspar and silica, that may be applied to igneous rocks or their light-colored minerals—namely the feldspars and silica minerals.

Foid—shortform term meaning feldspathoids and related minerals—namely leucite (and pseudoleucite), nepheline, sodalite, nosean, hauyne, cancrinite, and analcime.

Leuco—prefix, from the Greek *leukos* meaning white, used to designate a rock that is lighter in color, meaning it is more felsic, than the normal range (see Figure 4-10).

Mafic—mnemonic adjective (noun–mafite), from magnesium and ferric (or ferrous), that may be applied to igneous rocks or their dark-colored minerals—namely the olivines, pyroxenes, amphiboles, and biotite.

Mela—prefix, from the Greek *melanos* meaning black, used to designate a rock that is darker in color, meaning it is more mafic, than the normal range (see Figure 4-10).

-phyre—suffix indicating porphyry—for example, vitrophyre means a porphyry with a glassy groundmass.

Pyribole—mnemonic term, from pyroxenes and amphiboles, that is used to indicate a dark-mineral content of pyroxene and/or amphibole, which in some rocks are extremely difficult to distinguish from one an other by megascopic means.

PHANERITES

We have already mentioned that we have adopted the nomenclature recommended by the IUGS for plutonic rocks. In their statement on "Principles of Classification," however, the IUGS statement reads "By plutonic rocks we mean rocks with phaneritic texture, which are presumed to have crystallized at considerable depth." In this book, we use the designation phanerite in a strictly descriptive sense—that is, we believe that one should be able to name a rock whether or not the presumption of depth of crystallization is correct. The IUGS also noted that "By igneous rocks we mean 'igneous and igneous-looking rocks' . . . irrespective of the genesis of the rocks." In this book, we recommend exclusion of igneous-appearing rocks *known* to be of nonigneous origin.

The "Preliminary system" for megascopic identification is presented in Figures 4-8A, B, and C. The triangular diagrams are to be read as outlined in Chapter 1 (see Figure 1-2). Portions of the more extensive general classification that include the relatively common rocks are given as Figures 4-9, 4-10 and 4-20. Our descriptions, which follow, are in the numerical order given in Figure 4-9. Fields represented by rare rocks (e.g., No. 1b., the quartz-rich granitoids) are not described (see Figure 4-11).

Quartzolite (silexite of some geologists)—quartz > 90 percent
The silexite designation should be abandoned. The French use the term for chert (see page 217).

Dikelike, lenticular and irregularly shaped masses of milky to light gray or nearly colorless quartz occur within many igneous intrusives and their surrounding country rocks. Most of these quartz masses are no larger than a few meters in greatest dimension.

Many of the quartz "dikes" and lenses have been shown to be recrystallized, quartz-rich country rocks. None has ever been proved to have been formed by direct crystallization of a quartz magma. In fact, the conditions, especially the temperature required for a quartz magma, are essentially nonexistent within the earth's crust. Moreover, we know of no reported occurrence of a quartz mass where the adjacent rocks exhibit thermal effects that would be consistent with emplacement of a quartz magma.

Granitoids
The common phanerites that contain 20 or more percent quartz are all called granitoids (see Figure 4-8A). In the general classification, this includes alkali-feldspar granite, granite, granodiorite, and tonalite (see Figure 4-9). These four rocks, the most common of all igneous phanerites, resemble each other because of their quartz content (20 to 60 percent) and the fact that each is typically equigranular, medium- to coarse-grained, and light colored (see Figure 4-10).

Their typical interlocking texture (Figure 4-12) serves to distinguish granitoids from the sedimentary rock arkose with which they may, at first glance, be confused—arkoses consist of discrete fragments rather than interlocking grains. Their modes of occurrence and textural homogeneity permit distinction from most metamorphic rocks of similar composition—the minerals of the metamorphic rocks typically define a *foliation* (the term applied to a directional rock fabric manifesting a preferred orientation of constituents). In some cases, however, additional study—including microscopic and chemical investigations—may be required to distinguish granitoids from the metamorphic rocks they resemble.

Common granitoids. The mineralogical makeup of the granitoids, as shown on Figure 4-9, may be summarized as follows:

Alkali-feldspar granite
Felsics: quartz—20–60 percent

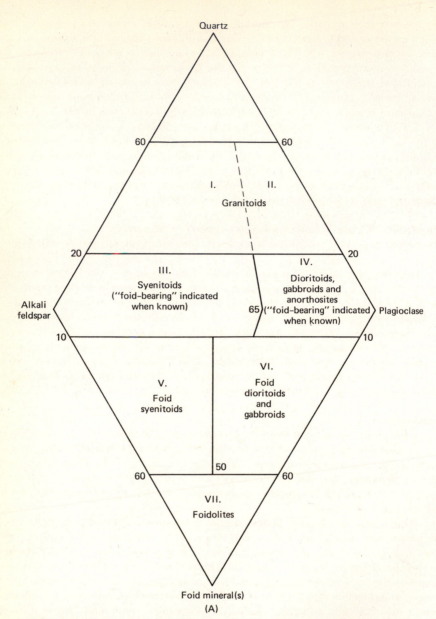

FIGURE 4-8 System for classifying the families of igneous phanerites. (A) Preliminary classification; (B) Gabbroic and ultramafic rocks; (C) Ultramafic rocks.

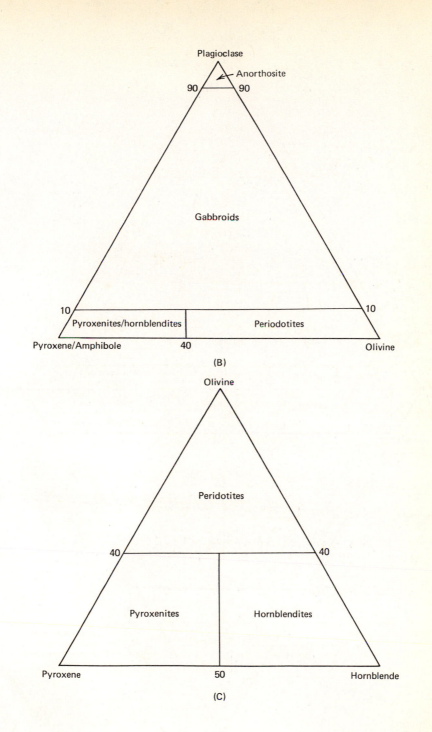

(B)

(C)

115

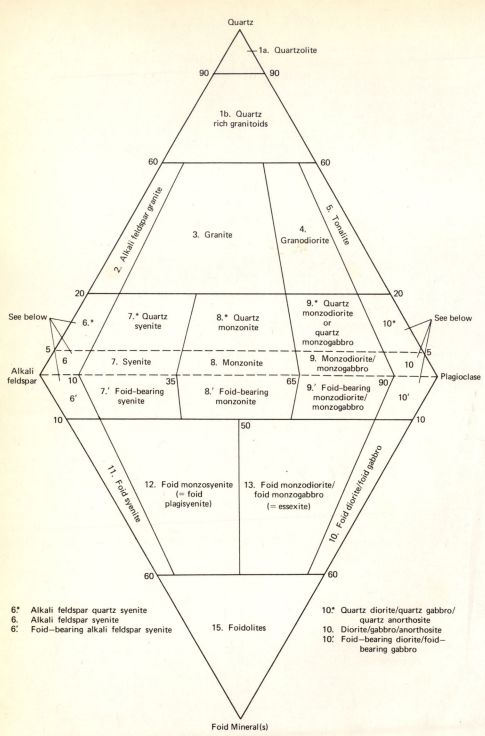

FIGURE 4-9 General classification and nomenclature of igneous phanerites.

	alkali-feldspar—90–100 percent of feldspars
	± plagioclase—< 10 percent of the feldspars
Mafics:	0–20 percent (typically biotite ± muscovite)

Granite

Felsics:	quartz—20–60 percent
	alkali-feldspar—35–90 percent of feldspars
	plagioclase—10–65 percent of feldspars
Mafics:	5–20 percent (typically biotite ± muscovite ± hornblende)

Granodiorite

Felsics:	quartz—20–60 percent
	plagioclase—65–90 percent of feldspars
	alkali-feldspar—10–35 percent of feldspars
Mafics:	5–25 percent (typically biotite and hornblende)

Tonalite

Felsics:	quartz—20–60 percent
	plagioclase—90–100 percent of feldspars
	± alkali-feldspar—< 10 percent of feldspars
Mafics:	10–40 percent (typically hornblende and biotite)

Although the preliminary system (See Figure 4-8A) suggests that all of the rocks of this group should be called granitoids in the field, our own experience indicates that the approximate proportions of the alkali- versus plagioclase-feldspars can often be determined megascopically. Therefore, many of the granitoids can be named according to the general classification in the field. Along this line, we anticipate that one of the problems that some geologists may have with the IUGS classification will deal with the granitoids that contain roughly equal amounts of alkali- and plagioclase-feldspars (i.e., rocks in the right-hand half of Field No. 3 in Figure 4-9). Many geologists, particuarly in North America, have long called these rocks either quartz monzonites or adamellites. Unfortunately, this use of quartz monzonite conflicts with the use recommended by the IUGS.

Color of granitoids. The overall rock color depends on the color of the predominant feldspar and the percentage of the dark-colored mafic minerals present. Alkali feldspars, typically perthites in the granitoids, tend to be flesh-colored, pink, buff, or off-white. The plagioclases, typically albite or oligoclase, are generally white, gray, or yellowish. The quartz is normally colorless, white, or light to medium gray. The common mafics are black (biotite), silvery (muscovite), or dark greenish gray (hornblende). In a few of the coarse-grained granitoids, accessory minerals such as bluish black magnetite, dark red garnet, black tourmaline, or golden brown sphene are also megascopically visible. In large exposures, most granitoids have been described as being white, gray, buff, or pink in color. In hand specimen, however, other adjectives and combinations of colors are frequently used—for example, mottled white and reddish brown. Some color varieties are even given names: light-colored alkali-feldspar granites are sometimes referred to as *alaskites* and leuco-tonalites may be called *trondhjemites*.

Texture of granitoids. In normal granitoids, grains of the mafic minerals and feldspars are euhedral or subhedral and quartz is anhedral. Porphyritic granitoids are not uncommon. In granite porphyries, the phenocrysts are generally a perthitic alkali-feldspar; in granodiorite and tonalite porphyries, the phenocrysts are more likely to be plagioclase. All these porphyries may contain quartz phenocrysts, but even where present, they tend to be subordinate in both size and abundance. In some granitoids, the mafic minerals are clustered and/or have a preferred orientation that apparently reflects flowage during consolidation. These rocks are referred to as flow-banded or gneissic. A few of the more exotic textures in fairly atypical granitoids have given rise to widely used varietal names.

Less common varieties of granitoids. As already mentioned, some granitoids have been given varietal names on the basis of their extremely low contents of mafic minerals. Descriptive varietal names have also been given because of certain mineralogical compositions (e.g., two-mica granite), chemical composition (e.g., soda granite), texture (e.g., graphic granite), and even because of some distinctive post-magmatic alteration (e.g., unakite). Some of the varieties warrant brief descriptions.

Alkalic granitoids differ from more common members of the granitoid group in that they contain distinctive and unusual mafic minerals such as the sodium- and iron-rich amphiboles and pyroxenes (e.g., riebeckite and aegirine). Unfortunately, it is sometimes

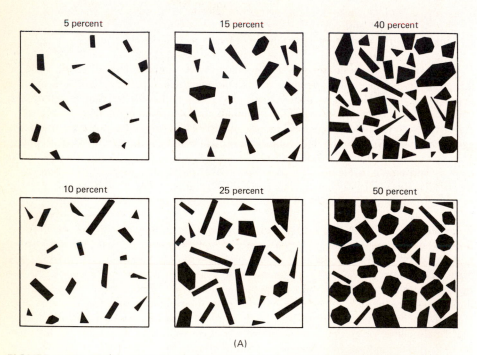

(A)

FIGURE 4-10 Mafic contents of phanerites. (A) Comparison chart for estimating mafic mineral contents. Grain shapes are similar to those commonly observed. (B) Mafic mineral contents of phanerites. If the mafic-mineral content is in the light area above the normal (stippled or darkened) field, the rock name should be preceded by the prefix leuco-; if the mafic-mineral content is in the light area below the normal field, the rock name should be preceded by the prefix mela-. For example, a granite with less than 5 percent mafic minerals would be a leuco-granite and a granite with more than 20 percent mafic minerals would be a mela-granite.

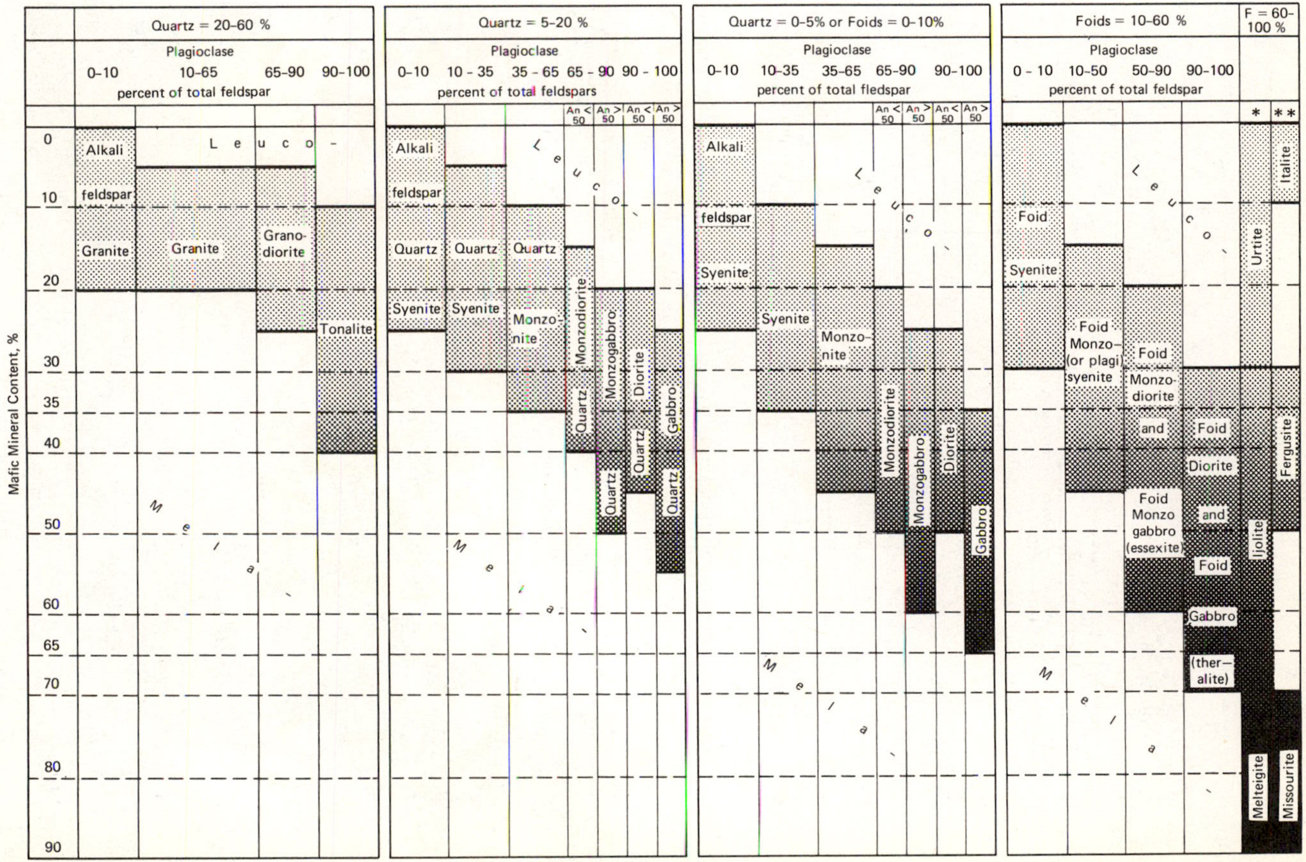

FIGURE 4-10B

*nepheline >> leucite or pseudoleucite
**leucite or pseudoleucite >> nepheline

119

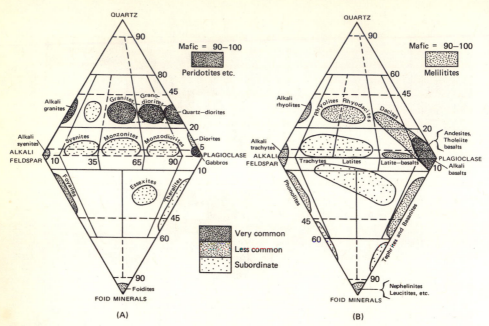

FIGURE 4-11 Estimated abundance of igneous rocks. (A) Phanerites; (B) Aphanites and aphanite porphyries. (After A. L. Streckeisen, N. Jb. Miner. Abh 107, p. 236.)

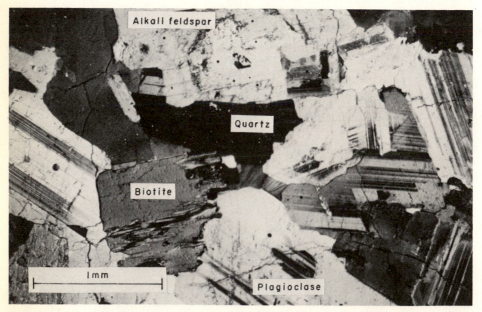

FIGURE 4-12 Thin section showing interlocking texture of minerals in a granodiorite from the Boulder Bathylith of Montana. (R. V. Dietrich)

difficult to distinguish minerals, such as riebeckite and aegirine, from other pyriboles. But, once this has been done in a given area, megascopic examination based on color is usually sufficient for additional identifications. In addition, many of these rocks have characteristic fabrics in that the feldspars are euhedral and the mafic minerals are subhedral or anhedral. Perhaps the most widely known alkalic granitoid in America is the Quincy Granite of Massachusetts, which was used in construction of the famous Bunker Hill Monument in Boston.

Aplites are white to buff or pinkish, fine-grained granitoids with sugary textures. The nearly equant feldspar grains are typically a pink or buff and white combination of roughly equal amounts of potassium-feldspar and sodium-rich plagioclase. And, even much of the quartz occurs as nearly equant grains rather than as anhedral grains filling interstices between other minerals. Sparse black specks, which are typically biotite or tourmaline, may be present. A few aplites have been found to be porphyritic. Most aplite occurs as dikes, ranging from less than a centimeter to a few meters thick, that cut through their parent pluton or through nearby country rock. An especially noteworthy example may be viewed from Owens Valley, California—aplite dikes are so numerous on the east side of the Sierra Nevada Batholith that they give the mass a striped appearance over an approximately 2400 meters vertical exposure. Aplites also occur intimately associated with some pegmatites (see below).

Charnockite is the name frequently applied to hypersthene granite. The rock was so-named because it constitutes the tombstone of Job Charnock, the English founder of Calcutta. *Charnockite series* is the term applied to a whole group of apparently related hypersthene-bearing phanerites including such diverse rocks as charnockite and norite (hypersthene gabbro). Actually, each of the rocks of the series can be named by merely adding hypersthene as a modifier to the correct rock name. Charnockite is typically rather dark colored. This is true because its quartz tends to be bluish and its feldspars are medium to dark gray. The hypersthene, which is generally discernible megascopically, may or may not have a bronzy appearance. At least some charnockitic rocks may be metamorphic rather than igneous. Among the better known North American localities for hypersthene granite and hypersthene granodiorite are the Sheridan District of Montana and Blue Ridge Province of Central Virginia.

Graphic granite consists of about 70 percent alkali feldspar and 30 percent quartz. The feldspar is present as large off-white, tan, or pinkish microcline perthite grains. The quartz is light gray and occurs as long, nearly parallel, wedge-shaped prisms within the feldspar. On certain microcline cleavage surfaces, cross-sections of the quartz prisms resemble cuneiform characters (Figure 4-13). Essentially all graphic granite occurs in pegmatite masses.

Miarolitic granitoids are characterized by crystal-lined cavities that appear to have been formed during consolidation of the parent magma. The cavities differ from cavities that have been filled after their enclosing rock was formed because the main crystals that extend into miarolitic cavities merge with their counterparts in the surrounding rock. Feldspar, quartz, topaz, tourmaline, and some relatively rare minerals characteristically line the cavities. Most miarolitic granitoids occur in masses that are thought to have solidified relatively high within the earth's crust. Some of the well-known crystals of smoky quartz and green microcline in museums that are labeled "Pike's Peak Region of Colorado" were collected from miarolitic cavities. .

Orbicular granitoids consist of diversely constituted spheroidal nodules, called orbicules, that are enclosed in matrixes of essentially normal textured granitoids. Because of

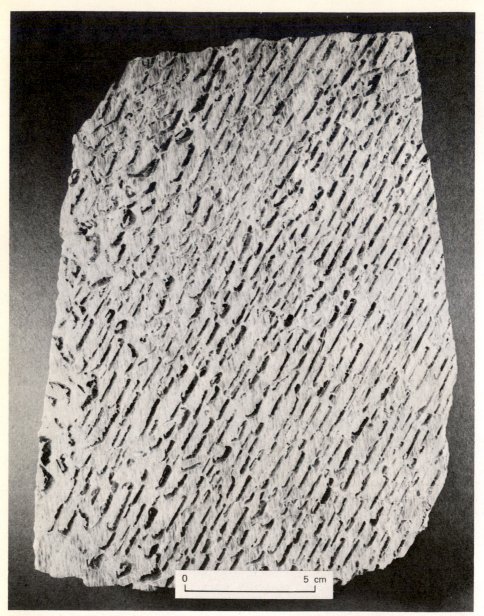

FIGURE 4-13   Graphic granite; white is feldspar, dark gray rod-like inclusions are quartz. (*Smithsonian Institution*)

their appearances, some orbicular rocks have been called "plum pudding stones." Well-developed orbicules, which range up to several centimeters in diameter, are made up of concentric shells in which one or more minerals predominate (Figure 4-14). Larger orbicules, in particular, tend to be rhythmically banded and in some masses, the arrangement of the bands correlates rather well from one to another orbicule. Orbicular representatives are known for syenitoids, dioritoids, gabbroids, and lamprophyres as well as for granitoids. The best-known orbicular granitoids occur in Finland, Sweden, and New Zealand. Among North American localities are those near Bethel and Craftsbury, Vermont.

Pegmatite, meaning "joined together," was first applied to graphic granite sometime before 1822. Subsequently, it has been extended to refer to any abnormally coarse-grained rock of overall igneous character. Unmodified, the name is generally accepted as meaning granite pegmatite and is referred to either the rock or to a mass made up of the rock. Nonetheless, it should be kept in mind that pegmatites with the gross compositions of other igneous rocks also exist—for example, there are syenite, nepheline syenite, gabbro, and even ultramafite pegmatites.

Most grains of pegmatites are more than 1 centimeter across; grains up to a meter or two across are relatively common; and individual crystals up to several meters in greatest dimension have been reported (e.g., a 15-meter spodumene at the Etta Mine, Keystone, South Dakota). In any case, no matter how large the grains, most pegmatites have typical igneous rock textures.

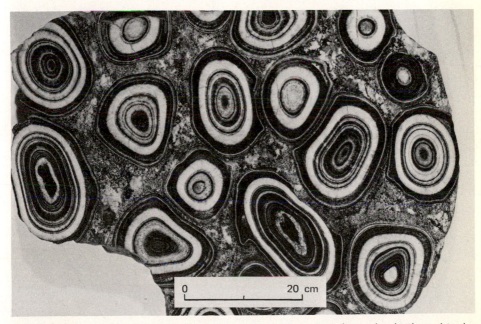

FIGURE 4-14 Orbicular diorite (polished slab) from Kangasala, Finland. The orbicules consist of a core (commonly a xenolithic fragment) surrounded by alternating bands of predominately light-colored plagioclase (An_{30}) and dark, biotite-rich bands. (*E. Halme*)

Individual pegmatite masses may be classified as simple or complex. The simple ones have an overall homogeneity and consist almost wholly of microcline perthite and quartz plus or minus minor amounts of biotite and/or black tourmaline. The complex pegmatites tend to be compositionally zoned and to contain, along with quartz and microcline, large quantities of clevelandite (the platy variety of albite), noteworthy amounts of muscovite, and well-formed crystals of such minerals as apatite, beryl, topaz, colored tourmaline, and spodumene, plus a number of less common minerals that contain elements such as lithium, niobium, tantalum, cesium, uranium, and the rare earths.

Most simple pegmatites occur as dikes within large igneous masses or their surrounding country rocks (Figure 4-15). Most complex pegmatites occur as lenticular pods or irregularly shaped masses within the country rocks surrounding large igneous masses or as apparently isolated masses within metamorphic rock terranes.

As already mentioned, graphic granite is found in some pegmatite masses and rather commonly aplite is intimately associated with pegmatite. Several hypotheses have been forwarded to account for the formation of pegmatites and for their rock associations. Most pegmatites are thought to have been formed from late stage igneous liquids. A few are thought to be high temperature veins filled by metamorphically derived solutions.

FIGURE 4-15   Granite pegmatite dike intruding medium-grained granite country rock near Bar Harbor, Maine. (Maine Dept. of Economic Development)

Simple pegmatites may be observed in or near many granitoid masses. There are many districts in North America that are world famous for their complex pegmatites. Among them are the Spruce Pine District of North Carolina, the Amelia District of central Virginia, the Middletown District of central Connecticut, the Keystone District of southwestern South Dakota, the Pala District of southern California, and the Winnipeg River Area of Manitoba, Canada. As well as being sources for fine mineral specimens and gem materials, several of the large complex pegmatite masses have been operated commercially to produce feldspar for the ceramic industry and muscovite for isinglass, electrical insulation, glitter, paint filler, and for various other uses.

Porphyry copper deposit is the name frequently applied to granitoid porphyries, typically altered granodiorites, that contain disseminated copper minerals. In practice, however, the name porphyry copper deposit has been extended to include any surrounding country rock that has been mineralized as well as the altered porphyry (Figure 4-16). Both the porphyry and country rocks are characteristically fractured and shattered on a scale of a centimeter or more and both also exhibit many types of alteration—for example,

0   1 cm

FIGURE 4-16 Porphyry copper. A brecciated granodiorite porphyry (polished surface), highly altered by hydrothermal solutions. Ore minerals that originally filled the fractures have been oxidized during weathering to form the dark limonite that is visible in the photograph. (B. J. Skinner)

silicification, albitization, sericitization, kaolinization, and chloritization—as well as copper mineralization. Some of the altered rocks consist almost wholly of the alteration products. The disseminated copper minerals appear to have been introduced after the fracturing and either contemporaneously with or subsequent to the alteration. They occur in veinlets that literally permeate the altered porphyry and adjacent country rocks. The most common copper minerals are chalcopyrite and bornite, but enargite, tetrahedrite, and chalcocite are also known in some deposits.

The first porphyry copper deposit recognized is the one still being mined in Bingham Canyon, Utah. Since it was discovered late in the nineteenth century, more than 100 additional porphyry copper deposits have been found around the world. In the Americas, they occur in a belt that trends roughly parallel to the western margin of the continents and extends from Alaska to central Chile. Currently, at some of the deposits, copper is being produced from rocks containing as little as 0.5 percent copper.

Rapakivi granite is a porphyritic granite consisting of rounded alkali-feldspar phenocrysts that are mantled with plagioclase (typically oligoclase, but in some cases albite or andesine) and are surrounded by a groundmass made up chiefly of medium-grained quartz and biotite and/or hornblende. Fluorite is a common, megascopically visible accessory. Typically, the phenocrysts are reddish salmon- to flesh-colored and range from two to three centimeters in longest dimension. The type locality for this rock is Kengis in southern Finland. Similar rock has been found as glacial boulders in Canada and Michigan and as bedrock on Deer Isle in Penobscot Bay, Maine. Rapakivi granite from the vicinity of Wiborg (Viipuri) in southeastern Finland is extremely massive and has been quarried in exceptionally large blocks. The 9-meter cube that was used for the base of the Alexander Column in Leningrad is a noteworthy example.

Unakite, named for exposures in the Unaka Range of the Great Smoky Mountains of eastern Tennessee and western North Carolina, is the name commonly applied to epidote-rich alkali feldspar granite. The feldspar is generally salmon-colored; the quartz is light gray; the epidote is a pistachio-to-bilious green. The grain size may be fine, medium, or coarse. Megascopically, the epidote appears to occur in veinlets and/or as disseminated grains. For a number of reasons, including the fact that unakite is commonly associated with the epidote-quartz rock *epidosite*, which is of metamorphic origin, many geologists believe that unakite is an epidotized granite.

Apparently because of its uncommon combinations of colors, unakite has gained widespread use in trinkets and costume jewelry. There are several exposures of such epidotized granite in the central and southern Blue Ridge Province (e.g., near Airpoint, Virginia). Similar rocks from various sources are common among the glacial and beach stones of Michigan and Wisconsin.

Occurrences of granitoids. As already mentioned, granitoids are the most common phanerites. Well-known examples underlie Mount Rushmore, South Dakota, where the gigantic heads of Jefferson, Lincoln, Washington, and Theodore Roosevelt are carved; Stone Mountain, Georgia, in which the huge bas-relief commemorating Confederate valor is carved; Half Dome in Yosemite National Park, California; and Pike's Peak, Colorado. The youngest known batholith in North America—the Early Miocene body beneath Mount Rainier, Washington—is a granodiorite. The largest intrusives in the world are masses of granite and/or granodiorite—for example the British Columbia, Southern California, Idaho, and Sierra Nevada composite batholiths of western North America, each of which extends over thousands of square kilometers (Figure 4-17). In addition, granitoid masses comprise

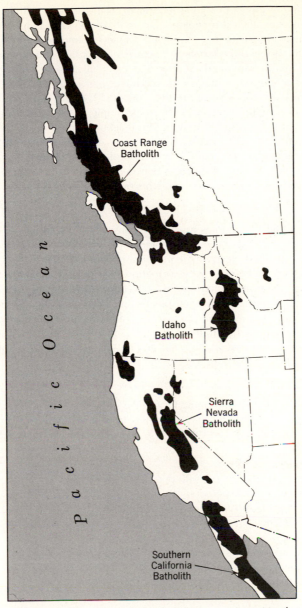

FIGURE 4-17 Granitic batholiths in western North America.

the cores of many of the earth's great mountain chains. In fact, drilling and geophysical evidence as well as geological mapping indicate that rocks of granitoid composition form the very foundations of the earth's continents. The less abundant granitoids, especially the alkali feldspar granites and the tonalites, occur mainly as *facies* of composite intrusives—for example, many predominantly diorite masses locally grade into tonalite. Facies, as applied to igneous intrusives, may be defined as a part of a mass that differs in texture and/or mineralogical composition from the typical rock of the main mass.

As the IUGS definitions of phaneritic rocks imply, some large masses of granitoid, commonly thought to be igneous, may not be igneous at all. Instead, they may represent pre-existing sedimentary rocks that have been converted to igneous-appearing rocks as the result of metamorphic recrystallization and replacement. Examination of hand specimens seldom, if ever, permits distinction between igneous and metamorphic rocks with granitoid characteristics. Instead, one must become involved in intensive field and laboratory investigations.

Uses of granitoids. Granitoids are used extensively as building stones. Cut and polished slabs for both internal and external facing are exemplary. Polished or honed blocks of granitoids are also used for more clearly ornamental purposes such as tombstones and pedestals for statues. Three especially well-known producing areas are near Barre, Vermont; Mount Airy, North Carolina; and Saint Cloud, Minnesota. Rough, irregular blocks are used as rip-rap. Crushed and sized pieces are used locally for cement and bitumen aggregate. A few of the less common uses of granitoids are for curbing stones, in filter plant beds, as the balls for ball-mill ore crushers, in costume jewelry, and for turkey grit.

Some rocks that are sold as polished granite are not only *not* granite, they are not even a granitoid. Instead, they are such rocks as syenite, diorite, gabbro, or a migmatite.

Syenitoids

Syenitoids are relatively uncommon rocks (see Figure 4-11). The low percentage of quartz is the characteristic that distinguishes syenitoids from granitoids. The general makeup of the syenitoids, as shown in Figures 4-8A, 4-9, and 4-10B may be summarized as follows:

Alkali-feldspar quartz syenite
Felsics: alkali-feldspar—90–100 percent of feldspars
            quartz—5–20 percent
            plagioclase—<10 percent of feldspars
Mafics: 0–25 percent

Quartz syenite
Felsics: alkali-feldspar—65–90 percent of feldspars
            quartz—5–20 percent
            plagioclase—10–35 percent of feldspars
Mafics: 5–30 percent

Alkali-feldspar syenite
Felsics: alkali feldspar—90–100 percent of feldspars
            plagioclase—0–10 percent of feldspars
            quartz—<5 percent
Mafics: 0–25 percent

Syenite
Felsics: alkali-feldspar—65–90 percent of feldspars

            plagioclase—10–35 percent of feldspars
            quartz—<5 percent
    Mafics: 10–35 percent
Monzonite
    Felsics: alkali-feldspar—35–65 percent of feldspars
            plagioclase—35–65 percent of feldspars
            quartz—<5 percent
    Mafics: 15–45 percent
Foid-bearing alkali-feldspar syenite
    Felsics: alkali-feldspar—90–100 percent of feldspars
            feldspathoids—0–10 percent
            plagioclase—<10 percent of feldspars
    Mafics: 0–25 percent

Color of syenitoids. Most syenites are buff, pink, or deep salmon red in color; a few are gray or yellowish. The monzonites tend to be of the same overall colors, but to appear mottled because of their mixed feldspars and relatively high mafic-mineral contents. Because the alkali-feldspar and plagioclase in syenitoids tend to be of different colors, we repeat the plea that concerted efforts should be made to estimate the proportions of the feldspars megascopically and thus to name these rocks according to the general classification (Figure 4-9). The common mafic minerals—biotite (black), hornblende and augite (both greenish black)—may occur singly or in any combination. Of the feldspathoids, nepheline and sodalite are most likely to be recognizable in the foid-bearing syenitoids. Sodalite is generally blue. Nepheline is most likely to be smoky gray. On fresh surfaces, nepheline resembles quartz; on weathered surfaces, it is likely to be etched because it is slightly soluble in acidic solutions, such as rainwater. Just as in the alkalic granitoids, the sodium- and iron-rich amphiboles and pyroxenes (such as riebeckite and aegirine) are present in many syenitoids, especially in those containing feldspathoids. Less common minerals such as astrophyllite, which looks like a golden mica, are also megascopically discernible in some of the quartz-free syenites.

Texture of syenitoids. Syenitoids, like the granitoids, tend to be equigranular and medium- to coarse-grained. In some syenitoids, the alkali feldspars are tabular and have a subparallel arrangement that may reflect magmatic flowage. Porphyritic, pegmatitic, and aplitic syenitoids occur. The phenocrysts are generally perthitic alkali feldspars in the syenite porphyries and perthite and plagioclase in the monzonites. Many of the deep salmon colored orthoclase crystals in mineral collections are phenocrysts from a syenite porphyry near Goodsprings, Nevada.

Occurrences of syenitoids. Syenites occur as marginal facies or apophyses of granitic masses and less commonly as relatively minor intrusives, such as stocks. Feldspathoid-bearing syenites tend to occur as facies of masses consisting chiefly of foid syenites (page 136). Most monzonites occur as marginal facies or apophyses of granites or granodiorites but they also occur as ring dikes. Perhaps the best known syenitoids in the United States are the quartz syenites that occur in the Adirondacks of northern New York. Similar syenites occur here and there in the Precambrian terrane of Ontario and Quebec.

Uses of syenitoids. Syenitoids are used in about the same way that granitoids are but in lesser amounts because of their more restricted occurrence. Sienite, as it was called by Pliny, was transported all the way from Syena, which is located at the cataracts of the Nile River, for use in Roman architecture and statuary. The attractive variety called larvikite (see below) is one of the most widely used facing stones in the world.

Less common varieties of syenitoids. As mentioned in the description of orbicular granitoids, orbicular syenitoids are known, but they are not common. Miarolitic syenite is relatively common. A few other varieties of syenitoids have been given special names. Two merit description here:

Larvikite is the bluish gray rock that seems to wink at you as you pass buildings faced by it. Because it is one of the world's most popular facing stones, you are likely to see it in just about any part of the world. This coarse-grained igneous rock that comes from the vicinity of Larvik, Norway, appears megascopically to consist almost wholly of one feldspar plus a small percentage of clustered mafics and a percentage or two of quartz or nepheline. Actually, the feldspar grains are intimate mixtures, on a submicroscopic scale, of oligoclase and alkali feldspar, so the overall composition of the rock is that of a monzonite. It is the character of the feldspar intermixture that gives the grains their beautiful opalescent quality. There are two relatively distinct commercial varieties of larvikite—one light bluish gray, the other dark bluish gray with golden brown overtones. The lighter one is sometimes marketed as "Norwegian Pearl granite." The dark variety commonly contains a black magnetic material, not nearly so hard as magnetite, called hisingerite.

Pulaskite is the name frequently applied to the foid-bearing alkali syenite that has been weathered to produce the bauxite deposits of Pulaski County in the Little Rock, Arkansas Region. It is light to dark bluish gray (in the latter case, it is sometimes erroneously called blue granite) and is either equigranular or somewhat porphyritic because of the presence of a few large grains of an alkali feldspar. The mafic minerals are diopside plus one or more of the sodium- and iron-rich pyriboles. Nepheline plus or minus sodalite, or locally nosean, may constitute up to five percent of the rock. The name is superfluous and thus should be abandoned.

Dioritoids, Gabbroids and Anorthosites

As is evident in Figures 4-8A and 4-9, there are three relatively common rocks in the composition field characterized by a predominance of plagioclase feldspar; they are diorite, gabbro, and anorthosite. The lack or near lack of quartz distinguishes these rocks from the granitoids; the absence or very low content of alkali feldspar distinguishes them from the syenitoids. The other rocks in the overall field—quartz monzodiorite, quartz diorite, and monzodiorite—are uncommon (see Figure 4-11).

Distinctions between diorites, gabbros, and anorthosites are straightforward but sometimes difficult to apply without a microscope. Anorthosite differs from diorite and gabbro because of its low (< 10 percent) mafic mineral content; diorite and gabbro cannot, strictly speaking, be told apart megascopically. This is true because the plagioclase composition, which cannot be determined in hand specimen, is definitive—diorite is defined as containing andesine or less calcic plagioclase, whereas gabbro is defined as containing labradorite or more calcic plagioclase. Nonetheless, many geologists do tentatively attempt to distinguish between the two rocks on the basis of a megascopic examination. They know, from experience that many diorites consist largely of a light-colored plagioclase and hornblende, whereas most gabbros are made up predominantly of a dark to violet or bluish gray plagioclase and augite. They also look especially carefully for olivine because they know that the plagioclase in olivine-bearing rocks is most likely to be labradorite or more calcic in composition.

The following tabulation summarizes the compositional differences among the rocks of this group:

Quartz monzodiorite
    Felsics: plagioclase—65–90 percent of feldspars
                  alkali-feldspar—10–35 percent of feldspars
                  quartz—5–20 percent
    Mafics: 15–40 percent

Quartz diorite
    Felsics: plagioclase—90–100 percent of feldspars
                  quartz—5–20 percent
    Mafics: 20–45 percent

Monzodiorite
    Felsics: plagioclase—65–90 percent of feldspars
                  alkali-feldspars—10–35 percent of feldspars
                  quartz—< 5 percent
    Mafics: 20–50 percent

Diorite
    Felsics: plagioclase—90–100 percent of feldspars
                  quartz—<5 percent
    Mafics: 25–50 percent (typically hornblende ± biotite ± augite)

Gabbro
    Felsics: plagioclase—90–100 percent of feldspars
                  quartz—< 5 percent
    Mafics: 35–65 percent (typically augite ± hypersthene ± olivine)

Anorthosite
    Felsics: plagioclase—90–100 percent of feldspars
                  quartz—<5 percent
    Mafics: 0–10 percent (typically augite)

Color of dioritoids, gabbroids, and anorthosites. The color of most diorites is an overall medium gray to greenish gray and may be seen on close observation to be a mixture of greenish black and off-white (see Figure 4-18). Plagioclase is typically off-white to light gray or buff in color; the mafic minerals are hornblende (greenish black or dark gray), plus or minus biotite (black), and/or augite (greenish black). Many diorites appear spotted because their dark colored mafic constituents are surrounded by the light colored plagioclase (Figure 4-18). Both leuco- and mela-diorites occur.

Most gabbros tend to be dark greenish and/or bluish gray to nearly black in color because both their plagioclase and their mafic minerals are dark in color. The greenish hue may originate from the color of the pyroxene, the olivine and/or its alteration product, serpentine, or even to saussuritization of the plagioclase. Grains of magnetite and/or pyrrhotite and/or ilmenite are megascopically discernible in many gabbros.

Anorthosites range from dark gray to bluish gray through light gray, off-white, or brownish hues. Some of the bluish gray varieties, which are the most common, exhibit a beautiful play of colors usually referred to as labradorescence. As a result, anorthosites may superficially resemble larvikite (page 130). Although many anorthosites appear

0 _____ 2 cm

FIGURE 4-18 Hand specimen of a diorite. White is plagioclase, black is hornblende. (B. J. Skinner)

megascopically to consist wholly of plagioclase, others contain minor amounts of megascopically distinguishable grains of other minerals such as pyroxene (augite and/or hypersthene), olivine, magnetite, and ilmenite. Anorthosites may, at first sight, look much like marble, coarse-grained quartzite, anhydrock, or even recrystallized limestone or dolostone. Fortunately, the greater hardness of plagioclase distinguishes anorthosite from all but the quartzite and that distinction can be made on the basis of cleavage in plagioclase and its absence in quartz.

Texture of dioritoids, gabbroids, and anorthosites. Most diorites and gabbros are equigranular and medium- to coarse-grained. Nearly all anorthosites are coarse-grained and some have been reported as having grains up to one meter in greatest dimension. Dioritic and gabbroic pegmatites are known, but are rare. There are diorite porphyries with phenocrysts of either plagioclase or hornblende, or both—generally in a fine-grained groundmass. Most porphyries of gabbroic composition consist of large plagioclase grains, some of which exhibit obvious breakage and apparent rounding, surrounded by fine-grained mixtures of plagioclase, mafic minerals, and, in rare cases, quartz. Megascopically discernible aggregates of magnetite plus or minus ilmenite, or of pyrrhotite, are sporadic in many gabbros. As described under "Occurrences," some gabbros and anorthosites are banded.

Occurrences of dioritoids, gabbroids, and anorthosites. Diorites and gabbros occur rather widely as stocks, dikes, sills, laccoliths, and other relatively small intrusives. Diorite is also rather common in border facies and apophyses of large granodiorite and gabbro masses. Gabbro is a common constituent of the large, layered intrusions called lopoliths (see Figure 4-7) and is also found in volcanic necks, and in the central parts of thick lava flows. Some geologists, however, are reluctant to use the designation gabbro for extrusive rock, no matter what its grain size. Instead, they call it coarse-grained basalt (page 150) or perhaps dolerite or diabase. We believe that they should overcome their reluctance and abandon unnecessary terms that compete with gabbro.

The gabbro portions of lopoliths and of other large intrusives tend to be layered or, alternatively, are said to be banded. Typical bands range from less than a centimeter to a few meters in thickness and may extend for several kilometers. The bands are defined by differences in the proportions of their constituent minerals—usually we observe light, plagioclase-rich layers and dark, mafic-rich layers. Boundaries between the layers may be relatively sharp or interlocking. Although the overall average of all layers is of gabbroic composition, some of the individual layers are actually anorthosites, pyroxenites, or even peridotites (page 138). North American examples of banded gabbro occurrences include portions of the Duluth Lopolith of northern Minnesota and adjacent Canada; the Muskox intrusive of the District of Mackenzie, Northwest Territories, Canada; the Stillwater Complex of south central Montana; and the Sudbury Lopolith of central Ontario. The Duluth mass, for example, is estimated to contain more than 200,000 cubic kilometers of gabbro.

Anorthosite tends to occur in large, rather ill-defined masses of batholithic dimensions and most of the masses are Precambrian in age. One notable group of anorthosite masses occurs in eastern Labrador, Québec and in the Adirondacks of New York. One of the anorthosite bedrock areas along the Saguenay River, north of Montreal, measures more than 15,000 square kilometers.

Uses of dioritoids, gabbroids, and anorthosites. Diorites have found little use except locally as rough building stone, fill, or crushed aggregate. Gabbros have also been used as dimension stones, including those that have been polished for monuments. Examples are the gabbros quarried near Duluth, Minnesota and near Keesville, New York. Anorthosite exhibiting labradorescence has been used in costume jewelry. An oligoclase anorthosite from the Piney River district of Virginia (marketed erroneously as aplite) is used as a raw material in the manufacture of ceramics and glass. Anorthosite, especially that in which the feldspar is bytownite or anorthite, is considered to be a potential source of aluminum when bauxite supplies must be supplanted. Concentrations of economically recoverable magnetite and/or ilmenite are associated with some anorthosite masses—for example, the deposits at Allard Lake, Quebec and those in the Adirondacks area of New York.

Varieties of dioritoids and gabbroids. Olivine-bearing gabbros are common; quartz-bearing gabbros are far from rare. Orbicular diorites and gabbros are uncommon, but do occur. Examples include the orbicular diorite from San Diego County, California and the so-called Corsican granite (also called corsite), which is the orbicular gabbro displayed in so many museums throughout the world. Miarolitic diorite is relatively common but is neither as common nor as readily recognized as miarolitic granites. The recognition difficulty is based on the fact that in diorites the central cavities tend to be filled with calcite. Three additional varieties—one texture-based, the others compositional—warrant description.

Diabase, dolerite, and trap rock are names that have been variously applied to fine-grained rocks that are transitional between medium-grained gabbro and its aphanitic equivalent, basalt. Because of the ambiguities involved in continued use of these terms, we believe that all should be abandoned in favor of the purely descriptive term fine-grained gabbro. Probably the most difficult hurdle to acceptance of this suggestion is the fact that many of these rocks constitute near-surface intrusives or even lava flows and the term gabbro is widely considered to refer only to plutonic rocks. We suggest that this difficulty can be overcome, at least in the literature, by clear statements such as "Lava flow number 37 consists largely of fine-grained gabbro."

Fine-grained gabbros are dark rocks—medium gray to nearly black, some tending to appear greenish. Along with the light gray feldspar laths and the black to greenish-black pyroxene grains, megascopic examination will generally reveal scattered grains of green olivine plus or minus bronzy-appearing flakes of biotite and small grains of magnetite, pyrrhotite, and/or ilmenite.

Some fine-grained gabbros are equigranular; others are porphyritic. The more or less equigranular ones commonly consist of laths of light gray feldspar with dark gray to greenish black pyroxene filling the interstices (Figure 4-19). Either mineral may predominate. Most of the porphyritic varieties have lath-shaped phenocrysts of feldspar in the groundmass like that just described. A few relatively rare fine-grained gabbro porphyries also have blocky augite phenocrysts. In many of these rocks, the plagioclase phenocrysts are greenish gray and have a greasy appearance because of saussuritization.

Fine-grained gabbro is a relatively common rock. Along with its occurrence in lava flows, in high level intrusives such as dikes and sills, and in volcanic plugs, fine-grained gabbro also occurs rather commonly as border facies of large coarse-grained gabbro masses. The sill that is exposed as the Palisades along the Hudson River in southern New York State serves as a good example of the many masses of predominantly fine-grained gabbro that occur within the Triassic basins of eastern North America. Good specimens of fine-grained gabbro can be collected at the trap rock quarries in these masses. There are several such quarries because the color and physical properties of this rock make it one of the best aggregate materials known.

Norite is a gabbro in which an orthopyroxene, typically hypersthene, is the predominant mafic mineral. Some geologists consider norite to be the gabbro member of the so-called charnockite series. Unless the orthopyroxene has a good characteristic bronzy appearance, it is difficult to distinguish a norite from a normal gabbro by megascopic examination.

Norite is a relatively common rock. One of the world's largest nickel deposits, located at Sudbury, Ontario, is enclosed within norite, the magma of which some geologists believe to have been intruded in response to meteoric impact.

Troctolite—also called forellenstein, which in German means trout rock in analogy to the speckling of trout—is the name applied to certain olivine plagioclase rocks that fit best into the gabbro category. These rather exotic appearing rocks typically consist of between 35 and 65 percent nearly white plagioclase, with scattered grains of green or nearly black olivine and/or its greenish, brownish, yellowish, or even reddish alteration products.

Troctolite is a rock that is included in many student study collections, even though the rock is relatively rare. Most specimens are from Volpesdorf, Silesia (now part of the German Democratic Republic). Similar rock occurs in the Wichita Mountains of southwestern Oklahoma and as layers in some lopoliths (e.g., near the middle of the Stillwater Complex in south central Montana).

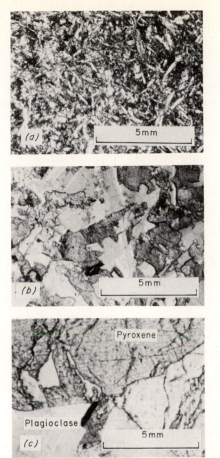

Fine grained

Medium grained

Pyroxene

Coarse grained

Plagioclase

FIGURE 4-19 Thin sections of fine-, medium-, and coarse grained gabbro from different parts of the thick Palisades Sill, New Jersey. (A) the fine-grained rock came from the rapdily cooled marginal zone; (B) the medium-grained variety from a slowly cooled portion 12 meters from the contact; (C) the coarse-grained variety 40 meters in from the contact. All sections are shown at the same magnification. (B. J. Skinner)

FELDSPATHOIDAL PHANERITES

None of the feldspathoidal phanerites is of common occurrence in the sense that granitoids and gabbroids are (see Figure 4-11). In fact, J. J. Sederholm, one of the great Finnish geologists, referred to these rocks as "the aristocrats" because he believed that the attention geologists had given them was out of all proportion to their abundance and importance.

On a simplistic basis, these rocks are like the granitoids, syenitoids, and gabbroids except for two facts: one or more of the feldspathoids occur instead of quartz; and sodium-

and iron-rich pyriboles are present instead of hornblende and augite. This, of course, means that the ratio of alkali-feldspar to plagioclase is fundamental to the root names (except for the diorite-gabbro pair), just as is true for the quartz-bearing phanerites. Therefore, once it has been determined that a feldspathoid is present and that quartz is absent, the descriptions given for the quartz-bearing equivalents are more or less applicable. On fresh surfaces, the nepheline-bearing phanerites, in particular, may be extremely difficult to distinguish megascopically from their quartz-bearing analogs. On weathered surfaces, however, nepheline-bearing rocks commonly weather to give pock-marked surfaces on which the altered nepheline is bluish-gray, has a dull luster, and occupies the depressions.

The foidolites, on the other hand, are not comparable to the quartzolites. Whereas quartzolites are nearly 100 percent quartz and thus light colored, the foidolites may have essentially any mafic mineral content. As shown on Figure 4-10B, the nomenclature of the foidolites depends upon the identity of the predominant feldspathoid—usually nepheline versus leucite or pseudoleucite—and the percentage of mafic minerals. The rock melilitolite, a phanerite made up almost wholly of the mineral melilite, is considered by some petrologists to belong to the foidolite group. Others, including the authors of this book, consider melilite to be a mafic mineral and the rock to be an ultramafite (page 138).

The general mineralogical compositions for the feldspathoidal phanerites, as shown on Figures 4-9 and 4-10B may be summarized as follows:

Foid Syenitoids
Foid syenite (e.g., nepheline syenite)
    Felsics: feldspathoids—10–60 percent
                    alkali-feldspar—90–100 percent of feldspars
                    plagioclase—<10 percent of feldspars
    Mafics: 0–30 percent

Foid Dioritoids and Gabbroids
Foid monzodiorite/Foid monzogabbro (Both = essexite)
    Felsics: foids—10–60 percent
                    plagioclase—50–90 percent of the feldspars
                    alkali-feldspar—10–50 percent of feldspars
    Mafics: 20–60 percent
Foid gabbros (= theralite)
    Felsics: foids—10–60 percent
                    plagioclase—90–100 percent of feldspars
                    alkali-feldspar—< 10 percent of feldspars
    Mafics: 30–70 percent
Foidolites
Foidolites (e.g., ijolite and italite—for other appropriate names, see Figure 4-10B)
    Felsics: foids—60–100 percent feldspars
    Mafics: up to 100 percent

In naming individual rocks in the foid-bearing groups, the names of the foid mineral or minerals are substituted for the term foid (e.g., a foid syenite that has nepheline as its feldspathoid becomes nepheline syenite). Similarly, instead of using the term foidolite for any given rock in which feldspathoids make up 60 to 100 percent of the light-colored mineral-content, the appropriate name given in Figure 4-10B should be used (e.g., a foidolite with a mafic mineral content of between 35 and 70 percent and more plagioclase than potassium-feldspar would be called ijolite).

Color of feldspathoidal phanerites. In overall color the feldspar-bearing feldspathoidal phanerites resemble their quartz-bearing analogs and the foidolites tend to resemble the quartz-bearing equivalents that contain similar percentages of mafic minerals. An especially noteworthy example of the latter relationship is the fact that the nepheline in some ijolites looks so much like labradorite that the rock really looks like a gabbro.

Despite the resemblances, many feldspathoidal rocks tend to be more colorful than their quartz-bearing analogs. This is true for two reasons: the feldspathoid minerals exhibit a greater variety of colors—for example, bright blue (sodalite), lemon yellow (cancrinite), and diverse greens (nepheline)—than typical rock-making quartz, and feldspathoidal rocks tend to contain a larger percentage and a more mineralogically varied group of accessory minerals. Among the accessories that are commonly identifiable with no more than hand-lens magnification are apatite, corundum, sphene, zircon, and cherry-red eudialyte.

Texture of feldspathoidal phanerites. The textures of these rocks resemble those of their quartz-bearing analogs, just as their overall colors do—for example, the foid syenite nepheline syenite may be aplitic or contain tabular alkali feldspar grains with subparallel arrangement, possibly reflecting magmatic flowage. Miarolitic, pegmatitic, and porphyritic representatives occur. The pegmatites of the Langesund Area of Norway and near Ivigtut, southern Greenland have furnished outstanding specimens of several rare minerals. The porphyries may have large phenocrysts of mafic minerals—for example, titan-augite—as well as of nepheline and alkali-feldspar.

Occurrences of feldspathoidal phanerites. Several different feldspathoidal phanerites commonly occur together in regions that, as a consequence, are called alkalic provinces. The rocks may occur in relatively large intrusives or in smaller stocks, dikes, and other such masses. Examples of such provinces include the Novanglian Province of New England, the Magnet Cove District of Arkansas, the Bearpaw and Highwood mountain areas of Montana, the Halliburton-Bancroft Area of south central Ontario, the Alnö District of Sweden, and the Kola Peninsula of the U.S.S.R. Feldspathoidal phanerites also occur locally as facies of normal granites, syenites, and gabbro. At many such occurrences, the foid phanerites appear to have been formed because of reactions between a normal, subalkalic magma and the surrounding limestone or marble country rock.

Two other modes of occurrence for these rocks are as layers in differentiated sills and as blocks ejected by volcanoes. Theralite (= foid gabbro) layers are fairly common in sills, such as the famous Lugar Sill of southwestern Scotland. Blocks of rocks, such as italite (see Figure 4-10B), have been ejected by a number of volcanoes in the Roman Province of Italy.

Uses of feldspathoidal phanerites. As is true for most rocks, several feldspathoidal phanerites have been used locally for building stones and as road metal. The Crawfordjohn rock of Scotland, which is used in many curling stones, is a porphyritic nepheline monzodiorite (essexite). Corundum-rich nepheline syenite, similar to that from Renfrew, Ontario, has been mined in South Africa for the production of abrasives. To the present, however, the most important use for feldspathoidal rocks has been as a raw material for the ceramics industry. Both Russian and Canadian rocks that are low in mafics and co-rundum have been used in the manufacture of ceramics, whiteware, and as a vitrifying agent in glass. And, as is true of the calcium-rich anorthosites, some of the foidolites are potential sources for vast quantities of aluminum.

Ultramafites

The term ultramafite refers simply to a rock that is rich in mafic minerals. Indeed, the rock may consist entirely of one or more mafic minerals. All ultramafic rocks have, as a con-sequence, low silica contents and this fact has led some geologists to extend the term, ultramafite, to include certain silica-free igneous rocks, such as carbonatites and magne-titites. The diagram given as a preliminary system for ultramafites (see Figure 4-8C) is instructive in two ways: It includes only the ultramafic phanerites that consist largely of common silicate minerals—that is, the peridotites, the pyroxenites, and the hornblendites; it indicates that within these three major classes the various members cannot be readily distinguished from each other by megascopic means. We follow the IUGS recommen-dations and also include magnetitite, chromitite, carbonatite, and melilitolite in the ultra-mafite category. We also maintain that dunite can be distinguished megascopically from the other varieties of peridotites and that most bronzititites can be distinguished mega-scopically from the other pyroxenites.

Magnetitite and chromitite are readily identifiable because their chief constituents are ore minerals. They can be told apart because magnetitite is strongly magnetic, whereas chromitite is not. Contrariwise, it is next to impossible to distinguish a magnetitite from some magnetite-rich metamorphic rocks, unless the geologic relationships are known.

Carbonatite is similarly difficult to distinguish from some marble (page 253) and even from some recrystallized limestone (page 216), unless the geological setting is obvious.

Naming a rock melilitolite depends only on identifying the mineral melilite.

Ultramafic silicate rocks (see Figures 4-8C and 4-20)
    Felsics: < 10 percent
    Mafics: 90 to 100 percent
Magnetitite and chromitite
    Felsics: < 10 percent
    Mafics: 90 to 100 percent (largely magnetite and chromite, respectively)
Carbonatite
    primary calcite: 90 to 100 percent
Melilitolite (actually an ultramafic silicate rock—see above)
    melilite: 90 to 100 percent

Color and texture of ultramafites. Because ultramafic rocks differ from one another in various ways, the color and texture of each group are dealt with separately.

Peridotites. *Dunite,* the peridotite that consists of 90 to 100 percent olivine, is light yellowish green in color, fine- to medium-grained, generally with an equigranular "sugary" texture. Most dunites look like a consolidated olivine sand because the grains are anhedral and nearly spherical (Figure 4-21). Black chromite grains are commonly present in small clusters or as scattered octahedra, typically of about pinhead size. Magnetite, ilmenite, pyrrhotite, and in rare instances, native platinum are megascopically discernible in some dunites. Upon weathering, dunites tend to develop chocholate-brown ferruginous coat-ings.

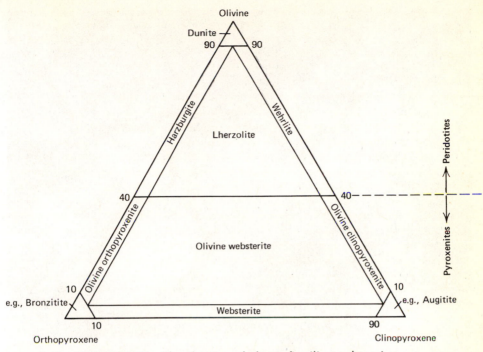

FIGURE 4-20   Classification of ultramafic silicate phanerites.

Peridotites other than dunite are dull green to black in color, are fine- to coarse-grained, and they commonly exhibit a distinctive texture, called poikilitic, in which each large grain of pyroxene and/or amphibole encloses several small spheroidal grains of olivine (Figure 4-22). The accessory minerals tend to be those just given for dunite but may also include scattered books of phlogopite. Many peridotites have been serpentinized—that is, they are now highly altered aggregates of serpentine plus or minus such other minerals as chlorite, talc, calcite, and a light tan-colored, asbestiform amphibole. Serpentinized peridotites appear waxy to dull green, are relatively soft, and are easily broken.

Pyroxenites are black, greenish black, or brown in color and tend to be medium- to coarse-grained. The *bronzitites* tend to have bronzy lusters which are a distinctive aid in their identification. Along with the accessories mentioned for dunite, some pyroxenites contain sulfides and a small percentage of calcic plagioclase. Some pyroxenites, like peridotites, have been altered to aggregates of serpentine plus or minus talc and chlorite. Others have been altered to masses that consist chiefly of vermiculite.

Hornblendites are black to greenish black in color and medium- to extremely coarse-grained. Most hornblendites contain identifiable amounts of pyroxene. Typical accessory minerals are magnetite, plagioclase, and biotite. In some so-called hornblendites, the shapes of the hornblende grains indicate that they have replaced preexisting pyroxene grains—that is, that the rocks are uralitized pyroxenites. Some petrologists think that most, perhaps all, so-called hornblendites are of metamorphic origin.

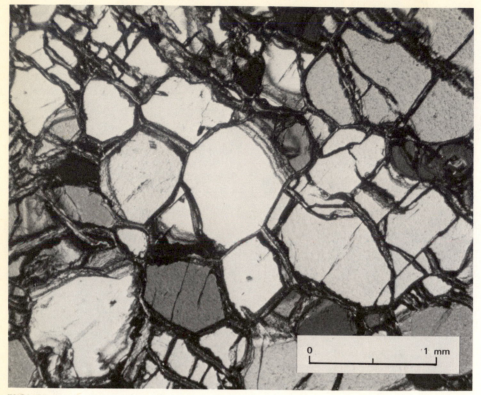

FIGURE 4-21   Dunite from the "Great Dyke" of Rhodesia made up of nearly all olivine grains, as it appears in thin section under polarized light. Dark rind around each grain is a secondary alteration product. (R. V. Dietrich)

Magnetitites and *chromitites* are black, fine- to medium-grained, granular rocks and because of their mineralogical compositions, they have high specific gravities. In some rocks, the magnetite and chromite are poikilitically enclosed in large bronzy-appearing pyroxene grains. Apatite is a relatively common accessory. Native platinum is present in some chromitites. Some of these rocks, particularly certain chromitites, crumble like only partially consolidated detrital sediments.

Carbonatites are off-white to light gray in color and typically medium-grained. The predominant minerals, calcite or dolomite, occur as interlocking grains or with a moasic appearance. Several different silicate, oxide, and sulfide minerals—in some cases, rather rare ones such as rare earth minerals—tend to be disseminated throughout these rocks. As a result, they may resemble marble altered by contact metamorphism. It has been suggested, in fact, that some rocks called carbonatites are really marbles that have taken on an intrusive aspect because of plastic flowage. The fact that carbonate lavas ($NaHCO_3$, rather than calcite or dolomite) were erupted from the volcano Oldoinyo Lengai in Tanzania in 1960–1961, is often cited as evidence supporting an igneous origin for carbonatites. Individual carbonatites may be distinguished, on the basis of their main constituents,

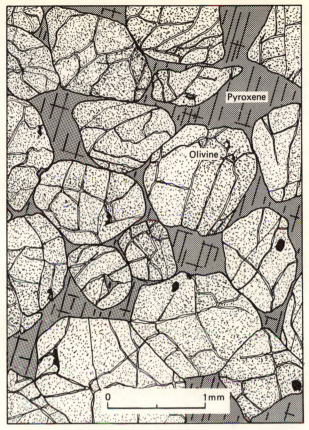

FIGURE 4-22   A poikilitic pyroxene with included olivine grains, as it appears in thin section. Isle of Rhum.
(R. V. Dietrich)

as calcite-, dolomite-, ferro-, or natro-carbonatites or even as, for example, calcite-dolo-
mite carbonatites.

Melilitolites may be fine-grained and look like basalts or fine-grained gabbros or they
may consist to a large extent of melilite crystals up to several centimeters across. Common
accessory minerals include apatite, augite, chromite, magnetite, phlogopite, and olivine.
It is noteworthy that the previously alluded to IUGS subcommission has stated that ''Many
melilitolites have been shown to be of metasomatic origin, but are of igneous aspect and
hence deserve an igneous name.''

Occurrences of ultramafites. Peridotites (including dunites), pyroxenites, and carbonatites occur as stocks, dikes, and other small intrusives. Examples are the dunite pipes
near Jefferson, North Carolina; the peridotite masses near Thetford, Québec; the pyroxenite
dikes in Cecil County, Maryland; and the carbonatite dikes transecting nepheline syenite
in the Magnet Cove, Arkansas Area.

One of the unusual circumstances under which peridotites are emplaced in the crust is by tectonic forces involving collisions of continental masses following movement of lithospheric plates. When such collisions occur, solid slices of the upper mantle, some as large as granitic batholiths, may be thrust up into the crust. Most of these masses of peridotite have been emplaced cold and have been serpentinized. Literally hundreds of peridotite bodies that are believed to be of this origin, each a few kilometers or less in length, occur sporadically along the trends of several of the world's fold mountain ranges (e.g., along the Alps and along the Appalachians from Newfoundland to Alabama). One of the large batholitic-sized masses is in Cuba; it is said to underlie an area in excess of 12,000 square kilometers.

Magnetitites and chromitites occur together with pyroxenites, dunites, anorthosites, and norites as cumulates in layers in many of the world's lopoliths (See Figures 4-7 and 4-23). Among these are the Bushveld Igneous Complex of Transvaal, South Africa; the masses that constitute the "Great Dyke" of Rhodesia; the Muskox Intrusive in the Northwest Territories, Canada; the Skaergaard mass of eastern Greenland; and the Stillwater Complex of south central Montana. Whereas the layers of magnetitite and chromitite range

FIGURE 4-23   (A) Layered anorthosite (light) and chromitite (dark) at Dwars River in the Bushveld Lopolith, South Africa. (B. J. Skinner) (B) graded bedding in an olivine pyroxenite at Duke Island, Southeastern Alaska (Scale, 6 inches long). (From H. P. Taylor, Jr. and J. A. Noble, Econ. Geol. Monograph 4, 1969)

(B)

from less than a centimeter to only a meter or so thick, some of the siliceous mineral layers are extremely thick—for example, there is a 1900-meter thick bronzitite layer in the Bushveld Complex.

Hornblende peridotite is present in the Cortlandt Complex of southern New York. Hornblendite, which is a rare rock, occurs as facies of some syenite masses just as pyroxenites occur as facies of igneous bodies made up largely of such rocks as mela-syenite, quartz monzogabbro, or gabbro.

All known carbonatites are spatially, and apparently also genetically, associated with feldspathoidal igneous rocks. Especially fine examples occur near Jacupiranga, southeastern Brazil; at Kaiserstuhl, near Freiburg, West Germany; at Alnö, Sweden; and near Fen, in the Telemark District of southern Norway.

Dunite occurs as nodules and angular fragments in some basaltic lavas—for example in several of the Hawaiian lava flows. At least some of these nodules appear to have been brought up from several kilometers deep within the earth's mantle. Others may have formed as cumulus rocks in shallow magma chambers.

Uses of ultramafites. Dunites attract commercial interest as a potential raw material for the manufacture of refractory bricks. Serpentinized peridotites (page 139) have been cut, polished, and marketed under the misleading name Verde Antique Marble, which is used widely as facing and trim stone. Vermiculite-rich alteration products of pyroxenites, which are relatively widespread throughout the world, are used in the expanded state as aggregates for plaster or concrete and also as an additive for potting and germinating soils. There is noteworthy production from several small masses centered around Macon County, North Carolina.

All of the world's chromium comes from chromitites or their weathered residua. Native platinum is recovered from some chromitites—for example, from the Merensky Reef of the Bushveld Complex. Magnetitites are not widely used as a resource for iron because the magnetite commonly contains trace elements in solid solution that are deleterious to smelting practices. In a few cases, the trace elements themselves are valuable. One instance of this is the recovery of vanadium from magnetitites in the Bushveld Complex. Nonetheless, magnetitites constitute a vast iron reserve.

In addition, noteworthy amounts of nickel and platinum have been and continue to be derived from peridotites. Carbonatites are of ever increasing economic interest because of their rare element concentrations.

Additional varieties of ultramafites. Varieties of ultramafites such as harzburgite and lherzolite can be defined on the identities of the component pyroxenes as clino- versus orthopyroxenes (Figure 4-20). Although uncommon in surface exposures, lherzolites, along with garnet peridotite, have rather recently gained widespread attention because of being a likely major component of the upper mantle. And, they do occur as nodules in kimberlites—for example, in the Frank Smith Pipe of South Africa and the Ming Bar Diatreme of Montana—where they are thought to have come from depths of more than 150 km. Microscopic study of thin sections is usually required to distinguish among the different pyroxenes. In some cases, however, extensive work with the rocks sometimes leads to an ability to identify them according to their proper name after only megascopic examination.

On the other hand, the four varieties next described can be identified rather easily by megascopic means because they have distinctive mineralogical compositions and/or textural characteristics.

Biotitite has been reported as having been ejected from a volcanic vent in South Africa. It was, however, interpreted as an inclusion. Although segregates of biotite occur in several igneous rocks, most rocks made up almost wholly of biotite are of metamorphic origin.

Kimberlite is a fine- to medium-grained, dull grayish green to bluish colored mica peridotite. Some of it, however, is porphyritic with abundant phenocrysts of olivine. The mica, either biotite or phlogopite, is generally poikilitic and rather large (up to about 5 millimeters across) as compared to the other constituents (typically 1–2 millimeters across). Chrome garnet, and ilmenite are relatively common accessory minerals. In many kimberlites, the mica has been chloritized and the olivine serpentinized and/or altered to some carbonate mineral or minerals. The most common occurrence of kimberlite is as dikes and steep walled pipes that may represent old eruptive conduits. Commonly the rock occurs in brecciated mixtures as the matrix around fragments from the mantle, the lower crust, and/or the surrounding country rocks (Figure 4-24). Kimberlite from South Africa has gained worldwide prominence because it is the host rock for a large percentage of the world's high quality diamonds. In the United States, a kimberlite pipe occurs near Murfreesboro, Arkansas and kimberlite dikes are widespread in rocks of the folded Appalachians and adjacent Allegheny Plateau Province, as well as here and there in several other

0   2 cm

FIGURE 4-24   Kimberlite from the Monastery kimberlite pipe, South Africa, (polished surface). Note reaction zones around fragments of pyroxene and garnet set in a serpentine matrix. (B. J. Skinner)

areas, such as in the Highwood Mountains of Montana, in southeastern Wyoming, and in Larimer County in Colorado.

Nelsonite is an equigranular, medium-grained apatite-ilmenite rock from Nelson County, Virginia. The nelsonite occurs in dikes but its origin remains in doubt. If it is of igneous origin, the rock is an ultramafite, so we have included it here.

Either ilmenite or apatite may predominate and much of the rock also contains rutile. Some nelsonite also contains megascopically discernible magnetite and/or chloritized biotite. Locally, the rocks grade into a rock consisting almost wholly of ilmenite. Some of the rutile-rich phases are essentially indistinguishable from the rutile-ilmenite rock, called urbainite, that occurs as lenses in anorthosite near St. Urbain, Québec—these masses constitute the world's largest known titanium deposit. Other superficially similar rocks include the Sanford Lake titaniferous magnetite rock, which is spatially associated with the Central Adirondack anorthosite mass. The Sanford Lake rock has been hypothesized to be metamorphic in origin by some geologists and igneous by others. Nelsonite has been mined and used as a source for titanium paint base.

Serpentinite (formerly called serpentine, the same as the mineral name) is the name given to rocks consisting almost wholly of one or more of the serpentine family minerals. Dr. Knopf once remarked that "These rocks show an infinite variety of forms. They are like Cleopatra—never stale." Most serpentinites are light greenish gray to greenish black in color and have waxy lusters. Some, however, are reddish colored, apparently because they are manganese-rich. Serpentinites may appear fairly homogeneous or be banded; they can be blotchy, streaked, or some combination of these. Although most serpentinites are rather compact, some exhibit relatively close-spaced, curved, and slickensided surfaces. Some serpentinites are also cut by veins of calcite, magnesite, talc, or asbestos. Chromite and magnetite are rather common, megascopically identifiable accessories; dolomite or ankerite occur as disseminated rhombohedral crystals in many serpentinites; chlorite is also commonly present. Because most, if not all, serpentinites are altered peridotites or altered pyroxenites, the occurrence of serpentinites is the same as that listed for the parent rocks.

Cut and polished serpentinite, usually marketed as Verde Antique Marble, has found widespread use as an interior and exterior facing stone. Perhaps the most beautiful varieties are those from the Lizard District of Cornwall, England—their predominantly dark green color is broken up by whitish, mahogany red, and/or chocolate brown blotches, streaks and/or veins. Noteworthy localities for similar serpentinite in the United States include Cardiff, Maryland; Rochester, New Hampshire; and Rutland County, Vermont. It also is worthy of note that the world's largest production of asbestos is from serpentinized ultrabasic rocks of the Thetford District of south central Québec.

Lamprophyres

Lamprophyres are dark-colored porphyries that occur mainly as dikes. Except for vogesite, a variety that is typically mica-free, the lamprophyres contain abundant phenocrysts of mica, either biotite or phlogopite, as well as phenocrysts of their other characteristic mafic minerals. The groundmass, which ranges from glassy through aphanitic to fine-grained phaneritic, consists of the same mafic mineral or minerals as the phenocrysts plus a feldspar. The phaneritic groundmasses tend to have aplitic textures.

Lamprophyres can be distinguished from most other dark porphyries by a characteristic shiny appearance that reflects their mica content. It is this appearance that led to the name lamprophyre (Greek, meaning shiny porphyry). Most lamprophyres are highly altered to calcite, chlorite, sericite, epidote and/or quartz. Some, in fact, contain so much calcite that they effervesce briskly with dilute hydrochloric acid. Many lamprophyres also contain zeolites.

Table 4-3 may be helpful in naming an unknown lamprophyre. If, however, the characteristic mafic mineral or minerals cannot be identified megascopically, it is best to call the rock merely lamprophyre.

Lamprophyres occur in many plutonic rock terranes. They are typically found as dikes cutting larger igneous masses and the surrounding country rocks. Most of the dikes range from a few centimeters to several meters thick. Lamprophyres have also been reported to occur in volcanic plugs, feeder dikes, and even as parts of lava flows. The minette of the Spanish Peaks of Colorado is a well known occurrence in the United States. An orbicular lamprophyre has been recently reported from Vesby in southeastern Norway.

APHANITES AND APHANITE PORPHYRIES

Aphanites are igneous rocks with grain sizes so small that none of the constituents can be distinguished megascopically. In the laboratory, the mineralogical or chemical composi-

TABLE 4-3   Compositions of lamprophyres.

Predominant Mafic Mineral	Predominant Feldspar		Feldspar-free (Commonly with Glassy Groundmass)
	Alkali-feldspar	Plagio-clase	
Biotite	Minette	Kersantite	Alnoite[a] (with melilite) Polzenite[b] (with melilite)
Hornblende/augite or diopside	Vogesite	Spessartite	
Alkalic amphibole/ pyroxene	Sannaite	Camptonite	Monchiquite[c]

[a]Mafic minerals >90 percent.

[b]Felspathoid is essential mafic minerals 70-90 percent.

[c]Titanaugite is common.

tion of an aphanite may be determined with a polarizing microscope and, consequently, may be given an appropriate name. In the field, however, only such characteristics as color, specific gravity, and geological associations can generally be determined and none of these serves as a satisfactory basis for more than gross classification.

Probably the most useful system is the twofold division whereby light colored aphanites are called felsic aphanites or *felsites* and the dark colored aphanites are called mafic aphanites or *mafites*. To be consistent with general practice, *light* includes white, light and medium gray, yellow, light and medium green, reds, purples, and browns whereas *dark* includes dark gray, dark green, black, and brownish black. From an empirical standpoint, we know that, so divided, the felsites include rhyolites, dacites, trachytes, latites, and most andesites (and also phonolite which tends to be medium gray-green) whereas the mafites include basalts, picrites, tephrites, basanites, and a few andesites.

On a chemical or mineralogical basis, the compositions of aphanites may be correlated with more or less equivalent phanerites as shown in Table 4-4.

For anyone who may wish to further distinguish the aphanites, the following names correlate with the compositions indicated by the numbers on Figures 4-8A and 4-9.

Figure 4-8A: (I) *rhyolitoids;* (II) *dacitoids;* (III) *trachytoids;* (IV) *andesitoids* and *basaltoids;* (V) *phonolitoids;* (VI) *tephritoids;* (VII) *foiditoids.*

Figure 4-9: (2) *alkali rhyolite;* (3) *rhyolite;* (4 and 5) *dacite;* (6*) *quartz-alkali trachyte;* (6) *alkali trachyte;* (6') *foid-bearing alkali trachyte;* (7*) *quartz trachyte;* (7) *trachyte;* (7') *foid-bearing trachyte;* (8*) *quartz latite;* (8) *latite;* (8') *foid-bearing latite;* (9's and 10's) *andesite* and *basalt;* (11) *phonolite;* (12) *tephritic phonolite;* (13) *phonolitic tephrite* (*basanite*); (14) *tephrite* (*basanite*); (15) *foidites.*

Many aphanitic igneous rocks are porphyritic. Some geologists refer to these rocks as aphanophyres. We prefer to call them aphanite porphyries. The names of the minerals that are present as phenocrysts may be used as modifiers—for example, a biotite, quartz, sanidine, aphanite porphyry. For many aphanite porphyries, more precise (although admittedly somewhat hazardous) naming is possible. This is true because it has been shown that the identity of a rock's phenocrysts tends to be indicative of the composition of its groundmass. Bearing in mind that exceptions exist, Table 4-5 may be used as a guide.

As can be seen by examining the table, abundant quartz phenocrysts indicate that

TABLE 4-4   Phanerite-aphanite equivalents.

rhyolite[a]	=	granite
dacite[b]	=	granodiorite
trachyte	=	syenite
latite	=	monzonite
andesite	=	diorite
basalt	=	gabbro
phonolite[c]	=	foid syenite
tephrite[d]	=	} foid diorite/foid gabbro
basanite[e]	=	
foidite (e.g., leucitite)	=	foidolite
melilitite	=	melilitolite

[a]Includes the quartz latites of some geologists.

[b]Expands former common usage, which was approximately equivalent to tonalite, to include former rhyoandesite of some geologists.

[c]Foid mineral is to used as adjective—e.g., leucite phonolite.

[d]With <10 perecent olivine.

[e]With >10 perecent olivine.

the aphanite porphyry is a rhyolite or dacite, whereas alkali feldspar phenocrysts, without accompanying quartz phenocrysts, indicate a trachyte, and so forth. In addition, some of the following generalities may be helpful.

1. Flowage banding, which is typically marked by color differences and/or alignment of phenocrysts, is common in rhyolites; fairly common in trachytes, dacites, and lightcolored andesites, but rare in basalts and dark colored andesites. (In fact, the name rhyolite comes from the Greek word *rhyax* meaning "a stream of lava.")

2. Trachytes, because of their texture, are often rough to the touch. (Their name comes from the Greek word *trachys,* meaning "rough.")

3. Thin slivers of glassy andesite may be translucent, whereas those of basalt are not. Glassy rocks tend to break with conchoidal fractures, whereas most lithic ones give rough, irregular surfaces.

4. Many andesite porphyries have speckled groundmasses because of the presence of microlites of mafic minerals.

5. Basalts and phonolites may ring or clink when hit with a hammer. (Phonolites were originally called Klingstein.)

6. Basalts are abundant, whereas the other dark-colored aphanites and aphanite porphyries are rare.

7. The plagioclase phenocrysts in many basalts are light green and greasy-appearing as a result of saussuritization.

The aphanites and aphanite porphyries also rather commonly exhibit certain gross features that are rare or absent in other rocks. Among the more common ones are:

TABLE 4-5   Typical phenocrysts in common aphanophyres. Here, x means commonly present; ± means sometimes present, sometimes absent; no means rarely present.

Rock	Quartz	Alkali-Feldspar	Plagio-clase	Mafic Minerals	Others
Rhyolite	x	x	±	± biotite	
Dacite	x	x	x	± biotite ± hornblende	
Trachyte	no	x	no	± biotite ± hornblende ± augite	
Andesite	no	no	x	± hornblende or augite (rare) ± biotite	
Basalt	no	no	x	± augite ± olivine (and rarely biotite, hornblende or magnetite)	
Phonolite	no	x (typically sanidine)	no	± aegirine augite	nepheline and/or leucite

Aa—blocky lava, typically basaltic.

Amygdule (adj., amygdaloidal)—a vesicle (see below) filled with one or more of such minerals as calcite, chalcedony, native copper, quartz (commonly agate), prehnite, and the zeolites (Figure 4-25). Amygdules are fairly common in basalts, less common in andesites.

Columnar jointing—prismatic jointing of igneous masses perpendicular to the masses' cooling surfaces and thought to have formed as a result of contraction during cooling (Figure 4-26). Columnar jointing is common in basaltic rocks, less common in the other aphanites and aphanite porphyries. Many groups of such columns have been named as if they are associated with Satan or some other superhuman—for example, Devil's Tower, Wyoming; Devil's Postpile, California; and Giant's Causeway, Northern Ireland.

Pahoehoe—lava, typically basaltic, with a ropy appearing surface (Figure 4-27).

Scoria—a basaltic or andesitic rock that consists of more than 50 percent vesicles.

Vesicle (adj., vesicular)—a roughly spheroidal cavity formed by the entrapment of a gas bubble during solidification of a magma (Figure 4-28). Vesicles are fairly common in basalt, less common in andesite, and rare in other aphanites.

Occurrences of aphanites and aphanite porphyries. Most of these rocks occur as lava flows. A few occur as volcanic plugs and as minor intrusives such as dikes and sills. Locally, they also comprise marginal facies of laccoliths and other relatively high-level intrusives. As is evident from the occurrences, all have developed their textures and grain sizes because of rapid cooling.

Several score, if not hundreds, of localities could be listed for the more common aphanites and aphanite porphyries. A few examples, chiefly for porphyries, are

Rhyolite—Mount Rogers, southern Virginia; Yellowstone National Park, northwestern Wyoming; Tonopah District, Nevada; Jemez Mountains, New Mexico; Plumas County, northeastern California.

0   2 cm

FIGURE 4-25   Amygdaloidal basalt. The minerals filling the
amygdules are calcite and zeolites. (B. J. Skinner)

Dacite—Crater Lake, Oregon.

Trachyte—Cripple Creek District of Teller County, central Colorado; Tuolumne County, east central California.

Andesite—widespread in the Cascades of western North America.

Phonolite—Devil's Tower, Wyoming.

Basanite and **Tephrite**—Roman Province of Italy.

Leucitophyre—Leucite Hills, central Wyoming.

Basalt—Whereas granitoids are the most abundant phanerite, basalts are predominant among the aphanites. Several large areas have basaltic bedrock—for example, Miocene basalts cover more than 500,000 square kilometers on the Columbia River-Snake River Plateau of eastern Oregon and Washington and southern Idaho. Similar large areas with basaltic bedrock occur in such widespread places as the Karroo Plateau of South Africa, the Parana Basin of Argentina, and the Deccan Plateau of India. On a different scale, nearly all of the Hawaiian Island lavas are basaltic.

Uses of aphanites and aphanite porphyries. The color, strength, and breakage tendencies, as well as its widespread availability have led to the utilization of basalt as a major source of aggregate and road metal. Much of the trap rock of commerce is basalt. The

FIGURE 4-26 Columnar jointing has formed the columns that constitute Devil's Post Pile National Monument in California. The columns are from 10 to 20 centimeters across and several meters long. (H. L. Mackay, from Design Photographers International, Inc.)

other aphanites and aphanite porphyries have found little other than local use for building foundations and road metal.

GLASSES

Glass is formed when magma is cooled so rapidly that its constituent ions do not have enough time to be arranged into minerals. Some rocks are made up wholly of glass; others consist of glass and minerals. The nearly pure glasses and the rocks that can be seen megascopically to consist predominantly of glass are included in this group. The latter, many of which are *porphyritic rocks with glassy ground masses,* may be called **vitrophyres.** Vitreous glasses do not occur in rocks more ancient than about the Cretaceous Period because, with sufficient time, glasses devitrify—that is they are converted to crystalline material. Devitrified glasses appear pitchlike or cherty (see page 217).

Obsidian
Obsidian, perhaps the most ancient rock name still in use, is natural glass. Compositions of obsidians range from that of a rhyolite, through andesite and trachyte to that of a

FIGURE 4-27   Pahoehoe. Lava from Kilauea volcano has flowed over a cliff in Hawaii. (D. Swanson, U.S. Geological Survey)

phonolite. The composition cannot be determined by hand specimen examination. Therefore, all of these glasses are simply referred to as obsidian. If, however, the chemical composition is known, the term obsidian should be preceded by the proper aphanitic rock name—for example, rhyolitic obsidian. It is noteworthy that a large percentage of the obsidians that have been analyzed have compositions that correspond to rhyolite.

Obsidians are typically dense but may be slaggy. They are dark gray to nearly black, red, or deep mahogany brown in color, have a vitreous luster, and generally exhibit magnificent conchoidal fractures (Figure 4-29). The colors are dependent upon uniformly

FIGURE 4-28   Vesicular basalt from Hawaii. Note the sporadic olivine crystals. (B. J. Skinner)

dispersed, submicroscopic particles of magnetite (black), hematite (red-brown), or tiny bubble holes (commonly giving a gold colored sheen). Individual pieces may be a solid color or color-banded, the banding reflecting magmatic flowage. Even black obsidian is transparent to translucent in thin slivers.

Most obsidians contain some crystalline material. *Spherulites, lithophysae,* or other crystalline materials generally occur as isolated grains or along flowage bands within the glass. Spherulites are spherical shaped masses, typically ranging from small shot-size to pea-size, that are made up of radiating fibers of a mineral such as feldspar (Figure 4-30A and B). They indicate very rapid crystallization, during which the fibers grew outward from the centers where they began to crystallize and continued until stopped by the increasing viscosity of the rapidly cooling magma. Lithophysae, meaning stone bubbles, are made up of concentric shells of minute crystals with open spaces between them and, in most cases, have hollow centers (Figure 4-30C). When exposed by the breaking of the rock, lithophysae resemble full-blown roses. The small crystals are typically quartz, tridymite, or feldspar or less commonly fayalite, topaz, garnet, or tourmaline. The origin of lithophysae is enigmatic. They may represent rhythmic crystallization in gas-rich magmas, with gas liberation accounting for both the open spaces and the perfection of the constituent crystals.

0   2 cm

FIGURE 4-29 Obsidian from Yellowstone Park, Montana, showing typical conchoidal fracture. (B. J. Skinner)

(A)   0   5 cm

FIGURE 4-30 Spherulites and lithophysae. (A) Spherulites in a clear, synthetic glass, showing radial growth of crystals from single sites of nucleation; (B) spherulites in a completely glassy obsidian from the Jemez Mountains, New Mexico; (C) lithophysae in a devitrified obsidian from Yellowstone Park, Montana. (B. J. Skinner)

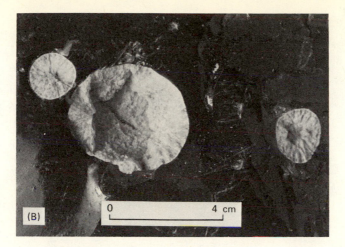

(B) 0   4 cm

(C) 0   5 cm

(A)

FIGURE 4-31   Pillow lavas, characteristic of lava extruded into or beneath water. (A) Pillow basalts, late Paleozoic in age, near Suhaylah, Sultanate of Oman. (Edgar H. Bailey, U.S. Geological Survey) (B) Precambrian aged greenstone (metamorphosed basalt) near Ishpeming, Michigan, showing typical cross sections of pillows on a glaciated surface. (M. I. Whitney)

Tachylyte

Tachylyte, sometimes called sideromelane, is glass of basaltic composition. It is typically greenish black to black and is essentially opaque, even in thin slivers. As compared to obsidian, its luster is greasy rather than vitreous and, as indicated by its name (Greek meaning "quickly soluble"), tachylyte is readily dissolved in acids. Variolites, the basaltic analogs of spherulites, and crystalline inclusions are relatively common.

Occurrences of glasses. Crusts on some lava flows and chilled marginal zones on dikes and sills that were intruded into cold rocks are glassy. A few thin dikes and sills consist completely of glass. The best known North American locality for obsidian is Obsidian Cliff in Yellowstone National Park, Wyoming, where some of the rock exhibits exceptionally fine spherulites. The obsidian from Glass Butte, Oregon, is well-known because of its stunning reddish brown and black-streaked appearance. The rinds of *pillows* that occur among lavas that have flowed into water are exemplary of tachylyte occurrences. Pillows are roughly cylindrical lobes of lava that have been extruded beneath or

(B)

flowed into water—for example, most submarine flows are made up of pillow lavas (Figure 4-31). In fact, considering the makeup of the crust beneath oceanic basins, pillow lavas of basaltic composition may very well be the most common igneous rock on the earth's surface.

Uses of glasses. Because of the way it breaks, obsidian was prized by primitive man for shaping his weapons and tools (Figure 4-32). Anthropologists report such use as dating back to at least 500,000 years ago. Today, especially in Mexico, obsidian is fashioned into charms, small carvings, and stones for costume jewelry. Pieces with included layers of gas bubbles often exhibit a golden play of color as they are turned in the light and, consequently, make particularly attractive decorative articles.

Varieties of glass. *Pumice* is the name applied to off-white, yellowish, brownish, light gray, or, in rare cases, red obsidian that has a silky luster and is frothlike. The froth consists of subparallel and entangled fibers of glass. Typically the fibers surround numerous holes and are wrapped around sparse phenocrysts. Pumice is so porous and light in weight that it floats on water.

Pumice occurs as crusts on some lavas and as fragments ejected from some highly explosive volcanoes. Because it floats, pumice fragments ejected onto water may be carried over long distances and washed ashore just about anywhere. Pumice from the Lipari Islands, just north of Sicily, has been used widely as an abrasive and as a polishing agent for such diverse purposes as removing bunions, scouring powder, and preparing wood for

FIGURE 4-32 Obsidian tool, 31 centimeters long, from the Pacific Coast of North America. (I. Friedman, U.S. Geological Survey)

final oiling, varnishing, or waxing. Pumice from Washington, Oregon, California, and New Mexico has also found use as lightweight aggregate and as an ingredient of acoustical plaster.

Pele's hair, sometimes called basaltic pumice, is the name given to brown threadlike fibers of basaltic glass that are found as sporadic matted masses on top of some lava flows. The individual fibers are generally less than a half millimeter in diameter and range up to a couple meters long. They are formed when bubbles of lava burst and the attenuated lava is then pulled out into threads of glass that can be blown and collected by the wind. Such masses are relatively common in the vicinity of Kilauea Volcano on the Island of Hawaii. In fact, the masses were named for the fire goddess associated in native myths with Kilauea Crater.

Perlite is a nearly colorless, gray, greenish, bluish, reddish, or brownish colored glass with a pearly to waxy luster. Its characteristic appearance comes from fractures formed along concentric shells ranging up to a few centimeters in diameter. The breakage along the concentric shells presents the pearl-like appearance that gives the rock its name. It is thought that the shells form in response to hydration of the glass and its consequent expansion. Some perlites exhibit flow banding outlined by small crystallites; a few contain phenocrysts of minerals such as sanidine, quartz, or tridymite; some contain glassy, more or less rounded masses (typically with concave indentations) that are called Apache tears. Perlite is sometimes heated until it is expanded to a frothy product that is marketed for use as lightweight aggregate, as a filter, or as a filler or extender. Unfortunately, the commercial product is also called perlite. Natural rhyolitic perlite occurs sporadically among many of the western United States lavas—two examples are in the Yellowstone National Park Region and in Taos County, New Mexico, where a noteworthy percentage of the raw material for the commercial product is quarried.

Pitchstone is a partly devitrified and hydrated obsidian that is characterized by a dull resinous or pitchlike luster. It is gray, black, olive green, brown, or red in color. Pieces may be one uniform color or they may be mottled or streaky. Most pitchstone is still translucent in thin slivers. Exemplary pitchstone occurs near Georgetown and at Silver Cliff in Colorado.

Palagonite is a hydrated glass derived from tachylyte just as pitchstone is derived from obsidian. It may be dull to greasy in luster and yellow, orange, brown, or nearly black in color. In most cases, it can be distinguished from pitchstone because palagonite is essentially opaque, even in very thin pieces. In other cases, the best criterion is its occurrence or the identity of its associated rocks—for example, it occurs as rinds on some ancient basaltic pillows.

PYROCLASTIC ROCKS*

When magma is erupted onto the earth's surface, it may either flow as a liquid or be ejected violently as loose fragments. Fragments extruded explosively are called *pyroclasts;* loose assemblages of pyroclasts are termed *tephra*; the rocks formed by cementation or welding of tephra are called *pyroclastic rocks.*

*The IUGS Subcommission is currently (1978) dealing with the nomenclature of pyroclastic minerals. The system we suggest is anticipatory of future actions of the group, the chairman of which has kindly supplied us with pertinent information from correspondence and meeting records.

Some geologists prefer to classify pyroclastic rocks as igneous; others prefer to call them sedimentary. Perhaps the most nearly correct suggestion is the one generally attributed to C. K. Wentworth, a geologist who spent much of his professional career observing volcanic activity in Hawaii: "They are igneous on the way up and sedimentary on the way down." In any case, these rocks constitute a good example of how rocks of even the major classes grade into one another and thus how classifications are often arbitrary. We include pyroclastic rocks here, at the end of the igneous rocks chapter because they are formed as the result of igneous activity. But, it also might be noted that this places them directly preceding the chapter on sedimentary rocks, the rocks to which they are so closely akin because of their similar modes of deposition and lithification and their stratification (Figure 4-33).

Pyroclasts and Tephra

Pyroclasts are named on the basis of their sizes; as a consequence, tephra and pyroclastic rocks are named on the basis of the size ranges and contents of their constituent pyroclasts—see Table 4-6 and Figure 4-34. As can be seen, however, the shape and/or origin of the large fragments is also taken into account. In addition, the general composition of the material may be indicated by using the name of the corresponding aphanite, for example, andesitic lapilli. Furthermore, the nature of the fragments may be indicated by utilizing the adjectives *vitric*, if the pyroclasts are chiefly glass; *crystal*, if chiefly mineral grains; *lithic*, if chiefly rock fragments; or *mixed* (Figure 4-35). Thus a complete designation might be, for example, "vitric rhyolite ash."

Individual pyroclasts may be described as follows:

TABLE 4-6   Pyroclasts, tephra, and pyroclastic rocks.

Size in Millimeters	Pyroclast (fragment)	Tephra (unconsolidated material)	Pyroclastic Rock (consolidated material)
> 64	Bomb[a]	Bombs	Agglomerate[c]
	Block[b]	Blocks	Pyroclastic breccia[d]
2[e]-64	Lapillus	Lapilli	Lapilli tuff
<2[e]	Ash grain	Ash	Ash tuff

[a]Fragment made up of material that was at least partly fluid when ejected (Figure 4-36)

[b]Fragment that was solid when ejected.

[c]Or bomb tuff.

[d]Or block tuff.

[e]Some geologists use 4mm as the cutoff

Bombs have twisted shapes (Figure 4-36) that indicate that they solidified from a fluid or partially fluid material while in flight through the air.

Blocks are large chunks of rock broken from the sides of the volcanic conduit or from a crust covering the underlying magma

Lapillus (plural *lapilli*) is the name given to individual fragments of mineral and/or rock (including glass) materials as well as to bomb- and/or block-like pyroclasts with mean diameters ranging between 2 and 64 millimeters.

Ash grain is a mineral, glass or rock fragment that is less than 2 millimeters in diameter.

FIGURE 4-33   Stratified ash-falls on the flanks of Oshima Volcano, Japan. The strata have not been folded—the dips shown are initial dips. The material is almost entirely basaltic in composition. Light colored layers are largely lapilli, darker colored layers are ash. (Richard S. Fiske)

All but the bombs and crystals may look like comminuted lava or pumice. The rock fragments tend to be angular but some, especially the large ones, may have broken-off corners because they were bumped or rubbed against each other or against the sides of the vent as they were ejected. The glass fragments, frequently referred to as shards, have rather characteristic shapes (Figure 4-37). Although most shards are microscopic, some can be recognized through a 10x handlens.

Any given tephra may or may not exhibit one or more of the following features:

Sorting may result in stratification and/or in recognizable lateral distribution patterns
   of fragments. Apparently in response to relative ease of movement during ejection,
   larger and heavier pieces tend to fall first and, barring strong winds, they also tend
   to fall nearest the source. Sorting ranges greatly—it may be so poor that it cannot
   be easily detected or it may show a remarkably high degree of perfection.

Fossils may be present in tephra and pyroclastic rocks. In fact, some of the best
   preserved nonmarine plants and animals yet found occur in volcanic tuffs. Examples
   include the famous fossil leaves in the Upper Miocene Middlegate Formation of
   western Nevada, and the people and other animals buried during the A.D. 79
   eruption of Pompeii.

Admixed rock materials may be of two origins: first, cognate inclusions and pieces
   broken off the country rocks or the vent walls through which the magma passed
   may be ejected and deposited along with pyroclasts; second, normal sediments—
   gravels, sands, silts, and clays—may be intimately intermixed with pyroclastic materials that are deposited in basins of active sedimentation. Deposits made up of
   the latter kind of mixtures are generally considered to be sedimentary rather than
   pyroclastic. As a consequence, they are given names such as tuffaceous silt or,
   more generally, are termed *tuffites*.

Interbedding of sedimentary and pyroclastic materials may occur where explosive
   volcanic activity takes place in a basin of active sedimentation. Alternations between tephra and lava are also relatively common around some volcanoes.

Pyroclastic Rocks

The conversion of tephra to rock generally involves compaction and/or cementation. In
some cases, pyroclasts are so hot when they are deposited that they are immediately fused
into solid rock. These rocks, which are generally called welded tuffs, are described in a
following section. As with sedimentary rocks, the cementing material may be one or more
of several minerals such as calcite, quartz, and/or one of the zeolites. The means by which
the cement is generally introduced is groundwater. Because of the various possibilities for
cement, you should not be surprised if, for example, a pyroclastic rock effervesces with
dilute hydrochloric acid (HCl).

Like other rocks, pyroclastic rocks may undergo alterations. In fact, most tuffs have
been altered—they tend to have a high porosity and permeability (see page 183) and the
sizes and shapes of their fragments afford large surface areas for attack and reaction.
Silicification, devitrification of glass shards, and chemical weathering are particularly common. It is especially noteworthy that vitric tuffs are fairly commonly opalized by circulating
water.

The relatively coarse-grained pyroclastic rocks are rather distinct when compared to
other rocks, including their sedimentary analogs. On the other hand, some tuffs can be
easily confused with other igneous rocks and also with mudstones, shales, and chalk (see
Chapter 5). Mixed tuffs, for example, may contain well-formed crystals and thus resemble
aphanite porphyries. Fortunately, in many tuffs, diligent search with a handlens will turn
up glass shards, broken crystals, or even small rock fragments (Figure 4-38). Also, most
tuffs feel rough because of their glass shards, whereas most of the equally fine-grained
sedimentary rocks feel smooth. In addition, because of the differences in the hardnesses

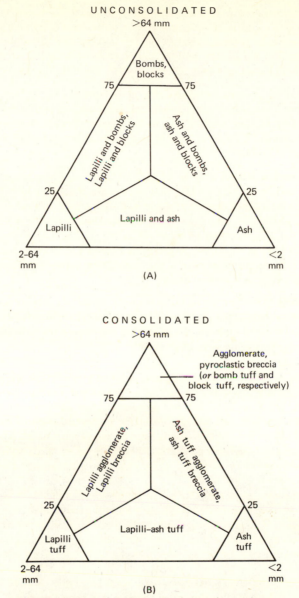

FIGURE 4-34 Classification of pyroclastic deposits and rocks that have a wide grain size distribution.

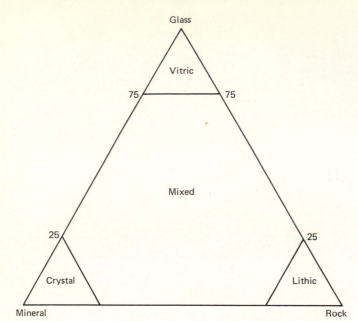

FIGURE 4-35 The nature of the fragments—glass, mineral or rock—of tephra and pyroclastic rocks are frequently indicated by the adjectives given on this triangle.

FIGURE 4-36 Volcanic bomb from Mauna Kea, Hawaii. (B. J. Skinner)

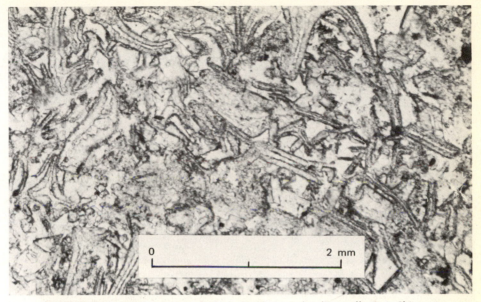

0   2 mm

FIGURE 4-37   Thin section of glass shards in a rhyolitic tuff. (B. J. Skinner)

of their constituents, tuffs will scratch coins whereas typical claystones and chalks will not. Nonetheless, some tuffs cannot be identified megascopically.

Just as mentioned for tephra, pyroclastic rocks should be named by using the appropriate terms given on Table 4-6 as the noun designators and by indicating the composition and crystallinity with the appropriate adjectives. For example, a consolidated tephra consisting of glassy ash grains of rhyolitic composition would be called a vitric rhyolite ash tuff. If the tuff is welded, that aspect should also be indicated. Adjectives such as tuffaceous should be used only to refer to sediments or sedimentary rocks with noteworthy pyroclastic contents—for example, a tuffaceous siltstone.

Occurrences of tephra and pyroclastic rocks. Pyroclastic materials occur in essentially all areas where volcanic activity has taken place. Agglomerates and pyroclastic breccias generally occur within less than a kilometer of their locus of ejection and in most places their lateral extents are no greater than their vertical thicknesses. A few occur within old vents. In marked contrast, many tuffs cover thousands of square kilometers.

In some instances, incredibly large volumes of pyroclastic materials have been ejected during single eruption phases. The culminating eruptions of Krakatoa—a volcanic island in Sunda Strait, east of Java—that took place August 26th and 27th, 1883, are particularly well documented. A few of the recorded facts follow: On the nearby sea, large masses of pumice were so thick that only the most powerful ships could navigate. Fist-sized pieces of pumice were thrown at least 40 kilometers from the island. Ashes covered an area of approximately 7.8 million square kilometers. An estimated 5 cubic kilometers of pyroclastic fragments were blasted out by the eruption—enough to cover all of Manhattan Island up to about the 25th floor of its skyscrapers. Some of the dust and fine ashes were blown some 25–30 kilometers high and one dust cloud reached a measured height of about 80 kilometers. Some of the fine dust circulated in the upper atmosphere and is

FIGURE 4-38   Pyroclastic rocks. (A) Lapilli and ash in a tuff from Clark County, Nevada; (B) mixture of rock types visible among lapilli in a tuff from Central Mexico.

generally thought to have been responsible for the exceptionally beautiful red sunsets and sunrises that were witnessed throughout the world during the late fall and early winter of 1883–1884. The accompanying tidal wave, up to 30 meters in height, travelled some 8700 kilometers to South Africa in less than 12 hours. Approximately two thirds of the original island area was subsequently under water, some as deep as 150 fathoms ($\sim$ 270 meters). And, according to recently compiled data, several prehistoric eruptions were of much greater magnitude.

   Uses of tephra and pyroclastic rocks. Where present, ash deposits constitute the best of all time-stratigraphic marker beds for use in correlation and in the reconstruction of past geologic history. This is so because these beds are deposited within so short a time span and in some cases over extremely broad areas. For example, there are three rhyolitic ash falls over much of the central Great Plains. They originated from Yellowstone 600,000 years ago and are, therefore, Pleistocene in age.
   Although pyroclastic rocks have found no large scale or unique commercial utilization in North America, they are used rather widely as building stones in a number of volcanic districts in other parts of the world—for example, in central France and in the vicinity of

(B)

0   5 cm

Rome and Naples in Italy. The peperino, an ash-gray pyroclastic material that occurs and is still used in west central Italy, was the main building stone used in Pompeii and Herculaneum.

Varieties of pyroclastic rocks. *Welded tuff* is the name applied to pyroclastic rocks, the fragments of which were plastic enough when they were deposited to have been fused. Some geologists call all such rocks *ignimbrites,* although that term should be restricted to refer only to welded tuffs of rhyolitic (obsidian) composition. Welded tuffs have been formed from both *ash falls* and *ash flows.* That statement should not, however, be taken to mean that all ash fall or ash flow deposits have become rock as a result of welding. Ash fall deposits are made up of volcanic ash that has been deposited directly from the air. Some are welded tuffs; some are not. Most such deposits and their consolidated products exhibit stratification as a result of sorting, typically expressed by graded bedding, of the constituent pyroclasts. Ash flow deposits are made up of pyroclasts that traveled rapidly along or near the ground surface after they were ejected. Most such deposits consist predominantly of ash grains, but also contain a wide size range including lapilli and blocks. Most of the deposits show very little, if any, evidence of sorting.

As might be expected, some welded tuffs exhibit flow textures. The constituent glass shards of welded tuffs may be flattened out as well as welded together (Figure 4.39). For many of these rocks, the flattening serves as the best criterion of origin. In others, the glass shards may have become so flattened and completely welded that essentially all traces of the shards have disappeared and the welded mass resembles an obsidian, particularly in

0   2 cm

FIGURE 4-39 Welded tuff from the Jemez Mountains,
New Mexico. Dark patches are fragments of obsidian;
rock fragment caught in the tuff is a rhyolite porphyry.
(B. J. Skinner)

hand specimens. Consequently, many welded tuffs have originally been mapped incor-
rectly as lava flows.

In many cases, hand specimens of welded tuffs from ash flow sheets cannot be
distinguished megascopically from welded tuffs formed from ash falls. Indeed some of
these rocks are even difficult to distinguish from similarly constituted aphanitic rocks
consolidated directly from lava. In most cases, field relationships are definitive. An exception is large ash flow sheets versus large ash falls; both may have essentially identical
geologic occurrences. Fortunately, the rocks representing ash flow sheets tend to be much
more uniform (i.e., unsorted) than those that represent ash falls. Therefore, even cursory
examination of the rock in outcrop may serve to differentiate between the two possible
origins.

Occurrences of welded tuff. Welded tuff formed from ash flows may cover relatively
small areas on the flanks of, or near to the source volcano (e.g., around the Valles Caldera
in the Jemez Mountains of New Mexico and on Mount Pélée on the island of Martinque
in the West Indies); they may constitute flows up to several tens of kilometers long (e.g.,
some of the pumice flows from former Mount Mazama, now Crater Lake, Oregon and

some of the flows in the Valley of Ten Thousand Smokes, Alaska); they also may cover extremely large areas, in which case they are referred to as ash-flow sheets (e.g., the deposits in Colorado, Nevada, New Zealand, and Asia Minor, each of which covers thousands of square kilometers).

Welded tuffs formed by ash falls may also cover areas ranging up to many thousands of square kilometers. Many such ash fall deposits, however, are only sporadically welded. One of the better known, rather extensive ash fall deposits of western North America originated about 6500 B.P. with the explosive phase of the catastrophic eruption of Mount Mazama, Oregon. That ash fall deposit, generally referred to as the Mazama Ash, has been found as remote from the source volcano as Athabaska in east central Alberta, some 1400 kilometers (almost 900 miles) to the northeast. And, still other ash fall deposits—for example, the Bishop Ash, which originated in east-central California and covered a wide area of the western and central United States—have been found to be even more extensive and to occur even farther away from their source volcanoes.

The great lateral extent of some ash flow and ash fall deposits, and the rocks formed from them, is especially noteworthy. Several individual ash flow sheets contain thousands of cubic kilometers of material. Therefore, these rocks may be considered to be the felsic analogs of the extensive plateau basalts.

Bentonite is an exemplary altered tuff. As already mentioned, tuffs are extremely susceptible to alteration, including weathering. Among the more common processes are devitrification, silicification (including opalization), and argillization (alteration to some clay mineral plus or minus sericite). Bentonites are tuffs that have been altered primarily to montmorillonite plus or minus beidellite. They are off-white to light gray and have a soapy feel. When moistened, they either swell to gelatinous masses that are several times their original volume or crumble to fluffy aggregates. Although some of the original pyroclastic texture is frequently preserved, it is generally difficult, if not impossible, to see it megascopically.

Occurrences and uses of bentonite. Tuff deposits that have been altered to bentonites once covered four rather large areas and several smaller areas in North America. One of the two largest areas is centered in central western Ohio and includes all, or parts of Minnesota, Iowa, Missouri, Illinois, Michigan, Indiana, Kentucky, Tennessee, Alabama, Ontario, New York, Pennsylvania, Maryland, West Virginia, and Virginia; the other, with an estimated volume of some 20,000 cubic kilometers, is centered in southeastern Montana and covers parts of North Dakota, South Dakota, Nebraska, Wyoming, Colorado, and Saskatchewan.

It has been reported that in pioneer days some of the Plains Indians fed swelling bentonite to previously starved captives as a mode of torture. Today, the swelling property is the basis for the use of bentonite as an absorbent of impurities from fats and oils and as a drilling mud that not only helps lubricate the bits but also helps lift cuttings from the holes. Such bentonite is recovered commercially in Mississippi, Texas, Montana, and Wyoming.

Useful References

Bayly, Brian (1968), *Introduction to Petrology*, Englewood Cliffs, N.J.: Prentice-Hall, Inc., 371 pp.

Daly, R. A. (1933), *Igneous Rocks and the Depths of the Earth*, New York: McGraw-Hill Book Company, 598 pp.

Dolbear, S. H. (Chairman, Editorial Board) (1949), *Industrial Minerals and Rocks,* New York: A.I.M.M.E., 1156 pp.

Harker, Alfred (1954), *Petrology for Students,* 8th ed., Cambridge, England: Cambridge University Press, 283 pp.

Hatch, F. H., Wells, A. K., and Wells, M. K. (1949), *The Petrology of Igneous Rocks,* 10th ed., London: Murby, 469 pp.

Heiken, G. (1979), *"Pyroclastic flow deposits,"* Amer. Scientist, Vol. 67, pp. 564-571.

Hyndman, D. W. (1972), *Petrology of Igneous and Metamorphic Rocks,* New York: McGraw-Hill Book Company, 533 pp.

Isachsen, Y. W., ed. (1969), "Origin of Anorthosite and Related Rocks," New York State Mus. and Sci. Services, Mem. 18, 466 pp.

Johannsen, Albert (1931–1938), *A Descriptive Petrography of the Igneous Rocks,* Vols. 1–4, Chicago: University of Chicago Press, 267 pp., 428 pp., 360 pp., and 523 pp., respectively.

McBirney, A.R., ed. (1969), Proceedings of the Anedesite Conference," *Ore. Dept. Geol. and Mineral Ind.,* Bulletin 65, 193 pp.

Merrill, G. P. (1903), *Stones for Building and Decoration,* 3rd ed., New York: John Wiley & Sons, Inc., 551 pp.

Ross, C. S. and Smith, R. L. (1961), "Ash Flow Tuffs: Their Origin, Geologic Relations, and Identification," U.S. Geol. Surv. Prof. Paper 366, 81 pp.

Schmidt, R. G. and Shaw, H. R. (1971), "Atlas of Volcanic Phenomena," *U.S. Geol. Surv.* 20 leaves.

Sørensen, H., ed. (1974), *The Alkaline Rocks,* New York: John Wiley & Sons, Inc., 622 pp.

Streckeisen, A. L. (1976), "To Each Plutonic Rock Its Proper Name," *Earth-Sci. Rev.,* Vol. 12, pp. 1–33.

Streckeisen, A.L. (1979), *Classification and nomenclature of volcanic rocks, lamprophyres, carbonatites, and melilitic rocks . . . ,"* Geology, Vol. 7, pp. 331-35.

Turner, F. J., and Verhoogen, J. (1960), *Igneous and Metamorphic Petrology,* 2nd ed., New York: McGraw-Hill Book Company, 694 pp.

Tuttle, O. F. and Gittins, J. (1966), *Carbonatites,* New York: John Wiley & Sons, Inc., 591 pp.

Tuttle, O. F. and Bowen, N. L. (1958), "Origin of Granite in the Light of Experimental Studies in the System $NaAlSi_3O_8$-$KAlSi_3O_8$-SiO_2-H_2O," *Geol. Soc. Amer.,* Mem. 74, 153 pp.

Wager, L. R. and Brown, G. M. (1967), *Layered Igneous Rocks,* San Francisco: W. H. Freeman and Company, Publishers, 588 pp.

Wilcox, R. E. (1965), "Volcanic-ash Chronology," in *The Quarternary of the United States,* VII INQUA Congress, Princeton, N.J.: Princeton University Press, pp. 807–816.

Williams, H., Turner, F. J., and Gilbert, C. M. (1954), *Petrography,* San Francisco: W. H. Freeman and Company, Publishers, 406 pp.

Wyllie, P. J., ed. (1967), *Ultramafic and Related Rocks,* New York: John Wiley & Sons, Inc., 464 pp.

CHAPTER 5
SEDIMENTARY AND DIAGENETIC ROCKS

Sediments are made up of materials derived from the physical and chemical breakdown of pre-existing rocks and from diverse organic processes. Sediments may be deposited physically as rock fragments or organic debris, chemically or biochemically as the result of precipitation from solution, or by flocculation of a colloidal suspension. Some of the chemical sediments are precipitated directly to solid aggregates. Most sediments, however, must be cemented or otherwise consolidated to form sedimentary rocks. Still others are largely to totally changed—mineralogically, texturally and/or chemically—to form diagenetic rocks.

In order to avoid possible confusion, it should be noted at the outset that the difference between most sedimentary rocks and diagenetic rocks is a matter of how much the original sediment has been changed by diagenesis. This is true because most sedimentary rocks have undergone at least some diagenesis and most diagenetic rocks retain some original sedimentary features. We distinguish the rocks as follows: Sedimentary rocks are rocks whose predominant textures *and* compositions have been formed as a result of either physical or chemical sedimentation. Diagenetic rocks are rocks whose predominant textures, compositions, or both have been imposed by low-temperature post-sedimentation processes, which are also termed diagenetic.

In any case, even though sedimentary and diagenetic rocks make up less than 10 percent of the earth's crust by volume, they cover some 75 percent of the continental surface and, as a consequence, are present in many roadcuts, quarries, and natural exposures.

Two features are frequently described as characteristically sedimentary—*stratification* (Figure 5-1A) and the presence of *fossils* (Figure 5-1B). **Stratification** is *the layering or bedding of deposited materials;* **fossil** is the name given to *evidence for former life preserved in rock*. Strictly speaking, however, even though both of these features are much more common in sedimentary than in other rocks, neither can be used as an absolute criterion for calling an unknown rock sedimentary. Lopoliths contain distinct cumulus layers of igneous rock; pyroclastic rocks are commonly layered and some contain fossils; and, some metamorphic rocks exhibit relict stratification and a few contain recognizable fossils. In addition, from the negative standpoint, several kinds of sedimentary rocks are not well stratified, at least not on the scale of a hand specimen or single outcrop, and many do not contain fossils.

Nevertheless, with a couple of noteworthy exceptions, which are mentioned later, most sedimentary and diagenetic rocks may be distinguished rather easily from rocks of the other major classes and also from each other. Just as for igneous rocks, compositions

(A)

FIGURE 5-1 Sedimentary rocks characteristically exhibit stratification and many contain fossils (A) Stratification exhibited by Upper Ordovician aged rocks of the Juniata Formation, Walker Mountain, west of Marion, Virginia (T. M. Gathright, Jr.) (B) Starfish, *Devonaster eucharis* (Hall) and other fossils on a slab of Devonian aged Hamilton Formation siltstone from Colgate University Quarry, Hamilton, New York. (Courtesy of G. A. Cooper and Smithsonian Institution)

and/or textural features generally provide the clues. And, these same properties, along with mode of occurrence, are also used both to classify the rocks and to interpret their histories.

Composition of Sedimentary and Diagenetic Rocks

The composition of a sedimentary rock reflects several things: first, its source materials; second, the erosion processes involved in the preparation and transport of the parent sediment; third, the physical and chemical conditions at the site of deposition; and fourth, postdepositional processes such as those responsible for lithification.

The source material for a sediment may be any other rock, any combination of other rocks, and/or any product of organic processes. That is to say, sediments may contain any of the earth's erosional debris, precipitates of materials dissolved in surface or near-surface waters and/or the remains of living matter. Therefore, fragments of igneous, metamorphic and previously formed sedimentary rocks, vein materials and unconsolidated overburden (including soil), precipitates from groundwater and salts from the sea, and both hard and replaced soft parts of organisms are all found in sedimentary and diagenetic rocks.

(B)

0   2 cm

When rocks or rock materials are brought close enough to the surface to be penetrated by the atmosphere and by percolating groundwater, they are subject to chemical decomposition and physical disintegration, generally referred to as *weathering*. The kinds of changes that take place depend upon the makeup of the rock material being weathered, the climatic conditions and, in some cases, the topographic character of the area. In cold and dry climates and for chemically resistant rocks, physical weathering is most important.

In hot and humid climates and for rocks that are relatively susceptible to chemical change, chemical weathering is more important. As might be expected, however, in many places physical and chemical weathering processes aid and abet each other.

Physical weathering results in the breaking of large pieces into small ones by processes such as frost heaving. As a result, although one mineral may be broken away from its surrounding rock—for example, a grain of quartz or feldspar from a granitic rock—no new substance is formed. Contrariwise, chemical weathering frequently involves formation of new minerals because percolating waters often cause rearrangement of constituent ions or even add and/or subtract substances from the rock material being weathered. As a consequence of chemical weathering, components of the percolating solutions and their potential activities are changed.

Weathering products that remain where they are formed are referred to as **residuum.** *Weathering products that are transported and deposited* elsewhere become **sediments.** Deposits of organic matter—for example, those that have become peat—are exemplary of residuum. Beach sand and river silt are examples of transported and deposited sediments.

Products of physical weathering are carried as fragments ranging from large boulders to extremely small particles. They are transported in direct response to gravity or by water, glacial ice, or wind. They are deposited whenever and wherever their transporting agent is no longer able to carry them. If the resulting deposits of gravel, sand, or silt are turned into rock, they become conglomerates, sandstones, or siltstones. Many things can be deduced about the environment of deposition of a sediment or its resulting sedimentary rock. This is so because the principles that determine relationships, such as those between the velocity of a transporting agent and the size and weight of fragments being carried versus those being deposited, are well known and can be tested in the laboratory.

Most products of chemical weathering are carried in solution. A few are carried in colloidal suspension. The transporting agent is either surface water or groundwater. Some of the same waters may also carry in solution materials that have been derived from the atmosphere and/or from organic and/or magmatic processes. Examples are carbon dioxide (CO_2), humic acids, and volcanic exhalations, respectively. It has been estimated that the groundwater, streams, and rivers of the world carry about 2.75 billion metric tons of dissolved materials from the continents into the oceans each year. It is of particular importance to the formation of rocks that minerals can be deposited from these natural solutions in any of a number of diverse environments—for example, in pore spaces and underground channels, around the orifices of springs, and within basins of sedimentation. In each case, the solution is chemically changed so that one or more of its components are precipitated to form deposits of, for example, calcite, aragonite, or silica gel. Subsequently, many of these precipitates become rocks or parts of rocks such as limestone, rock salt, and chert. Some precipitation is promoted by biological activities and is termed biochemical, as opposed to strictly chemical, precipitation. Because chemical precipitation and flocculation take place in accordance with well-known principles of chemistry, the identities of the deposited minerals indicate ranges for the physical and chemical conditions that existed during their deposition. Nonetheless it must always be kept in mind that once formed, chemical sediments do not necessarily remain where they were originally deposited; instead, they may be broken up, transported, and redeposited elsewhere— in some cases in environments quite different from those in which they were originally formed and deposited.

Mixtures of physically and/or chemically transported materials are relatively common. The following terms are used to call attention to noteworthy minor constituents of such mixtures: *sandy* sediments or rocks are sometimes referred to as being *arenaceous; clayey* ones are *argillaceous; calcite-bearing* ones are *calcareous; carbon-bearing* ones are *carbonaceous; iron-bearing* ones are *ferruginous;* and *quartz-bearing* ones are *siliceous.* For most cases, we recommend use of the first of each of the italicized, paired terms.

Another composition-based characteristic that may be indicative of conditions during sedimentation is the color of the resulting rock. This is especially true for rocks made up largely of fine sand, silt, or clay because nearly all of these rocks would be off-white if they did not contain at least trace amounts of organic matter and/or one or more mineral pigments. Fortunately, once one has become familiar with certain characteristic hues, the identities of pigments can be suggested with confidence, even though most cannot be discerned megascopically. The more common color indicators are:

Reds and *reddish browns* are attributable to hematite, which is most frequently formed in sediments that are intermittently oxygenated. Oxidizing conditions of this type are more common in continental environments than within marine basins.

Yellowish to *rusty browns* are dependent upon the presence of limonite, which is generally formed under oxidizing *and* hydrating conditions. Well drained, nonmarine or transitional areas that are barren of vegetation appear most favorable.

Light bluish and *greenish grays*, which more nearly resemble the true colors of the sedimentary particles themselves, persist in environments where neutral to slightly reducing conditions prevail. It is rather generally thought that marine environments are indicated.

Dark greens are due to the presence of ferrous minerals; *dark grays* or *blacks* represent incompletely decomposed organic matter or, in some rocks, fine particles of pyrite and/or other iron sulfides, each of which is generally suggestive of reducing conditions. Stagnant marine basins (e.g., the present-day Baltic Sea) and both tidal and nonmarine swamps and bogs are exemplary.

Many geologists take special pains when describing color of sedimentary rocks because of the possible genetic significance of the color. Some geologists report the colors of their rocks on the basis of matching them with colors on the *Rock-Color Chart* (1963), distributed by the Geological Society of America.

Where present, fossils may also constitute clues as to the environment of sedimentation. This is so because certain animals and plants only live (and die) in specific habitats. A few generalizations, such as the likelihood that animals with thick shells can withstand pounding surfs, whereas animals with thin shells cannot, may be readily deduced. Additional data about animals and plants that are fairly frequently found as fossils are given in a number of the introductory books about paleontology, especially those that deal with paleoecology.

Diagenesis

This term is widely applied to low temperature changes that take place in sediments prior to and often contributing to their *lithification* (i.e., conversion into rock). The changes include all chemical, physical, and biologically induced modifications and transformations of sediments except those attributable to metamorphism or subaerial weathering. Especially important diagenetic processes are solution, deposition, replacement, recrystallization, compaction, and cementation. The changes may take place as soon as a sediment is deposited or any time thereafter. They may take place at, close to, or well away from the sediment-water interface—that is to say, they may take place under either submarine or subaerial conditions and under the influence of sea water, vadose water, or ground water. All are controlled by the physical and chemical makeup of the sediment and the physical and chemical conditions at the site of change. They tend to take place whenever and wherever the constituents of the original sediment are not stable under the existing conditions.

Minerals that are soluble in solutions percolating through sediments may be partially or wholly dissolved and removed or they may be replaced. Open spaces may be filled by minerals precipitated from interstitial fluids. Overgrowths on already present minerals are exemplary. Unstable minerals or aggregates may be replaced by or recrystallized to more stable ones. Replacement is widely conceived to involve essentially simultaneous solution of the original material and precipitation of the new. Therefore, it generally results in both chemical and mineralogical changes—for example, calcite and aragonite are often replaced by dolomite or chert. Recrystallization is thought to involve solution and reprecipitation of one and the same chemical material. It may or may not result in a change of the mineralogical composition as well as of the texture of the sediment—for example, fine calcareous mud, made up of particles of either aragonite or calcite, may be recrystallized to coarse interlocking grains of calcite. Both replacement and recrystallization may be partial or complete and may or may not destroy preexisting features such as sedimentary laminae (layers 1.0 millimeter or less in thickness) and fossils.

As already noted, some sediments become solid rocks upon deposition. Some evaporites and most cave and spring deposits are examples. Most sediments, however, have to be lithified. The diagenetic processes most commonly responsible for lithification are compaction, recrystallization, and cementation.

Compaction is sufficient to cause some clay-rich sediments to become solid rock. It occurs when the weight of the overlying sediments is enough to remove much of the entrapped water, thus reducing the pore space and consequently pressing the platy clay particles so closely together that they adhere to each other because of interparticle attraction (Figure 5-2). Other than removal of entrapped water, compaction does not change the composition of sediment being lithified.

Recrystallization frequently results in the formation of interlocking or melded grains and thus in lithification. As already noted, true recrystallization short of metamorphism may result in mineralogical changes, but not in chemical changes.

Cementation is the filling of open spaces with mineral matter that will hold the particles together (Figure 5-3). It is accomplished by deposition of compounds from the aqueous solutions that circulate through the connected open spaces. The cementing material may be derived from within the sediment itself or it may be carried in from external sources. Thus, cements may be of the same general composition as the sediment or of a completely different composition—for example, a quartz sand may be cemented by quartz, by calcite or even by some less common mineral, such as hematite or siderite. As a consequence, cementation may or may not change the overall composition of the resulting rock.

In many rocks it is possible to recognize diagenetic changes by megascopic observation. Every attempt should be made to do this and thus to elucidate still another chapter in the history of the so-affected rocks.

FIGURE 5-2 Triassic aged shale, as seen in thin section, lithified chiefly in response to compaction from Hamden, Connecticut. (B. J. Skinner)

As will be evident from the discussion of metamorphic processes in Chapter 6, diagenesis grades into low temperature metamorphism. Therefore, diagenetic processes serve to exemplify how processes as well as rocks may straddle a boundary between major rock groups.

It should be evident from what has been said in this rather brief account that the composition of either a sedimentary or a diagenetic rock (see Table 5-1) may indicate a relatively simple or an extremely complex history. It should be equally clear that a simple composition does not necessarily indicate a simple history—for example, it is quite possible that a pure, off-white colored, quartz-cemented sandstone could have had a much more complex history than a red, calcite-cemented, clay-rich, arkosic sandstone. Furthermore, many rock histories cannot be deduced satisfactorily until the texture of the rock is also taken into consideration.

Texture

Sedimentary and diagenetic rocks display two fundamentally different kinds of textures: *clastic* textures, which arise when transported fragments have been compacted and cemented together; and *mosaic* or *interlocking* textures, which are attributable either to direct crystallization of sedimentary minerals from aqueous solutions or to recrystallization. Each of these textural types has variants that can be discerned megascopically.

Clastic textures. Clastic textures are characterized by discrete bodies of rock material, generally termed *clasts*. The clasts may be fragments derived by terrestrial weathering and erosion of preexisting rock materials—for example, sand grains; complete or broken-off pieces of biochemically produced bodies—for example, shell fragments; or particles

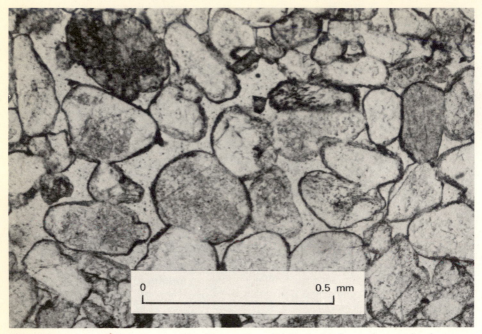

FIGURE 5-3 Sandstone, as seen in thin section, lithified chiefly as the result of cementation. Rounded grains are mostly quartz. Cement is calcite. (B. J. Skinner)

formed by submarine breakage of chemically or biochemically precipitated detritus—for example, pebble-sized tablets of partially consolidated, fine lime mud. The sediments and resulting rocks may consist of any one or some combination of the different kinds of clasts. The actual textures are generally described on the basis of grain shape, grain size, sorting, packing, and how the rock was lithified. Differences in one or more of these features, plus or minus layer to layer compositional differences, account for stratification. Each of these aspects of clastic texture warrants individual consideration.

   Grain shape is described on the basis of two parameters: *roundness* and *sphericity*. Roundness is the degree of abrasion as indicated by the sharpness of the corners and edges of fragments. It is generally described by the terms *angular, subangular, subrounded,* and *rounded* (Figure 5-4). Sphericity is the degree to which a fragment's shape approaches the form of a sphere. It has been defined in several ways, including some that use complicated geometry. For most purposes, terms such as *spheroidal,* meaning roughly equidimensional; *disclike,* meaning platy; *rodlike,* meaning prismatic; and highly irregular should suffice (Figure 5-5). Both roundness and sphericity depend upon the original shape of the fragment first broken from its parent mass, the physical properties of the fragment (such as the grain size and grain distribution of its constituents), and the effective process or processes responsible for its modification during transport.

   In general, the degree of rounding of a fragment varies directly with the distance it has been carried—that is, a fragment tends to become more and more rounded the farther (and/or more slowly) it is transported. The sphericity, on the other hand, tends to reflect the inherent physical properties of a fragment. Nevertheless, a few fragments do have

TABLE 5-1   Megascopically distinguishable minerals in sedimentary and diagenetic rocks.

Detrital Rocks	Chemical Rocks	Organic Rocks	Diagenetic Rocks
As clasts:	Anhydrite	Carbon-rich	Apatite
Calcite	Aragonite	mineraloids	Calcite
Clay minerals	Calcite		Dolomite
Feldspars	Dolomite		Glauconite
Micas	Gypsum		Hematite
Quartz	Halite		Pyrite
(including	Silica		Pyrrhotite
chert)	(chert)		Silica
[Rock frag-	Other salts		(chert)
ments]			
As cement:			
Calcite			
Hematite			
Limonite			
Quartz			

shapes that characterize modes of formation—for example, wind-abraded ventifacts and glacially faceted stones (Figure 5-6). In any case, it should be remembered that roundness and sphericity are not directly correlative. Rounded does not indicate spherical (a rod-shaped fragment with no corners or edges is rounded) and spheroidal does not indicate rounded (a cube has a relatively high degree of sphericity.).

Another aspect of shape that is sometimes instructive is the surface character of the constituent grains. Descriptive terms that are widely used include *polished, frosted, striated, pitted* or *grooved,* and *percussion marked.* Nearly all surficial features, however, may be formed by more than one process.

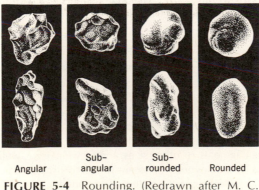

| | Sub- | Sub- | |
| Angular | angular | rounded | Rounded |

FIGURE 5-4   Rounding. (Redrawn after M. C. Powers, Jour. Sedimentary Petrology, v. 23, 1953)

FIGURE 5-5   Sphericity and rounding. These arkose fragments were collected from a stream gravel near New Haven, Conn. As arranged, they indicate what might be expected when a disc- (or plate-) shaped fragment (upper right) and a rod- (or spindle-) shaped fragment (upper left) are subjected to progressive abrasion. As shown, either might end up as a well-rounded spheroidal pebble. (B. J. Skinner)

Grain size may be measured. It is usually based on the smallest cross-sectional area or some mean diameter of a grain. Thence, the individual clasts, the loose sediments made up largely of the clasts, and the consolidated rock equivalents may be classified and named as shown on Table 5-2. Individual deposits of sediments and their consolidated rock analogs, however, may range from very poorly sorted to very well sorted and thus should be given more descriptive names (Figure 5-7).

Sorting is a measurement of how well the fragments of one size and or weight have been separated from fragments of other sizes and/or weights. A well sorted sediment is one that consists largely, if not wholly, of grains of essentially the same size and/or weight.

Both grain size and the degree of sorting are important in interpreting the history of a sediment or its lithified equivalent. We know, for example, that in water laid deposits

TABLE 5-2 Detrital fragments (clasts), detrital sediments and detrital sedimentary rocks.

Size, Mean Diameter	Clast (fragment)	Loose Sediment	Rock	Remarks
>256 mm	Boulder	Boulder gravel[a]	Boulder conglomerate[b]	
64–256 mm	Cobble	Cobble gravel[a]	Cobble conglomerate[b]	
2–64 mm	Pebble	Pebble gravel[a]	Pebble conglomerate[b]	Clasts between 2 and 4 mm are sometimes called granules
$1/16$–2 mm	Sand grain	Sand	Sandstone	The following subdivisions are often used: 1–2 mm, very coarse $1/2$–1 mm, coarse $1/4$–$1/2$ mm, medium $1/8$–$1/4$ mm, fine $1/16$–$1/8$ mm, very fine
$1/256$–$1/16$ mm	Silt grain	Silt	Siltstone	
<$1/256$ mm	Clay particle	Clay	Claystone, mudstone or shale[c]	

[a]Rubble if fragments are angular.

[b]Breccia if fragments are angular.

[c]If fissible.

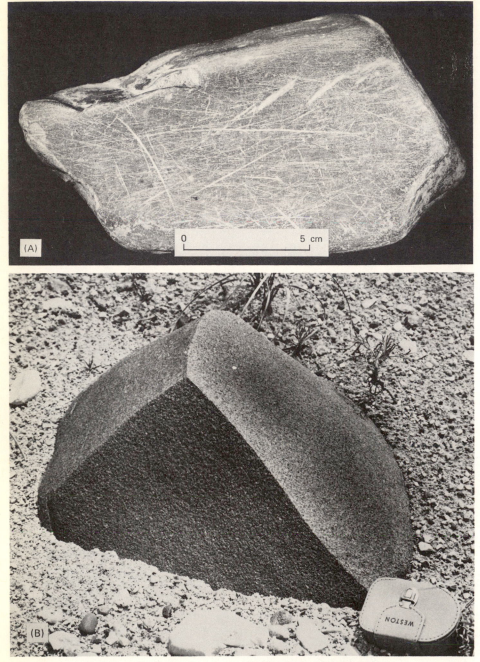

FIGURE 5-6 (A) Glacially faceted and scratched cobble of dolostone from a Wisconsin stage moraine near Winn, Isabella County, Michigan. (R. V. Dietrich) (B) Ventifact of fine-grained gabbro, from Sleeping Bear Dune, Leelenau County, Michigan. Exposure meter case in lower right-hand corner is approximately 7 centimeters wide. (M. I. Whitney)

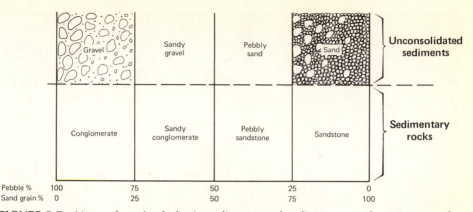

FIGURE 5-7 Names for mixed clastic sediments and sedimentary rocks. Mixtures other than those shown would be named in a similar way—for example, a sedimentary rock consisting of 25 to 50 percent clay and 50 to 75 percent silt would be a clayey siltstone.

the velocity of the transporting water controls the maximum size that a clast can have and still be transported. We also know that a mountain torrent can transport large as well as small clasts, whereas a sluggish meandering stream can carry only small ones. As a consequence, we know that size is often a rough guide to the distance a clast is located from its source area—that is, we know that most large fragments have not traveled as far from their source as most small ones. We also know that abrupt decreases in velocity tend to cause deposition of poorly sorted mixtures of fragments, whereas continual working and reworking by similar currents tend to give well-sorted sediments. As already implied, many sedimentation principles are well-known or can be deduced and experimentally tested.

Packing is the geometrical expression of the character and amount of filled versus open space in a sediment. It refers to the arrangement and spacing as well as to the sizes of the sedimentary particles and the surrounding voids. Packing is dependent upon the size, shape, sorting, and orientation of fragments. Terms such as floating grains, point contacts, long contacts, and imbricate arrangement are used (Figure 5-8). The sorting and orientation, in particular, reflect the mode of deposition and, therefore, the physical conditions that prevailed during deposition.

In most cases, when a sediment is first deposited, it tends to be rather loose-packed—that is, to have a relatively high percentage of open space. Later, as the sediment is disturbed by vibrations—for example, by earthquakes—and/or is compacted because of the weight of overlying sediments, it tends to become tighter (close-packed). Thus loose packing versus close packing in a rock may indicate early versus late cementation.

Along with grain shape and sorting, packing controls two extremely important and quantitatively measurable properties, *porosity* and *permeability*. Porosity is the percentage of open (or pore) space per unit volume. Permeability is the capacity of a material to transmit fluid. If pore spaces in a rock are not connected, the permeability may be quite low even though its porosity is high; if the pore spaces are connected, both the porosity and the permeability may be high. The permeability, in particular, is important so far as the movement and recovery of groundwater, oil, and gas.

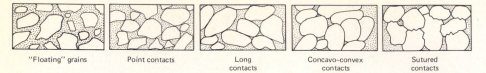

"Floating" grains   Point contacts   Long contacts   Concavo-convex contacts   Sutured contacts

FIGURE 5-8 Types of grain contacts in clastic sedimentary rocks.

Rough impressions about the packing in a sediment or a sedimentary rock may be gained from megascopic study of the nature of grain contacts or, in some cases, even by noting some characteristic such as fluid absorption tendencies. Along with such descriptive terms as close- and loose-packed, the terms dense and porous are also rather widely used to roughly describe packing.

Character of lithification refers to changes in texture that take place during diagenesis and lithification. Some changes can be discerned megascopically; some can be inferred on the basis of dependent characteristics; some can only be determined by utilizing relatively sophisticated laboratory procedures. In coarse-grained clastic rocks, boundaries between adjacent grains and between grains and their matrix of smaller grains and/or their cementing material can generally be seen with the naked eye or through a handlens. For these rocks, both the character of the materials and the overall textures can be described. For other fragmental sedimentary rocks, the way they break is often indicative—for example, a calcite-cemented sandstone will tend to break along irregular surfaces from which individual sand grains can be easily broken, whereas a claystone consisting mainly of flakelike particles with their nearly flat surfaces essentially parallel to bedding will tend to break parallel to that bedding.

Interlocking textures. Interlocking textures, which are characteristic of some sedimentary rocks, are similar to the interlocking textures of phaneritic igneous and some metamorphic rocks. Included are textures that are formed by such diverse processes as direct crystallization from aqueous solutions, certain types of cementation, recrystallization, and replacement. In describing these textures, the grain size should be stated and the terms euhedral, subhedral, and anhedral used for grain shapes. In addition, terms such as mosaic and sutured mosaic (see Figure 5-8) can often be used.

Other features of sedimentary rocks, mainly structures that can best be seen in outcrop and in large specimens, deserve mention. Among the relatively common ones are fossil mudcracks, raindrop prints, ripple marks (Figure 5-9) and the following:

Armored mudball—a relatively large (typically 5–10 centimeters in diameter), subspherical mass of mud (clay ± silt) that is studded with sand or gravel. Armored mudballs are formed when chunks of mud are broken from banks and rolled along stream beds or beaches, thereby accumulating their armor. When incorporated in sediments and lithified, they are sometimes mistaken for concretions.

Concretion—a mass or aggregate of mineral matter that has distinct boundaries with the rock within which it was formed and is enclosed (Figure 5-10A). Concretions, which are most common in shales, typically have roughly oblate spheroidal shapes but also rather commonly assume all sorts of rather odd shapes (Figure 5-10B).

FIGURE 5-9 Current ripple marks in an Upper Cambrian dolostone of Tazewell County, Virginia. (W. E. Moore)

Cross bedding (and cross lamination)—stratification at an angle to the overall layering of the unit within which it occurs (Figure 5-19).

Cut-and-fill (also termed scour-and-fill)—a sedimentary structure that consists of a scoured-out channel filled by later deposition (Figure 5-11).

Dendrites—secondary mineral growths, commonly surficial films of manganese or iron hydroxides, that branch irregularly like a tree (Figure 5-12).

Geopetal structure—any feature or fabric that can be used to determine the original top and bottom of a sedimentary layer or other rock unit. Cut-and-fill structures and graded bedding are exemplary. Robert Shrock (1948), in his classic compilation *Sequence in Layered Rocks*, describes and illustrates many such original structures.

Graded bedding—layering in which the grain size in individual beds gradually changes from coarse to fine, bottom to top (Figure 5-13).

Imbricate structure—shinglelike arrangement of roughly tabular or discoidal clasts (Figure 5-14). In nearly all cases, the clasts lean down-current.

Stylolite—a thin irregular, interdigitated contact seam, most commonly occurring in limestones or dolostones, that is expressed on relatively flat surfaces by dark gray or greenish zig-zag lines that consist of concentrations of relatively insoluble materials such as clay, carbon, or pyrite (Figure 5-15). Stylolites appear to form as the result of solution and compression during diagenesis.

Unconformity—a surface that marks a gap in continuity between the rock units below and above (Figure 5-16). The gap represents a period of either subaerial or subaqueous erosion.

Vug—an irregularly shaped, generally crystal-lined cavity in a rock (Figure 5-17). Rocks with many vugs are said to be vuggy.

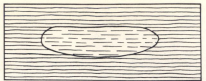

A

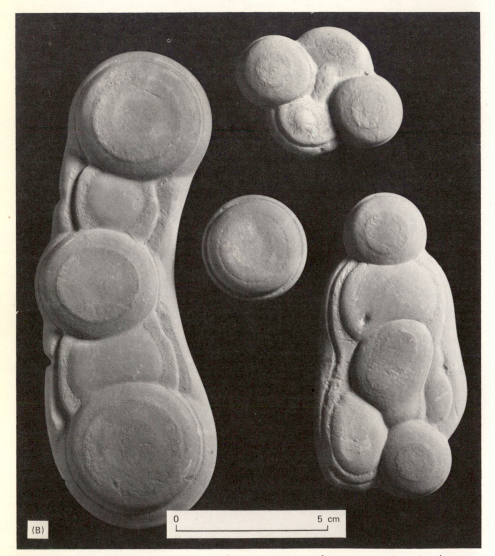

FIGURE 5-10 Concretions (A) Vertical cross sections of two concretions in claystone showing different times of origin relative to deposition of enclosing sediment. Concretion on left formed contemporaneously with sediment; concretion on right formed after sedimentation. (B) Calcareous concretions from Pleistocene lake sediments in Connecticut. (B. J. Skinner)

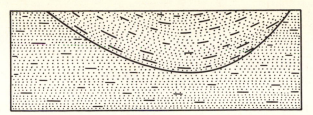

FIGURE 5-11 Cut and fill structure in sediments.

Classification

Sedimentary and diagenetic rocks can be divided into three main categories: (1) *detrital sedimentary rocks*, which consist largely of loose rock and mineral fragments derived by weathering and erosion of preexisting rocks—these are named on the basis of features such as grain size, grain shape, and/or grain composition; (2) *chemical and biochemical sedimentary rocks*, which are made up largely of precipitated materials, both those that have remained where they were originally deposited and those that have later been transported and deposited as intrabasinal clastics—these rocks are subdivided on the basis of their mineralogical contents, in some cases modified by considerations of their origins; and (3) *diagenetic rocks*, which form as the result of wholesale prelithification recrystallization, replacement, or other chemical or biochemical modification of the original sediments—these rocks are named on the basis of their compositions.

Some sedimentary and diagenetic rocks have questionable origins; others may be formed in more than one way. As a consequence, a few rocks that appear essentially identical in handspecimens may be, for example, either chemical sedimentary rocks or diagenetic rocks. We have tried to make this clear in our descriptions but do not describe or even list all such rocks under all pertinent subheadings.

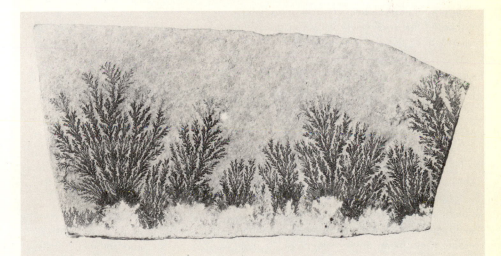

FIGURE 5-12 Dendrites. Tree-shaped deposits of pyrolusite are relatively common on some rock surfaces. (Smithsonian Institution)

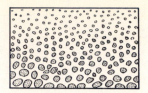

FIGURE 5-13 Graded bedding.

A list of the common sedimentary and diagenetic rocks within the three main categories, is shown in Table 5-3. We use the classification as a basis for the descriptions of the rocks in the remainder of this chapter.

TABLE 5-3   The common sedimentary and diagenetic rocks.

Detrital Sedimentary Rocks

Conglomerate and sedimentary breccia (and tillite)
Sandstone (including fossil placers, arkose, graywacke, sedimentary quartzite, and tar
  sand)
Siltstone (including loessite)
Claystone, mudstone, and shale (including argillite, clay ironstone, phosphatic and oil
  shales)

Chemical and Biochemical Sedimentary Rocks

Clastic limestone (calcirudite, calcarenite, and calcilutite; fossiliferous, oolitic and
  lithographic limestones; coquina and chalk)
Nonclastic limestone (reef rock, stromatolitic limestone, travertine, calcareous tufa, and
  marl)
Chert and siliceous sinter (radiolarian chert and diatomite)
Evaporites (gyprock, anhydrock, rocksalt, etc.)

Diagenetic Rocks

Recrystallized limestone
Dolostone
Replacement chert (flint, jasper, fossiliferous and oolitic chert, novaculite, porcelanite,
  and tripoli)
Phosphorite
Glauconitic sandstone (greensand)
"Sedimentary ore" (including certain iron, manganese, and lead-zinc-copper ores)
Organic rocks (peat; lignite; bituminous, cannel, semianthracite, and anthracite coals;
  guano)

DETRITAL SEDIMENTARY ROCKS

The fragments in detrital sediments and detrital sedimentary rocks are derived from preexisting rocks that have undergone subaerial weathering, erosion, and transport. Many geologists refer to these sediments and rocks as terrigenous, indicating that they consist predominately of material eroded from the land. Conglomerates, sedimentary breccias, sandstones, siltstones, and claystones are included.

A widely used classification scheme for naming the individual clasts, the unconsolidated sediments, and the sedimentary rocks of this category is given in Table 5-2. The basis of the classification scheme is a geometric scale, generally termed the Wentworth Scale or Wentworth-Udden Scale, with a $2\times$ multiplier and the boundary between coarse and very coarse sand set at 1.0 millimeter.

Conglomerates and Sedimentary Breccias

As shown in Table 5-2 and Figure 5-18, conglomerates are made up of 50 or more percent rounded pebbles, cobbles, and/or boulders, whereas sedimentary breccias are made up of 50 or more percent angular pebble-, cobble-, and/or boulder-sized fragments (Figure 5-18). The term breccia, alone, should never be applied to known sedimentary breccias.

FIGURE 5-14 Imbricate arrangement of pebbles. (R. V. Dietrich)

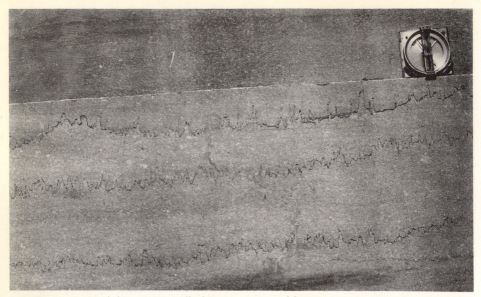

FIGURE 5-15 Stylolites in so-called Tennessee marble. Surveying compass is approximately 10 centimeters on an edge. (Photograph by T. N. Dale, from L. V. Pirsson collection)

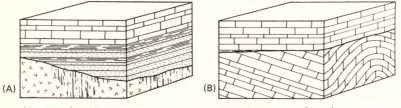

(A) Nonconformity

(B) Angular unconformity

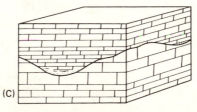

(C) Disconformity

FIGURE 5-16 Unconformities: (A) nonconformity–sediments overlie igneous and/or metamorphic rocks; (B) angular unconformity–sediments overlie folded and truncated (by weathering and erosion) sedimentary rocks; (C) disconformity–sediments above and below the surface of erosion have essentially the same orientation in space. (From C. O. Dunbar, and J. Rodgers, Principles of Stratigraphy © John Wiley & Sons.)

FIGURE 5-17   Vug lined with calcite crystals. (R. V. Dietrich)

Otherwise, they might be misinterpreted as pyroclastic breccias (page 160) or tectonic breccias (page 244), neither of which is a sedimentary rock.

Conglomerates and sedimentary breccias may be of just about any color or combination of colors. This is a consequence of the fact that their fragments may be just about any rock and their matrixes may consist of one or more of several different minerals or rocks or both. Stratification is, at best, crude in most conglomerates and sedimentary breccias and fossils are rare.

In general practice, adjectives, varietal names, or combinations of the two are used to make conglomerate and sedimentary breccia designations more meaningful. Most of

the frequently used adjectives refer to size (e.g., cobble conglomerate) or to composition
of clasts (e.g., quartzite conglomerate or polymictic sedimentary breccia). The term
polymictic is used rather widely to indicate that the fragments are of several different kinds
of rocks and/or minerals. (The complementary terms oligomictic, meaning fragments of
only one kind of rock, and monomictic, meaning fragments of only one kind of mineral,
are seldom used. Instead, the name of the rock or mineral is usually noted.)

   Varieties of conglomerates and sedimentary breccias. As can be seen, the following
representative varietal names are genetically based.

Basal conglomerates are those deposited as the first sediment on top of a surface of
   erosion—that is, they mark a surface of unconformity.
Collapse breccias consist of cemented fragments formed as the result of the foundering of
   the roof of a cave or a volcanic caldera.
Intraformational conglomerates (and breccias), sometimes referred to as edgewise conglomerates (or breccias), consist of tabular or discoidal clasts that are broken pieces of
   some coherent or partially coherent sediment that was deposited during the same sedimentary cycle as the underlying and overlying units. They are typically intrabasinal in
   origin.
Fanglomerates are cemented alluvial fan deposits.
Tillites are consolidated glacial tills. Many tillites are not really conglomerates or sedimentary breccias. Rather they are conglomeratic or brecciatic siltstones or mudstones
   (see Figure 5-7).

   Unfortunately, the use of varietal names has led to some ambiguity so far as use of
the general terms. To some, conglomerate and sedimentary breccia indicate "... of no
known origin"; to others, they indicate "... of some origin other than as alluvial fan
material, glacial till, ... (etc.). This dilemma may be avoided by appropriately indicating
either the established origin or the lack of knowledge of the origin—for example, "a
sedimentary breccia formed in the surf zone along a sea cliff" or "a polymictic conglomerate of unknown origin."
   Several origins other than those indicated for the named varieties have been suggested.
Among them are: lag concentrates produced by subaerial weathering or deflation by the
wind, near-shore wave action along rocky coasts, concentrations of ice-rafted cobbles and
boulders, and talus or other deposits formed by mass wasting. No matter how formed,
conglomerates and sedimentary breccias are of great geological interest. In many cases,
their clasts may be correlated with a bedrock source and their overall composition and
relationships with spatially associated sedimentary rocks may be used to interpret the
climatic and/or tectonic conditions that existed when their parent gravel or rubble was
deposited.

   Occurrences of conglomerates and sedimentary breccias. Conglomerates and sedimentary breccias are relatively common in many sedimentary rock sequences. A few
examples may be given: In the sedimentary sequence of the central part of the Appalachian
fold belt, there are almost pure quartzite conglomerates of Late Precambrian and Early
Mississippian ages; a polymictic cobble conglomerate of Middle Ordovician age; several

polymictic pebble conglomerates, some that contain coal pebbles, of Mississippian and Early Pennsylvanian ages; several intraformational, edgewise sedimentary breccias of Cambrian through Late Ordovician ages; and several less noteworthy occurrences. In the Late Cambrian Potsdam Sandstone of northern New York, there are lens-shaped masses of boulder conglomerate that represent stream deposits. In the Devil's Icebox, near Norway in Michigan's Upper Peninsula, there is a Late Cambrian basal sedimentary breccia that contains pebble- to boulder-sized fragments of banded iron ore. Some of the Middle Cenozoic Bishop Conglomerate of southern Wyoming is fanglomerate. The emerged stacks in and around St. Ignace on the Straits of Mackinac, Michigan, are thought to consist of Lower Devonian collapse breccia. The Middle Ordovician age Cow Head Breccia of Newfoundland is thought to represent deposition by submarine density currents. The handsome boulders of polymictic conglomerate and conglomeratic argillite that are so widespread in the Pleistocene drift in the upper midwestern states are from a central Ontario exposure of a metamorphosed Precambrian tillite, the Gowganda Tillite. The Miocene San Onofre Breccia of western California is an exemplary sedimentary breccia.

In the Lake Superior District, some of the Late Precambrian Keweenawan conglomerates are copper-bearing. The world renowned Witwatersrand Conglomerates of South Africa, from which so much gold has been mined, are interpreted by some geologists as representing Precambrian stream deposits and by others to represent beach or delta deposits. The list could go on almost indefinitely.

Uses of conglomerate and sedimentary breccia. Like most other rocks, conglomerates and sedimentary breccias have been used here and there for building foundations and to fulfill other local needs. A few of these stones have been used more widely—two examples are the rather gaudy appearing "Calico rock," a coarse polymictic Triassic conglomerate once quarried in the vicinity of Washington, D.C., and the "Jasper puddingstone," an attractive red and white Precambrian metamorphosed conglomerate-breccia that crops out near Sault Sainte Marie, Ontario and occurs widely in the glacial drift, especially in Michigan, Indiana, and Ontario. Both have been used as facing stones and as accent stones in buildings and for other decorative purposes. In addition, some quartz pebble conglomerates and conglomeratic sandstones have been quarried and fashioned into millstones—for example, the Mississippian Cloyd Conglomerate of southwestern Virginia and the Mississippian Marshall Grindstone near Grindstone City, Michigan.

Sandstones

Sand deposits consist of a framework of sand grains, plus or minus matrixes of finer particles, with intergranular voids. Sandstones consist of sand deposits, the grains of which have been cemented together. The overall appearance of a sandstone depends upon the identity, size, shape, and arrangement of its constituent grains, including any matrix present, plus the color and identity of its cement. Each of these aspects should be considered in describing a sandstone—for example, a sandstone that is made up largely of quartz grains ½ to 1 millimeter in size, that has a calcite cement and that appears banded because the grains of some of its layers are coated with hematite might be termed "a red and white banded, coarse-grained, calcite-cemented (or calcareous) sandstone."

Most sandstones are white, light gray, buff, reddish or yellowish brown in color; a few are greenish, bluish or purplish. In some sandstones the colors are different from layer to layer or are arranged so the rock has a mottled or spotted appearance. The apparent

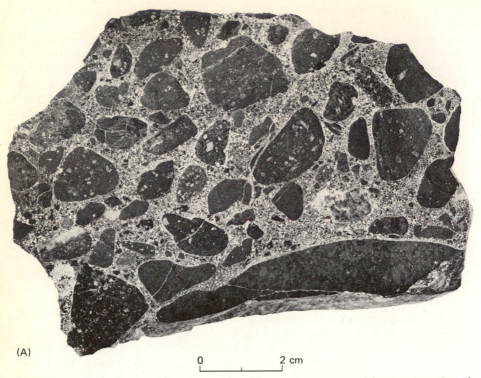

(A)

0 ⊢——⊣——⊣ 2 cm

FIGURE 5-18   (A) Conglomerate—arkose pebbles set in a matrix of finer grains; (B) polished surface of a sedimentary breccia—fragments are marble and matrix is a mixture of calcite and fine-grained silicate minerals. (B. J. Skinner)

color of many sandstones is dependent upon the composition of thin coatings on the sand grains, of matrix material or of cement, rather than of the sand grains themselves. The fairly common reddish brown coatings are generally hematite and the yellowish browns are limonite. Sandstones that are so pigmented are frequently referred to as ferruginous. The most common matrix minerals are the clay minerals and silt-sized quartz grains; the most common cementing minerals are calcite, dolomite, and quartz. Sandstones with these constituents may be indicated as, for example, clayey or argillaceous, silty, calcite-cemented or calcareous, dolomitic and silica-cemented, respectively. Many sandstones contain more than one of these kinds of minor constituents and are then referred to as, for example, a calcareous *and* argillaceous sandstone (or, more simply, a calcite-cemented clayey sandstone).

Sandstones may be well laminated or thin- to thick-bedded. Many are so thick-bedded that they appear homogeneous in hand specimen and even in some outcrops. The layering of sandstone may express differences in color, percentages of different mineral constituents, grain size, grain shape, mode of packing or some combination of these features. Color and grain size differences are most frequently reported.

(B)

Cross-bedding, graded bedding, and ripple marks are more likely to occur in sand-stones than in other sedimentary rocks. Some sandstones, for example, those made up of windblown sand, may exhibit little if any layering other than cross-bedding (see Figure 5-19).

Quartz is the predominant mineral in most sandstones. In fact, the term sandstone, unmodified, is generally understood to mean quartz sandstone. The reason quartz is so predominant is that it is abundant in many rocks and it is chemically stable and physically durable under most weathering and transporting processes.

Among the other minerals commonly present as sand grains are the feldspars, mag-netite, garnet, tourmaline, and mica (as flakes). A few sandstones, like the already de-scribed conglomerates, contain economically important amounts of heavy minerals such as gold, platinum, cassiterite, monazite, magnetite, chromite, ilmenite, rutile and the gem-stones diamond, ruby, sapphire, spinel, and zircon. These mechanical stream and strand concentrations are sometimes called *fossil placers*. In still other sandstones, sand sized rock fragments may be common. In general, when grains other than quartz make up more than 25 percent of a sandstone, that fact is referred to in the name—for example, a garnetiferous sandstone. A few such impure sandstone compositions are so widely distributed that they have been given varietal names that have gained rather broad acceptance.

Varieties of sandstone. *Arkose* is a feldspar-bearing sandstone, commonly conglomeratic or brecciatic, that resembles a granitoid. Most arkoses consist of 25 or more percent of poorly sorted angular to subangular fragments of potassium feldspar and quartz plus or minus mica and/or plagioclase. The shapes of the grains as well as their compositions indicate derivation of most arkoses from a nearby granitoid or granitic-composition metamorphic rock that was undergoing chiefly physical weathering. This deduction can be drawn because chemical weathering breaks down feldspar. The color of arkoses is typically reddish, indicating that many of them have been deposited in nonmarine or transitional oxidizing environments.

Graywacke (also spelled greywacke) is a field designation for dense, gray to greenish gray colored, impure sandstones (frequently termed dirty) that consist of 25 percent or more angular to subrounded feldspar grains *and* dark colored minerals and/or rock fragments. Most graywackes consist of poorly sorted mixtures of gravel, sand, silt, and clay. Those made up largely of rock fragments have been termed lithic graywackes, or even lithic sandstones by some geologists. The most common rock fragments are mafic volcanics, slate, chert, and phyllite. Many graywackes have very little cement; instead, they contain relatively large percentages of a well compacted, typically dark colored, clay or clay plus chlorite matrix. In some graywackes, the matrix appears to be clastic; in others, the matrix appears to have been formed within the original sediment as a result of diagenetic alteration. Cement, where present, is generally quartz or calcite. Nearly all graywackes give off a clayey odor when breathed on. Although some graywackes may at first glance resemble igneous rocks, handlens examination generally suffices to show their detrital character.

Tar sand is the name given to sandstones in which there are relatively large quantities of intergranular, highly viscous, asphalt-like hydrocarbon compounds. In some areas, these rocks are called by such names as bituminous rock or asphalt rock. Many, if not all, of these rocks appear to be oil-bearing sandstones from which the more volatile constituents have escaped.

Sedimentary quartzite, unlike the just described compositional varieties, is named on the basis of how it fractures. When most sandstones are broken, the fracturing tends to take place in the cement. This causes some of the sand grains to stand in relief and thus to make the surface appear and feel like sandpaper. Some sandstones, however, are so well cemented by either coarsely crystalline or chalcedonic quartz (Figure 5-20), that they fracture indiscriminately across the grains and the cement. Many such rocks exhibit conchoidal fractures similar to those of quartz and obsidian (see Figure 4-29). Some geologists apply the term orthoquartzite to these rocks in order to distinguish them from quartzites of metamorphic origin, which they call metaquartzites. A few geologists use the designation, quartz arenite. We think that the term sedimentary quartzite is preferable. In any case, it is impossible to distinguish many cabinet specimens as either sedimentary or metamorphic quartzites unless their occurrences or the identities of their associated rocks are known.

Occurrences of sandstones. Sandstones are relatively common in nearly all sequences of sedimentary rocks. For example, in the Appalachian region noted under the conglomerates and sedimentary breccias, there are several different sandstone formations—includ-

FIGURE 5-19 Cross bedding (sometimes referred to as cross-strata) in wind-blown Jurassic sand consolidated to form sandstone. (Tad Nichols)

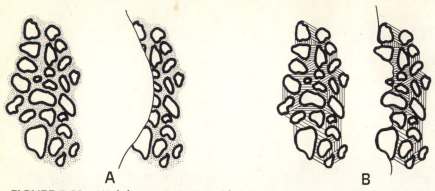

FIGURE 5-20   (A) left, quartz grains with interstitial quartz cement; right, relatively smooth conchoidal fracture cutting indiscriminately across the sand grains and the cement. (B) left, quartz grains with interstitial non-quartz cement; right, rough surface caused by fracture that is characteristically within the cement and thus around the sand grains.

ing a number of sedimentary quartzites, several calcite- and hematite-cemented sandstones, and some graywackes—with an aggregate thickness of more than 1500 meters.

Probably the most famous sandstone in the world is the slab called the Stone of Scone (also known as the Coronation Stone and the Stone of Destiny). This slab, which monarchs of Great Britain sit on when they are crowned, is said by legend to be the pillow used by Jacob when he dreamed of the ladder to Heaven.

Widely known arkoses occur in the Pennsylvanian age Fountain Formation of Colorado and the redbed sequences in the Triassic basins of the Atlantic seaboard area of North America. Well known graywackes occur in the Jurassic age Franciscan Group of the Coast Range of California and the Upper Jurassic Mariposa Formation of the Sierra Nevada. The best known and possibly the largest tar sand deposits in the world are the Cretaceous age Athabaska Tar Sands that underlie approximately 75,000 square kilometers in northern Alberta, Canada. Two other large tar sand deposits are the Orinoco deposit of Venezuela and the Olenek deposit of north central Siberia.

It may be of interest to collectors that almost every ridge in the Appalachian Valley and Ridge Province is capped by Clinch-Tuscarora Sedimentary Quartzite of Silurian age.

Uses of sandstones. Sandstones have been used for flagstones, grindstones, rip-rap, and as building stone, particularly in the past. Historical accounts indicate that the Triassic sandstone, called brownstone, from Portland, Connecticut, was the first stone quarried in the United States. Large quantities were used before 1665 and later the rock was used in the famous brownstone mansions so well known in eastern cities and even in San Francisco whence the stone was shipped via Cape Horn. Another widely used sandstone is the Upper Cambrian Potsdam Sandstone from northern New York and adjacent Ontario—it was used, for example, to face several of the buildings of Columbia University and for the Dominion Houses of Parliament in Ottawa. Today, a few sandstones like the well known Crab Orchard stone from Pennsylvanian age strata of western Tennessee, are still used rather widely in building, especially as trim stone. The durability of quartz-cemented sandstones is, by the way, almost legendary. As an example, when St. Peter's Church at Lamerton, England burned, the tower that was made up of so called freestone, actually a sandstone, remained intact even though the six large bells in the belfry were melted.

As we have already mentioned, placers and fossil placers have served and still serve as the source for many mineral resources. A few examples are the gold of Sutter's Mill, California, and of the Klondike District; the platinum of the Urals, Columbia and Tasmania; diamonds from central India, eastern Brazil and many areas in Africa; rubies, sapphires, spinels, and zircons from eastern Burma and Ceylon; cassiterite from the Maylayan Peninsula; and ilmenite, rutile, monazite, and zircon from eastern Australia and from several small deposits in the Piedmont and Coastal Plain provinces of Virginia, North Carolina, South Carolina, and Florida.

Asphalt from tar sand was used by Sumerians as a cement in works of art as early as about 3000 B.C.; by ancient Egyptians as a preservative for mummification about 2500 B.C.; and by the Babylonians for caulking and water-proofing before 700 B.C. Today, it is used in a few places as a natural macadam and it is also considered to constitute a potentially large oil reserve. This is the oil generally called "heavy oil". Examples are the natural macadam that is quarried, pulverized, and crushed for use as paving in west central Kentucky, southern Oklahoma, and in Carbon and Uinta counties, Utah; and the aforementioned Athabaska deposit that is even now being mined and processed near Fort McMurray, Alberta to produce about 6,500 metric tons of oil daily.

A few very pure silica sandstones—for example, the Early Mississippian-aged Berea Sandstone of northern Ohio and the Early Devonian Oriskany Sandstone of southern New York and adjacent Pennsylvania—are used in the manufacture of glass. Some others—for example, the Early Cambrian-aged Erwin Sedimentary Quartzite of southwestern Virginia—have been used as one of the raw materials for production of the alloy ferrosilicon.

Perhaps the newest use of sandstone involves utilizing certain underground sandstone formations that have relatively high porosities and good permeabilities as reservoirs for the storage of oil and gas.

Siltstones

Siltstones are, strictly speaking, silt deposits that have been lithified. In practice, however, the name siltstone is often applied to mudstones that feel gritty. Rather fittingly, such grittiness is generally dependent upon the presence of angular broken fragments, predominantly quartz, of silt and/or very fine sand size. Nonetheless, it should be realized that many rocks that are called siltstone on the basis of only megascopic examination are really silty or sandy claystones. One way to avoid such misnaming is to follow the nomenclature system advocated by some petrographers whereby the term *mudrock* is used as a field designation and/or class term to apply to both siltstones and claystones—that is, to all detrital rocks made up of fragments finer than sand.

Siltstones tend to be buff to yellowish or orange-tan, gray or greenish in color. They are commonly finely laminated and in some the laminations exhibit small-scale cross-bedding and cut-and-fill structures. Siltstones tend to be harder and more dense than mudstones and to be slabby rather than fissile like shales (page 200).

The term *loessite* has been proposed for siltstones and mudstones that consist of unlithified windblown dust, widely known as loess. Although many deposits of loess have been recognized, the existence of loessite remains to be proved. Loess is generally pale to buff-yellow or brownish gray in color. It is characteristically well-sorted, gritty, and relatively porous. Some of it is partially cemented by calcite. Most loess lacks stratification but, instead, has a tendency to break along essentially vertical fractures. It commonly forms nearly vertical banks along stream valleys. Concretions of calcite and limonite are present in many loess deposits.

Occurrences of siltstones. Most siltstones occur as interbeds within sedimentary sequences that are chiefly sandstone or shale. Those of the Devonian-aged Portage Group of central New York have often been cited as exemplary. Siltstones are also common in gradational zones between shale and sandstone units—for example, within the upper part of the Hampton Shale and the lower part of the overlying Erwin Sedimentary Quartzite units of the Lower Cambrian in the central Appalachians.

Loess deposits made up of windblown fragments of glacially ground rock flour occur here and there, especially along the lee side of large river valleys, in proglacial areas of the midwest United States, Western Europe, New Zealand, and Argentina. The previously mentioned nearly vertical fracturing is particularly well exhibited along the Missouri River between Council Bluffs, Iowa and Omaha, Nebraska.

Uses of siltstones. Locally, but rather rarely, siltstones have been crushed and used as road metal. In the past, some siltstones have been used as whetstones.

Claystones, Mudstones, and Shales

Each of these rock names has been used in more than one way. We subscribe to the usage whereby *claystone* is the overall designation for detrital sedimentary rocks made up chiefly of clay-sized particles; *shale* is used for claystones with fissility; and *mudstone* is used for claystones without fissility. *Fissility* is the tendency to split along closely spaced, roughly planar surfaces that are essentially parallel to bedding. It depends on the identity, crystallinity, abundance, and orientation of constituent clay minerals. The orientation, a preferred arrangement of the typically flaky or lath-shaped clay minerals with their longer axes in the plane of the bedding, is gained during sedimentation and enhanced during compaction (Figure 5-21). As a rule, claystones that consist largely of illite, montmorillonite, and/or chlorite are fissile, whereas those made of kaolinite are not.

Shales and mudstones are frequently named on the basis of their color, some compositional characteristic, or the degree of development of their fissility; examples are red shale, calcareous mudstone, and paper shale, respectively. Mineralogical designations, such as illitic shale, can only be given after microscopic or X-ray study.

Most claystones are gray, bluish, greenish, reddish, brownish or some blotchy combination of two or more of these colors. A few that are rich in organic carbon and/or fine particles of pyrite are nearly black. Although claystones may consist almost wholly of clay minerals or contain a noteworthy percent of admixed grains of other minerals, such as quartz and the micas, their grain sizes are so small that they appear to be homogeneous. Most clay minerals are produced by chemical weathering. It is these minerals that give clays and claystones their characteristic odor when they are damp or breathed on. Most of the nonclay particles are formed as a result of physical fragmentation of sand and larger pieces of preexisting rock. Their presence is sometimes indicated by a grittiness. Most shales are soft and brittle or crumbly. Many feel smooth because they consist almost entirely of clay minerals. Most mudstones exhibit blocky breakage and feel gritty because they contain higher percentages of irregularly shaped fragments than shales do. Many are

FIGURE 5-21 Early Mississippian aged, Antrim Shale, from Central Alpena County, Michigan, showing well-developed fissility. Handlens is approximately 2 centimeters in diameter. (R. V. Dietrich)

silty and thus might well be termed mudrock in the field, as noted under the siltstone subheading.

Black shales are frequently referred to as *carbonaceous shales*. Many contain pyrite or marcasite, which are thought to be of diagenetic origin with their sulfur derived from the hydrogen sulfide that was given off by putrid organic matter buried in the parent clay. When sulfide-bearing shales are altered, gypsum and/or alum family minerals are often deposited as white crusts on both natural and man-made exposures of the rocks. Consequently, such shales have often been called *alum shales*.

Concretions with an overall argillite (see below) character are relatively common in some shale units (see Figure 5-10). In most cases, the concretions are concentrated at certain horizons and occur in relatively large groups. Although most concretions measure 50 centimeters or less in greatest diameter, now and then one measuring a meter or more across is found.

Many shales have been lithified solely as the result of compaction—that is, without addition of cementing material. Some shales, however, are calcareous, with at least some of the calcite serving as cement. Calcareous shales grade into marls (page 210) and argillaceous (or shaly) limestones.

Some shales have such good fissility that they resemble their metamorphic successors, slate. In most cases, however, hand specimens of shale may be distinguished from hand specimens of slates, even when their geological occurrences are not known. This is possible because most shales give off a clayey odor when damp, but slates rarely do; slates tend to be harder than shales and many slates have greasy or satin-like lusters, whereas most shales have pearly or dull lusters. In addition, many slates exhibit angular relationships between their cleavage and the original sedimentary layering (see Figure 6-16) whereas shales never show an angular relationship between their fissility and the sedimentary layering.

The fossil content of some nonmarine and mixed (marine and fresh water) environment shales is particularly interesting—for example, in the Late Jurassic age Morrison Formation near Como Bluffs, Wyoming, there are fossils of about 70 species of dinosaurs and some 25 species of primitive mammals.

Varieties of Claystones. *Argillite* is the name given to extremely compact, nonfissile claystone. At least some argillites are probably slightly metamorphosed claystones in which there has been no development of slaty cleavage. Some argillites are essentially indistinguishable in hand specimen from aphanitic igneous rocks.

Bentonite, claystone formed by alteration of volcanic tuffs, is described in the section on pyroclastic rocks (page 169).

Clay ironstone is a compact brown or dark gray sedimentary rock that consists of siderite with about 30 percent or less clay. It generally occurs as thin layers of nodules or as concretions that are spatially associated with carbon-rich rocks, including coals.

Oil shale is the name applied to shales that contain relatively large percentages of solid organic material that will yield both gaseous and liquid petroleum when the rocks are destructively distilled. They are potential sources of large quantities of petroleum products. Yields as high as 240 gallons of petroleum per ton of shale have been reported for some of the richest oil shales.

Phosphatic shale is any shale that contains abnormally large percentages of phosphorus, generally more than 7.5 percent P_2O_5. Much of the phosphate in these shales appears to have been derived from phosphatic brachiopods, crustaceans, or from the teeth, bones, and/or scales of fish or other vertebrates. Some of it, however, may be of secondary origin—that is, introduced during diagenesis. Phosphatic shales can seldom be distinguished from ordinary shales by megascopic means.

Conglomeratic and brecciatic mudstones may be formed by the lithification of certain glacial tills and of other clay-large clast mixtures such as those deposited by landslides, mudflows, and turbidity currents. In many of these rocks, the pebble-sized and larger clasts "float" in the clay or silty clay matrix. Some geologists refer to these rocks as *diamictites*.

Occurrences of claystones. It has been estimated that approximately 50 percent of all sedimentary rocks are claystones. The parent muds were deposited in such diverse environments as estuaries, lagoons, tidal flats, inland seas, relatively deep marine water, and freshwater lakes (including proglacial lakes). Indeed, shale may be found in most sedimentary rock sequences throughout the world.

Mudstones and argillites are relatively rare. Clay ironstones are fairly common in some coal measures. The Rock of Gibraltar, perhaps the most widely known rock in the world, owes its shape—in fact, its very existence—to the presence of a capping of Jurassic shale. If it were not for the shale, the largely cavernous limestone promontory would have been long since eroded away. Probably the best known oil shale is the Eocene Green River Shale of Wyoming, Colorado, and Utah. Some of the Permian age Phosphoria Formation of Idaho, Montana, Utah, and Wyoming consists of phosphatic shale.

Uses of claystones. In the past, the Sioux Indians used a brownish red claystone to carve into their peace pipes and various other articles. This rock, sometimes called catlinite, occurs at several localities near Pipestone City, Minnesota, and Flandreau, South Dakota. They and other American and African aborigines also used clays and claystones for war paint.

Today, clays and claystones that consist almost entirely of clay minerals are used as pigments, fillers, and as raw material for the manufacture of brick, tile, and other ceramic products. Shales are mixed with limestone and calcined to manufacture cement. Some shales will bloat when heated to high temperatures and the resulting cinder can be used as light weight aggregate in concrete. Oil shales, such as the Eocene age Green River Shale of Wyoming, Utah, and Colorado constitute an estimated petroleum reserve of several hundred billion barrels. Phosphatic shales are mined locally as sources of phosphorus, most of which is used as fertilizer. A number of black shales such as the Cretaceous age Pierre Shale of South Dakota and Nebraska, and the Lower Mississippian Chattanooga Shale of central Tennessee and adjacent states may someday be worked as low grade uranium deposits because in places they contain as much as 0.006 percent Uranium.

CHEMICALLY AND BIOCHEMICALLY DEPOSITED SEDIMENTARY ROCKS

The rocks described under this heading are, with a few noted exceptions, made up either completely or largely of materials that have been formed by chemical precipitation (in some cases as a result of evaporation), by biochemical precipitation, or by flocculation of colloidal suspensions. *Chemical precipitation* occurs when a solution becomes supersaturated with a substance because of a change in the chemical properties of the solution. *Evaporation*, when extensive, frequently causes solution concentrations that promote precipitation. *Biochemical precipitation* is precipitation that takes place either directly or indirectly in response to chemical activities of living organisms. *Flocculation* is the process whereby colloids, which are essentially molecular sized particles in suspension, are deposited, generally as gels that may be desiccated to solid masses of micro- or crypto-crystalline substance.

As already stated in the section dealing with the overall classification of sedimentary and diagenetic rocks, chemical and biochemical sediments that have undergone physical transport within the basin where they were formed as well as those that have not moved since original deposition are included in this category. The coverage is such that limestones of both origins are described first, followed by chert and siliceous sinter, and than by the common evaporites and anhydrock, much of which may be of diagenetic origin.

Clastic Limestones

Many limestones are made up largely of calcium carbonate-rich fragments that have been transported since they were initially precipitated. On the basis of the size of their constituent fragments, these rocks may be called calcirudites, calcarenites or calcilutites—which correspond, respectively, to the already described detrital rocks called conglomerates, sandstones, and silt- or claystones.

Chemically and biochemically precipitated carbonate grains have a special class name—*allochem*. As already implied, some allochems have been deposited and subsequently lithified in place; others have been formed and, prior to lithification, transported and redeposited elsewhere within the basin in which they were formed. There are four distinct kinds of allochems that are common: intraclasts, fossils, oolites (sometimes termed ooliths), and pellets (Figure 5-22). *Intraclasts* are fragments made up of lithified to semi-lithified fragments of calcite or aragonite mud. Most intraclasts are of sand or pebble size; although they may be of just about any shape, most of the larger ones are roughly tabular. *Fossils,* as allochems, include both complete and fragmental skeletal remains. Fragmentation may occur as a result of such processes as wave and current transport or passing through certain animals' digestive tracts. *Oolites* are ellipsoidal masses, typically between 0.2 and 2.0 millimeters in longest diameter, with concentric and/or radial structures. Generally found in tidal environments, most oolites resemble fish roe. *Pellets* are ellipsoidal masses of the same or smaller size than oolites, but with no apparent internal structures. Many pellets are thought to represent fecal material from diverse carbonate mud-ingesting invertebrates; some may be algal spores or nodes. Some geologists apply the term pelletoids to pellets of unknown origin.

A few, probably less than one percent on a world-wide basis, of the fragments termed intraclasts may have been derived from preexisting limestones by mechanical weathering. If a clast is so identified, it should be called a *lithoclast* and recognized as terrigenous detritus. Unless certain fossil contents or other characteristic features are contained in such clasts, however, lithoclasts and intraclasts may be indistinguishable. Thus some geologists use the less specific designation *lime clast.*

In most clastic limestones, the transported allochems are surrounded by an extremely fine-grained carbonate matrix called *micrite* and/or by a coarsely crystalline, typically clear, carbonate cement that is sometimes referred to as *sparite*. Some limestones are almost wholly microcrystalline carbonate and are properly referred to as merely micrites.

Some geologists combine the root terms for the allochems (*intra, bio, oo* or *pel*) and for the matrix materials (*mic* or *spar*) plus or minus the appropriate grain-size stem (*-rudite, -arenite* or *-lutite*) to name rocks of this category—for example, intramicrudite (meaning a breccia made up of intraclasts within a fine-grained matrix), biosparite (a fossiliferous limestone consisting of fossils cemented by coarsely crystalline calcite) and pelmicrite (a pelletiferous calcilutite). An alternative classification scheme, which also includes names

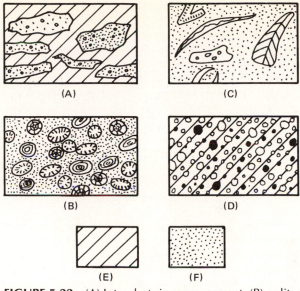

FIGURE 5-22 (A) Intraclasts in sparry cement; (B) oolites ($\sim 3\times$) in microcrystalline calcite (micrite) matrix; (C) fossils in micrite matrix; (D) pellets ($\sim 3\times$) in sparry cement; (E) sparry calcite cement; and (F) micrite matrix.

for limestones made up of nontransported chemical and biochemical calcium carbonates, is given in Table 5-4. As can be seen, that scheme is based primarily on depositional fabric, with the chief concern being whether the constituent grains were or were not in mutual contact when originally deposited. Also, the terms calcirudite, calcarenite or calcilutite plus qualifying adjectives or clarifying phrases can be used—for example, an oolitic calcarenite with a microcrystalline matrix (instead of oomicarenite). We prefer the longer, less cryptic designations.

Clastic limestones may be nearly white, gray, bluish, greenish, reddish, brownish or nearly black in color. They may range from micro- to coarsely crystalline with grains up to a few centimeters across. Some of these limestones are extremely pure calcium carbonate; others are clayey, sandy, dolomitic, glauconitic or some combination of these and thereby grade into calcareous shales, calcareous sandstones, and so forth. Many clastic limestones are fossiliferous and a few consist almost wholly of fossils.

Both natural outcrops and man-made exposures of limestone tend to be rounded because of the relative ease with which limestone dissolves in even weak natural acids, such as rainwater.

Varieties of clastic limestone. *Fossiliferous limestones* may be made up of many different kinds of fossils or of predominantly one or a few species. The latter are often given specific names such as crinoidal or coralline limestone.

Coquina consists of very loosely packed and cemented shell fragments (Figure 5-23). Most coquina is white with some of the constituent shells sporadically stained buff or tan.

Chalk is made up largely of calcareous powder that consists of various mixtures of

TABLE 5-4. Classification of limestones according to depositional texture. Modified after R. J. Dunham, 1962. (With permission of the American Association of Petroleum Geologists.)

Depositional Texture Recognizable					Depositional Texture Not Recognizable
Original components were not bound together during deposition				Original components were bound together during deposition	
Contains mud[a]			Lacks mud[a]		
Mud-supported		Grain-supported	Grain-supported		
Less than 10 per-cent grains	More than 10 per-cent grains				
MUDSTONE	WACKESTONE	PACKSTONE	GRAINSTONE	BOUNDSTONE	CRYSTALLINE CARBONATE[b]

[a] Particles of clay and fine silt size.
[b] To be subdivided according to classifications designed to bear on physical texture or diagenesis.

0   2 cm

FIGURE 5-23 Coquina is the name commonly given to this kind of fossiliferous calci-rudite (or biomicrudite), from St. Augustine, Florida. (B. J. Skinner)

microorganisms. Under the microscope chalks may be seen to include such things as calcareous exoskeletons of foraminiferans, plates and discs of algae, plus or minus some minor percentage of siliceous diatoms, radiolarians, and/or sponge spicules. Most chalk is white but some is gray, buff, or flesh colored. Typically, it is friable and rather porous. Nodules of dark gray chert (flint) occur in many chalk formations.

Oolitic limestone typically consists almost wholly of calcium carbonate oolites.

Lithographic limestone is the name applied to dense, homogeneous, extremely fine-grained limestones that are typically pale creamy to buff or light gray in color and tend to break along conchoidal fractures. Whether these limestones consist of precipitated calcium carbonate mud, of extremely fine bioclastic fragments, or of some combination of the two, can rarely be determined megascopically.

Occurrences of clastic limestones. Clastic limestones ranging in age from Precambran to Recent occur in thick sequences of marine sedimentary rocks throughout the world. With a little searching in areas underlain by such bedrock, several varieties of limestone can usually be found.

One of the world's most famous fossiliferous limestones is the Eocene aged rock used as the facing stone for the Great Pyramid of Cheops near Giza, Egypt. It is reported that tests of a foraminifer, nummulites, within a matrix of fine-grained comminuted fossil debris make up most of the 2.5 million two-ton blocks that were used.

Chalks are especially common in formations of Cretaceous Age. In fact, the name Cretaceous comes from the Latin word *creta,* which means chalk. Exemplary Cretaceous chalk formations are the famous White Cliffs of Dover in England; the similar high bluffs of eastern Denmark (e.g., Stevns and Møns klints); the Selma Chalk of Alabama, Mississippi and Tennessee; and the Niobrara and Fort Hays chalk formations of Nebraska and Kansas.

One of the best known coquinas—mainly because of its widespread use in introductory geology teaching laboratories—is that from the Pliocene and more recent formations of southeastern Florida. For the same reason, and also because it is used widely as a trimstone, the Mississippian age Indiana Limestone from the vicinity of Bedford in southern Indiana is an especially well known oolitic limestone.

The Jurassic age Solenhofen Limestone of Bavaria is a world famous lithographic limestone. It is known not only because of its former use in high-quality lithography but also because of its remarkable fossil preservation. Approximately 500 species have been discovered including insects, jelly fish and even impressions of fleshy parts and bird feathers (Figure 5-24).

Uses of clastic limestones. Limestones constitute one of the most widely used rock materials. The following gives the more important uses plus a few exemplary lesser uses.

Limestone is used widely as road metal, as aggregate for both macadam and concrete mixes, and as building stone. The already mentioned Indiana Limestone is used for statuary as well as for trimstone. The Middle Ordovician age Holston Limestone from Knoxville, Tennessee, is an example of the many limestones that take a good polish and are marketed under the incorrect term *marble* (see page 253). Another misnomer is the light buff to gray colored Tennessee marble, which contains striking stylolites, that has been used as sanitary enclosures in so many public lavatories in North America.

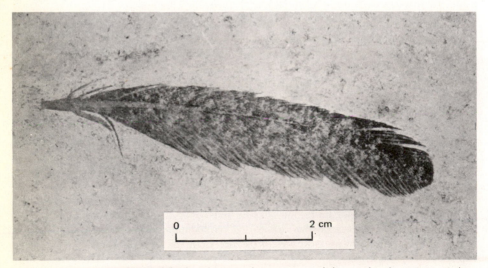

0   2 cm

FIGURE 5-24   Impression of feather from Archaeoptryx, in lithographic limestone, Solenhofen, Bavaria. (John Ostrom)

Limestone is used as a flux in many open-hearth iron smelters. It is one of the basic raw materials for the manufacture of Portland cement. It is the chief source for chemical lime and is ground for use as agricultural lime. It is used as the inert ingredient in some pharmaceutical materials. It is also ground and pressed to make blackboard chalk.

Nonclastic Limestones

Chemically and biochemically precipitated calcitic and/or aragonitic materials that have not been transported since original deposition comprise the rocks of this subclass. These limestones have been formed in both marine and nonmarine environments.

One group of marine limestones that belongs to this group has already been described under the preceding heading "Clastic Limestones." These are the limestones that are made up of oolites and/or pellets or, in rare cases, even fossils that have not been transported laterally since deposition. Actually, in most cases, the matter of whether these allochems have or have not been transported is difficult, if not impossible, to ascertain. In any case, the descriptive terms applied to the corresponding clastic limestones are generally also used for this kind of nonclastic limestones.

Other rocks of this nonclastic limestone subclass are named on the basis of their textures and/or modes of formation.

Reef rocks. In many instances, the remains of active reef-building organisms and/or the products of sediment-binding organisms have been bound together since deposition. Included are biohermal *reef limestones* and algal mat *stromatolitic limestones*.

Reef limestones are products of communities of marine organisms, most of which have secreted calcareous skeletal matter. Among the organisms that have been primarily responsible for the construction of different reef rocks are algae, corals, bryozoans, foraminiferans, and mollusks. The resulting rocks generally consist largely of a framework of loosely knit, intergrown skeletal matter, most of which is still in its original, respective growth position. The rocks are commonly full of open spaces that are either coated with fine calcite crystals or filled or partially filled with sediment. Many reef rocks appear, at first glance, to be highly fossiliferous breccias.

Stomatolitic limestones exhibit fine laminae, typically a couple of millimeters or less thick, that have the shapes of various convex-upward, hemispherical forms, such as those of inverted shallow bowls and bulbous cabbageheads. The laminae are composed predominately of calcareous clasts, ranging from clay to fine sand size, that have been trapped and bound together by an algal mat. In essence, then, the lamination is merely stratification that has been modified by shallow water algal activities. In most stromatolitic limestones, the laminations are different shades of gray, apparently reflecting different organic matter contents.

Primarily because of their importance to petroleum production, these rocks have been studied rather intensively. As an indirect consequence, several terms have been applied to them. Along with those mentioned in the preceding paragraphs are the more general terms, biolithite and boundstone (see Table 5-4).

Travertine. Solution-deposited calcite and/or aragonite in caves or around springs and seeps, is called travertine. In caves, travertine forms stalactites, stalagmites, and other dripstone formations (Figure 5-25). On the surface, where it is sometimes called *calcareous tufa*, travertine forms flow stone with diverse shapes and commonly encloses vegetation, such as fallen leaves. On freshly broken surfaces, travertine is white, tan, yellowish,

FIGURE 5-25 Cave travertine approximately 6 meters high, Luray, Virginia. (Courtesy of Luray Caverns, Virginia.)

creamy, or some combination of these colors, typically banded. On weathered surfaces it is generally dirty gray in color. Travertine ranges from dense and compact to porous, cellular, or spongy and from microcrystalline to very coarsely crystalline. Some geologists restrict the term travertine to the dense varieties and apply the term calcareous tufa to the porous and cellular varieties. Mexican onyx is the name frequently applied to a dense, translucent, and commonly banded variety of travertine that takes a good polish. Most travertine is apparently chemically precipitated. Some calcareous tufa appears to be bio-chemical in that it is thought that its precipitation has been enhanced by activities of fresh water algae.

Marl. Marl is a variously defined term that is applied to many different materials. Generally it is used for loosely consolidated, earthy-appearing mixtures that consist largely of calcium carbonate and clay. Included are such diverse rocks and deposits as shell and clay mixtures (shell marl), slightly indurated calcareous sands (sandy marl and glauconitic marl), fresh water bog lime, and even poorly cemented argillaceous limestones. We think that if the term is used at all, it should be restricted for use as a gross field designation.

Occurrences of chemically precipitated limestones. Reef rock masses ranging in size from a meter or so up to more than 1000 meters across and more than 100 meters thick occur in many marine sequences of Paleozoic and later age. Some noteworthy examples in North America are the Silurian age Niagaran reefs of the Great Lakes Region, the oil-bearing Devonian reefs of Alberta, the Mississippian and Pennsylvania age biohermal reefs of New Mexico, and the Permian complex reefs of the Guadalupe Mountains of Texas and New Mexico. Stromatolitic limestones that range from Precambrian to Recent in age, appear to be best developed in Precambrian and Early Paleozoic age rocks. One frequently cited example is a stromatolitic reef, measuring approximately 65 meters across and 20 meters thick, that occurs near Great Slave Lake in the Northwest Territories of Canada.

Most known travertine deposits are of Pleistocene or Recent age. They are relatively common in areas of hot springs (e.g., in Yellowstone National Park, Wyoming) and in regions where there are caves (e.g., in the Appalachian Valley and Ridge and the Allegheny Plateau provinces of the eastern United States). In caves, at least some of the precipitation appears to take place as a result of a change in partial pressure of CO_2 rather than as a consequence of evaporation.

Marls of diverse compositions are especially common among the loosely consolidated Cenozoic age sediments of the Atlantic Coastal Plain sequence. Bog lime occurs in many fresh water lakes—for example, those of the upper midwestern United States and adjacent Canada—where some plants (e.g., *Chara*) produce calcium carbonate in their fruits, leaves and stems.

Uses of nonclastic limestone. Reef rock limestones have many of the same uses already listed for clastic limestones. Travertine, especially that from Tivoli, Italy, has been used as a building material since ancient times—for example, many buildings of ancient Rome, including the exterior of the Colosseum (*amphitheatrum Flavium*), were made of this rock. It is still being widely used as an interior accent stone. So-called Mexican onyx, most of which is from the area just southeast of Pueblo, Mexico, is carved into ornaments and marketed throughout the world. Marl has been used both as a fertilizer and in the manufacture of Portland cement.

Cherts and Siliceous Sinter

Although much chert appears to be of diagenetic origin, some cherts, like the already described limestones, are of chemical or biochemical origin. Like their biochemical and chemical limestone analogs, these cherts may be either clastic or nonclastic, but this aspect is seldom discernible. Siliceous sinter is analogous to calcareous tufa.

Chemical chert. Some cherts may have been formed as the result of the flocculation of colloidal silica. One present-day occurrence of colloidal silica is on the deep ocean floor of, for example, the central Pacific and in a belt between approximately 45 and 60 degrees south latitude, nearly encircling Antarctica. The general characteristics of chert are described under diagenetic rocks (page 217).

Biochemical chert. These cherts, most of which were originally made up of opaline silica, consist predominantly of microscopic diatoms, radiolarian tests and/or sponge spicules. On the basis of microscopic examination these cherts would be called, for example, *radiolarian chert* or *diatomaceous chert* (or diatomite).

Diatomaceous earth is a name widely applied to a loosely coherent, chalklike sediment made up of fragmentary and complete shells of diatoms (Figure 5-26). Diatoms are free-swimming, one-celled aquatic plants that secrete microscopic, opaline-silica shells. To give an indication of their size, it has been calculated that a thumb-sized piece of

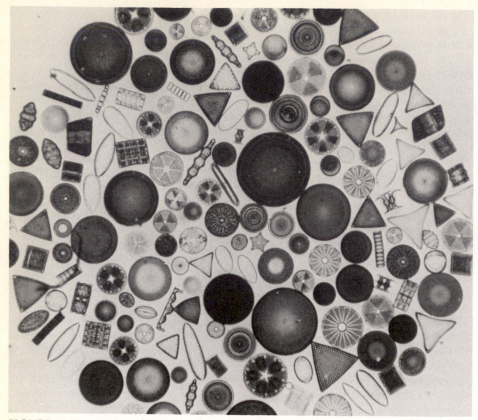

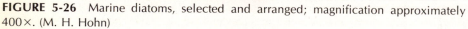

FIGURE 5-26   Marine diatoms, selected and arranged; magnification approximately 400×. (M. H. Hohn)

diatomaceous earth would contain about a quarter of a billion diatom shells. The material is typically white but may be pale yellow, gray, or tan in color. It is generally so light that it will float on water. Diatomaceous earth can be distinguished from chalk because it does not effervesce with acid, and from clay by its lack of a clayey odor when breathed on.

Siliceous sinter. Opaline silica is sometimes precipitated by the hot waters issuing from hot springs and geysers. The general name for the resulting rock material is siliceous sinter; that deposited from geysers is often called *geyserite*.

When pure, opaline silica is white. More commonly, it is variously tinted because of the presence of diverse impurities. Most siliceous sinters occur as incrustations around the orifices of springs or geysers and range from loose to compact and from porous to fairly dense. Deposits of siliceous sinter are in several ways the siliceous analogs of deposits of calcareous tufa. Siliceous sinter occurs along with calcareous tufa in Yellowstone National Park, Wyoming.

Occurrences and uses of cherts. Some of the silicic oozes being deposited in the ocean basins today consist largely of radiolarian tests. The Mesozoic age Franciscan Chert of California is a fine example of a radiolarian chert. Other well-known radiolarian cherts are present in the Lower Carboniferous section of Great Britain and Germany and in the Jurassic rocks of the Austrian Alps.

Diatomaceous earth occurs widely in fresh water lake deposits. In fact, at nearly all latitudes there are swamp deposits that include layers of diatomaceous earth. In addition, diatomaceous earth and diatomite of marine origin comprise a nearly 1600 meters thick Miocene age formation that crops out in the Coast Ranges of southern California. The correlative Monterey Chert of central California is a diatom-rich sediment that has been altered to chert.

Diatomite, mostly from the Lompoc District of Santa Barbara County, California, is used rather widely as an insulating material, a polishing agent, a filler, and as a filter for many purposes.

Evaporites

Evaporites, as already implied, are formed when an aqueous solution is totally or in a large measure evaporated. Although evaporites have been formed from inland lake water as well as from seawater, most of the really extensive deposits have been formed from seawater. Therefore, evaporites deposited in former lake basins are not described as such in this book. Suffice it to say that each rock formed by lake evaporation is generally referred to by the name of its predominant mineral constituent—for example, glauberite, mirabilite, and trona.

The fundamental constituents of evaporites are the ions which were dissolved in the water that was evaporated. In seawater, the most common ions are sodium Na^{+1}, calcium Ca^{+2}, chlorine Cl^{-1}, sulfate $(SO_4)^{-2}$, and carbonate $(CO_3)^{-2}$. When evaporation takes place, salts are deposited in a predictable order that is controlled by both the solubilities of the salts and the ever changing composition of the solution. The order for typical seawater is calcite or aragonite (limestone), gypsum and/or anhydrite (gyprock and/or anhydrock), halite (rock salt), and then the relatively rare salts of magnesium, potassium, and the other ions present, also in a set order. In general, however, evaporite deposits exhibit relationships that clearly show that interruptions and repetitions occurred during their deposition. In some basins the latter relationships are interpreted by some geologists as related to some cyclic phenomenon.

There are a number of especially noteworthy problems associated with the evaporites. Perhaps the most puzzling ones relate to their tremendous thicknesses. Consider, for example, that total evaporation of typical seawater with a depth of more than 100 meters would yield only about 0.08 meters of gypsum and 1.4 meters of halite, yet several known deposits are hundreds of meters thick. To date, the only reasonable suggestion to account for such thicknesses involves basins in which the rate of evaporation is equal to or exceeds the rate of inflowing solution.

Another question relates to the fact that in many evaporite deposits the proportions of the evaporites differ markedly from those that would be logically expected from evaporation of a column of seawater.

Also, there is the already posed question as to whether or not anhydrock may be of diagenetic origin. Briefly stated, some geologists have interpreted certain field relationships, such as the presence of gypsum at shallow depths and of anhydrock deeper down within the same individual deposits, to indicate that gypsum was the originally deposited sulfate and that the anhydrock was formed by subsequent diagenetic dehydration of the gypsum. The often suggested process involves reflux activity of circulating pore solutions. A few geologists, however, still appear to favor the older hypothesis, whereby at least some anhydrock is produced by evaporation, just as gyprock is. We subscribe to the hypothesis involving diagenesis. Nevertheless, we describe both rocks in this section in order to facilitate comparing and contrasting them with each other and to avoid duplication of statements about them.

Carbonate evaporites. Some limestones and dolostones have very likely been formed as evaporites. Unfortunately, most of them cannot be recognized as such by megascopic examination. Some have been interpreted as evaporites because of some definitive field relationship. Others have been so interpreted on the basis of containing crystals of some typical evaporite mineral—for example, the fine grained Silurian limestones of the Michigan basin that contain cavities that appear to have once been occupied by halite crystals, which are thought to have been deposited along with the parent calcaneous sediment.

General descriptions of limestones and dolostones are on pages 204 and 217, respectively.

Gyprock and anhydrock. These two rocks are made up predominantly of gypsum and anhydrite, respectively. Some geologists prefer to call the rocks as well as the minerals by the mineral names. Others call them rock gypsum and rock anhydrite, by analogy to rock salt.

Both rocks are typically white, but may be yellowish to reddish brown or gray in color, and consist of granular or interlocking grains. Most anhydrock is fine- to medium-grained and relatively homogeneous or finely laminated. Gyprock may be fine- to coarse-grained and either homogeneous or texturally heterogeneous, containing such features as sporadic fibrous aggregates (selenite) with the overall appearance of cross-fiber veins. Fairly large gypsum crystals, apparently formed by recrystallization and/or hydration, may occur in either gyprock or anhydrock, giving the rocks a porphyritic or porphyroblastic appearance (pages 108 and 242). Both gyprock and anhydrock may occur interlaminated with rock salt, dolostone, shale, or mudstone (commonly bituminous in nature). Some geologists have interpreted the paired layers as representing varves (annual deposits). Both rocks also commonly occur as nodules within shale, thereby comprising breccia-like mixtures sometimes referred to as chicken-wire arrangements (Figure 5-27). Some gyprock exhibits highly contorted layering thought to represent volume increases that took place in response to hydration of preexisting anhydrock. Apparently different diagenetic processes may cause the gypsum-anhydrite conversion to go in different directions.

Gyprock may be distinguished from anhydrock and also from similarly appearing limestones and dolostones by its inferior hardness. Anhydrock may be distinguished from limestones and dolostones by its lack of effervescence with dilute hydrochloric acid.

Occurrences of gyprock and anhydrock. Gyprock and anhydrock of various ages are widely distributed throughout the world. They are generally associated with each other and with rock salt, dolostone, limestone, and shale in marine sequences. The caprock of many salt domes consists of anhydrock with or without gyprock and/or sulfur-bearing limestone. The sulfur is formed diagenetically as the result of the reduction of calcium sulfate by subsurface anaerobic bacteria of the genus *Desulfovibrio*.

Perhaps the best known commercial gyprock deposits in North America are those in the Silurian age Salina Formation of western New York, Pennsylvania, eastern Ohio, and northern West Virginia; in the same unit and also in some of the Devonian and Mississippian formations of the Michigan Basin of Lower Michigan and adjacent southern On-

FIGURE 5-27   Nodular gyprock in shale, from Alabaster, Iosco County, Michigan. (R. V. Dietrich)

tario; and in the Permian Castile formation of western Texas, adjacent New Mexico, and Mexico. There also is noteworthy production of gypsum from beds ranging in age from Mississippian to Jurassic in Nova Scotia, southwestern Virginia, western Kansas, and southern California. The Rann of Cutch in western India is a well-known present-day saltpan in which evaporites are being deposited.

Uses of gyprock and anhydrock. Gyprock has several uses. Probably its best known use is in the manufacture of plaster of Paris and, of course, of plaster board. It also is frequently used where soft fillers are needed (e.g., in crayons) and very locally as a fertilizer, generally called land plaster. Some high quality white or variously tinted fine-grained gyprocks, usually referred to as *alabaster,* were used as interior facing stones and for small statues and carved decorative objects found in Egyptian pyramids. Today, replicas and modern art objects made from alabaster are widely marketed in either their natural color or stained.

Rock salt. Rock salt is made up almost wholly of the mineral halite. It typically consists of a granular aggregate or mosaic of coarsely crystalline grains, ranging from 5 to 100 millimeters across. The grains may be transparent or translucent, colorless, or some tint of blue or orange. Halite is commonly admixed or interlaminated with gypsum, anhydrite, and/or clay. The taste of rock salt is characteristic and serves to distinguish it from all other rocks.

Occurrences of rock salt. The occurrences given for gyprock and anhydrock also pertain to salt. The aforementioned Salina Basin, which underlies an area of more than 2.5 million square kilometers, is estimated to contain about 185 million tons of rock salt.

The salt is reported to have a total thickness of about 95 meters at Syracuse, New York, and about 180 meters at Detroit, Michigan and Windsor, Ontario.

In addition, salt underlies domes that are the surficial expressions of masses of salt that have been intruded upward from their parent strata into the overlying formations. Most salt domes are nearly circular in plan and generally less than a couple miles in diameter. They are well-known features along the Gulf Coast of Louisiana, Texas, and Mexico.

Uses of rock salt. Archeological evidence indicates that a salt deposit in Nevada was worked nearly 3000 years ago. Historical records show that one of the Romanian salt mines has been worked nearly continuously since the early days of the Roman Empire.

Today, salt is mined as rock salt; is recovered from subsurface brines, both natural and artificially produced; and is precipitated from seawater channeled into man-made salt pans. It is marketed as either a solid or as brine. The best known uses of salt are for seasoning and preserving food and to inhibit freezing on highways and walkways. In addition, salt is required for many different purposes in the chemical, metallurgical, ceramics, and agricultural industries as well as in the field of medicine. Currently, there is much debate about the possible future use of abandoned salt mines to store nuclear wastes.

DIAGENETIC ROCKS

Diagenesis, as defined on page 175, includes all the low temperature changes that take place in sediments prior to, and commonly contributing to, their lithification. The rocks we include in this category are those that have formed as a result of low-temperature recrystallization and/or replacement of original materials in the parent sediment. Strictly speaking then, diagenetic processes and the resulting rocks are transitional between those generally agreed upon as sedimentary and those defined as metamorphic. The basis for subdividing and naming diagenetic rocks is their mineralogical composition.

Limestones

Calcium carbonate rocks formed by recrystallization of preexisting lime sediments or limestones occur in both unmetamorphosed and metamorphosed sequences of rocks. Those in sedimentary sequences are diagenetic limestones; those in metamorphic sequences are marbles. In general, megascopically recognizable recrystallization is indicated by relatively large interlocking crystals. In some rocks the recrystallized grains transect original sedimentary features such as bedding laminae or boundaries between fossils and their matrixes. In others, recrystallization has destroyed all or most of the original sedimentary features.

As previously noted, limestones can be distinguished from similarly appearing anhydrocks and dolostones by checking their reaction to dilute hydrochloric acid. Contrariwise, as already implied, it is extremely difficult (if not impossible) to distinguish some recrystallized limestones from similarly appearing marbles unless their occurrences are known.

Occurrences and uses of limestones. Occurrences and uses listed under the clastic limestones on pages 206 and 207 apply. In fact, the so-called Tennessee marble that is mentioned there appears to be a fine example of diagenetic recrystallization.

Dolostones

Some geologists call the rock, as well as the mineral, dolomite. That usage is confusing and should be abandoned. In any case, dolostones consist predominantly of dolomite.

Although a few dolostones may consist of dolomite that was either chemically or biochemically precipitated, most exhibit features that indicate their replacement origin. The coarse-grained textures of some dolostones appear best explained by recrystallization. It is because of features such as these, along with considerations of laboratory data relating to dolomite synthesis, that dolostone is placed in the diagenetic rock category.

Dolostones may have the same colors, grain sizes, and textures as limestones (see page 204). Therefore, except when one is familiar with a certain rock to the point that its identity is known, dolostones cannot be distinguished megascopically from limestones until they are checked for reactions with cold, dilute hydrochloric acid. Pure dolomite reacts only when powdered or freshly scratched and then only with a slow smouldering effervescence; calcite, on the other hand, effervesces briskly. Along with some fairly pure limestones and dolostones, however, there are many rocks that are mixtures of the two minerals and these tend to give ambiguous or misleading reactions. As outlined in Chapter 2, staining techniques have been developed to distinguish between the two minerals in such rocks. Fortunately for the field geologist, in many areas, even the relatively fine-grained mixtures can be directly recognized megascopically because the two minerals react differently to weathering processes. In many areas, for example, weathered surfaces of dolomite resemble a chamois cloth.

Dolostones can be distinguished from similarly appearing anhydrocks by the acid tests. Just as is true for limestones and calcitic marbles, however, field relationships must be known if one is to distinguish between handspecimens of some dolostones and similarly appearing dolomite marbles.

Occurrences of dolostones. Considering the likelihood that many dolostones are formed by replacement of preexisting calcium carbonate sediments, it is not surprising that most dolostones have the same range of occurrences as limestones. Perhaps the best known locality for dolostones is the Dolomite Alps of the eastern Tyrol of southwestern Austria and northern Italy. Dolostones are also common in the Ordovician rocks of the folded Appalachians and they are the predominant constituent of the Silurian rocks of the famous Niagara escarpment that rims so much of the Great Lakes shoreline.

Uses of dolostones. Dolostones are used for crushed stone and as dimension stone, especially as rough facing stone. Some of the so-called commercial marbles are actually dolostones. Relatively pure dolostones are being used more and more in lieu of limestones as fluxes in iron blast furnaces. This use is based on the fact that the slag produced when dolostones are used will not slake and thus can be used as lightweight aggregate. Dolostones are also used as sources for both chemical and agricultural magnesium, as conditioners, and as inert fillers. Dead-burned dolostones are crushed and used as a refractory material; calcined dolostones are used as soft abrasives.

Cherts

Cherts are made up of microcrystalline and/or cryptocrystalline quartz with or without opaline silica. As already mentioned, cherts appear to be of several different origins.

Most cherts are white, gray, or tan in color. Some, however, are pink, red, yellowish, greenish, bluish, brown, or black and some specimens may even be banded—for example, concentrically arranged white and gray. Cherts appear microcrystalline in hand specimen and have lusters ranging from subvitreous through porcelaneous to dull. Most cherts are dense and have conchoidal or splintery fractures. The hardness (~7) distinguishes cherts from rocks such as obsidian and the aphanitic felsites, which some cherts may roughly resemble.

When a chert contains inclusions of other minerals, for example, dolomite or calcite, that fact is noted by the use of adjectives to give names such as dolomitic chert. One fairly common impurity is dolomite that commonly occurs as isolated rhombohedral crystals. On weathered surfaces, the crystals are usually etched out to leave cavities called *dolomolds* (Figure 5-28).

Chert also is present in minor amounts in other rocks so that the rocks are termed cherty—for example, cherty limestone.

Varieties of chert. *Flint* is the term for tough, dark gray to black chert that was widely used by aborigines for tools and weapons. There is good evidence that flint was so used at least 25,000 years ago and that at least 14,000 years ago Neolithic inhabitants of Great Britain actually dug shaft mines into the Cretaceous chalk to obtain unweathered flint nodules.

Jasper is the name often applied to red, yellowish or brownish colored, ferruginous chert. It is commonly, but not always, associated with iron ore. The similar term *jasperoid* has been applied to silicified limestones in the Tri-State zinc mining district of Missouri, Kansas, and Oklahoma.

Fossiliferous cherts are of two main types: those, already mentioned, that consist of originally siliceous biochemically deposited materials (diatom shells, radiolarian tests, or sponge spicules) and those made up of fossils that have their present composition because of silica replacement. Only the latter belong in this diagenetic rock subcategory. Some of these fossiliferous cherts contain macrofossils that may be easily recognized and identified megascopically.

Oolitic chert consists of siliceous oolites in a chert matrix. In some of these cherts, some of the oolites have quartz grains as cores and thus are thought to be concretionary. Most chert oolites, however, are probably calcium carbonate that has been diagenetically replaced by microcrystalline silica.

Novaculite is the name given to a white to pale-gray colored, bedded chert from Arkansas that once was widely marketed for use as hone stones. At least some novaculite may be thermally metamorphosed, radiolarian chert.

Porcelanite is the name sometimes applied to impure cherts with fractured surfaces that resemble unglazed porcelain. The most common impurities are calcite, clay, silt, or tuffaceous particles.

Tripoli is the name given to predominantly chalcedony rocks that appear to represent impure calcite- and/or dolomite-bearing cherts from which the carbonates have been leached. It is sometimes called rottenstone. It may be of just about any color but is most commonly gray, buff, or reddish. Most tripoli has a harsh feel.

Occurrences of cherts. The two most common occurrences of chert are as nodules in limestones and dolostones (See Figure 5-29) and as layers interbedded with carbonaceous shales, phosphorites, or altered submarine basalts. Some chert nodules exhibit a roughly concentric color banding. Although the nodules may be of just about any shape,

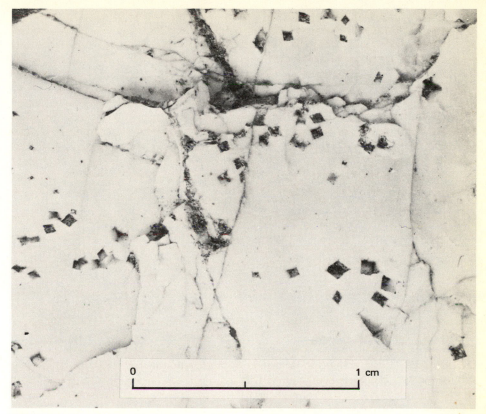

FIGURE 5-28 Dolomolds in dense white chert. Cambro-Ordovician aged Copper Ridge Formation, Mountain Lake Road, Giles County, Virginia. (R. V. Dietrich)

most are more or less disc-shaped and have their long dimensions parallel to bedding. Typically, the nodules are concentrated in certain layers or zones. In many places, nodules of one horizon may be seen to be bridged to nodules in other horizons. At some localities, nodules may be seen to coalesce to form irregular layers. Some bedded cherts have sharp boundaries with their adjacent formations; others grade imperceptibly into them. A few bedded chert units have been reported to be several hundreds of meters thick.

Chert nodules are relatively common in carbonate rocks of all geological ages. Among the better known are those of Cambro-Ordovician age in the Appalachians, of the Silurian-aged Niagaran Group of the upper midwestern United States, and of the Mississippian-aged Ste. Genevieve Limestone in the midcontinent area. Several of the Appalachian cherts are oolitic. Perhaps the best known flint occurs as nodules in Cretaceous chalks of western Europe. Bedded chert occurs in many sequences—for example, in the Ordovician age Normanskill Formation of central New York, the Devonian Woodford Formation of Oklahoma, and the Permian Phosphoria Formation of Idaho and Montana, and as the predominant rock of the Jurassic aged Franciscan Chert and the Miocene Monterey chert of California.

FIGURE 5-29 Chert nodules in dolostone (same location as Figure 5-28). The key is approximately 5 centimeters long. (R. V. Dietrich)

Novaculite of Middle Paleozoic Age occurs in the Ouachita River Region of western Arkansas, and in adjacent Oklahoma and Texas.

Tripoli occurs locally in several areas of the United States. An especially noteworthy deposit is near Seneca in southwestern Missouri.

Uses of cherts. Cherts have found little use other than for tools, weapons, flints in flintlocks, and jewelry. In a few instances, however, cherts have been used in lieu of sand or sandstone as the source of silica in the production of vitrified bricks. Actually, some ceramic engineers consider cherts to be preferable for certain ceramic uses because they are more reactive than coarsely crystalline quartz. Novaculite, which means razor stone in Latin, formerly found extensive use as a hone for sharpening razors, knives, and so forth. Tripoli has been recovered and marketed for such uses as cleaning and polishing metals and stones, and also as an inert and chemically stable filler.

Phosphorite

Rocks made up largely of microscopic or submicroscopic fluorapatite and other phosphate minerals are called phosphorite or, less often, rock phosphate or phosphate rock. Like chert, phosphorites may be of diverse origins, including chemical and biochemical precipitation as well as by replacement.

Phosphorite is black or brownish, has a dull luster and appears either microcrystalline or, if constituted by oolites, granular. Some phosphorites contain such materials as shell fragments, hydrocarbons, calcite, dolomite, marcasite, clay, and chert. Phosphorite may be distinguished from limestones and dolostones, which it resembles, by employing the acid test. Phosphorite does not effervesce with cold, dilute hydrochloric acid. In addition, with a little practice, the higher specific gravity of phosphorite ($\sim$3.1 versus $\sim$2.7 and $\sim$2.85 for limestone and dolostone, respectively) can be readily recognized by hefting. Also, on weathered surfaces phosphorite commonly exhibits a bluish white skin.

The phosphorus of phosphorites is probably largely derived by solution of animal excreta. Some phosphorites may even have been formed wholly as a result of biochemical precipitation. Others contain phosphatic materials obviously formed by replacement of preexisting calcium carbonate sediments. Such replacement appears to have occurred penecontemporaneously with sedimentation and/or during diagenesis.

Occurrences of phosphorite. Phosphorite occurs as layers up to 2 meters thick in the Permian Phosphoria Formation of Idaho, Montana, Utah, Wyoming, and southern Alberta. Other concentrations of phosphatic materials occur at several North American localities such as in Marion and Polk counties, Florida and in eastern South Carolina and central Tennessee. The largest phosphorite deposits discovered so far are in northern Africa.

Uses of phosphorite. Phosphatic rocks and deposits are used principally in the production of fertilizers and in the chemical industry. The world's largest production is from Algeria, Morocco, and Tunisia. The phosphate-rich rocks of Florida, South Carolina, and of the Phosphoria Formation may someday become important sources of uranium. Although the deposits are of very low grade, over 500 million tons of uranium are estimated to be present.

Glauconitic Sandstones

Sand-size sedimentary rocks that consist of 25 or more percent glauconite pellets are generally called greensands or, less commonly, green sandstones. Many of these rocks also contain noteworthy percentages of shell fragments.

Some glauconite is thought to be of marine, biochemical origin, probably representing fecal pellets. Most of it, however, very likely represents calcium carbonate pellets that have undergone diagenetic replacement on the sea floor.

Sandstones made up largely of glauconite are distinctly green; those with lesser percentages of glauconite tend to have a salt and pepper appearance. Upon weathering, some glauconite tends to turn orange-yellow in color.

Occurrences and uses of glauconitic sandstones. Poorly consolidated glauconitic sandstone (greensand) beds are relatively common in the Cretaceous and Tertiary formations of the Atlantic Coastal Plain wedge of sediments of the eastern United States. Sporadic layers of glauconitic sandstones and other glauconite-bearing sedimentary rocks occur in marine sequences throughout the world.

Greensands of the Atlantic Coastal Plain, especially from Cretaceous beds of New Jersey, have been used locally as fertilizers because glauconite gives the rock relatively high potassium and phosphorus contents. They also are used as water softeners because they have high base exchange capacities and regenerate rapidly.

Sedimentary and Diagenetic Ores
The term sedimentary ore is often applied to certain sedimentary and diagenetic rocks that contain unusually high contents of iron, manganese, lead, zinc, and/or copper. Only a few of the rocks are ores in the sense that they are sufficiently rich to be mined and processed for their metal contents. In the generic sense, the term is therefore a misnomer.

Iron formations. Any sedimentary rock containing more than 15 percent iron is termed an iron formation. The term is cumbersome and includes rocks of many different origins. Most are chemical sedimentary rocks and contain, as their principal iron minerals, limonite, hematite, magnetite, siderite, chamosite, or greenalite. Some that contain pyrite, pyrrhotite or marcasite, are clearly diagenetic rocks because the iron minerals have formed after deposition of the host sediment. Many have undergone metamorphism (see page 258). Iron formations are typically, but not necessarily, thin-bedded, commonly with interlayers of chert and an iron mineral (Figure 5-30). Cherty iron formation is more common in Precambrian age sequences. Carbonate-rich iron formation, much of it oolitic, is more common in later sequences.

There is a certain amount of disagreement as to exactly how most of the iron formations were formed. Among the important processes contributing to the formation of at least some iron formations are chemical and biochemical precipitation, replacement dur-

0   20 cm

FIGURE 5-30 Precambrian banded iron formation from Transvaal System, South Africa. Chert-rich bands (light gray) alternate with hematite-rich bands (dark gray). (B. J. Skinner)

ing diagenesis, low-grade metamorphic reactions, and residual concentration during weathering. Table 5-5 summarizes data for some of the most important iron formations.

Manganese ore. Analogous to iron formations, manganese-rich rocks are encountered in many sedimentary environments. The primary manganese minerals, all of which contain manganese in its most oxidized (Mn^{+4}) state, are pyrolusite, psilomelane, cryptomelane, birnessite, and todorokite. All the manganese minerals apparently form as chemical precipitates when a solution containing Mn^{+2} is oxidized. Manganese-rich sediments form in three principal environments: first, as thin, cherty beds, interlayered with submarine volcanic rocks, typically basaltic in composition; second, as a carbonate and/or organic-rich sediments deposited under shallow water conditions; and third, as nodular growths (Figure 5-31) on lake bottoms and on the deep-sea floor.

Copper-lead-zinc ores. There is no certain, confirming evidence to prove that copper, lead or zinc minerals precipitate as primary chemical sediments. Considerable evidence exists to support the notion that the minerals are formed during diagenesis.

Copper, lead, and zinc diagenetic ores are typically thin-bedded, originally clastic sediments that are rich in organic matter and carbonates as well as containing up to 20 percent of copper, lead, and zinc sulfide minerals. The most important minerals are chalcocite, chalcopyrite, bornite, galena, and sphalerite. Pyrite is a common associate mineral.

Occurrences and use of sedimentary and diagenetic ores. Some of the sedimentary and diagenetic iron formations, many of which have undergone metamorphism, are of

FIGURE 5-31 Photograph of a field of ferromanganese nodules on Pacific Ocean floor at −5320 meters M. S. L. (Lamont-Doherty Observatory of Columbia University)

TABLE 5-5   Sedimentary and diagenetic iron ores (not including placers and glauconite)

Chief Mineral(s)	Common Features	Depositional Environment	Examples and/or Remarks
Goethite	Oolites ± concentrically banded chamosite	In marshy environments close to water table (e.g., in bogs)	Principle mineral of many post-Precambrian deposits; Jurassic of Europe; in many glacial lakes; as hardpans
Hematite	Oolites (some with sand cores); replaced fossils; commonly interbedded with chert (magnetite is common); may have ripple marks, mudcracks, and so forth.	Oxidizing, shallow marine	Precambrian with chert; Silurian fossil ore (Clinton)
Magnetite	Impure layers interlayered with chert	Oxidizing, shallow marine; many deposits have undergone mild metamorphism	Mostly Precambrian; probably metamorphic, possibly diagenetic
Siderite ± ankerite	Spherulites, disseminated; abundant in Fe-bearing sediments; concretions (and clay ironstones); typically altered to limonite in outcrop	In presence of organic matter, e.g., bogs (including brackish swamps)	Many in Gogebic and Marquette districts (Michigan); as ironstone in coals and shales–especially of Carboniferous age
Chamosite or greenalite	May be primary; stilpnomelane often present; oolitic to compact	Shallow marine, *not* strongly oxidizing	Wabana, Newfoundland (in part)

TABLE 5-5   Sedimentary and diagenetic iron ores (not including placers and glauconite) (continued)

Chief Mineral(s)	Common Features	Depositional Environment	Examples and/or Remarks
Pyrite/marcasite	Bedded with black shale; scattered crystals; disseminated 'dust'; replacing fossils, nodules, and so forth.	Swamps and other shallow water reducing environments (stagnant marine/ brackish) usually diagenetic	In coal measures and in some graptolitic shales of Wabana district

great economic importance. Examples in North America include the Ordovician age Wabana chamositic ores of Newfoundland, the Silurian age Clinton Formation hematite ores of the Birmingham Region of Alabama, and the Precambrian metamorphosed cherty iron ores of the Lake Superior Region. The largest manganese-producing deposits in the world—at Chiaturi, Georgia and at Nikopol, Ukraine (both U.S.S.R.)—are of sedimentary origin. The famous copper-rich shale, the late Permian age Kupferschiefer, which has been mined near Mansfeld, East Germany for nearly a thousand years, is interpreted as a diagenetic rock by many geologists. Other important ores of apparently similar origin are the great Zambian copper deposits, the lead and zinc areas of Mt. Isa in Australia, and the copper deposits in the vicinity of White Pine, Michigan. Deposits within hot brine pools on the floor of the Red Sea may represent future copper-lead-zinc rocks of this type.

Organic Rocks

We refer to the accumulated and consolidated remains of plant and animal matter as organic rocks. These rocks are diagenetic in that all represent sediments from which volatiles have been driven off. The environments in which the parent materials first accumulate are fresh water swamps on deltas or coastal plains or in inland lake basins. Subsequently, such swamp deposits have frequently undergone chemical and physical changes and thus progressed through one or more stages, the products of which are called peat, lignite, bituminous coal, and anthracite.

The first step, deposition, involves the growth and death of plants such as horsetails, rushes, sedges, trees, and peat mosses. Actually, more than 3000 plant species have been identified from coal beds. The basic ingredients are cellulose [polysaccharoids of $(C_6H_{10}O_5)_n$] plus lesser quantities of nitrogen with or without sulfur and mineral matter—for example, wind-blown dust. The next step, incomplete decomposition, takes place mainly under subaqueous anaerobic conditions where oxidation is precluded and involves removal of carbon dioxide, methane (marsh gas), and even water of constitution to form peat. Burial and subsequent increases in temperature and pressure cause additional changes that result in concentration of carbon and decreases in hydrogen and oxygen as peat progresses first to lignite, then to bituminous coal. In response to continued concentration of carbon and decreases in volatiles, commonly during tectonic folding, anthracite is formed.

Although there is a general correlation between degree of coalification and geological age, it is not a firm rule. Among noteworthy exceptions are the relatively high rank coals in the Tertiary rocks of Alaska and in the Miocene sequence of Antarctica.

The coaly substances, sometimes called lithotypes, that make up lignites and the different kinds of coal can be divided into two groups: *anthraxylon* is the name widely applied to all bright lustrous components; *attritus* is the companion term that may be applied to all dull appearing components. These can be broken down further into four designations that suffice to describe the materials usually distinguishable megascopically:

Clarain is laminated, has a silky or glossy luster and a smooth fracture that is essentially perpendicular to the bedding, and is clean to the touch.

Durain is more or less homogeneous, has a dull matte luster and a granular fracture, and generally appears lead-gray or brownish black.

Fusain, also called mineral charcoal, is friable to powdery and highly cellular or porous, has a satiny or silky luster, and is dirty to the touch.

Vitrain is homogenous, has a vitreous luster and conchoidal fracture, is brittle, and is clean to the touch.

In addition, minor quantities of such minerals as one or more of the clay family minerals, siderite, and pyrite or marcasite are present in many coals. The pores in fusain are commonly filled with calcite or pyrite. The iron minerals, in particular, tend to be present as disclike nodules or concretions.

Even though coals of different rank grade into one another, each, with the exception of semianthracite and bituminous coals, may be distinguished from the others, as well as from other rocks, by megascopic examination. This is so because certain physical characteristics tend to change with the fixed carbon content that serves as the fundamental basis for classifying the coals into their different ranks (Figure 5-32).

Peat. This is the name given to a light tan or dark brown colored spongy mass of matted, partly decomposed plant remains. Upon drying, it tends to be crumbly and burns readily.

Lignite. Compaction and lithification of peat produces lignite, which is chocolate brown to nearly black in color and has a dull to pitch-like luster. It ranges from dense and compact to earthy and fragile. Partially decayed woody fibers can usually be seen embedded in the finer carbonized material. When dried, lignite commonly exhibits shrinkage cracks or even crumbles to small pieces. Dried lignite burns with a smoky yellow flame and gives off a strong odor. Lignite grades into sub-bituminous coal, which will coke whereas lignite will not.

Coal. Bituminous coal differs from lignite and sub-bituminous coal in that it does not crumble and disintegrate upon exposure to the air and it does not contain megascopically recognizable vegetable matter. Bituminous coal is dark gray to velvet black in color and is typically banded because of alternating layers with dull, pitchy, or vitreous lusters (Figure 5-33). It is brittle and because of prismatic jointing more or less perpendicular to its banding tends to break into blocks. Bituminous coal burns readily with a smoky yellow flame and gives off an oily odor. Bituminous coal is usually marketed as soft or coking coal.

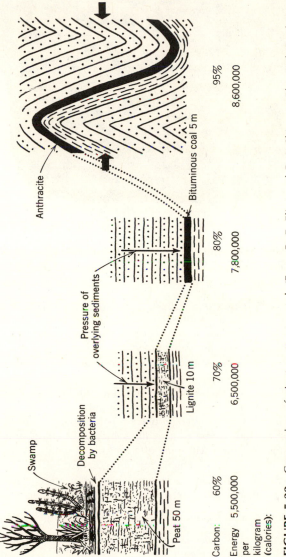

Swamp

Decomposition
by bacteria

Peat 50 m

Pressure of
overlying sediments

Lignite 10 m

Bituminous coal 5 m

Anthracite

Carbon:	60%	70%	80%	95%
Energy per kilogram (calories):	5,500,000	6,500,000	7,800,000	8,600,000

FIGURE 5-32 Conversion of plant matter to coal. (From R. F. Flint and B. J. Skinner, Physical Geology, 2nd. ed. John Wiley and Sons, 1977.)

0   2 cm

FIGURE 5-33 Bituminous coal from Pocahontas, West
Virginia. (G. K. McCauley)

Cannel coal, which is bituminous in rank, is a dull, compact, homogenous coal that
tends to break along conchoidal fractures. Under the microscope, it can be seen to consist
almost wholly of spores and pollen. *Boghead coal* is a similarly appearing coal that consists
largely of algae. Both burn readily with smoky yellow flames and give off kerosenelike
odors. *Jet*, sometimes classified as a variety of cannel coal, is a relatively hard lustrous
coaly material that occurs sporadically as isolated masses in bituminous (coaly) shales.
    Semianthracite coal is megascopically indistinguishable from bituminous coal. In
commerce, the name indicates that the coal will not coke.
    Anthracite is a lustrous dark gray to jet black nearly homogeneous coal characterized
by a subconchoidal fracture. Some of it exhibits iridescent colors and is spoken of as
peacock coal. Anthracite ignites with difficulty and burns with a nearly smokeless and
odorless blue flame. It is marketed, chiefly for domestic use, as hard coal. Because the
transition from bituminous coal to anthracite appears to require temperatures and pressures
attained during tectonic deformation, some geologists classify anthracite as a metamorphic
rock.

Occurrences of organic rocks. Coals are relatively rare, though widespread, in sedimentary sequences of all ages since the early Devonian. They occur on a worldwide basis in
Carboniferous aged rocks and with lesser but noteworthy distribution in rocks of Permian,
Triassic, Jurassic, and Cretaceous ages. Beds range from thin films up to tens of meters
thick with an average of about a half meter. Beds of greater than 3 meters thickness and
wide extent are rare. The thickest known coal bed in the United States is at Adaville,
Wyoming; it is about 24 meters thick. Probably the best known coal bed in North America

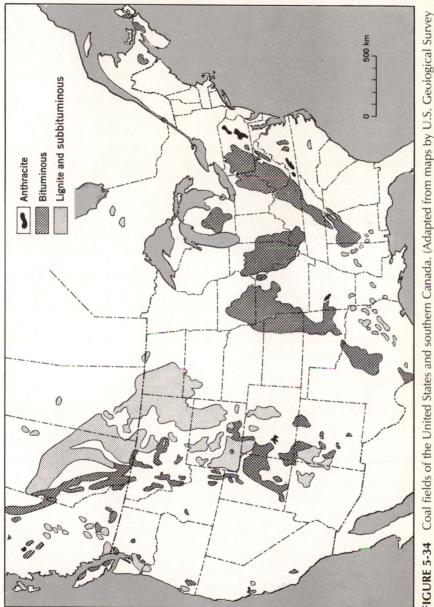

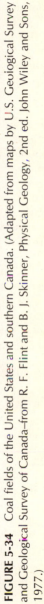

FIGURE 5-34 Coal fields of the United States and southern Canada. (Adapted from maps by U.S. Geological Survey and Geological Survey of Canada—from R. F. Flint and B. J. Skinner, Physical Geology, 2nd ed. John Wiley and Sons, 1977.)

is the Pittsburgh seam of western Pennsylvania and adjacent West Virginia and Ohio. Ranging between 1.8 and 3.0 meters thick, it is reported to have an areal extent of between 50 and 60 thousand square kilometers. Most of the world's lignite is of Late Mesozoic or of Cenozoic age. Some of the more important coal and lignite fields of North America are shown on Figure 5-34. Most peat is of Pleistocene or Recent age. It occurs sporadically in many boggy areas, especially in northern Europe, in glaciated areas of the northern United States and southern Canada where there are numerous lakes and swamps, and here and there along the southern Atlantic Coastal Plain of the United States (peat that averages about 2 meters thick underlies about 5700 square kilometers of the Dismal Swamp Area of southeastern Virginia and adjacent North Carolina).

Uses of organic rocks. Coal is a major source of heat and power. Anthracite is an especially desirable fuel for domestic use because of its smokeless burning quality. Bituminous coal, the most utilized coal, is used in the production of coke, gas, light oils, tar, ammonia, and several other organic byproducts. Lignite is gaining more and more use for many of the same things that bituminous coal is being used. Peat is recovered here and there as a relatively inexpensive, locally available fuel. A somewhat related material, called peat moss, is used widely as a soil conditioner. Coal is now thought to have several important future uses. For example, coal liquefaction, to produce petroleumlike products, is considered to be a potentially large industry and coal seam degasification is thought likely to become the basis for recovery of large quantities of now wasted natural gas.

Guano. Phosphate-rich deposits formed as the result of the leaching of excrement, generally from birds, occur at many localities, especially in arid regions such as on some of the islands off the coast of Peru, off the coast of western Africa, and in the Caribbean. Most of the deposits are only poorly consolidated and would not be considered rock as such. Identifiable feathers and bones are commonly present in the deposits. A few deposits are mined for use as phosphatic fertilizer.

Useful References

Bathurst, R. G. C. (1972), *Carbonate Sediments and Their Diagenesis,* New York: American Elsevier Publishing Co., Inc., 700 pp.

Blatt, H., Middleton, G., and Murray, R. (1980), *Origin of Sedimentary Rocks,* 2 nd ed., Englewood Cliffs, N.J.: Prentice-Hall, Inc., 634 pp.

Braitsch, O. (1971), *Salt Deposits, Their Origin and Composition,* New York: Springer-Verlag Inc., 297 pp.

Carozzi, A. V., ed. (1974), *Sedimentary Rocks. Concepts and History,* New York: Academic Press, Inc., 464 pp.

Dunbar, C. O., and Rodgers, J. (1957), *Principles of Stratigraphy.* New York: John Wiley & Sons, Inc., 356 pp.

Fuchtbauer, H. (1975), *Sediments and Sedimentary Rocks,* Halsted Press Div., New York: John Wiley & Sons, Inc., 464 pp.

Garrels, R. M. and Christ, C. L. (1965) *Solutions, Minerals, and Equilibria,* New York: Harper & Row Publishers, 450 pp.

Ham, W. E., ed. (1962), "Classification of Carbonate Rocks, a Symposium," *Amer. Assn. Pet. Geol.,* Mem. 1, 279 pp.

Hatch, F. H., Rastall, R. H., and Greensmith, J. T. (1971), *Petrology of the Sedimentary Rocks,* 5th ed., New York: Hafner Publishing Co., 502 pp.

Ivanov, M. V. (1964), "Microbiological Processes in the Formation of Sulfur Deposits," *Israel Prog. Sci. Trans.* (1968), Jerusalem, 298 pp.

James, H. L. (1966), "Chemistry of the Iron-rich Sedimentary Rocks," *in Data of Geochemistry,* 6th ed., U.S. Geol. Surv., Prof. Paper 440W, 61 pp.

Larsen, G. and Chilingar, G. V., eds. (1967), *Diagenesis in Sediments;* New York: American Elsevier Publishing Co., Inc., 551 pp.

Murchison, D. and Westoll, T. S., eds. (1968), *Coal and Coal-bearing strata,* New York: American Elsevier, Publishing Co., Inc., 418 pp.

Pettijohn, F. J., Potter, P. E., and Siever, R. (1973), *Sand and Sandstone,* New York: Springer-Verlag, Inc., 618 pp.

Pettijohn, F. J. (1975) *Sedimentary Rocks,* 3rd ed., New York: Harper & Row Publishers, 628 pp.

Rigby, J. K., and Hamblin, W. K., eds. (1972), "Recognition of Ancient Sedimentary Environments," *Soc. Econ. Paleo. and Min.,* Spec. Pub. No. 16, 340 pp.

Schafer, W. (1972), *Ecology and Palaeoecology of Marine Environments* (transl. by I. Oertel; G. Y. Craig, ed.), Chicago: University of Chicago Press, 568 pp.

Scholle, P. A. (1978), "A Color Illustrated Guide to carbonate Rock Constituents, Textures, Cements and Porosities," AAPG, Mem. 27, 241 pp.

Schrock, R. R. (1948), *Sequence in Layered Rocks,* New York: McGraw-Hill Book Company, 507 pp.

Selley, R. C. (1970), *Ancient Sedimentary Environments (A Brief Summary),* Ithaca, N.Y.: Cornell University Press, 237 pp.

Selley, R. C. (1976), *An Introduction to Sedimentology,* New York: Academic Press, Inc., 408 pp.

Stewart, F. H. (1963), "Marine Evaporites," *in Data of Geochemistry,* 6th ed., U.S. Geol. Sur. Prof. Paper 440Y, 52 pp.

Valentine, J. W. (1973), *Evolutionary Paleoecology of the Marine Biosphere,* Englewood Cliffs, N.J.: Prentice-Hall, Inc., 511 pp.

Valeton, I. (1972), *Bauxites,* Amsterdam, The Netherlands: Elsevier Publishing Co., 226 pp.

CHAPTER 6
METAMORPHIC ROCKS AND MIGMATITES

Metamorphic rocks are formed by transformation of preexisting rocks while they remain in the solid state. The term *metamorphism*, first applied to rocks in 1820, is derived from two Greek words, *meta* meaning after or change and *morphe* meaning form. Metamorphism is now applied to all of the processes which, under changing temperatures and pressure, cause sedimentary and igneous rocks to be transformed to metamorphic rocks. The processes take place in solid, or essentially solid, rock at temperatures and pressures higher than those under which diagenesis takes place and lower than those under which the rocks in question would melt. Not only igneous and sedimentary rocks but also previously metamorphosed rocks may be metamorphosed.

The transformations may be textural, mineralogical, or more commonly both and may or may not involve changes in the overall chemical composition of the rock. The most common kinds of chemical changes are the driving off of volatiles such as water and carbon dioxide. High temperatures, high pressures and/or chemically active pore fluids or diffusing ions promote the metamorphic changes. Recognizing that increased temperature, physical deformation, and chemical rearrangement are the primary driving forces, geologists usually refer to the main types of metamorphism as thermal metamorphism, dynamic metamorphism, and, depending upon the main source of the fluids or diffusing ions, either isochemical metamorphism or metasomatism.

Metamorphism takes place whenever the minerals in the preexisting rocks have sufficient time to adjust their mineralogical assemblages and textural configurations so that they are more nearly in equilibrium with a new chemical and physical environment. The sufficient time requirement offers a simple explanation of the otherwise anomalous observation that most metamorphic rocks show little or no signs of readjustment reflecting changes from high pressure and temperatures to atmospheric pressure and temperature conditions. This is not to say that metamorphic rocks can only exhibit features representative of one set of metamorphic conditions. Indeed, many metamorphic rocks have features representative of relatively high temperature and pressure conditions imprinted on features indicative of earlier lower intensity metamorphism and there also are rocks that have relatively low intensity features imprinted on higher ones. The former are generally said to have gone through *progressive metamorphism,* whereas the latter are said to have undergone *retrograde metamorphism*, sometimes termed *diaphthoresis*. In both cases, the rocks were held under the later metamorphic conditions long enough for some changes to occur but for less time than that necessary for complete equilibration.

Environments of metamorphism include zones of dislocation (faults), contact zones between magmas and their surrounding country rocks, and relatively deeply buried zones involved in mountain building activities. The causative processes are generally referred to as dislocation metamorphism (or *cataclasis*), contact metamorphism, and regional metamorphism, respectively. In cataclasis, the predominant agent is differential stress, generally called shear. In contact metamorphism, transformations may take place in response to essentially pure thermal metamorphism, to metasomatism or to both. In most large areas where regionally metamorphosed rocks are exposed, there are evidences for increased pressure (both hydrostatic and shear), for increased temperature, and also for activities attributable to percolating pore fluids. This kind of metamorphism is sometimes referred to as dynamothermal.

Rocks formed within the different metamorphic environments tend to be rather distinctive: cataclastic rocks exhibit shearing, commonly granulation; contact metamorphic rocks tend to have a nearly random arrangement of their constituent minerals; and many metamorphosed rocks in regional tracts are foliated—that is, they have a preferred orientation of their constituent tabular and platy minerals (Figure 6-1). In a few instances, however, aureoles of contact metamorphic rocks around igneous masses have also been foliated and can only be distinguished from metamorphic rocks in regional tracts when their occurrences are known.

In contact aureoles the intensity of metamorphism generally decreases with increased distance from the actual contact between the igneous mass and the surrounding country rock. This decrease in intensity, largely dependent upon the dissipation of the heat as it is conducted away from the cooling magma, is revealed by differences in mineralogical composition. Some minerals are particularly temperature-sensitive.

The term *metamorphic facies* is used to refer to contrasting assemblages of minerals that have attained equilibrium within a specific range of temperature-pressure conditions.

Several mineral assemblages that are commonly observed in different metamorphosed

0   5 cm

FIGURE 6-1   Gneiss with rough foliation marked by preferred orientation of platy biotite grains (black). (Ward's Natural Science Establishment, Inc.)

rock sequences formed at many different times throughout geological history have been so carefully studied that the range of temperature-pressure conditions they represent are now well established. The widely recognized facies shown on Figure 6-2A were named for the mineral assemblages that formed during progressive metamorphism of rocks of basaltic composition, as follows:

Blueschist facies—the rocks tend to be bluish in color because of the presence of the blue amphibole glaucophane and mottled bluish gray lawsonite.

Greenschist facies—the rocks are green because of the presence of chlorite, actinolite and/or epidote.

Amphibolite facies—the rocks contain noteworthy percentages of dark green or black hornblende plus gray plagioclase, typically andesine.

Granulite facies—the rocks contain anhydrous minerals, primarily pyroxenes and a dark red garnet with a composition between almandine and pyrope.

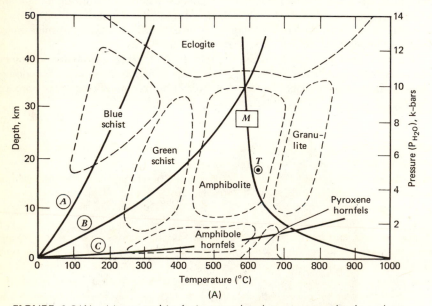

FIGURE 6-2(A)   Metamorphic facies as related to pressure/depth and temperature. Boundaries are gradational. Curve A is the geothermal gradient developed in strata that are buried so rapidly that thermal equilibrium cannot be maintained. Curve B is a normal continental geothermal gradient typically developed during slow burial of a pile of strata. Curve C is a typical thermal gradient surrounding an intrusive igneous magma that is causing contact metamorphism. Curve M indicates the temperature pressure conditions for the beginning of melting of "wet" granite. Point T is the position of the triple point shown in Figure 6-2B.

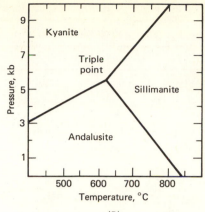

(B)

FIGURE 6-2(B) Stability fields for the polymorphic forms of Al_2SiO_5. The position of this triple point has been given different values by different experimenters. Among other things, it has been shown to vary if impurities are present. The one shown is from S. W. Richardson, M. C. Gilbert, and P. M. Bell (1969, *Amer. Jour. Sci.*, v. 267, p. 270).

Eclogite facies—these are heavy, granular rocks that consist largely of jadeitic pyroxene and pyrope garnet.

Hornfels facies—these are dense rocks, commonly so fine grained that they appear horn-like; microscopic examination shows them to be characterized by the presence of ortho- and clino-pyroxenes.

It must be kept in mind that the mineralogical makeup of any given rock in any given metamorphic facies is controlled by the bulk chemistry of its precursor, as well as by the temperature-pressure conditions of metamorphism. As a consequence, different rocks yield different mineral assemblages at the same pressure and temperature. Some of the more common metamorphic rocks can be correlated with the classical facies as shown in Table 6-1.

Fortunately, in some rocks key minerals such as the polymorphs kyanite, sillimanite, and andalusite may be used as temperature-pressure and thus facies indicators (Figure 6-2B). Even when two or three of the polymorphs occur together there is generally some indication that one or two were in the process of being changed to another. Results are now available from laboratory studies of many different minerals and mineral groups. From the results, it is possible to assign close limits to the conditions under which most mineral assemblages have formed.

Before leaving the subject of metamorphic facies, two low temperature and low

TABLE 6-1   Common mineral assemblages in metamorphic facies.

Facies	Precursor Rock Type		
	Basaltic	Argillaceous	Calcareous
Blueschist	Glaucophane, lawsonite, pumpellyite, chlorite, jadeite	Glaucophane, lawsonite, chlorite, aragonite, quartz, muscovite	Tremolite, aragonite, muscovite, glaucophane
Greenschist	Chlorite, actinolite, epidote, albite	Chlorite, muscovite, albite, quartz	Calcite, dolomite, tremolite, phlogopite, epidote, quartz
Amphibolite	Hornblende, intermediate plagioclase, epidote, almandine	Biotite, muscovite, quartz, garnet, sodic plagioclase	Calcite, diopside, grossular, ± forsterite; or calcite, diopside, scapolite, phlogopite
Granulite	Diopside, hypersthene, garnet, intermediate plagioclase	Garnet, orthoclase, intermediate plagioclase, quartz, kyanite (or sillimanite)	Calcite, plagioclase, diopside
Eclogite	Jadeitic pyroxene, pyrope, rutile, ± kyanite		
Hornfels	Diopside, hypersthene, plagioclase	Biotite, orthoclase, quartz, cordierite, andalusite	Calcite, wollastonite, grossular

pressure facies not shown in Figure 6-2A must be mentioned. These are the *zeolite facies* and the *prehnite-pumpellyite facies*. The conditions indicated are those generally believed to exist where sedimentary and volcanic rocks have been buried only a few kilometers. In general, the assemblages indicative of such metamorphism are only recognized in certain rocks, such as basaltic and andesitic volcanic piles and graywackes. In many cases the indicator minerals can only be observed in the matrix portions of the rocks, which means they frequently cannot be recognized in hand specimen. Recognition of these low-grade metamorphic rocks in the field is further hampered because most of the rocks retain their original sedimentary, igneous, or pyroclastic features and, except for a few rocks of the prehnite-pumpellyite facies, have not developed any obvious foliation. In light of the fact that these rocks can so seldom be recognized in hand specimen, we shall not describe them further. In many ways, rocks of the zeolite and prehnite-pumpellyite facies may be considered to be transitional between rocks that are universally recognized as metamorphic and rocks that have undergone marked diagenesis.

Metamorphic facies develop both by contact and by regional metamorphism. In the field, we generally map the first appearance of a mineral as we go from unmetamorphosed rocks into metamorphosed rocks or from low pressure and temperature to higher temperature and pressure conditions. For example, in going from unmetamorphosed to metamorphosed siltstones we may plot the first appearance of chlorite, then the first appearance of biotite, and so forth. But, it must be kept in mind that, in most cases, the appearance of one mineral does not necessarily require the disappearance of another. For instance, in the example just given, chlorite may also be present in rocks encountered on the high temperature-pressure side of the biotite *isograd*. Isograd is the name applied to a line on a map that connects the locations of the first appearances of a mineral as just described. This term was chosen because within metamorphic terrains we frequently designate the rocks as representative of, for example, a low versus high *grade of metamorphism*. Isograds give an overall view of the distribution of temperature-pressure conditions during metamorphism (see Figure 6-3).

As implied in the chapters dealing with igneous and sedimentary rocks, the characteristics that permit one to distinguish most metamorphic rocks from most igneous and sedimentary rocks are composition and texture. As also noted, however, some marbles and some quartzites cannot be named for sure unless their geological occurrences are known.

Composition of Metamorphic Rocks

The bulk chemical composition of a metamorphic rock depends on the composition of the original rock and the composition of the substances, if any, that were added and subtracted by percolating pore fluids or diffusing ions. The mineralogical composition

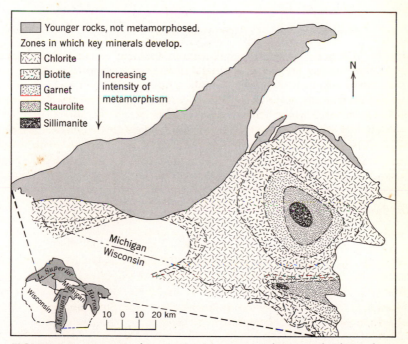

FIGURE 6-3 Metamorphic zoning in upper Michigan took place about 1.5 billion years ago. There are two well-defined centers of intensity. (After H. L. James, Geol. Soc. Amer. Bull., v. 66, p. 1455, 1955)

depends on the temperature and pressure conditions at the time of recrystallization. Some minerals that are fairly common in metamorphic rocks are extremely rare or nonexistent in igneous and sedimentary rocks (Table 6-2).

Metamorphic recrystallization may involve only the formation of different grains of one or more of the minerals already present in the preexisting rocks, the formation of new minerals, or both. In general, rocks consisting entirely, or largely, of one mineral will simply recrystallize—for example, chert becomes quartzite, pure limestone becomes a calcite marble. On the other hand, rocks made up of two or more minerals frequently have their elements recombined into new minerals—for example, a quartz-rich dolostone might be recrystallized to a diopside-rich rock:

$$CaMg(CO_3)_2 + 2SiO_2 \rightarrow CaMg(SiO_3)_2 + 2CO_2 \uparrow$$

$$\text{dolomite} \qquad \text{quartz} \qquad \text{diopside} \qquad \text{carbon dioxide}$$

Some of the new minerals may also contain substances introduced into the rock by percolating pore fluids or diffusing ions.

Considering the diversity of possible parent rocks, of the migrating fluids and diffusing ions, and the variability of conditions under which metamorphism can take place, it is hardly surprising that there are a great many different metamorphic rocks.

This, of course, means that to interpret the history of a metamorphic rock, one should know its mineralogical composition, including the chemical composition of its minerals and of possible precursor minerals, and the chemical and physical conditions under which

TABLE 6-2   Common minerals of metamorphic rocks

Minerals that occur as major components in common metamorphic rocks are in column A; minerals that are common varietal constituents in fairly common metamorphic rocks and/or are major components of rather rare metamorphic rocks are in column B; minerals that typically occur as sporadic accessories but are locally abundant are in column C. The minerals whose names are preceded by an asterisk also occur as predominant constituents in one or more of the common igneous and/or sedimentary rocks.

A	B	C
*Amphiboles (especially actinolite, hornblende and tremolite)	Andalusite	Chondrodite
	Chloritoid	Hematite
	Cordierite	Magnesite
Biotite	Epidote/zoisite	Phlogopite
*Calcite	Garnet (especially almandine and grossular)	Pyrophyllite
Chlorite		Scapolites
*Dolomite	Graphite	Sphene
Muscovite	Kyanite	Spinel
*Plagioclase	*Pyroxenes (especially diopside)	Stilpnomelane
*Potassium feldspar		Tourmaline
*Quartz	Sillimanite	Vesuvianite
Serpentine	Staurolite	Wollastonite
	Talc	Zeolites

its minerals may form and persist. With such knowledge, the probable parent and history of a metamorphic rock can generally be deciphered (Table 6-3), together with the range of possible conditions within which the metamorphism took place (see Figure 6-2).

Texture of Metamorphic Rocks

The shapes and arrangements of grains in metamorphic rocks commonly reflect the conditions of metamorphism—for example, a texture characterized by many pulverized grains indicates formation in response to dislocation metamorphism, whereas a texture characterized by a three-dimensional mosaic of nearly equidimensional grains indicates formation under relatively static conditions.

Metamorphic rocks range in grain size from submicroscopic to coarsely crystalline. Individual grains may be euhedral to anhedral and of almost any shape. The grains may be arranged in a more or less random fashion; be roughly segregated by species, grain size, and/or shape; or have some preferred orientation. A few metamorphic textures are of such common and widespread occurrence that they have special names. The following adjectives are used to describe those textures that can frequently be recognized during megascopic examination (see Figures 6-4 and 6-7):

Cataclastic—containing many grains that have been broken, fragmented, and/or granulated in response to dislocation metamorphism.

Crystalloblastic—an overall term indicating recrystallization under the influence of directed pressure.

Granoblastic—characterized by more or less equidimensional grains, typically with well-sutured boundaries.

Lepidoblastic—containing a noteworthy proportion of platy or flaky mineral grains (e.g., mica or chlorite) that exhibit a foliation.

Nematoblastic—containing a noteworthy proportion of prismatic mineral grains (e.g., amphibole) that exhibit a preferred alignment, lineation.

TABLE 6-3   The principle metamorphic rocks and their common parent rocks.

Metamorphic Rock	Parent Rock
Cataclasite	Any Rock
Hornfels	Any rock but typically an impervious one such as a shale
Tactite	Any rock but typically an impure carbonate rock, e.g., an argillaceous dolomitic limestone
Gneiss and schist	Granitoid or aphanitic equivalent, arkose, siltstone or shale
Greenstone	Basalt or andesite
Amphibolite and amphibole schist	Gabbroid or aphanitic equivalent, graywacke or siliceous dolostone
Phyllite and slate	Shale or felsic tuff
Metaquartzite	Sandstone or chert
Marble	Limestone or dolostone
Soapstone/serpentinite	Peridotite or pyroxenite

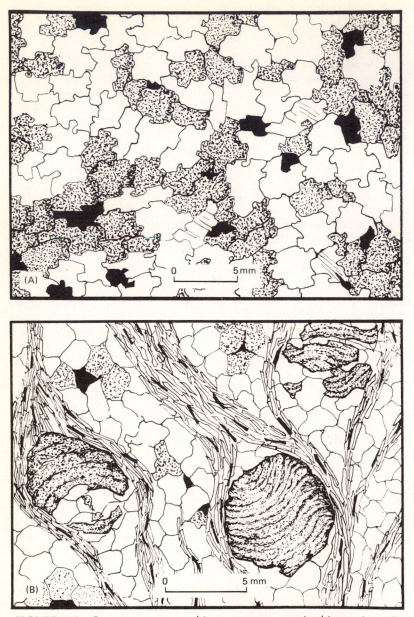

FIGURE 6-4 Common metamorphic textures as seen in thin section. (A) Granoblastic texture in a Precambrian hypersthene, diopside, plagioclase, magnetite hornfels from the Brier Hill Quadrangle, St. Lawrence County, New York. (B) Crystalloblastic texture in a Precambrian garnet schist, part

of the Lynchburg Gneiss, Floyd County, Virginia. (C) Lepidoblastic texture in a biotite schist horizon in the Lynchburg Gneiss, Floyd County, Virginia. (D) Nematoblastic texture in a zoisite amphibolite unit of the Lynchburg Gneiss, Floyd County, Virginia.

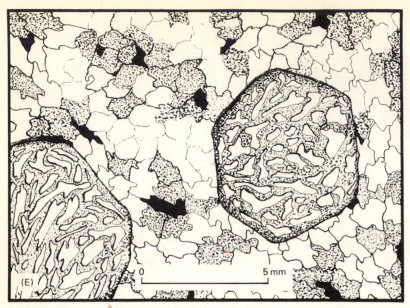

FIGURE 6-4   (E) Poikiloblastic texture of garnets in a garnet gneiss of the Lynchburg Gneiss, Floyd County, Virginia.

Poikiloblastic—having megacrysts (see below) that are riddled with inclusions of other minerals. (This is sometimes referred to as sieve texture.)

Some additional, rather common terms that relate to certain special metamorphic textural features are

Augen—eye-shaped (lenticular) megacrysts (Figure 6-5).

Cataclast—a relatively large remnant of fragmentation, typically surrounded by a much more finely granulated matrix.

Idioblastic—term sometimes applied to euhedral grains formed by metamorphic recrystallization.

Megacryst—any grain, no matter what its origin, that is significantly larger than its surrounding grains.

Porphyroblast—megacryst formed as a result of metamorphic recrystallization (see Figures 6-4B and 6-14).

Xenoblastic—term sometimes applied to anhedral grains formed by metamorphic recrystallization.

Classification of Metamorphic Rocks (Including Eclogites) and Migmatites

Metamorphic rocks are classified genetically according to their environment of metamorphism: those produced in response to dislocation metamorphism, those metamorphosed in contact zones surrounding igneous masses, and those metamorphosed in regional tracts during mountain building activities. In addition, we also include some problematical rocks that may only be partly of metamorphic origin in this chapter. The coverage is as shown in Table 6-4.

TABLE 6-4 Metamorphic rocks and migmatites.

Local Metamorphic Rocks
    Cataclasites
        Tectonic breccia
        Mylonite
        Phyllonite
        Pseudotachylyte
    Contactites
        Hornfels
        Natural coke
        Tactite (skarn)
        Pyrometasomatic ores

Regional Metamorphic Rocks
    Nonfoliated
        Marble (calcitic and dolomitic)
        Quartzite
        Metaconglomerate
        Granulite
        Metamorphosed iron formations (jaspilite and taconite)
    Foliated
        Gneiss
        Amphibolite and amphibole schist
        Schists, (mica schist, greenstone,
           talc schist, and soapstone)
        Phyllite, slate, and argillite
        Eclogite

Migmatites
    Arterite
    Metasomatite
    Venite
    Anatexite

CATACLASITES

These rocks are formed as the result of mechanical breakage and distortion that occur during crustal movements generally referred to as either tectonic or diastrophic. Cataclasites may be derived from essentially any rock and consequently may consist of just about any mineral assemblage and be nearly any color. Among the diverse rocks reported to have undergone cataclasis are anorthosite, anthracite coal, arkose, gabbro, gneisses of different compositions, granite, granodiorite, hornfels, quartzite, sandstone, shale, and a few ultramafic igneous rocks.

Cataclasites are characterized by fragmented and/or distorted grains (Figures 6-6 and 6-7). Some predominantly cataclastic rocks, however, also show evidence of some re-

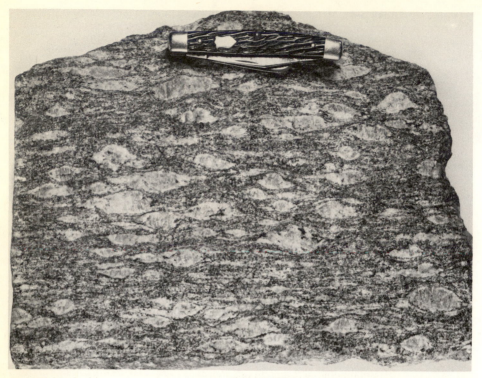

FIGURE 6-5   Augen gneiss from the Precambrian aged Grayson Gneiss, Grayson County, Virginia. Augen are feldspar; Knife is 84 millimeters long. (R. V. Dietrich)

crystallization, plastic deformation, or even new mineral growth. Typically, the changes involve the formation of chlorite and/or sericite. It is thought that the water contained in these minerals was very likely sucked in during cataclasis and that frictional heat enhanced their formation. Plastic deformation is sometimes megascopically discernible because of such features as bent cleavage surfaces in calcite.

Many of the rocks of this group cannot be distinguished in hand specimen from similarly appearing igneous, sedimentary, or metamorphic rocks of other origins unless their geological occurrences are known. Most cataclasites occur in relatively restricted zones of deformation such as fault zones or along axial zones of folds in brittle rock. A few, however, have been injected away from where they were formed into adjacent rocks. These cataclastic dikes have led to all sorts of problems in the interpretation of both their origin and the overall geological relationships within the areas where they occur.

The rocks of this group are named on the basis of the degree of fragmentation, expressed by grain size and arrangement, and the coherency or compactness of the aggregate fragments. In most cases, the coherency appears to be a reflection of how high the confining pressure was during the mechanical granulation.

Tectonic Breccia

This term—synonymous with the terms dynamic breccia and pressure breccia, used by some geologists—may be used to include fault breccia, fold breccia, crush breccia and

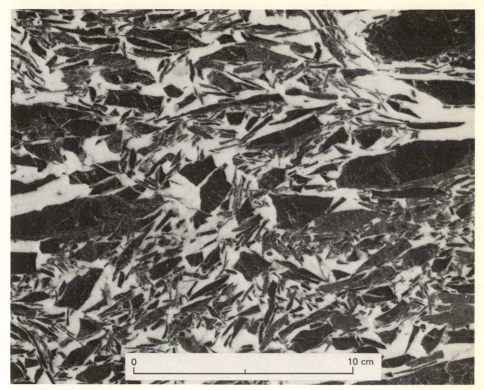

FIGURE 6-6 Cataclastic breccia. Black marble fragments cemented by white calcite deposited from groundwater. (B. J. Skinner)

conglomerate, friction breccia, cataclastic breccia, and some shatter and crackle breccias. All of these rocks are made up of broken fragments, typically with a haphazard arrangement, in a matrix consisting of smaller fragments and pulverized rock generally called gouge. Most are only loosely coherent and, as a consequence, are thought to have formed under relatively low confining pressures. The larger fragments may range up to several meters in greatest dimension. The pulverized matrix is commonly of powdery clay- or silt-sized constituency. Although tectonic breccias are usually described as made up of angular fragments, some contain many or even a predominant percentage of rounded fragments that appear to have been formed by attrition during movement within the zone of dislocation.

As indicated in the introductory statement, some of these rocks are extremely difficult, if not impossible, to distinguish megascopically from their sedimentary counterparts unless their field relationships are known. Two characteristics that are highly suggestive of cataclasis rather than sedimentation are the presence of fragments that have polished and striated surfaces, slickensides (Figure 6-8), and the inclusion of fragments that are fractured, especially if two or more nearby fragments can be matched—that is, the fragments can be seen to have once been parts of a single larger fragment.

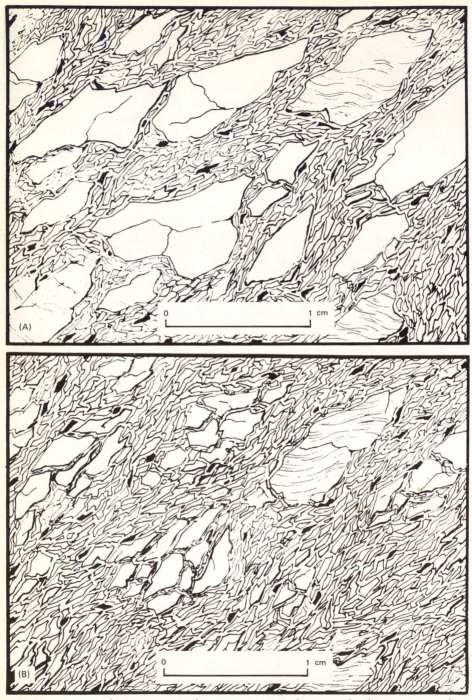

FIGURE 6-7   Cataclasis as seen in thin section: (*A*) Early stage of pulverization; (*B*) later stage. Samples are both quartz-feldspar rocks from Fries Fault zone, southwestern Montgomery County, Virginia.

A few tectonic breccias that occur along fault zones consist almost wholly of pulverized gouge. These loosely- to noncoherent masses of granulated rock material are usually called *fault gouge*.

Tectonic breccias tend to be highly permeable as well as highly porous. Thus, they serve as channelways for percolating solutions. Consequently, exposures are commonly marked by springs or water seeps. In addition, tectonic breccias are commonly mineralized and become ore deposits. Galena, sphalerite, and other sulfide minerals occur disseminated through the matrixes or replacing the matrixes and/or the fragments of tectonic breccias at many localities. Among the mining regions in the United States where mineralized tectonic breccias and shear zones are encountered are the ore deposits of the Coeur d'Alene district of northern Idaho and parts of the Mascot, Tennessee and the famous Tri-State zinc deposits of Kansas, Missouri, and Oklahoma.

Mylonites

The name, mylonite, is derived from a Greek word meaning through the mill. It is applied to cataclastic rocks that appear to have been formed as the result of granulation, pulverization, and smearing out of minerals under high confining pressures.

Many mylonites are extremely fine-grained and dense and thus resemble chert or some aphanitic igneous rock. Those that contain porphyroclasts (residual fragments that are notably larger than the surrounding pulverized material) roughly resemble porphyritic aphanites. In fact, they have been called pseudoporphyries by some petrologists. In general, the porphyroclasts are ellipsoidal in shape and have their two longer axes nearly parallel to the surfaces of major movement, which in turn are marked by streaks. The streaking, based on color and/or grain size and/or compositional differences, is especially evident on surfaces that have been etched during weathering. Some pseudoporphyritic mylonites grade into augen gneisses.

Phyllonite is a mnemonic term frequently given to mylonites that resemble phyllites (page 265). Shiny mica and graphite are common constituents. In hand specimen, most phyllonites are indistinguishable from true phyllites except when their occurrences are known.

Pseudotachylyte, also termed *ultramylonite,* is so fine-grained that it appears glassy (see tachylyte, page 156). X-ray studies are almost always required to show that they actually consist of submicroscopic, minutely pulverized mineral and rock fragments. These relatively rare rocks are doubly difficult to distinguish from igneous rocks because they tend to occur as dikelet-like masses extruded into relatively unaffected country rock.

Occurrences of cataclasites. Cataclastic rocks have been reported from many localities throughout the world. Two examples are: the tectonic breccias that occur along many of the faults exposed in the unmetamorphosed part of the Appalachians and the mylonites along some of the border faults bounding the Triassic basins of the eastern United States and within several other fault zones in the crystalline part of the Appalachians. Some of the latter are phyllonites. The San Andreas Fault of California is marked by a zone of cataclastic rocks approximately 1000 kilometers long and up to nearly 3.5 kilometers thick.

Uses of cataclasites. Several cataclastic rocks, especially carbonate-bearing tectonic breccias, have been quarried and polished for use as decorative marbles. All have unique appearances—some are rather attractive; some are rather garish. Those, such as the "Fantastica di Lasa," from the Alps of northern Italy are exemplary.

FIGURE 6-8   Slickensides. A slickensided fault surface in Triassic rocks near Washington, D.C. (T. M. Gathright, Jr.)

CONTACTITES

When hot magma is intruded into relatively cool rock or extruded onto the surface of the earth, the adjacent country rocks may be heated and metamorphosed (Figure 6-9). The most common changes are: a color change—for example, a red rock may turn light gray as the result of a reduction of its hematite (Fe_2O_3) pigment; minerals with relatively low melting temperatures may be melted; water vapor and other gases, such as carbon dioxide, may be driven off—for example, a coal may be degassed to form natural coke; partial to complete recrystallization may occur, resulting chiefly in textural changes; reaction may produce mineral assemblages more nearly at equilibrium with the higher temperature conditions; rock compositions may be changed by fluids emanating from the magma— new material can be added and/or existing material removed from the rock; and, of course, rocks may be changed in more than one way as a result of two or more processes acting either together or sequentially.

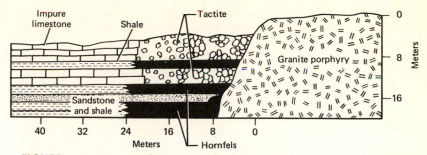

FIGURE 6-9 Metamorphism around a hypothetical granite porphyry intrusive. Sandstones and shales have been baked to fine-grained hornfels. Impure limestones have been converted to tactite containing new metamorphic minerals such as garnet.

In some cases, the magma itself and the igneous rock formed by its cooling may be changed because of reactions with and/or assimilation of country rock. The effects on the country rocks are termed *exomorphism*, whereas those on the magma and the resulting igneous rock are referred to as *endomorphism*.

The formation of hornfelses, tactites, and pyrometasomatic ore deposits are particularly noteworthy examples of exomorphism. Hornfelses form as the result of pure thermal metamorphism. The metamorphism is generally marked by mineralogical changes that. involve at least some recombination of elements of the original rock but little or no evidence for the introduction of any new material. Some hornfelses have been formed near contacts with apparently dry magmas—that is, magmas that have given off little or no volatiles; other hornfelses appear to represent country rocks such as shales or slates or other relatively dense fine-grained rocks that were either impermeable to or incapable of reacting with percolating volatiles. Tactites, on the other hand, are characterized by minerals whose compositions indicate that some of their elements have been added by magmatic volatiles. Many tactites represent impure calcareous rocks that were permeable and relatively easily replaced as well as susceptible to recrystallization. Some pyrometasomatic ore deposits, principally of copper and iron minerals, appear to consist largely of magmatically derived materials; others appear also to include material derived as a consequence of a redistribution of elements within the original country rock.

Contact metamorphic zones range from a few millimeters to as much as two kilometers thick. Both their sizes and shapes depend upon differences between the temperatures and compositions of the magma and those of the country rocks and, as just implied, may be correlated roughly with such properties as the conductivity, permeability, and chemical reactivity of the original country rock. Hornfelses tend to form continuous aureoles more or less parallel to their igneous rock contacts and to exhibit continuous transitions from highly metamorphosed to unaltered rocks, outward from their contacts. Tactites and associated ore deposits tend to be rather sporadically arranged, commonly with localization along or near fracture zones, around the causative igneous masses and to show abrupt transitions from highly altered to essentially unaffected country rocks.

Hornfelses

Nearly all hornfelses are hard, dense, nearly homogeneous, microcrystalline to fine-grained rocks, with or without scattered, relatively large porphyroblasts of such minerals as andalusite, cordierite, corundum, epidote (or clinozoisite), garnet (generally grossular or almandine), hornblende, hypersthene, plagioclase, sillimanite, spinel (magnetite or pleonaste), staurolite, and vesuvianite.

Hornfelses may be black, gray, greenish or nearly white. Like many other dense nearly homogeneous rocks, they tend to break with conchoidal fractures. The sporadic larger grains, which range from nearly euhedral to very irregular and commonly contain many minute inclusions, give some hornfelses spotty or knotty appearances.

Some very fine-grained hornfelses resemble cherts, felsites, andesites, or basalts. Remarkably, some hornfelses look like the rocks from which they were derived—for example, a nearly pure diopside hornfels from the contact aureole of the Boulder Bathylith of Montana closely resembles its cherty dolomite precursor (Figure 6-10). Perhaps even more remarkably, some hornfelses look like completely different rocks—for example, a spotted cordierite hornfels also from the Boulder Bathylith contact zone looks very much like a vesicular basalt, especially on weathered surfaces. Because of their great diversity, hornfelses are extremely difficult to identify by megascopic means, but not by microscopic means, unless their field occurrences are known.

Hornfelses are generally named on the basis of their mineral content (e.g., a cordierite hornfels) or on the basis of some chemical characteristic (e.g., a calcic hornfels). Except for those of which the scattered megascopic grains can be identified, the former method is useful only after microscopic study. Unless the unit can be traced into its parent rock, the latter method is hazardous without chemical analysis.

Novaculite

As already mentioned (page 219), at least some novaculite may represent thermally metamorphosed chert.

Natural Coke

Coke produced naturally is also called *carbonite*. It is formed, albeit rather rarely, as the result of thermal metamorphism or as a result of natural combustion. Natural coke is lustrous to dull, dark gray to black, and slightly to markedly vesicular. As compared to somewhat similarly appearing vesicular basalt, natural coke is softer, lighter in weight, and more easily broken. As compared to man-made cokes, natural coke tends to exhibit much less overall homogeneity. This is corroborated by analyses that show deposits of natural coke to have large ranges in fixed carbon, ash, and volatile contents. Natural coke tends to have ignition and burning characteristics more like those of semianthracite coal than of any of the man-made cokes.

Tactites

These medium to very coarse-grained contact metamorphic rocks consist almost wholly of calcium-bearing silicates such as tremolite, diopside and epidote, with or without calcite. In addition, a special group of minerals such as axinite, fluorapatite, phlogopite, scapolite, and tourmaline are typically present. It is because of the presence of these minerals, in fact, that tactites are considered to be at least partly metasomatic in origin— each of the minerals contains one or more elements such as boron, chlorine, fluorine or phosphorus, known to occur as volatiles driven off from igneous magmas.

As already noted, most tactites are formed by replacement of impure (siliceous and/ or argillaceous) calcitic or dolomitic country rocks. Additional minerals that are rather characteristic of tactites are andradite (garnet), hedenbergite (pyroxene), and wollastonite.

FIGURE 6-10   Diopside hornfels from contact aureole of the Boulder Bathylith of Montana. This rock, originally an impure dolomite containing chert nodules, is now largely diopside. (R. V. Dietrich)

And, among the other several additional minerals reported to occur in these rocks, corundum, epidote (and clinozoisite), fluorite, graphite, humite, magnesite, magnetite, monticellite, olivine (typically forsterite), plagioclase (especially anorthite), scheelite, sphene, spinel, several sulfides, topaz, tremolite, and vesuvianite are fairly common.

Although tactites tend to have compositions that differ rather markedly, even within individual hand specimens, some consist of only one or two minerals and have been given names like garnetite, magnesite rock, and wollastonite marble. For those that would be given names already used for rocks of some other origin—for example, pyroxenite (page

139)—the name of the predominant mineral (or minerals) is used as a modifier to the term *tactite*—for example, pyroxene tactite.

Skarn is a name that has been applied to a great many different rocks, including a number of tactites. The term has been used in so many different ways that its continued use leads to confusion. Therefore, the term should be abandoned or used only when and where it is clearly defined for the purpose at hand.

Pyrometasomatic Ores

Some calc-silicate rocks in contact aureoles of intrusive igneous masses contain clusters, stringers, and/or veinlets of ore minerals. The most commonly associated gangue minerals are andradite (less commonly grossular) and a diopside-hedenbergite pyroxene plus or minus calcite and/or quartz. Relatively common ore minerals include cassiterite, gold, hematite (generally specularite), ilmenite, magnetite, bornite, chalcopyrite, galena, molybdenite, pyrite, pyrrhotite, sphalerite, scheelite, and wolframite. Like the tactites, a large percentage of these rocks appear to have been formed within or to have replaced calcareous rocks. The sulfides, in particular, exhibit features indicating that they have replaced earlier-formed calc-silicate or oxide minerals.

Some geologists think that the ore minerals were deposited by hydrothermal solutions; others favor transfer by diffusion. Whatever the mechanism, large quantities of materials are introduced and moved during the formation of these deposits.

Occurrences of contactites. Baked contacts are relatively common next to lava flows and near-surface intrusives. In the Crazy Mountains of Montana, the hardened rocks of one baked zone stand as ridges and peaks around the more deeply eroded igneous mass. Adjacent to some of the Triassic dikes and sills of eastern North America, the normally red arkosic country rocks have been bleached light gray or nearly white in color.

Hornfelses occur in the contact aureoles of many igneous masses, especially granitoids. As shown on Figure 6-2, hornfelses generally form at relatively low pressures. Noteworthy occurrences are associated with some of the igneous masses in the White Mountains of New Hampshire and with the Sierra Nevada complex of California, as well as with the already mentioned Boulder Bathylith of Montana.

Natural coke has been recorded from localities where coal beds have been transected by basaltic dikes. Two well-known examples occur in the Traissic age Midlothian Basin near Richmond, Virginia and in the Book Cliffs coal field near the north end of the Wasatch Plateau in central Utah.

Tactites are relatively common in crystalline rock terranes where both granitoids and impure marbles occur. The Grenville Province of northern New York, eastern Ontario, and adjacent Québec is exemplary. Some tactites have become world famous because of both the variety and the quality of their minerals. Examples include the Crestmore, California, and Magnet Cove, Arkansas mineral localities and some of the Burmese rubies and sapphires.

Associated ore deposits have been prospected or worked for several different products. Some in North America are: iron—Cornwall, Pennsylvania, Iron Springs, Utah and Fierro, New Mexico; copper—some of the deposits of Morenci and Bisbee, Arizona and of Bingham, Utah; zinc—Hanover, New Mexico, and Long Lake, Ontario; lead—Magdalena, New Mexico and Inyo County, California; tin—Yak, Alaska; tungsten—Mill City, Nevada and Bishop, California; molybdenum—Buckingham, Québec; graphite—Adirondacks of New York, Clay County, Alabama and Buckingham, Québec; gold—Cable, Montana and

Hedley, British Columbia; emery–Peeksville, New York; corundum–Peeksville, New York and Chester, Massachusetts. Also noteworthy are garnet from North Wilmot, New Hampshire and wollastonite from Willsboro, New York.

Uses of contactites. As is apparent in the preceding section, tactites and associated ore deposits include many mineral resources. Many other examples could be listed. Sillimanite is one of the few mineral resources recovered from apparently pure thermal metamorphic rocks; it is used in the manufacture of refractory materials such as spark plug casings.

REGIONAL METAMORPHIC ROCKS

Dynamothermal metamorphism takes place during mountain building activities. The designation, "regional," directs attention to the fact that the resulting rocks comprise extensive volumes of material that underlie regions of many thousands of square kilometers, whereas cataclastic and contact metamorphic rocks occur over relatively restricted zones that typically constitute the bedrock of areas measurable in less than a few or a few tens of square kilometers.

Regional metamorphism generally involves recrystallization and new mineral growth under directed pressure, with some of the changes enhanced by percolating fluids and diffusing ions. The new mineral assemblages are indicative of the temperature-pressure conditions of the metamorphism that produced them. (See Figures 6-2 and 6-3). In addition, because recrystallization takes place under directed pressure, the minerals tend to be somewhat segregated by species and to grow with preferred orientations.

In some metamorphic rocks, the preferred orientation of mineral grains is not obvious and can only be determined by petrofabric studies that involve statistical analysis of microscopically determined crystallographic or shape orientations; in many metamorphic rocks, however, mineral orientations are readily apparent as a megascopic foliation.

Our discussion of regional metamorphic rocks is based on the presence or absence of megascopic foliation. Rocks that do not exhibit megascopic metamorphic banding or foliation—the marbles, quartzites, and granulites—are described first. Then, the banded or foliated rocks are described in a sequence starting from those with the least developed foliation and ending with those with the best developed foliation.

Two additional facts are worthy of note: some of the marbles, quartzites, and granulites are banded, but that banding appears to represent original compositional bands inherited from the parent sedimentary rocks rather than metamorphic segregation; and almost any rocks of this group may grade into any other rock of the group or into its unmetamorphosed sedimentary or igneous parent rock.

Marbles
Marble is a metamorphic rock that consists predominantly of calcite and/or dolomite. Unfortunately, the business world has corrupted the word marble to refer to almost any carbonate rock—including limestones and dolostones—that will take a good polish. In this book, we use the term, marble, in the purely geological sense.

Marbles may be snow white, gray, black, buff, yellowish, chocolate, pink, mahogany-red, bluish, lavender, or greenish in color. The color may be nearly uniform, splotchy, vein-like, or have a so-called marbled appearance. Marbles may be essentially pure carbonate rocks or may contain one or more of a great variety of disseminated minerals.

Typical impurities include brucite, diopside, epidote (or clinozoisite), feldspars, forsterite, graphite, grossular, humite, periclase, phlogopite, pyrite, quartz, scapolite, serpentine, sphene, spinel, talc, tremolite, vesuvianite, and wollastonite.

Both calcite and dolomite marbles range from very fine- to coarse-grained. Within a given unit, however, the grains tend to be of rather uniform size. Also, where calcite and dolomite marbles occur together, the calcite varieties are generally the coarser. Most calcite marbles can be seen to have interlocking grains with mosaic or sutured interrelationships (Figure 6-11A). Most dolomite marbles tend to be granular or saccharoidal (Figure 6-11B).

In coarse-grained marbles, the carbonates may be seen to have rhombohedral cleavage. This, along with their hardness and their reactivity with dilute hydrochloric acid, permits distinction of marbles from similarly appearing anorthosites and anhydrocks but not from some diagenetically recrystallized limestones and dolostones. To make the latter distinction, the identity of the associated rocks or the geological occurrence needs to be known. On the other hand, marbles that are impure are relatively easily distinguished from nearly all other rocks, including diagenetically recrystallized calcareous rocks. This is so because of the impurity-mineral content of the impure marbles. Most of the minerals mentioned above form only during metamorphism and just do not occur in the other rocks. Furthermore, in some cases, the impurity minerals can also be used to place their host marbles into their appropriate metamorphic facies. As should be expected, however, both pure and impure marbles formed during regional metamorphism may be impossible to distinguish from their contact-metamorphosed analogs except when the identities of their associated rocks or their geological occurrences are known. About the only other indicative feature is that marbles in regional metamorphic tracts are more likely to exhibit foliation than those formed under the relatively static physical conditions that are usually associated with contact metamorphism. Finally, some marbles of high metamorphic rank— particularly those that contain accessory minerals like pyrochlore—are practically impossible to distinguish from carbonatites (page 140).

Whereas essentially all dolomite marbles are formed by metamorphism of dolostones, calcite marbles may be derived from either limestones or dolostones. Dedolomitization of a siliceous dolostone, for example, may result in the formation of a calcite marble containing such minerals as diopside, forsterite, periclase, tremolite, and talc. In fact, several chemical equations can be given to support the possibility that many impure marbles may represent metamorphic recombination and recrystallization of sandy (or cherty) and clayey, calcitic or dolomitic rocks *without* noteworthy changes in the rocks' overall chemical compositions. For example, as already noted

$$1 \text{ dolomite} + 2 \text{ quartz} \quad \rightarrow \quad 1 \text{ diopside} + 2 \text{ carbon dioxide} \uparrow$$

and

$$3 \text{ dolomite} + 4 \text{ quartz} + 1 \text{ } H_2O \quad \rightarrow \quad 1 \text{ talc} + 3 \text{ calcite} + 3 \text{ carbon dioxide} \uparrow .$$

That is to say, a dolomitic sandstone might yield a talc-diopside marble.

Occurrences and uses of marbles. Marbles commonly exhibit plastic flow features and/or folding (Figure 6-12). Many marbles have attractive appearances when cut and polished. Relatively pure marbles are easy to cut and shape because of their relative softness ($H = 3$). Consequently, marbles have found use in statuary and architecture since prehistoric times. For the most part, pure white marbles are used for statues and carvings,

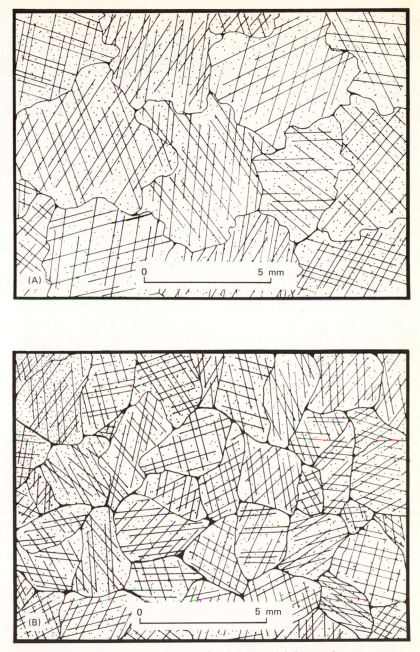

FIGURE 6-11 Marbles, as seen in thin section, exhibiting diverse textures.
(A) Sutured texture of Precambrian aged Grenville, calcite marble from Ma-
comb, St. Lawrence County, New York; (B) granular or saccharoidal texture
of Middle Cambrian, Stissing Dolomite marble, Dutchess County, New York.

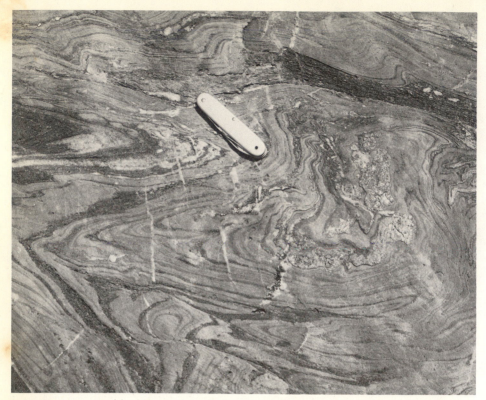

FIGURE 6-12   Marble commonly exhibits plastic flowage and/or folding. Outcrop near Val Malenco, Northern Italy. Pocket knife is approximately 75 millimeters long. (Kurt Bucher)

whereas marbles having relatively uniform colors or some particularly striking features are used in architecture. Currently, those with sublinear patterns that are amenable to cutting and matching that resembles quarter-sawed lumber are in great demand.

Probably the most widely known marbles are those from Greece and Italy. The world-famous ancient Greek statues and buildings, including the magnificent Parthenon, exemplify use of the nearly pure, white marble found in Greece. The great variety of marbles from the quarries in the Appenines of northern Italy is almost beyond belief; several of them are marbles in the geologic sense as well as from the commercial standpoint.

In North America, the belts of metamorphic rocks in the Grenville Province of Quebec, Ontario and New York, and in the Appalachians and Rocky mountains have supplied large quantities of commercial marble. Lesser quantities have been recovered in several other states including Alaska, Arkansas, California, and Minnesota. The largest present-day production in North America is from near Proctor, Rutland County, Vermont where marbles with a great variety of colors—white, black, gray, blue, green, and varicolored—are quarried; near Sylacauga, Talladega County, Alabama where a fine-grained white marble is the main product; and in the vicinity of Tate and Marble Hill, Pickens County,

Georgia where medium- to coarse-grained white, pink, bluish, and gray varieties are recovered. An interesting folk tale frequently repeated about the Georgia pink marble holds that it was white before being stained by blood shed during the American Civil War.

The Washington Monument in the District of Columbia is faced by three different marbles: the bottom 152 feet (~ 46 meters) is a rather coarse-grained calcitic marble from Texas, Maryland; directly above that, there is some marble from Lee, Massachusetts; and the top approximately 400 feet (~ 120 meters) is a fine-grained magnesium-rich marble from Cockeysville, Maryland. The differences, which are quite apparent, reflect the construction schedule that was broken by the Civil War and then not resumed until after the United States Centennial.

The handsome Yule Marble that occurs along Yule Creek, south of Marble, Gunnison County, Colorado is also noteworthy if for no other reason than the fact that it was used for the Lincoln Memorial (but not for the famous statue in the memorial) and for the Tomb of the Unknown Soldier in Arlington National Cemetery. In addition, however, the Yule Marble is thought by some of the geologists who have worked in the area to represent recrystallization of limestone in response to pure thermal contact metamorphism.

Marble has also been used for rip-rap, aggregate in terrazzo, agricultural lime, as a source for chemical lime, as whiting, and as filler. The Cambrian Stissing Dolomite, a dolomitic marble of central eastern Dutchess County, New York, exemplifies the use of very pure marble as a filler.

Metamorphic Quartzites

As already noted, the term *quartzite* has been applied to both metamorphosed sandstone and silica-cemented sandstones that fracture indiscriminately across their grains and cement (see Figure 5-20). Therefore, the appropriate adjective, either metamorphic or sedimentary, should be used to indicate the true identity of each given quartzite.

Quartzites may be white or just about any color; the most common colors are gray, reddish, or some shade of brown. Quartzites may be finely laminated or massive, thin- or thick-bedded. Many of the color and grain size descriptions given for sandstone (page 193) pertain to quartzites. A few quartzites have undergone so complete a recrystallization that it is impossible by megascopic means to tell whether they were derived by metamorphism of sandstone or of chert. Other modifications characteristic of some metamorphic quartzites involve the development of closely spaced slickensided surfaces in cataclastically deformed zones and the development of metamorphic minerals in some of the more impure quartzites—for example, biotite, chlorite, hematite (specularite), kyanite, magnetite, muscovite, and sillimanite. Just as with marbles, the identity of these minerals may permit the placing of their host quartzites into their appropriate metamorphic facies. This, of course, is more likely to be possible with rocks such as metamorphosed arkoses and graywackes than with the more common metamorphosed quartzites that consist almost wholly of quartz.

Metamorphosed Conglomerates

These rocks, also called metaconglomerates or quartzite conglomerates, have the same general relationships to conglomerates that metamorphic quartzites do to sandstones. In essence, most of them are conglomerates with metamorphosed matrixes. A few have also had their larger clasts physically stretched and/or chemically modified. Metamorphosed conglomerates and conglomeratic rocks of many different origins are known—for example, metamorphosed tillites.

Occurrences of metamorphic quartzites and metamorphosed conglomerates. Metamorphic quartzites are relatively common in many metamorphic terrains. Well-known examples include the Precambrian Mississagi Quartzite near Blind River, Ontario and several quartzite units that occur here and there in the Precambrian Grenville sequence— for example, near Brier Hill and Hammond in Saint Lawrence County, New York. *Itacolumite*, a peculiar flexible rock that is a mica-rich quartzite, occurs in the Sauratown Mountains of western North Carolina. A metamorphosed conglomerate containing stretched pebbles occurs in the Littleton-Moosilauke District of western New Hampshire. The Precambrian age Lorrain Metaconglomerate and the Gowganda Metatillite, both of which crop out near Sault Sainte Marie, Ontario, are especially well known because of their widespread occurrence as glacial erratics in the upper midwestern United States.

Uses of metamorphic quartzites and metamorphosed conglomerates. High-silica quartzites have found use as the primary raw material in the manufacture of glass and refractory bricks and in the production of ferrosilicon alloys. They have also been used as dimension stones and locally as crushed stone.

Granulite

This term should probably be abandoned as a rock designation because it has been applied to at least four different kinds of rocks as well as to one of the major metamorphic facies (see Figure 6-2). If the term is to be retained for rocks, we believe that it should be restricted to use as a field term to be applied to medium- to coarse-grained granular metamorphic rocks, other than marbles, that lack obvious foliation.

Metamorphosed Iron-rich Rocks

Rocks of this subclass are formed either by regional metamorphism of iron-rich sedimentary rocks or by metasomatism during contact metamorphism. The nomenclature of the resulting rocks is confused by local terms introduced by miners and is not widely agreed upon. The following names and descriptions are consistent with some past usage and will permit megascopic naming of the relatively common varieties.

Banded iron formations are made up of alternating layers of fine-grained quartz and gray-colored layers of magnetite or reddish colored layers of hematite. The rocks have been given such names as *jaspilite* and *taconite*. Many have the overall appearance of argillites with mineral grains too small to be identified megascopically; some are coarse-grained.

Banded iron formations are best known in Precambrian terrains—for example, in the Lake Superior Region of Minnesota, Wisconsin, Michigan, and Ontario; in Minas Gerais, Brazil; in the Hamersley Range of Western Australia; and in the Transvaal, South Africa.

Hematite schist, sometimes called *itabirite,* has the overall appearance of a mica schist (page 262) with flakes of specular hematite rather than of mica. The original siliceous sediment, probably chert, has been recrystallized to megascopically distinguishable quartz grains while the iron minerals have been recrystallized to specular hematite plus or minus some magnetite.

Rocks of this kind also occur in the Lake Superior District as well as at several other localities throughout the world.

Gneisses

The term *gneiss* is a generic name for medium- to coarse-grained, banded, or roughly foliated crystalline rocks in which granular minerals are more abundant than minerals with platy habits (see Figure 6-1). Gneisses may be just about any color: most of the relatively homogeneous gneisses are light to dark gray, pink, or reddish because of their high feldspar contents; most of the banded gneisses consist of the same colors plus or minus black in alternate bands (Figure 6-13).

Quartz and potassium feldspar, generally microcline or microcline perthite, plus or minus a sodium-rich plagioclase and, in rare cases, calcite, are the common granular minerals in most gneisses; cordierite, garnet, and staurolite are abundant granular minerals in a few gneisses. Each of these minerals may range from nearly equidimensional to roughly lenticular in shape. Biotite, muscovite, and hornblende—alone or in combination—are the most common minerals that clearly define the foliation. Their preferred orientation may give a planar texture, a linear texture, or both. A few gneisses tend to break parallel to their foliation and thus expose mica-coated surfaces that give them schist-like appearances.

FIGURE 6-13   Banded gneiss from Kongshavn, near Kristiansand, Norway. (R. V. Dietrich)

Although much foliation appears to be essentially parallel to original discontinuities such as bedding, some foliation quite obviously transects original structures. The foliation ranges from poorly defined in the fairly homogeneous gneisses to extremely well defined, and recognizable over distances of several meters, in banded gneisses. Some of the banded gneisses, in particular, exhibit well-defined structures such as folds and faults.

Some gneisses contain relatively large grains of feldspar or other minerals such as almandine garnet, andalusite, or staurolite set in relatively fine-grained matrixes. Although a few of these megacrysts may be remnants of originally larger rock units such as sedimentary pebbles, most are porphyroblasts that grew during metamorphism. As mentioned for marbles and quartzites, the megacrysts may often be used to determine the appropriate metamorphic facies for their host rocks. The megacrysts may be euhedral, subhedral, or of some other fairly regular or irregular shape. Some of the large feldspar grains tend to be lenticular and thus are called augen after the German word meaning eye. (See Figure 6-5.)

Variety names of gneisses are based on several different characteristics: texture—for example, augen gneiss; overall appearance—for example, banded gneiss; mineral content (other than quartz)—for example, biotite-hornblende gneiss; or rock composition—for example, granite gneiss. In addition, the prefixes *ortho-* and *para-* are often used to distinguish between gneisses formed from igneous and sedimentary rocks, respectively. The adjective gneissic is used when the foliation is known or thought to be of metamorphic origin; the adjective gneissoid is used if the foliation is known or thought to be of nonmetamorphic origin. The latter includes foliation formed as the result of magmatic flowage and injection as is involved in the formation of some migmatites (page 270).

Most gneisses are of amphibolite facies or of higher metamorphic rank. Although they may be derived from a great range of igneous and sedimentary rocks, most gneisses appear to have been derived from granitoids and their aphanitic equivalents and from arkoses, feldspathic sandstones, siltstones, or shales.

Occurrences and uses of gneisses. Mica gneisses are both abundant and widely distributed in most metamorphic terranes. In North America, gneisses are well represented in many areas—for example, in the crystalline Appalachians of New England and in the Central Atlantic states and here and there in the Rocky Mountain Region.

Some relatively massive gneisses have been used as rip-rap, aggregate, and even as dimension stone. For the most part, however, such use has been restricted to areas where generally better suited rocks were not readily available.

Amphibolites and Amphibole Schists

Foliated rocks made up predominately of amphibole are called amphibolites if the other main constituent is feldspar and amphibole schists (or in some cases, amphibole gneisses) if it is quartz. The term amphibolite was introduced because this rather common gneissic-to-schistose rock contains very little if any quartz, once considered as specific for both gneisses and schists. As shown in Figure 6-2, the term amphibolite is also applied to one of the widely recognized metamorphic facies.

Most of the amphibole-rich rocks have fairly high specific gravities and are dark colored—typically different shades of green, greenish gray, or nearly black. Several have a silky sheen on foliated surfaces. In many, the nonamphibole constituents are practically masked by the amphiboles and can only be seen with the aid of a handlens on surfaces that cut across the foliation. Rocks of both kinds may be fine-, medium- or coarse-grained and exhibit essentially no to very good foliation, plus or minus lineation. Tabular grains of amphibole that range from hairlike and only a few millimeters long up to matchlike and 20 to 30 millimeters long are characteristic of the well-foliated amphibole-rich rocks. More nearly equidimensional amphibole grains, which appear to have replaced pyroxene, are common in poorly foliated or nonfoliated varieties.

As indicated by their prevalent colors, the common amphibole in these rock types is hornblende or actinolite. Less commonly, glaucophane, anthophyllite and/or cummingtonite occur. The feldspar in most amphibolites is plagioclase in the oligoclase-andesine range; the feldspar in most amphibole schists is microcline, a sodium-rich plagioclase or perthite, which occur individually or in any combination. Although amphibolites may grade into amphibole schists and vice versa, most amphibolites contain little or no quartz, whereas amphibole schists tend to contain as much or more quartz than feldspar. Because of their granularity, however, the feldspars and quartz are rather difficult to distinguish from each other in all but the relatively coarse-grained amphibole schists. Other minerals that occur in some of these rocks in grains large enough to be identified by megascopic means include calcite, chlorite, epidote (or clinozoisite), garnet (typically, deep red-colored almandine), magnetite (and/or some other opaque mineral or minerals), mica (biotite and/or muscovite), pyroxene (generally, diopside or augite), siderite, and sphene. Quartz and the common carbonate minerals may occur as veinlets as well as grains.

Amphibolites are named on the basis of some obvious constituent or constituents other than the amphibole or plagioclase—for example, a garnet amphibolite or an epidote amphibolite. Amphibole schists are named by the identity of the amphibole, sometimes with additional mineral name modifiers—for example, a biotite glaucophane schist.

It appears that amphibole-rich rocks are formed from several different rock types under conditions ranging from moderately low to moderately high grade regional metamorphism or, in some cases, in response to contact metamorphism. Among the parent rocks known to have been metamorphosed to amphibolites are dioritoids and gabbroids and their pyroclastic and aphanitic equivalents (especially basalt), ultramafites (such as some of the pyroxenites and peridotites) certain graywackes, and also various dolomitic and clayey sedimentary rocks.

Amphibole-rich rocks that occur as cross-cutting masses can be safely identified as former igneous dikes. Those that are interpreted to be metamorphosed diorites are sometimes called epidiorites. The origins of most amphibole-rich rocks that occur interlayered with schists and gneisses are difficult to interpret, even on the basis of fairly extensive laboratory studies.

Occurrences of amphibolites and amphibole schists. Both of these rocks, especially amphibolites, are extremely common rocks in many metamorphic terranes. Among the thousands of occurrences in North America, especially noteworthy examples occur in the Halliburton-Bancroft District of Ontario, where amphibole-rich rocks have been interpreted to represent contact metamorphosed impure marbles; in the Blue Ridge Province of southwestern Virginia and adjacent North Carolina, where there are relatively large cross-cutting dikes and also several different varieties of layered amphibole-rich rocks of undetermined parentage that are interbedded with gneisses and schists; in the Coast Ranges of California and Oregon, where there are glaucophane schists and similarly constituted slatelike rocks with origins that are still unproved; and in several other localities in the Sierra Nevada of California, near the bottom of the Grand Canyon of the Colorado in Arizona, in the Beartooth Mountains of Wyoming and Montana, and in the Biwabik District of northeastern Minnesota.

Uses of amphibolites and amphibole schists. A few of these rocks have been used for road metal. Some massive amphibolites surpass ASTM standards set for quality aggregate and are so used. Locally, some well-foliated amphibole-rich metamorphic rocks have been quarried, split, and marketed for use as flagstones.

Schists

Schist is the name given to medium- to coarse-grained, well-foliated metamorphic rocks in which platy minerals predominate (Figure 6-14). Schists grade into gneisses and phyllites. They may be named on the basis of their mineralogical composition—for example, garnet muscovite schist; their overall composition—for example, ferruginous schist; or some particular textural or appearance aspect—for example, spotted schist (a schist in which graphite, for example, is aggregated into sporadic dark spots). The following are relatively common varieties of schist and closely related rocks.

Mica schists include muscovite schists, biotite schists, and biotite-muscovite (commonly referred to as two-mica) schists, all of which are widespread and abundant. Paragonite (sodium mica) and fuchsite (chromium muscovite) schists also occur, but are rare. Muscovite and paragonite are typically silvery-white in color, biotite is brownish black or bronzy, and fuchsite is light bluish green. In the most common two-mica schists, biotite and muscovite occur as discrete grains or intimately intergrown so that some individual grains appear to be partly biotite and partly muscovite. The preferred orientation of the flakes, which are typically anhedral, or of aggregates of mica define the most obvious foliation in these schists. Some foliation surfaces and even individual mica grains may be curved or crenulated.

Quartz, the other major mineral in most schists, generally occurs in dense to saccharoidal, lens-shaped aggregates of grains with the long dimensions of the aggregates parallel to the overall foliation. In some schists, the predominately quartz aggregates contain grains of feldspar and/or calcite. Some mica schists contain such minerals as almandine garnet, staurolite, or sillimanite, which occur typically as idioblastic porphyroblasts that range up to several centimeters long. Other megascopically discernible minerals that occur in many mica schists are actinolite or hornblende, chlorite, epidote (including clinozoisite), graphite, and kyanite. The graphite tends to be in calcite-bearing schists. Nearly all mica schists have compositions and occurrences that indicate that they have been formed as the result of regional metamorphism of argillaceous sedimentary rocks such as siltstones and shales of felsic volcanic tuffs. Because of their overall grain size, the minerals that characterize metamorphic facies are rather readily identified in most schists. Mica schists form under conditions of the greenschist facies through amphibolite facies of metamorphism.

Chlorite schist and greenstone. *Chlorite schists* are foliated; *greenstones* are not. Both are green, typically yellowish green. Where the two rocks are spatially associated, the schists are often referred to as greenstone schists. Some chlorite schists are fine-grained and grade into phyllites. Nearly all of these rocks contain a sodic plagioclase and epidote. In some, the epidote occurs both as disseminated grains and as veinlets. A few contain actinolite. The chlorite schists, especially those that are fine-grained and transitional into phyllites, contain sericite, the fine-grained variety of muscovite. Some chlorite-rich rocks closely resemble, but are much harder than serpentinites.

True chlorite schists are much less common than either mica schists or chlorite phyl-

FIGURE 6-14 Porphyroblastic schists. Knife is 84 millimeters long. Top sample is a Precambrian-aged Lynchburg staurolite schist, from near Stuart, Patrick County, Virginia. Bottom sample is a Lynchburg two-mica, garnet schist from Burke's Fork, Floyd County, Virginia. (R. V. Dietrich)

lites. Greenstones are locally abundant as metamorphosed basaltic lavas. Amygdules are still readily recognized in some greenstones. The chemical composition of the rocks of this group supports the interpretation that most are formed by metamorphism of rocks of basaltic or ultramafic composition. Their mineralogical compositions indicate formation under relatively low-grade dynamothermal conditions that are characteristic of the greenschist facies.

Talc schist and **soapstone** consist predominately of talc. If the flakes, or plates of talc have a preferred orientation, the rock is called talc schist. If the rock is more or less massive, it is called soapstone or sometimes steatite.

Talc schists are generally light-colored—white, yellowish, greenish, or gray in color. Most soapstones are medium gray or fairly dark greenish gray in color. Some soapstone resembles certain serpentinites and pyrophyllite-rich rocks. Nonetheless, both soapstone and talc schist are relatively easy to identify because talc is so soft (H = 1)) and feels like soap.

Additional minerals that occur in talc-rich rocks include chlorite (in some cases the reddish purple chromitiferous kammererite), chromite, olivine, serpentine, enstatite, fuchsite, tremolite, magnetite, magnesite, quartz, and dolomite. In general, the additional minerals are megascopically discernible in talc schists but not in soapstones.

The common igneous rocks that are precursors of talc schists and soapstones are peridotite and pyroxenite; the most likely sedimentary rock parent is a dolomitic marl. The conditions of metamorphism under which talc-bearing rocks form are low- to medium-grade dynamothermal metamorphism in the greenschist or low amphibolite facies or, less commonly, by contact metamorphism.

Occurrences of schists. Mica schists are almost as common as gneisses. They occur here and there in essentially all areas of regional metamorphism—for example, in the Grenville Province of Canada and adjoining northern New York, in the Crystalline Appalachians of eastern North America, and in the Rockies and Coast Ranges of western North America. Although of much less common occurrence, the other schists and related rocks also occur sporadically in most regional metamorphic terranes. The following list, along with localities noted in the next section on "Uses" gives an exemplary North American locality or two for each of the other schists and related rocks: chlorite schist and greenstone—in the vicinity of Chester, Vermont and along the Menominee River in the Upper Peninsula of Michigan; hornblende schist—in the Van Horn Area of western Texas; chloritoid schist—in Lancaster County, Pennsylvania and Mariposa County, California; piemontite schist—near Pilar in northern New Mexico; pyrophyllite schist—in central North Carolina; staurolite schist—near Windham, Maine and in Patrick County, Virginia; and stilpnomelane schist—in the Blue Ridge Province of southwestern Virginia and in Mendocino County, California.

Uses of schists. Mica and chlorite schists have found little use other than as local building stones. The famous Firestone Library at Princeton University is faced by a rather striking mica schist known as the Wissahickon Schist.

Flake graphite has been recovered from some mica schists and gneisses. The deposits in Chilton, Clay, and Cossa counties in east central Alabama and in the Llano-Burnet area of central Texas are examples.

Dense greenstone has been used locally for crushed stone. A massive actinolite-chlorite rock quarried in Lynchburg, Virginia is marketed widely for uses as an ornamental and accent stone. Greenstones from Michigan, Pennsylvania, and Wisconsin are marketed in both their natural condition and as artificially colored granules for asphalt roofing. A few saccharoidal textured, epidote-rich varieties that resemble epidosite (page 126) have been taken from exposures of the Late Precambrian age Catoctin Greenstone near Luray, Virginia, for cutting and polishing as cabachons or scarabs for use in costume jewelry.

Talc schists serve as a primary source for commercial talc. Large tonnages of talc are used annually in the paint industry, as an extender for cold-water paints; in ceramics, as an additive; in the roofing, rubber, and insecticide industries, as a filler; and in all sorts of cosmetics such as creams, powders, rouges, and soap. Lesser quantities are used for such diverse things as a dusting agent in the manufacture of nails, as a polishing agent for glass and cereal grains, as an absorbent for odors and fluids from wounds, and as a base for crayons and for certain waxes and polishes. The largest production in North America is from deposits near Talcville, Saint Lawrence County, New York.

Because soapstone is so easily cut and shaped and because it is heat and acid resistant, it has been used for many different purposes since prehistoric times. Only a few uses follow: Prehistoric man fashioned it into cooking bowls and ornaments. Canadian Eskimo and native African artists carve some of their widely marketed statuettes from soapstone. Because it retains heat, it has been used for footwarmers, griddles, and fireless cooker stones. Because it is acid- and fire-resistant, soapstone has found widespread use for chemical hoods, table tops, and sinks in chemical and photographic laboratories. It is also used here and there by the building construction industry for such things as spandrels, wainscoting, and even floor tile. Today, nearly all North American production is from deposits near Schuyler, Nelson County, Virginia.

Kyanite, andalusite, and sillimanite from schists have served widely as raw materials for the production of refractories used in the ceramic, chemical, electrical, and metallurgical industries—for example, for chemical porcelain, furnace linings, and spark plugs. In North America, there has been noteworthy production of kyanite from schists and so-called schistose quartzites from the Piedmont Province of Virginia, North Carolina, and Georgia. Andalusite has been recovered from a sericite schist at White Mountain, Mono County, California. Sillimanite, although known to be fairly abundant in some of the schists of the Piedmont Province of North and South Carolina and Georgia and at scattered localities in New Hampshire, South Dakota, Colorado, New Mexico, and Washington, has not been recovered in commercial quantities from any of them. It has been recovered commercially from schists in Assam and Pradesh states, India.

With regard to the other schists, uses for graphite-bearing schists and hematite schists have already been mentioned. In addition, pyrophyllite from schists is used in many of the same ways as talc and pyrophyllite-rich soapstonelike rocks are often used in lieu of talc soapstone for refractory blocks. Piemontite schist is used locally as a rather attractive reddish violet accent stone.

Phyllites, Slates, and Argillites

Phyllites are very finely crystalline and well foliated. Slates are microcrystalline and so well foliated that they split readily into thin plates. Argillites resemble slates except that they do not cleave. The foliation of phyllites and the rock cleavage of slates may be parallel to or at any angle to the stratification of their sedimentary or pyroclastic parent rocks. Fossils, commonly distorted, may be preserved in these rocks, especially in slates and argillites.

Depending on one's viewpoint, phyllites may be considered as extremely fine-grained schists or as glossy slates. The minerals that define the foliations are muscovite (variety sericite), chlorite, and graphite. The grain size of these minerals, which essentially coincides with the cut-off between grains that are and are not discernible through a $10\times$ handlens, gives phyllites their typically glossy appearance. In general, silvery gray to light greenish gray colored phyllites are sericitic, green ones are chloritic, and dark gray to nearly black ones are carbonaceous (commonly graphitic). A phyllite may be distinguished from similarly appearing slates by its satin-like luster, its tendency to contain porphyroblasts and the fact that its foliation surfaces are commonly crenulated (Figure 6-15). In addition, quartz grains may be visible on cross fractures. Among the minerals reported as porphyroblasts are andalusite, biotite, chlorite, chloritoid, cordierite, garnet, magnetite, pyrite, staurolite, and stilpnomelane. As previously mentioned, occurrence data are often required to megascopically distinguish phyllites from phyllonites (page 247).

Slates are characterized by a cleavage that approximates mineral cleavage in perfection. They appear dull on cross fractures and dull to slightly shiny on cleavage surfaces. Slates may be nearly any color; the more common colors, correlated with the mineral or other material most likely to be responsible for the color are blue gray—sericite and/or illite; black—carbonaceous matter, generally graphite; red—hematite; green—chlorite and muscovite; and brown to yellowish brown—limonite. Many slates are spotted, streaked or mottled—for example, many predominantly red slates are partly green and/or purple. Some slates contain scattered crystals of pyrite or marcasite. A few contain concretions.

Some slates, shales, and devitrified rhyolite tuffs resemble each other. Among possibly distinguishing characteristics are the tendencies for slates to be firmer than shales, for slates to split at angles across stratification rather than parallel to it like shales (Figures 6-16 and 6-17), and for pyroclastic fragments to be etched out of devitrified rhyolite tuffs.

As just mentioned, argillites look like slates except that they do not exhibit slaty cleavage. As also previously noted (page 202), some argillites may be sedimentary, whereas others are metamorphic. Just as with some quartzites, it is essentially impossible to distinguish between argillites that are sedimentary and those that are metamorphic unless their geological occurrences are known.

Phyllites, slates, and argillites represent metamorphosed siltstone, shale, mudstone, or felsic pyroclastic rocks. Slates and argillites are formed under conditions generally attributable to the greenschist or low amphibolite facies. Most phyllites are formed under greenschist facies conditions. Some phyllites appear to have been formed by retrograde metamorphism.

Occurrences of phyllites, slates, and argillites. Phyllites and slates occur at least sparsely in most terrains of regional metamorphism. Perhaps the best known slates in the world are those from the Cambrian and Silurian formations of northern Wales. They have been shipped to every continent. In North America, slate is produced from quarries in central Maine, eastern Vermont, eastern Pennsylvania, northern Maryland, and central Virginia and is known to occur in potentially commercial deposits in Arizona, Arkansas, California, Colorado, Georgia, Minnesota, Nevada, New Jersey, Tennessee, Texas, Ontario, New Brunswick, and Nova Scotia.

Some commercial slates are phyllites. Other phyllites have been recorded from many rather widely separated localities in the James River Synclinorium near Lynchburg, Virginia; on the Blue Ridge Upland of Floyd County, Virginia; near Orange in southern

FIGURE 6-15 Phyllite (A) Hand specimen of Wills Phyllite, Floyd Co., Virginia. (R. V. Dietrich) (B) Thin section of Wepawaug Phyllite from Woodbridge, Connecticut. (B. J. Skinner)

FIGURE 6-16   Slates commonly exhibit rock cleavage—that is, they have a metamorphic texture that causes them to split readily across original sedimentary layering. From northern Vermont. (B. J. Skinner)

Connecticut; in the Mother Lode District of the western foothill belt of the Sierra Nevada in central California; and in the Sierra Diablo foothills of northwestern Texas.

Meta-argillites are less common rocks. A good example of an argillite of metamorphic nature is the red and green banded rock with the general appearance of a varved sediment that occurs in the Precambrian age Mount Rogers Sequence in the Blue Ridge Province near the commonpoint of North Carolina, Tennessee, and Virginia. Another example occurs in the Late Precambrian Belt Series of northwestern Montana.

Uses of slates and phyllites. Slates are quarried and cleaved for use as roofing, flagging, billiard tables, blackboards, table tops, hearth stones, and floor tile. The pyrite- and marcasite-bearing varieties are not used because they tend to become iron-stained upon weathering. Smaller pieces of slate and phyllite are ground and used as nodules for asphalt roofing and are heated until they bloat, with the end-product being marketed as lightweight aggregate.

ECLOGITES

The name eclogite comes from a Greek word meaning a choice selection, apparently in allusion to its attractive appearance. Eclogite is a rather rare, typically granular rock that was originally defined as consisting largely of a pyropic (pyrope + almandine ± grossular) garnet and an omphacitic (jadeite-diopside) pyroxene. Subsequently, some geologists have extended the term to apply to all crystalline rocks made up chiefly of garnet and pyroxene, no matter what their varietal compositions. We believe that this latter use of the term should be avoided.

Eclogites are rather striking rocks because they typically consist of a medium-grained, granular to saccharoidal mass of deep green pyroxene grains studded with nearly spherical

FIGURE 6-17   Slatey cleavage. This panel of slate, cleaved from the Ordovician aged Arvonia Slate of Virginia, exhibits bedding (upper right to lower left) at an angle to the natural splitting surface. (Holsinger Studio, Charlottesville, Virginia)

grains of reddish colored garnets. Some of these rocks have a crude foliation because of a preferred orientation of the pyroxene grains; others appear to be nonfoliated.

Some eclogites contain megascopically identifiable kyanite, rutile, diamond, epidote (or zoisite), hornblende (or some other amphibole), and plagioclase. The last three probably indicate retrograde metamorphism.

Some eclogites appear to be of igneous origin, whereas others are metamorphic. Among the diverse associations are (1) in kimberlite, as fragments apparently transported upward from some 100 to 250 kilometers deep within the mantle; (2) in ultramafic sequences of rocks, as streaks and lenses, probably formed by magmatic crystallization but possibly representing masses transported in from deep-seated loci (as in No. 1); (3) in migmatites of the granulite or high amphibolite metamorphic facies, as lenses and irregular-shaped masses; and (4) with glaucophane schists of metamorphosed orogenic zones, as the metamorphic products after basaltic rocks, including pillow lavas.

The fact that most eclogites are anhydrous and consist largely of minerals with high specific gravities—so-called space-saving minerals—suggests that, whether metamorphic or igneous, eclogites are formed under conditions of high confining pressure over a broad range of temperature. Many petrologists accept an eclogite metamorphic facies (see Figure 6-2).

Occurrences and uses of eclogites. Small masses of eclogite are rather widespread. A few examples are the fragments in South African and Siberian kimberlites, as streaks and lenses in ultramafic igneous masses of the Caledonian Range of western Norway and northwestern Scotland, and within the glaucophane schists of the Franciscan Series of California and of the Pennine Alps of northwestern Italy.

Some eclogites have been cut and polished and used for decorative purposes—for example, as table tops.

MIGMATITES

Migmatites, like pyroclastic and diagenetic rocks, serve to emphasize the fact that some rocks are transitional between the major rock families—in this case, between those designated metamorphic and those termed igneous. By definition, migmatites are composite mixtures of metamorphic and igneous or igneous-appearing components. A very large percentage of migmatites consist of a dark colored, metamorphic rock such as amphibolite and a light colored crystalline rock of granitoid composition. In field exposures, the dark colored rock generally appears to have once been physically and/or chemically less mobile than the light colored rock material (Figure 6-18).

Almost a hundred terms have been introduced to apply to migmatites of different origins and/or appearances and associated processes. In essence, however, there are only four main processes involved in the formation of migmatites. The end-products may be designated as follows:

Arterite—a migmatite, the mobile portion of which was injected magma.

Metasomatite—a migmatite, the mobile portions of which were tenuous fluids and/or diffusing ions introduced from an external source such as a magma.

Venite—a migmatite, the more mobile portion of which was formed by exudation (lateral secretion) from the rock itself.

Anatexite—a migmatite, the mobile portion of which was formed in response to partial melting—that is, the low melting temperature constituents became magma and were segregated from the remaining minerals.

FIGURE 6-18 Migmatite. A polished cenotaph of the so-called Morton Gneiss from the Minnesota River Valley, is really a Precambrian migmatite that is widely used as a decorative building stone. (R. V. Dietrich)

In many cases, it is impossible to determine which mode or modes of formation obtained without extensive field and laboratory studies. Unless the genesis is obvious, it is best to call the rock just plain migmatite. If one wishes to distinguish between the light- and dark-colored components of migmatites, it is best to use their proper rock designations. Short of this, sometimes the terms *leucosome* and *melasome* are used for the light- and dark-colored components, respectively. In addition, some petrologists use the terms *neosome* to refer to the more mobile constituent and *paleosome* for the relatively less mobile or immobile constituent.

A number of interesting features are most commonly found in migmatites. Two of them are noteworthy: *ptygma* is the name applied to granitoid material that occurs in the form of tortuous folds (Figure 6-19); *schlieren* are roughly tabular to irregular, relatively dark colored inclusions most of which appear nebulous and seem to represent xenoliths that have been soaked with granitoid material.

Occurrences of migmatites. Migmatites are especially common in terrains thought to represent the deepest levels of the Earth's crust. They also occur in contact zones of some of the relatively large intrusives such as batholiths and as discrete masses that appear to have been injected as *migma* (the name given to mobile or potentially mobile mixtures of solid rock material and rock melt).

The rocks first called migmatites occur in the Precambrian terrain of southern Finland. Subsequently, migmatites have been recognized in many parts of the world—especially in the Precambrian Shields. In America, there are several excellent exposures of migmatites

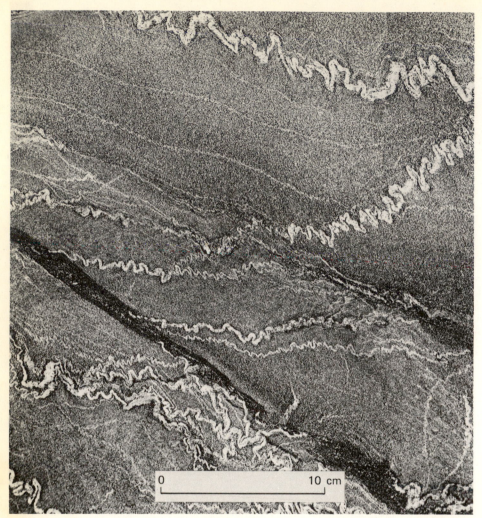

FIGURE 6-19   Ptygma. Polished surface of specimen from Little Hammond, Saint Lawrence County, New York. (R. V. Dietrich)

in the Canadian Shield and the northwest Adirondacks; near Lithonia, just east of Atlanta, Georgia; and in the contact zones of a number of the western North America batholiths—for example, the Chelan Batholith in north central Washington. Several intruded masses of migma are recorded from eastern Greenland. As with some of the other rocks, a comprehensive list of migmatite localities would fill many pages.

Uses of migmatites. Migmatites, like most other rocks, have been used locally as crushed stone for road metal and railroad ballast and also as rip-rap. The Morton Gneiss, a migmatite from the Minnesota River Valley of southwestern Minnesota, is widely used as polished ashlar and, to a lesser extent, for monuments. Each piece is unique and generally quite handsome with its red, black, gray, and nearly white hues arranged in rather flamboyant patterns.

Useful References

Dietrich, R. V. (1974), "Migmatites—A Résumé," C.E.G.S. Short Review No. 24, *Jour. Geol. Educ.,* Vol. 22, pp. 144–156.

Ernst, W. G., ed., (1975), *Metamorphism and Plate Tectonics Regimes.* Benchmark Papers in Geology, No. 17., New York: Halsted Press, 440 pp.

Fyfe, W. S., Turner, F. J., and Verhoogen, J. (1958), "Metamorphic Reactions and Metamorphic Facies." *Geol. Soc. Amer.,* Mem. 73, 259 pp.

Harker, A.(1939), *Metamorphism,* 2nd ed., New York: E. P. Dutton & Co., 362 pp.

Mehnert, K. R. (1968) *Migmatites and the Origin of Granitic Rocks,* Amsterdam: American Elsevier Publishing Co., Inc., 393 pp.

Miyashiro, A. (1973), *Metamorphism and Metamorphic Belts,* New York: John Wiley & Sons, Inc., 479 pp.

Nockolds, S. R., Knox, R. W. O'B, and Chinner G. A. (1978), *Petrology for Students,* Cambridge, England: Cambridge University Press, 435 pp.

Turner, F. J. (1968), *Metamorphic Petrology—Mineralogical and Field Aspects,* New York: McGraw-Hill Book Company, 403 pp.

Winkler, H. G. F. (1967), *Petrogenesis of Metamorphic Rocks,* 2nd ed., New York: Springer-Verlag, Inc., 237 pp.

CHAPTER 7
OTHER ROCKS AND PSEUDO-ROCKS

Some rocks present even greater difficulties to fit into the three major rock families than do pyroclastic rocks, diagenetically modified sedimentary rocks, or migmatites. Such rocks, plus a number of pseudo-rocks, which are man-made materials that resemble and can easily be mistaken for rocks, are described in this chapter in the following order.

Veins and products of wallrock alteration
Rocks produced by weathering and groundwater
Meteorites
Impactites and Tektites
Fulgurites
Pseudo-rocks
  Asphalt mixes
  Brick and Tile
  Cinders
  Coke
  Concrete
  Glass and Porcelain
  Slag
  Terrazzo

VEINS

Veins are mineral masses that have been deposited in tabular or sheetlike openings in rocks by hot, aqueous (hydrothermal) solutions (Figure 7-1). The openings may have been fissures caused by jointing or faulting, spaces in loose breccias, partings along bedding planes, or solution cavities. Veins may range up to several kilometers in length and from less than a millimeter to several meters in thickness; be of uniform thickness or range greatly from place to place; have relatively simple shapes or constitute an intricately braided network; occur singly or in groups with parallel, intersecting, or other regular geometric relationships; be solid or contain voids, commonly with crystals protruding into them.

Veins may have sharp walls or grade through a transitional zone of alteration and/or replacement with their surrounding country rock. Nonetheless, even where veins have so-called gradational margins, the veins are easy to distinguish from their enclosing rocks

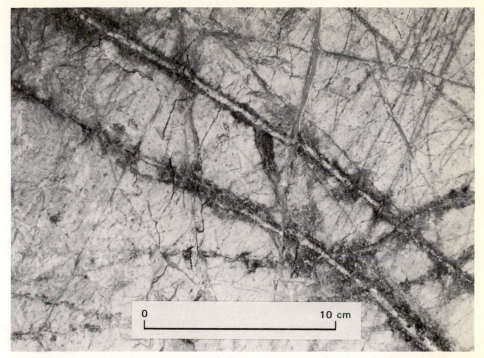

FIGURE 7-1 Veined limestone, Gaspé Copper Mine, Québec. Hydrothermal solutions moved through fractures, depositing ore minerals and altering adjacent wallrocks. (John Allcock)

because of differences in textures and/or compositions. The grain sizes of vein minerals can range from very coarse-grained to cryptocrystalline (e.g., from so-called bull quartz to chalcedonic silica). Many veins exhibit features generally interpreted as indicating growth in open space—for example, elongate crystal units approximately perpendicular to walls, rough or interrupted banding nearly parallel to walls, and/or the presence of well-formed crystals either enclosed on all but one side by another mineral or protruding into voids.

Veins may contain only one, two, or several minerals. Quartz is the most common vein mineral; calcite is also relatively common; other minerals include various native elements, sulfide, sulfate and carbonate minerals, and many others. Some individual veins have different mineralogical compositions from section to section—for example, a so-called galena-sphalerite vein at the surface may pass downward through a chalcopyrite- and pyrite-rich zone into a lower massive pyrite ($\pm$ magnetite) zone before pinching out. Other veins, which may or may not be more or less homogeneous individually, may be seen to present still a different type of zoning—one often referred to as regional or district zoning. In this latter type of zoning, apparently related veins of different compositions exhibit some regular and predictable distribution pattern—for example, a concentric arrangement of galena-sphalerite veins around chalcopyrite-pyrite veins. Some zoned districts cover 500 or more square kilometers.

Veins are best named on the basis of their compositions—for example, a quartz vein or a galena-bearing calcite vein. In the past, however, many veins have been characterized on the basis of their interpreted temperature and/or depth of formation by names such as high temperature or hypothermal veins, and moderate temperature or mesothermal veins. Such terms involve interpretation based on models and assumptions that are questionable, so the terms should be avoided.

In rare cases, veins may resemble sedimentary strata or igneous dikes or sills. They may be distinguished from sedimentary strata and most tabular igneous masses on the basis of their compositions and/or textures. There is, however, disagreement as to whether some pegmatite masses (page 124) are igneous dikes or veins; in fact, a few especially prudent geologists apply the curious term vike to such masses.

Although much remains to be learned about the origin of veins, a few generalizations can be made. The fundamental requirements for vein formation are the existence of hot aqueous solutions, flow channels for circulation, sites where deposition may occur, and physical and chemical conditions that will promote deposition.

The water may be groundwater, sea water that was entrapped within sediments, or water given off by cooling and crystallizing magma. The ore metals may also be magmatic in origin or they may be leached from the rocks through which the hydrothermal solutions passed. Regardless of the sources of either the metals or the water, samples of the solutions that have been caught in tiny bubbles inside vein minerals (Figure 7-2) show that the solutions are brines that are as salty as, or even more salty, than sea water. And, it can be

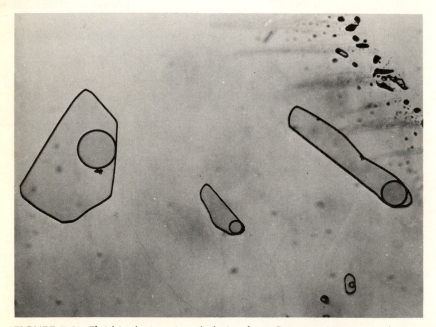

FIGURE 7-2 Fluid inclusions in sphalerite, from Cananea, Mexico. Inclusions contain saline water, a round vapor bubble, and tiny crystals of daughter minerals deposited from the cooling solution. Magnification 100×. (Edwin Roedder)

shown that such brines, especially at elevated temperatures, are potent solvents for many materials.

The depositional sites may be merely open spaces such as those just mentioned or they may be some particularly reactive substrate. Indeed, in many places, certain vein minerals occur more commonly, if not exclusively, where the vein transects some certain rock and/or zone rich in some certain alteration product. Additional chemical and physical controls include pressure, temperature, and concentration, acidity (pH), and state of oxidation (Eh) of the solution.

Wallrock Alteration

Vein forming solutions commonly modify at least some of the rocks through which they migrate. The changes, generally referred to as wallrock alteration (Figure 7-3), may involve isochemical redistributions of elements within the rocks and/or additions to (and almost always complementary subtractions from) the original rocks. Several such changes are so common that they have been given well recognized and accepted names (Table 7-1). Wallrock alterations often provide geologists with good clues about the fluids that were active and thus to the identity of possibly associated mineral deposits.

FIGURE 7-3 Wallrock alteration is indicated by bleached zones surrounding fractures within dark gray, unaltered limestone, Gaspé Copper Mine, Québec. (John Allcock)

TABLE 7-1   Rock types formed by wallrock alteration.

Process Designation	Common Minerals in Alteration Zones	Rock Often Affected	Typical Changes
Argillization (including kaolinization)	Clay minerals ± alunite, sericite, pyrite, topaz, tourmaline	Dioritoids and andesites	Alteration of feldspars to clays
Greisenization	Topaz, lepidolite, tourmaline, fluorite	Granitoid compositions, including metamorphics	Especially feldspar and muscovite alteration
Propylitization	Epidote-family minerals, carbonates, chlorite, serpentine, ± albite, quartz, sericite, sulfides, zeolites	Dioritoids, andesites	Mafic minerals are altered to calcite, chlorite and serpentine; plagioclase may be altered to albite and epidote
Sericitization	Sericite ± quartz, pyrite, and clay minerals	Feldspar-rich rocks	Felsic minerals to sericite and quartz ± clay minerals
Silicification	Quartz, chalcedony (including jasper), opaline silica	Any rock	Impregnation and/or replacement by silica

Occurrences and uses of veins. Veins are present in many igneous, sedimentary, and metamorphic rocks. They are especially common in metamorphic rocks and adjacent to contacts between relatively large igneous intrusives and the rocks they intrude. Veins may be associated with and grade into rocks with vesicles or other pore spaces that are filled with the same minerals as the veins.

Many famous mineral deposits are based on production from veins. Included are deposits of gold, silver, copper, lead, zinc, tungsten, tin, antimony, mercury, and bismuth as well as deposits of other mineral resources like fluorite and barite. The following are exemplary deposits in North America: *Gold*–Mother Lode, California; Cripple Creek, Colorado; Porcupine and Kirkland Lake, Ontario. *Silver*–Coeur d'Alene, Idaho; Comstock Lode, Nevada; Cobalt, Ontario; and Tintic, Utah. *Copper*–Kennicott, Alaska; Bisbee, Arizona; and Butte, Montana. *Lead* and *zinc*–San Juan, Colorado and the Tri-State District of Kansas, Missouri and Oklahoma. *Tungsten*–Atolia, California and Mill City and Silver Dyke, Nevada. *Mercury*–New Almaden and New Idria, California. *Uranium*–Great Bear Lake, Northwest Territories, Canada. *Asbestos*–Thetford Mines, Québec. *Barite*–Washington

County, Missouri. *Fluorite*–southeastern Illinois and adjacent Kentucky. And, there are, of course, many other vein deposits not only in North America but throughout the world.

ROCKS PRODUCED BY WEATHERING AND GROUNDWATER

Weathering involves both physical distintegration and chemical changes. Nearly all of the chemical changes involve groundwater solutions and include such processes as solution, oxidation, reduction, and hydration. Among the several things that may happen either individually or in combination are: original minerals may be decomposed; new minerals may be formed; mineral matter in solution may be added to the original rock; and, minerals may be dissolved and subtracted from the original rock.

Both original and new minerals may become parts of new mineral assemblages. Predominantly physical processes may produce lag concentrates, placers or clastic sediments. Predominately chemical processes may lead to residual concentrations, supergene enrichment or other chemical precipitation.

In this section, brief descriptions are given for two relatively common rock groups formed by residual concentration (residual clays and laterites) together with a group of rocks formed by leaching and enrichment of ore deposits (gossans, oxidized, and supergene ores) and a number of special rocks formed by precipitation from groundwater solution (duricrusts and hardpans). Travertine and siliceous sinter, previously described on pages 209 and 211, respectively, are also formed by groundwater precipitation.

Residual Clays

Clay is the name applied to more or less consolidated masses of one or more of the clay minerals. The different mineral species cannot be identified megascopically. Probably the most abundant species are kaolinite and montmorillonite.

When pure, clays are white; when stained by minute quantities of iron, managanese, and/or organic compounds, they may be just about any color—for example, gray, buff, pink, red, yellowish, greenish, light purple, brown or nearly black. Most residual clays feel smooth, stick to the tongue and have a musty (clay-like) odor when damp—for example, when breathed on. Some clays contain impurities such as gritty quartz grains.

Many residual clays are essentially indistinguishable from transported clays. Some residual clays may be traced downward through transitional zones of partly weathered material into their nonweathered parent rock. Typical parent rocks include granitoids, syenitoids, gneisses, and shales, all of which contain one or more high-aluminum minerals, such as feldspar, that tend to weather to a clay mineral.

Residual clays are formed by normal chemical weathering in areas with relatively humid temperate climates. Most of the processes involve the conversion of feldspar to clay and the removal of other minerals in solution.

Bentonite forms from tuff that has been altered to montmorillonite, plus or minus beidellite, and is described under the pyroclastic rocks (page 169).

Occurrences of clays. Residual clays in North America occur in at least small quantities in most of the United States south of the limit of glaciation. The best known occurrences are in the Appalachian Piedmont Province from Delaware to Georgia. The deposits overlying pegmatite masses in western North Carolina are exemplary. Lesser deposits, apparently derived from impure dolomites, occur here and there near the eastern edge of the Appalachian Valley and Ridge Province and in southeastern Missouri.

Uses of clays. Clay was one of the earliest mineral commodities to be used on a large scale—burned clay figurines identified as probably Aurignacian (30,000 to 20,000 B. C.) have been found in Moravia and fine pottery dating back to at least 10,000 B. C. has been unearthed in Egypt. Bricks, made by firing clay, have been made since at least the early days of the Babylonian Empire (~2800 B. C.).

Today, clays are the basic raw material of the ceramic industry and are used widely as fillers and in drilling muds.

Laterites and Bauxites

Laterite is the general term for highly weathered rock material from which nearly everything except hydrous oxides of ferric iron and/or aluminum has been leached. Laterites are typically earthy, poorly to well consolidated, medium soft to hard (gibbsite has a hardness of 2.5 to 3.5 whereas diaspore has a hardness of 6.5 to 7), and they break with an uneven to conchoidal fracture.

Laterites have three different textural variants, each of which may occur alone or with one or both of the others in a given deposit: (1) pisolitic, (2) massive, and (3) spongy. Pisolites are spheroidal nodules that resemble pebbles but actually are concretionary (Figure 7-4). They may be widely spaced or closely packed within typically massive lateritic material. Most pisolites are less than 2 centimeters in diameter. In a given deposit they may range greatly or be of a fairly uniform size. They tend to be of the same color or slightly darker than their surrounding matrix. Internally, pisolites may appear concentric, radiating fibrous or massive. The massive pisolites resemble their fine-grained and compact matrix material. The spongy type of laterite has been alternatively described as cellular. Obviously porous, it commonly consists of closely spaced spheroidal cavities, each up to about a centimeter across. In some places, laterites have retained certain elements of the textures of their parent rocks.

The most common aluminum hydroxides are gibbsite and diaspore. The common iron minerals are hematite and limonite. Laterites made up predominantly of aluminum hydroxides are called *bauxites*. Laterites made up predominately of iron minerals are called *iron laterites*. Frequently, the two can be distinguished by overall color—many, but not all, bauxites are off-white, light gray, cream, pink-buff or tan colored, whereas most iron laterites are dark brown, dark red or almost black. Both may contain several other minerals—for example, quartz, the clay minerals kaolinite, halloysite and nontronite, plus the titanium and manganese oxides, and the phosphate minerals.

Although laterites can be seen in the process of formation today, the complicated processes are far from being completely understood. The main controls appear to be: (1) permeable parent rocks that contain iron- and/or aluminum-bearing materials, (2) a tropical, monsoonal climate, (3) slightly acid, leaching solutions, (4) low topographic relief (to prevent rapid erosional removal), and (5) ample time. The fact that many laterites are spatially associated with clay suggests that the formation of clay may represent an intermediate step.

Occurrences of laterites and bauxites. Because of the required climatic conditions and the tendency for rapid removal of the products of chemical weathering by erosion, most laterites occur in Late Mesozoic or more recent deposits and are confined to relatively low latitudes—for example, in the East Indies, northern Australia and southeastern Asia, in the West Indies and northern South America, in West Africa, and in the jungles of Brazil. In North America, apparently reflecting former climatic conditions, fossil laterites

FIGURE 7-4   Bauxite from the Lightner deposit, 4 kilometers west of Spottswood, Augusta County, Virginia, exhibiting typical concretionary pisolites of gibbsite with minor amounts of diaspore and traces of kaolinite. (R. V. Dietrich)

occur beneath Cretaceous and later sediments on Long Island and bauxites occur in many places, such as near Little Rock in central Arkansas, in the Appalachians of Alabama and Georgia, and in northwestern Oregon. The Cuban laterites are developed on serpentinite; the Arkansas bauxites overlie nepheline syenite; the Alabama and Georgia bauxites are derived from residual clay; and the Oregon material is formed from ferruginous basalt of Middle Miocene age.

Uses of laterites and bauxites. Laterite got its name from the Latin word *later*, meaning brick, because it could be made into extremely durable building stones by merely cutting it into blocks of the desired shapes and sizes and then wetting and drying them. In the drying process, colloidal sized particles of hydrous ferric hydroxide in the laterite are partly and irreversibly dehydrated to limonite.

Bauxites are the basis of a large percentage of the world's aluminum production.

Gossans, Oxidized Ores, and Supergene Ores

As can be seen in Figure 7-5, gossans and oxidized and supergene ores are genetically related—metallic elements subtracted from above produce secondary enrichment below. In the general process, ground water dissolves pyrite (FeS_2) to form sulfuric acid (H_2SO_4) and the residual iron oxides that make up the gossan; the acid dissolves other metallic minerals and carries them away in sulfate solutions; the solutions may deposit native metals, oxides, sulfates, carbonates, and silicates as oxidized ore above the water table; and, as the result of loss of oxygen, the modified solutions that enter the saturated zone below the water

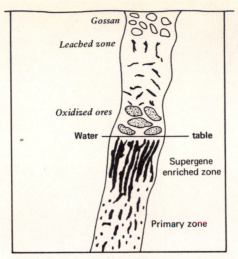

FIGURE 7-5 Relationships among gossan, oxidized ore, supergene ore, and primary ore in a vein.

table may deposit secondary sulfide minerals to form supergene ore—in most cases, directly below the water table.

Gossans are typically dense to cellular rocks that consist chiefly of limonite family minerals (Figure 7-6). The limonite is generally a fine-grained mixture of megascopically indiscernible goethite and hematite plus or minus jarosite [$KFe_3(SO_4)_2(OH)_6$]. It is variously colored yellowish to seal brown or maroon. It may have any of several textures ranging from fine-granular and massive to honeycombed. The patterned voids of gossans are called boxworks. They may be rounded and resemble vesicles or they may be prismatic with a shape characteristic of the mineral that once occupied the space.

Oxidized ores are most frequently formed low in the zone of oxidation just above the groundwater table. Deposition occurs in response to concentration by evaporation or to reactions of the descending solutions with other solutions or rock materials. Although many minerals that occur in oxidized deposits also occur in primary deposits, several minerals are thought to form only under oxidizing conditions—for example, the copper carbonate minerals azurite [$Cu_3(CO_3)_2(OH)_2$] and malachite [$Cu_2(CO_3)(OH)_2$]; the lead and zinc carbonates cerussite ($PbCO_3$) and smithsonite ($ZnCO_3$); the oxide minerals psilomelane [$BaMn_9O_{16}(OH)_4$] and wulfenite ($PbMoO_4$); the silicates chrysocolla ($CuSiO_3 \cdot 2H_2O$) and hemimorphite [$Zn_4(OH)_2Si_2O_7 \cdot H_2O$]; and the sulfate minerals anglesite ($PbSO_4$), antlerite [$Cu_3(SO_4)(OH)_4$], brochantite [$Cu_4(SO_4)(OH)_6$] and chalcanthite ($CuSO_4 \cdot 5H_2O$).

Supergene ores occur where descending metal-bearing solutions percolate through sulfide-bearing rock below the zone of oxidation—that is, below the groundwater table. These ores are characterized by replacement of sulfides and other minerals in the primary ore by sulfide minerals introduced by the percolating solutions. The replacements usually involve removal of iron in solution and substitution of other metals with greater affinities for sulfur. The order from greatest to least affinity for sulfur is mercury, silver, copper,

FIGURE 7-6 Gossan. (A) Massive, botryoidal limonite derived from a massive pyrite-bearing primary ore. Gardiner Mine, Bisbee, Arizona. (B) Cellular, spongy boxwork derived from sphalerite. Empire Zinc Mine, Hanover, New Mexico. (From Roland Blanchard, 1968, Bull. 66, Nevada Bur. Mines)

bismuth, lead, zinc, nickel, cobalt, iron, and manganese—which means, for example, that supergene chalcocite will tend to replace primary pyrite and chalcopyrite. The degree of replacement, which in some of these rocks is observable with handlens, ranges from incipient to complete and from selective to all pervasive. Incipient replacement is marked by surface tarnish, thin crusts, and/or fine veining. Pseudomorphs are formed in many supergene ores—for example, chalcocite after chalcopyrite, and covellite after galena are both common.

In most zones of supergene enrichment at least some of the original sulfides and/or other primary minerals have persisted. These serve to indicate the composition of the underlying primary ore.

Uses of gossans, oxidized ores, and supergene ores. Gossans are important as possible indicators of underlying ore deposits. Extensive studies have indicated that different colors and textures of the limonite boxworks may be correlated with the minerals that were leached out and thus may be used to predict the identity of both the primary mineral suites and the subsequently deposited supergene minerals. In addition, in bygone days, some gossans were used as local sources of iron—for example, pots and pans made during the early 1800s from a gossan in Floyd County of the Blue Ridge Upland of southwestern Virginia had so much copper in them that they were a copper-iron alloy. Their users said "they rang like a bell and far outlasted other ironware."

The utilization of oxidized ores dates back several centuries. In fact, one of the oldest underground mining operations in the world was in a malachite-rich deposit in the Negev Desert of southern Israel. That mine, which includes a multilevel, rather complex network of drifts and shafts (some apparently dug as ventilation tubes), has been dated as late Bronze Age, approximately 3400 B.P.

Supergene ores are usually small, but very rich, compared to the mass of primary ore below. Thus a primary ore that contains less than 1 percent copper may, in the supergene zone, be enriched to 10 percent copper or more. As a result, supergene ores have often been the rich plums that have provided the profits and capital used to develop the underlying large, but low grade, deposits—for example, the huge copper mine at Bingham, Utah, now the largest copper mine in the world, started operation on rich supergene ores, but is now based on primary ore containing as little as 0.5 percent copper.

Duricrusts and Hardpans

These partially to well-consolidated rock materials consist of unconsolidated overburden that has been cemented and/or otherwise aggregated by percolating groundwater solutions. Some are formed on top of the land surface; others are formed below. Those that consist largely of sand and gravel resemble conglomerate or concrete. Others look like normal limestone, impure gyprock, cemented soil, sandstone, or other clastic sedimentary rocks, including sedimentary quartzite. A few are nothing more than thin efflorescent crusts. Typical colors are off-white, buff, rusty, or reddish brown. In some of the coarser grained types, the cement may be seen to occur as successive crusts on the larger fragments.

The nomenclature for these rocks is somewhat confused. We suggest that the term *duricrust* be restricted to rocks of this type that are formed on the surface and that *hardpan* be used for those formed below the surface. Thence, either can be modified by the name of the cementing material—for example, gypsiferous duricrust and limonitic hardpan. Alternatively, the following rather widely employed terms can be used: *calcrete* for calcium carbonate-cemented duricrust; *gypsum earth* or *gypsite* for gypsum-rich duricrust;

ferricrete for iron oxide- (limonite- and/or hematite-) cemented duricrust; *silcrete* for silica-cemented duricrust; *claypan* for clay-rich, hardpan-like soil layers; *fragipan* for dense silt- and sand-rich hardpan-like subsurface soil layers; *ironpan* for iron oxide-cemented hardpan; *limepan* for calcium carbonate-cemented hardpan; and *moorpan* for ironpan that is rich in peat or bog materials. The highly ambiguous term caliche should be abandoned because it has been applied rather indiscriminately to both calcium carbonate-cemented duricrusts and hardpans and also to the well-known sodium nitrate-cemented gravels and soils of northern Chile and Peru.

Duricrusts are deposited by groundwater solutions that move upward, at least in part, by capillary action, and evaporate at the surface. The composition of duricrust reflects the composition of the groundwater, which, in turn, is influenced by the compositions of the underlying rock materials. Hardpans are formed by similar chemical action below the surface. In some cases, hardpans are deposited by rising water in interstices within the capillary fringe at the top of the groundwater table. In others, they are formed by more typical soil-forming processes that involve leaching by descending solutions and deposition lower down within the vadose zone.

Occurrences of duricrusts and hardpans. Duricrusts are relatively common in semi-arid regions. Especially noteworthy examples are to be seen on some of the tablelands of the countries of the Middle East and in the southwestern United States. For example, the Bethlehem stall in which Christ was born was dug in a calcium carbonate duricrust.

Hardpans occur sporadically in both semiarid and semihumid areas. Where present, hardpans essentially preclude cultivation because roots cannot penetrate them and water cannot percolate through them.

A few duricrusts have been recognized in relatively ancient rock units. Examples include a Precambrian silcrete in the Lake Superior Iron District, a calcrete in the Devonian age Old Red Sandstone of northern Wales, and another in the Mississippian age Mauch Chunk Formation of eastern Pennsylvania.

Uses of duricrusts and hardpans. Gypsum duricrusts have been used in Egypt for land plaster (fertilizer) and as a raw material for plaster of Paris. The occurrence is one of the very few mineral deposits known that is continually renewing itself.

Some of the iron-rich duricrusts and hardpans—for example, one near Seney in Michigan's Upper Peninsula—have been used for local iron production and/or as pigments. In general, however, hardpans are only a curse to farmers, as the often applied term, "plow-sole," implies.

METEORITES

Solid fragments of extraterrestrial origin that have fallen on Earth are called meteorites. Despite the fact that meteorites have been falling on Earth throughout geologic history, as late as 1808 the usually sagacious Thomas Jefferson is said to have questioned their existence. There is an unsubstantiated suggestion that when Jefferson heard that Benjamin Silliman and James L. Kingsley, both professors at Yale, had reported a meteorite fall at Weston, Connecticut, he remarked: "It is easier to believe that Yankee professors would lie, than that stones would fall from heaven."

Although there are meteorites with all sorts of irregular shapes, many are roughly conical and exhibit grooves and pits formed by inflight ablation as they passed through the atmosphere (Figure 7-7). In any case, most meteorites—even as freshly broken fragments that were not seen to fall—have megascopic features that distinguish them from terrestrial rocks.

Several kinds of meteorites have been given special names relating to their compositions. All may be placed into three general categories.

Iron Meteorites

These are the meteorites made up almost wholly of metallic iron-nickel alloys. The most common type consists largely of alternating lamellae of kamacite and taenite. These natural alloys, along with sulfide minerals and nonmetallic minerals, constitute the three main categories of irons. The classes are based on nickel percentages: *hexahedrites* - 4–6 percent Ni, *octahedrites* - 6–12 percent Ni, and *ataxites* - >12 percent Ni. When polished and etched by dilute acid, the octahedrites—the most common iron meteorites—often exhibit

0   5 cm

FIGURE 7-7 External surface of a meteorite found at Weston, Conn. Smooth, fluted surface was produced by ablation as the meteorite fell through the atmosphere. The internal texture can be seen on the sawed face. (Smithsonian Institution)

Widmanstätten patterns (Figure 7-8), which express the arrangement of the lamellae parallel to octahedral faces.

When found, some iron meteorites have thin (~ 1 mm) outer coatings of brownish iron oxide. Iron meteorites tend to be large compared to stony meteorites. Many that weigh several tons have been found—for example, one discovered in West Africa was nearly 100 meters long and weighed upwards of a million metric tons.

Stony-Iron Meteorites

Sometimes called siderolites, these meteorites constitute the transitional group in the more or less continuous series between the iron and stony categories. There are two general types the pallasites, which have the appearance of a metallic matrix or continuum studded with spheroidal, nometallic mineral grains (Figure 7-9), and the mesosiderites, which look like breccias of nonmetallic minerals and mineral aggregates with much disseminated metallic material. The spheroidal mineral grains in the first type average about 5 millimeters across and are typically olivine but may consist of combinations of such minerals as bronzite and tridymite. The common metallic constituents are the Fe-Ni alloys kamacite and taenite, plus troilite. Stony-iron meteorites up to several hundred kilograms have been found.

Stony Meteorites

These meteorites, sometimes called stones or aërolites, consist predominately of silicate minerals—for example, plagioclase, clino- and/or ortho- pyroxene and olivine. Many of them also contain the metallic minerals kamacite, taenite, and troilite. Less common constituents include chromite, magnetite, graphite, and diamond plus some chloride,

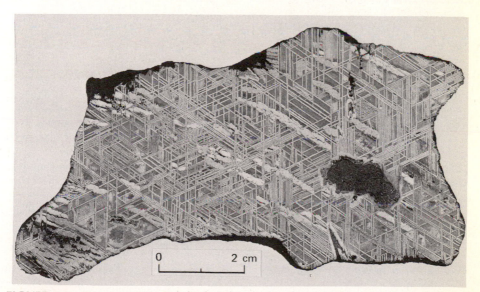

FIGURE 7-8   Iron meteorite. Polished and etched surface of Edmonton, Kentucky, octahedrite. Narrow white bands are kamacite; gray angular areas enclosed by bands are plessite. (Smithsonian Institution)

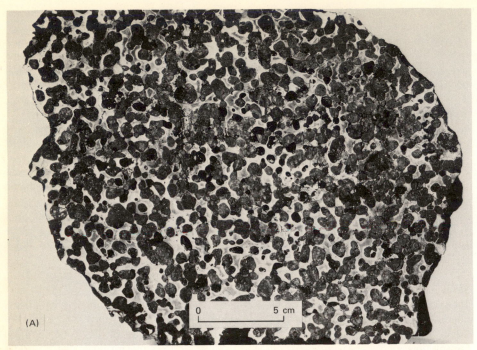

FIGURE 7-9 Stony-iron meteorites. (A) Polished surface of Brenham pallasite, showing rounded crystals of olivine (gray to black) in a matrix of nickel-iron (white). (B) Polished surface of the Huckitta pallasite, showing angular fragments of olivine (black) up to 6 centimeters long in a matrix of nickel-iron. (From Brian Mason, The Pallasites; American Museum Novitiates, No. 2163, 1963)

phosphide, and carbide minerals that are not known, or are extremely rare in terrestrial rocks.

When found, stony meteorites generally have a thin (~ 1 millimeter) black ablation crust (brownish when weathered) and a light gray interior with sporadic black spots, shiny flecks of metallic iron-nickel and/or pinhead to pea-sized gray to brownish spheroidal masses. The overall texture is fine-grained granular to aphanitic. The metallic flecks are malleable. The spheroidal masses, called chondrules (Figure 7-10), are easily broken, most with conchoidal fractures that have shiny lusters. Actually, however, the chondrules have many different internal textures and compositions. With handlens, most of the larger ones may be seen to consist of radiating fibers of orthopyroxene, of more or less parallel plates of olivine with intercalated light brown glass, of porphyritic masses consisting of small crystals of olivine in a glassy groundmass, or of chiefly granular olivine. Stones that contain chondrules are called *chondrites*; those without chondrules are called *achondrites*. Chondrites make up more than 75 percent of the stony meteorites recorded as having been observed while falling.

Although stony meteorites—especially the achondrites—resemble terrestrial rocks, either the presence within them of a few chondrules or of flecks of malleable iron-nickel generally suffices to distinguish them from terrestrial rocks.

(B)

0   5 cm

Even though it is rather generally thought that some, perhaps a large percentage, of the meteorites that have fallen on Earth are fragments from a small disrupted planet now represented by the belt of asteroids between Mars and Jupiter, some scientists believe otherwise. Regardless of their original location within the Solar System, all meteorites apparently orbit the sun and were formed at the same time as Earth and the other planets. Because of their great age—about 4.6 billion years—and certain of their features, some scientists have suggested that unmetamorphosed chondrites represent not just the oldest planetary matter known but perhaps the actual primordial material of our solar system.

Meteorites are named on the basis of their identity and the name of the place where they fell to Earth—for example, the Copper Valley siderolite. It has been reported that when meteorites fall, they make a luminous streak across the sky, followed by a trail of smoke, that they give off a startling sound like rapid gunfire until they land or darken, and that they sometimes explode above the surface with the resulting fragments subsequently giving off hissing sounds as they fall. The latter phenomenon, when hundreds of pieces are involved, is called a meteorite shower—an example would be the Holbrook, Arizona Fall of 1912 that is reported to have involved more than 14,000 stones that ranged from about 1 to 15 centimeters across and had a total weight of about 225 kilograms.

There undoubtedly are many meteorites, especially stony ones, yet to be found. This claim is supported by three facts: (1) among the meteorites that have been observed to fall, there is a predominance of stony meteorites; (2) in collections there is a predominance of iron meteorites; and, (3) whereas iron meteorites do not resemble common rocks and

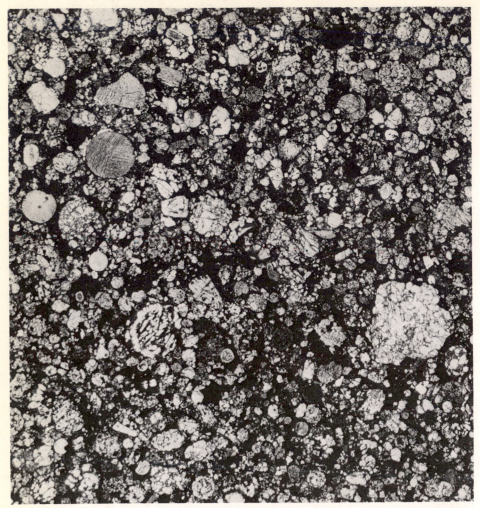

FIGURE 7-10 Stony meteorite. Photomicrograph of thin section of the Clovis chondrite, showing spherical chondrules (average ~1 millimeter in diameter) of olivine and/or pyroxene in a fine-grained groundmass. (Smithsonian Institution)

thus are noticed, stony meteorites do superficially resemble common rocks and thus are frequently not recognized unless they are seen falling.

Occurrences of meteorites. Because of their origin, occurrences appear to be of little more than historical interest. It is noteworthy, however, that meteors frequently form craters when they land. Small craters only a few meters across and a few centimeters deep as well as craters up to more than a kilometer across and several meters deep have been formed. In North America, two well known craters are the Barringer Crater near Winslow, Arizona, and the crater now occupied by Clearwater Lake, near Hudson Bay in western

Québec. The latter, apparently of Precambrian age, is approximately 30 kilometers in diameter.

Uses of meteorites. Iron meteorites were used to make tools long before man learned how to smelt iron ore. In addition, meteorites have been venerated for eons. The black stone of Kaaba (in Mecca), perhaps the most holy object of the Moslem world, may be a meteorite; in Acts (19:35) of the New Testament, there is reference to what must have been a meteorite—"... what man is there who does not know that the city of Ephesians is temple keeper ... of the sacred stone that fell from the sky?" (translation quoted—*Holy Bible*—Revised Standard Version); and it is reported that a fall near Ensisheim, southwestern Germany, in 1492 was believed by Maximilian I of the Holy Roman Empire to be a divine exhortation and was responsible for his leading a crusade against the Turks.

IMPACTITES AND TEKTITES

The impact of high velocity meteorites with the surface of a large planetary body causes pulverization, shattering, impact metamorphism (also called shock metamorphism) and even melting. The products of this process are called impactites. Tektites may or may not also be products of such impacts.

Impactites

These are discrete masses of rock material, typically a few centimeters to a little less than a meter in greatest dimension (but ranging up to about 200 meters thick and spread over areas with diameters of up to 65 kilometers), that are usually identified on the basis of their occurrence and certain distinctive characteristics. Some impactites, however, may be identified even though their mode of occurrence is unknown.

Impactites occur in and around craters formed as the result of collisions between high-velocity projectiles, such as large meteorites or comets and, for example, the Earth or the moon. Those that are readily recognized megascopically consist of brecciatic mixtures of melted and/or partially melted rock and fractured and/or crushed rock material plus or minus minor amounts of meteoric material. Those that are essentially impossible to identify megascopically without occurrence data lack the meteoric component.

The melted rock may be glassy or appear as an aphanitic or fine-grained crystalline crust on a coarser grained fragment of the target rock material. If glassy, the vitreous phases generally show no evidence of flow. The rock may or may not be vesicular. It may occur as discrete pieces that appear to have been ejected from the impact crater, as the matrix of the brecciatic mixtures or as dike- or sill-like masses that have been injected into the otherwise essentially unaffected adjacent rock material. The name *fladen* is sometimes applied to disc-shaped, glass-rich impactites that resemble volcanic bombs. The term, *impact melt,* has been applied to some of the dike- and sill-like masses of fused rock that occur around some impact craters.

The fractures, which may occur in both rock fragments and in individual mineral grains, tend to be discontinuous, lenticular, tensionlike breaks that in cross-section are up to a few millimeters in width and a few centimeters long. Kink bands are relatively common in some fragments.

The comminuted particles may contain space-saving minerals, high-pressure polymorphs such as coesite and diamond, that indicate shock metamorphism. In most cases, however, these minerals are present as grains that are too small to be recognized by megascopic means.

The meteoritic material is as described on pages 285-290.

Occurrences of impactites. As already noted, if masses of impactite-like rock occur near an impact crater, they are called impactites. Conversely, if a crater or crater-like feature is found to have impactite-like masses spatially associated with it, the feature is generally interpreted to be an impact crater. The latter type of inference may be hazardous if the masses do not contain meteoritic material.

Perhaps the most widely known occurrences of impactites in North America are those in and around the Barringer Meteor Crater near Winslow, Arizona and those around the fossil "meteor craters" at Kentland in northwestern Indiana and near Sinking Spring in south central Ohio. To the present, several tens of impact craters have been recognized on Earth—more than half in North America, but not less than two on each continent.

Tektites

These small (typically 1 to 3 centimeters, but ranging up to at least 7.5 centimeters, across) masses of yellowish to dark green, dark brown, or black-colored glass occur in well-defined geographic belts and in groups, but without any obvious genetic relation to nearby geological formations. Their shapes, rather varied, tend to be roughly globular, teardrop-shaped, or dumb-bell-like (Figure 7-11). Because of their shapes, some tektites were considered by Australian aborigines to be emu eyes. The surfaces of tektites range from smooth to rough with many grooves and pits. Both the shapes and surface features are suggestive of sculpturing and shaping under the influence of aerodynamic forces. Chemical analyses of tektites are more like those of shales than those of typical obsidians, so the chances of a volcanic origin are remote.

Although the origin of tektites is not known definitely, the two favored alternatives both involve vitrification in response to impact. One hypothesis holds that tektites have been formed and splashed up by the impact of relatively large, high velocity meteorites that have hit the Earth. This is thought to account for the fact that their compositions are similar to that of shale, the most common sedimentary rock. The alternative hypothesis retains an impact origin, but holds that tektites come from extraterrestrial sources—for example, that they represent moon splashes that escaped the moon's gravitational pull. The great majority of scientists who have closely studied tektites now incline to a terrestrial origin.

Occurrences of tektites. Tektites have been found at only a few rather widely separated localities—for example, near the Moldava River in the Bohemia District of Czechoslovakia, where they are called moldavites, and in a northwest-southeast trending belt running from Indochina, through Java and the Philippines and across Australia, where they are called indochinites, philippinites, australites, and so forth. In Australia, millions of tektites are strewn over an area of some 5 million square kilometers. No tektites have been recorded as having been observed to form or to fall.

Uses of tektites. A few tektites have been fashioned into carved cameos or simple cabachon stones and mounted into costume jewelry. The appeal appears to be their conversation-piece value rather than any truly appealing or unique appearance.

FIGURE 7-11   Tektites. Well-preserved Australian tektites showing a variety of forms. (From R. O. Chalmers, E. P. Henderson, and Brian Mason, 1976, Smithsonian Contributions to Earth Science, No. 17)

FULGURITES

Silica glass formations produced where lightning has caused melting and fusion are generally referred to as fulgurites (from the Latin word meaning "thunderbolt"). There are two kinds: tubes formed in sand and crusts formed on solid rocks.

Sand Fulgurites

These are hollow, roughly cylindrical masses of glass and sand (Figure 7-12). Although the diameters of the cylinders generally decrease downward, many exhibit bulges, knobs and other irregularites and here and there they may deflect around such things as pebbles. Many also branch out downwards. Terminations are typically crumbled or flattened sack-like enlargements. One mineralogist has reported fulgurites up to 7 centimeters across and about 20 meters long; more typically, they are 3 centimeters or less across and less than 1 meter long. The typical sand fulgurite is lined with smooth glass, is paper thin to 2 millimeters thick and has a rough exterior made up of adhering sand grains. Nearly colorless, light gray to black and buff or yellowish brown colored glasses have been reported. The color differs along the length of some individual fulgurites, apparently reflecting slight compositional differences in the layers of the penetrated sand.

(A)

FIGURE 7-12 Fulgurite. (A) Excavated fulgurite in a sandhill, Lake Congamond, Connecticut. The fulgurite is 4 meters long. (Yale Peabody Museum) (B) Portion of fulgurite, from beach sand along Lake Michigan, showing glassy central portion and sandy exterior. (R. V. Dietrich)

Rock-crust Fulgurites
These are merely glassy surficial coatings on rock outcrops that have been hit by lightning.

Occurrences of fulgurites. Fulgurites are relatively common. The requisite conditions for the formation of sand fulgurites—loose dry quartz sand above a wet layer—are fairly widespread. In North America, several fulgurites are formed each year along the Atlantic and Lake Michigan coasts where there is sand atop a relatively shallow water table. One especially interesting report, dating back to 1790, tells of a fulgurite found while workers were excavating beneath a tree in order to replace the foundation for a memorial tablet that warned bypassers not to get beneath trees during thunderstorms. Rock fulgurites are said to be fairly common on the high peaks of some mountain ranges. An Austrian geologist has reported, for example, that outcrops near the summit of Little Ararat in Armenia have overall glassy appearances because of lightning fusion. In North America, rock fulgurites have been recorded as occurring on Mount Theilsen, Oregon.

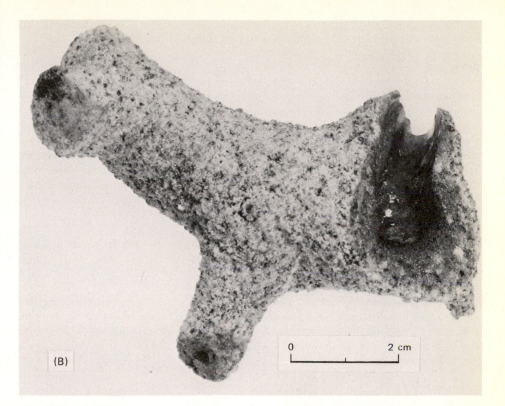

(B)

0   2 cm

Uses of fulgurities. Save museum exhibitions, the only use known to us involved the use of a fulgurite as evidence in a court case. Raymond Murray has recorded the fact that in a criminal case involving suspected arson the accused was cleared when a fulgurite was found and lightning was thereby shown to have caused the fire.

PSEUDO-ROCKS

A few man-made materials resemble rocks. Their shapes and/or occurrences generally suffice to identify them as man-made. Nonetheless, those that are found as well-rounded beach stones or as isolated field stones may confuse even the expert. Although full descriptions for pseudo-rocks seem unwarranted, a review of the characteristics that may be used to help distinguish them from the rocks they resemble may prove useful. The coverage is alphabetical.

Asphalt Mixes
Asphalt mixes used for paving may be megascopically indistinguishable from natural asphalt-impregnated sandstones and limestones that are commonly referred to as bituminous sandstones, tar sands, or asphalt rock. They are easily distinguished from other

conglomerates and breccias because of their tarlike matrix that is soluble in organic solvents, such as carbon disulfide, and because they soften on heating.

Bricks and Tiles

Bricks and tiles may roughly resemble siltstone, tuff, or even some aphanitic lavas. Whereas the various brick-red colors are generally distinctive when compared to either limonite- or hematite-cemented or -pigmented rocks, some of the brick buffs and tans are not. Bricks and broken surfaces of even glazed tile have much duller lusters than typical aphanites. Whereas siltstones and some tuffs are finely bedded or laminated, bricks show no good layering and the layering of pressed tile tends to be discontinous and to have the appearance of having been smeared. Most bricks have sporadic, spheroidal holes unlike siltstones or even vesicular aphanites. Many tile fragments, even when well-rounded, have distinctive flat, commonly curved shapes.

Cinders

Cinders from furnaces may be essentially indistinguishable by megascopic means from scoria. A few furnace cinders contain extraneous materials such as nails.

Cokes

Cokes from coke ovens do not really look like any rock, including natural coke. They are medium gray in color and have a spongy appearance. The cavities, typically of about the same size in individual specimens, range from about a half millimeter to a centimeter across. Many have irregular shapes. Cross fractures have a dull luster; cavity linings appear pearly to vitreous or steel-like.

Concretes

Depending on the aggregate used, concretes may appear to be calcite-cemented sandstones, conglomerates, breccias, or some pyroclastic rock. The calcite-cemented aspect is suggested because concrete effervesces briskly with dilute hydrochloric acid. In general, however, concretes tend to be tougher than similarly appearing calcite-cemented natural rocks. In addition, the matrix portion of essentially all concretes can be seen to have sporadic holes that represent air bubbles formed during curing (Figure 7-13).

Glasses and Porcelains

Some man-made glasses closely resemble quartz. Some porcelains look like chert.

The colors of colored glass tend to be deeper than those of quartz, except for the manganese-bearing varieties that have been turned to a light violet. Most beach abraded glass has a characteristic frosted appearance. The hardness of most glasses is about 5½, whereas that for quartz is 7.

Some porcelains are essentially indistinguishable from some cherts by megascopic means. In general, however, their lusters are fairly distinctive.

A large percentage of glass and porcelain "stones" are flat fragments with one dimension much less than the others, whereas quartz and chert pebbles tend to be more nearly equidimensional.

Slags

Most slags only very superficially resemble any natural rock. Nonetheless, a great many specimens believed by their finders to be meteorites actually turn out to be slag.

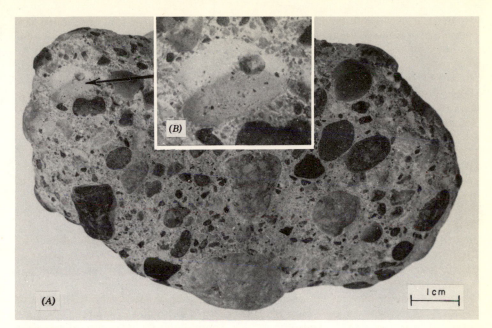

FIGURE 7-13 Concrete (A) A pseudo-rock that resembles conglomerate. (B) Insert shows typical air bubbles developed around larger pieces of aggregate during curing. (R. V. Dietrich)

Most slags are one of two types—essentially solid or highly porous. Either may be one or more of many colors including several shades of red, yellow, green, blue, purple, gray, or brown. Most slags exhibit flowage, the porous ones commonly having elongate holes.

Terrazzos

A few terrazzos resemble brecciatic or conglomeratic rocks with fine-grained or aphanitic matrixes. The larger fragments are generally angular, of only one or a few colors, and of but one or two fairly restricted size ranges. Most are marble chips that have either their original color or have been stained just about any imaginable color or black. The typical mean dimension of the chips is between 1.5 and 7.5 millimeters but some may range up to 25 millimeters. The matrixes, actually binders, are commonly white, buff, or light tan, but may be tinted with other colors. Most are white cement, some resinous material (e.g., epoxy or polyester), or a cement with resinous and/or other additives.

Terrazzos are perhaps the least likely of the pseudo-rocks to be found associated with beach stones or in other natural environments. This is true because even though some terrazzos are precast and thus have to be transported and, in some cases, sized where used, most are produced right where they are used, generally indoors. In any case, even if terrazzo is found with natural stones, most of it may be readily recognized because essentially all precast terrazzo contains reinforcement bars and/or wire mesh. Terrazzos with cement binders are neither chemically resistant nor physically durable, so they are unlikely to persist except on beaches where most of the natural stones are, for example, limestone. Terrazzos with resinous binder, which is fairly inert chemically and tough (but not hard) physically, will tend to have their marble chips weathered or abraded out and, as a consequence, will no longer resemble rock. Cement-bound terrazzo fragments that do persist will generally have one dimension less than about 12 millimeters (the poured maximum is almost always between 10 and 12.5 millimeters), will tend to be tabular or discoid in overall shape, may have one polished surface, and will have matrixes with sporadic spheroidal holes like those described for concrete.

Useful References

Barnes, V. E. and Barnes, M. A., (1973), *Tektites,* New York: Academic Press, 458 pp.

Bateman, A. M. (1950), *Economic Mineral Deposits:* 2nd. ed., New. York: John Wiley & Sons, Inc., 916 pp.

Blanchard, R. (1968), "Interpretation of Leached Outcrops," *Nevada Bur. Mines Bull.,* Vol. 66, 196 pp.

Frondel, Clifford (1962), *Dana's System of Mineralogy,* 7th ed.. Vol. 3, *Silica Minerals,* New York: John Wiley & Sons, Inc., 334 pp.

King, E. A. (1977), "The Origin of Tektites: A Brief Review," *American Scientist,* Vol. 65, pp. 212–218.

Maighiem, R. (1966), *Review of Research on Laterites,* Liège, Belgium: UNESCO, 148 pp.

Mason, B. (1962), *Meteorites,* New York: John Wiley & Sons, Inc., 274 pp.

McCall, G. J. H., ed., (1977), *Meteorite Craters,* Stroudsburg, Pa.: Dowden, Hutchinson and Ross, 384 pp.

Patterson, S. H. (1967), "Bauxite Reserves and Potential Aluminum Resources of the World," *U.S. Geol. Sur. Bull.,* 1228, 176 pp.

Short, N. M. (1966), "Shock Processes in Geology," C.E.G.S. Short Review No. 4, *Jour. Geol. Educ.,* Vol. 14, pp. 149-166.

Simonson, R. W. (1968) *Concept of Soil:* Advances in Agronomy, Vol. 20, pp. 1-45.

Skinner, B. J. (1976), *Earth Resources,* 2nd ed., Englewood Cliffs, N.J.: Prentice-Hall, Inc., 152 pp.

Stefferud, A., ed. (1957), "Soil," *The 1957 Yearbook of Agriculture* U.S. Dept. Agriculture, 784 pp.

chapter 8
identification tables for rocks

You may wish to name a rock in the field or in the laboratory. In both places, megascopic examination will usually lead to a fundamentally correct and acceptable identification. Subsequently, if more precise names or further information are needed, microscopic and/ or other laboratory investigations may be undertaken.

With experience, most hand specimens may be identified in a fairly routine manner. The only ones that are likely to be confusing are specimens that have features characteristic of two or more kinds of rock—for example, some sedimentary and metamorphic quartzites or certain recrystallized limestones and marbles. A few specimens may prove to be so difficult that you cannot name them unequivocally unless their geological relationships or the identity of their associated rocks are known. Fortunately, there are very few such cases.

There have been many attempts to outline the mental processes used in identifying and naming a rock. The attempts have rarely been useful. In part this is so because the procedures outlined are seldom the ones actually used by professional geologists. Most professionals, in fact, do not consciously go through any set procedure—rather, they identify rocks much as they recognize their friends. Nonetheless, our experience indicates that a good first step is to use charts like Tables 8-1 and 8-2 and a procedure as outlined in the examples given below. By so doing, most students will fairly quickly build up the necessary background so that they, too, can then identify and name most rocks in a more or less routine manner.

The tables should not, however, be considered a panacea. Only the rather common rock types are included. Therefore, two points must always be kept in mind. First, a specimen may fit better between than within any of the broad categories given on the tables, as, for example, a sandy limestone. Secondly, the less common rocks cannot be classified and named without consulting the main text.

THE TABLES

Table 8-1 is for rocks whose main constituents occur as grains that can be identified with the naked eye or with the aid of a 10× handlens, plus or minus a few simple tests. Table 8-2 is for rocks whose constituents are too small for such identification.

On both tables, there are two main subdivisions based on hardness, then additional subdivisions based on genesis. The former are indicated by a division (8-1A and 8-1B) or a horizontal line; the latter are separated by vertical lines. On Table 8-1, there also are broader subdivisions that are based on overall textural characteristics; they are separated by double vertical lines. Finally, there are remarks about each of the individual rocks and page references to their descriptions that are given in the main text.

Porphyries, some of which are fairly common rocks, are not included on the charts. To name porphyries, attention is directed to the suggestions given on page 147. Alternatively, the groundmass can be identified by using the charts and then the rock can be named as *groundmass-name porphyry*.

The two hardness categories are based on the hardness of a geologic pick (hammer) for two reasons: 1) geologists generally carry a hammer in the field and have one available in the laboratory; and 2) a large percentage of the common rock-forming minerals and other constituents are markedly softer or harder than the typical hammer (H = 5–5½). The hardness differences noted were determined empirically by several students and geologists who checked at least ten specimens of each rock type. As was done by them, anyone using the charts should determine a rock's hardness by using the rock to scratch the hammer (*not* the reverse, whereby the hammer is used as the scratcher). So long as that method is used, the sometimes misleading disaggregation of relatively incoherent rocks can be avoided (see page 21). In addition, care must be taken to try a number of corners or edges of each rock so that some rare constituent grain will not give a false impression of the general hardness of the overall rock. And, for some rocks that break up rather easily, it may be necessary to examine the hammer surface with a handlens to see if it has or has not been scratched.

The genetic subdivisions are based on those used in the main text: igneous, pyroclastic, sedimentary, diagenetic, metamorphic, and migmatitic. To facilitate presentation and use of the tables, diagenetic rocks are combined with sedimentary rocks and migmatites, most of which are mixtures of a granitoid and an amphibolite or some other relatively dark colored metamorphic rock, are not given. Inclusion of the genetic classes on the charts emphasizes the fact that, ideally, a rock should be seen as part of an exposure in the field. When such is possible, one can frequently see larger scale relationships, including the identity of the associated rocks, that clearly indicate a rock's genetic class. As a consequence, similarly appearing rocks of other origins may be automatically eliminated from consideration.

Attention is directed to Figures 4-12 and 4-19, to 6-1 and 6-14, and to 5-18 and 5-30 for illustrations of what is meant by the headings "interlocking grains," "foliated," and "fragmental and/or layered," respectively. The fact that many of the rocks in the column for foliated rocks also consist of interlocking grains is noteworthy.

The remarks give simple tests and/or other information that will help distinguish a rock from rocks that it may resemble. The remarks deal with such characteristics as fracture, mineral content, and solubility.

Two examples of how the tables may be used follow.

I. A. The rock has megascopically discernible grains—use Table 8-1.
    B. The hardness is less than that of a hammer—go to Table 8-1B.
    C. The texture is interlocking with no obvious preferred orientation—note left third of the chart.
    D. The rock is one of the following—
        1. Rock salt, if it has a salty taste;
        2. Gyprock, if it can be scratched with a fingernail;
        3. Limestone, calcite marble, or carbonatite if it effervesces briskly with dilute HCl;
        4. Dolostone or dolomite marble, if it effervesces slowly with dilute HCl;
        5. Anhydrock, if it does none of the above.

    E. If it is one of the rocks in group No. 3 or group No. 4, the descriptions in the text should be consulted.

II. A. The rock consists of grains too small to be seen megascopically—use Table 8-2.

    B. The hardness is greater than that of a hammer—go to the top half of the chart.

    C. The rock is one of the following—felsite, basalt, obsidian, pumice, ash tuff, chert, shale, diatomite, slate, phyllite, greenstone, or mylonite.

    D. Each may be distinguished from the others on the basis of the remarks—for example, an obsidian could be distinguished from the others because of its color, luster, and translucency.

TABLE 8-1A   Identification of rocks with megascopically discernible grains; HARDNESS > HAMMER.

Interlocking Grains			Foliated	Fragmental and/or Layered		
Igneous	Sedimentary/ Diagenetic	Metamorphic	Metamorphic	Igneous/ Pyroclastic	Sedimentary/ Diagenetic	Metamorphic
After constituent minerals are identified, see Figs 4.8, 4.9 & 4.20. Compositions noted below are typical, **not** inclusive. Q = quartz, Alk = alkali feldspar, Plag = plagioclase, M = mafics. Granitoid, p. 113 Q, 20–60%; Alk > = < Plag; M, 10–40%.		All rocks, except phyllite, in the next ("Foliated") column also may consist of interlocking grains. Quartzite, p. 257 H-7; vitreous, conchoidal fracture. Epidosite, p. 126 Chiefly green epidote. Eclogite, p. 268 Red garnets in mass of green pyroxene.	Quartz is common in all of these except amphibolite. Gneiss, p. 258 Streaked or banded; chiefly granular grains. Amphibolite, p. 260 Dark gray to greenish black; medium-grained; lacks quartz Schist, p. 262 Enough platy constituents to	The first four rocks are named on basis of size of the clasts that make up 50 or more percent of the volume of the rock. Agglomerate (Bomb tuff), p. 163 Clasts are bombs >64 mm. Pyroclastic breccia (Block tuff), p. 163 Clasts are blocks >64 mm.	Rocks consist chiefly of clasts with mean diameters of noted lengths. Conglomerate, p. 189 Rounded clasts > 2 mm. Sedimentary breccia, 189 Angular clasts > 2 mm. Sandstone, p. 193 1/16–2 mm; quartz > 75%	Quartzite, p. 257 Chiefly quartz; conchoidal fracture; may be sedimentary—see p. 196 Metaconglomerate, p. 257 Pebbles, cobbles and boulders in a metaquartzite matrix.

Syenitoid, p. 128
Q < 20%; Alk, up to 100%; M < 45%.
Dioritoid, p. 130
Q < 5%; light Plag > 50%; M < 50% (hornblende).
Gabbroid, p. 130
Q < 5%; dark Plag < 50%; M > 50% (pyroxene).
Anorthosite, p. 130
Bluish gray Plag, 90–100%.
Ultramafites, p. 138
One or more mafic minerals, 90–100%.

give good foliation.
Phyllite, p. 265
Very fine grained; foliation surfaces have glossy sheen; commonly corrugated.

Lapilli tuff, p. 163
Clasts 2–64 mm.
Ash tuff, p. 163
Clasts <2 mm; rough to touch.
Dunite, p. 138
Looks like an olivine sandstone.

Arkose, p. 196
1/16–2 mm; feldspar > 25%; resembles granite
Graywacke, p. 196
1/16–2 mm; mafics ± rock clasts > 25%; clay odor when damp.
Siltstone, p. 199
1/256–1/16 mm; gritty between teeth.

TABLE 8-1B Identification of rocks with megascopically discernible grains; HARDNESS < HAMMER.

	Interlocking Grains			Foliated	Fragmental and/or Layered		
	Igneous	Sedimentary/Diagenetic	Metamorphic	Metamorphic	Igneous/Pyroclastic	Sedimentary/Diagenetic	Metamorphic
	Carbonatite, p. 138 Brisk effervescence with dilute HCl; typically contains disseminated silicates, oxides and sulfides, commonly some rare ones.	Rock salt, p. 215 Has salty taste. Gyprock, p. 214 Can be scratched with fingernail. Anhydrock, p. 214 H—3½ Limestone, p. 204 Brisk effervescence with dilute HCl. Dolostone, p. 217 Slow smoldering effervescence with dilute HCl.	Marble, p. 253 May be calcitic to dolomitic; commonly contains disseminated graphite and/or silicate minerals; with HCl; effervesces as noted in column to left.	Talc Schist, p. 264 Can be scratched with fingernail; soapy feel; is foliated. Soapstone, p. 264 Like talc schist but nonfoliated. Serpentinite, p. 146 Typically green; H–2½–3½; waxy to greasy appearance.		Clastic limestone, p. 204 Contains fragments including intraclasts, fossils, oolites and/or pellets; effervesces briskly with dilute HCl. Dolostone, p. 217 As above but effervesces slowly with dilute HCl.	

TABLE 8-2 Identification of rocks that are microcrystalline or glassy.

	Igneous	Pyroclastic	Sedimentary/ Diagenetic	Metamorphic
Hardness > Hammer	*Felsite*, p. 147 Light colored (p. 147); stony appearance. *Basalt*, p. 150 Dark gray to greenish black; commonly vesicular or amygdaloidal. *Obsidian*, p. 151 Glassy; dark gray, brown or streaked; translucent in thin pieces; vitreous luster. *Pumice*, p. 157 Glassy; froth-like.	*Ash tuff*, p. 163 Consolidated ash; rough feel.	*Chert*, p. 217 Porcelaneous luster; conchoidal fracture. *Shale*, p. 200 Disaggregates easily; is fissile; clay odor when damp. *Diatomite*, p. 213 Gritty feel; light–floats on water; no clay odor or effervescence with acid.	*Slate*, p. 265 Parallel rock cleavage that may be at an angle to bedding. *Phyllite*, p. 265 Glossy sheen on foliation surfaces; commonly corrugated. *Greenstone*, p. 262 Olive green color; dull luster; subconchoidal fracture. *Mylonite*, p. 247 see below.
Hardness < Hammer			*Coal*, p. 226 Black color and streak; dull and/or bright luster; brittle. *Gyprock*, p. 214 Can be scratched with fingernail. *Anhydrock*, p. 214 H–3½. *Limestone*, p. 204 Brisk effervescence with dilute HCl. *Dolostone*, p. 217 Slow smoldering effervescence with dilute HCl. *Claystone*, p. 200 Clay odor when damp; smooth feel; sticks to tongue; no effervescence with acid.	*Mylonite*, p. 247 Smeared-out appearance; commonly includes sheared fragments.

index

Asterisks indicate illustrations.

Aa, 149
Achondrite, 288
Actinolite, 56
Adamellite, 117
Aegirine, 53, 54
Aegirine-augite, 54
Aërolite, 287
Agglomerate, 160, 163
Alaskite, 117
Albite, 34
Alkalic igneous rocks, see Feldspathoidal
     phanerites
Alkali feldspar, 34, 38*
Allanite, 61
Allotriomorphic form, 109*
Allochem, 204
Almandine, 62
Alnoite, 147
Alteration, 106, 278
   argillization, 278
   chloritization, 106
   greisenization, 278
   kaolinization, 278
   propylitization, 278
   saussuritization, 106
   sericitization, 278
   serpentinization, 106
   silicification, 278
   spillitization, 106
   uralitization, 106
   wallrock, 277*
Alunite, 79
Amber, 86
Amphibole, 56, 57*
   actinolite, 56
   anthophyllite, 56
   arfvedsonite, 57
   cummingtonite, 56
   glaucophane, 56
   hornblende, 56
   pyribole, 53, 59
   riebeckite, 57
   schist, 239, 260

   tremolite, 56
   uralite, 59
Amphibolite, 239, 260
   facies, 234, 236
Amygdule, 149, 150*
Analcime, 44
Anatexite, 270
Andalusite, 64, 235
Andesite, 148
   chemical composition, 101
Andradite, 62
Anhedral form, 11, 12*, 109*
Anhydrite, 78
Anhydrock, 214
Ankerite, 82
Anorthoclase, 35
Anorthosite, 114, 115, 130, 142*
   quartz, 116
Anthophyllite, 56
Anthracite, 228
Anthraxylon, 226
Antiperthite, 35
Apatite, 83
Aphanites and aphanite porphyries, 146
   andesite, 148
   basalt, 148
   basanite, 148
   dacite, 148
   felsite, 147
   foidite, 148
   latite, 148
   leucitite, 148
   mafite, 147
   melilitite, 148
   phonolite, 148
   rhyolite, 148
   tephrite, 148
   trachyte, 148
Aphanophyre, 147
Aplite, 121
Aragonite, 83
Arenaceous rock, 175
Arfvedsonite, 57